Deutsch im Blick

Table of Contents

THE UNIVERSITY OF TEXAS AT AUSTIN

Center for Open Educational Resources and Language Learning

for an open world

Deutsch im Blick, *http://coerll.utexas.edu/dib/*, the web-based German program developed and in use at the University of Texas since 2004, and its companion site, **Grimm Grammar** (2000) *http://coerll.utexas.edu/gg/* are open acess sites, free and open multimedia resources, which require neither password nor fees. **Deutsch im Blick**, used increasingly by students, teachers, and institutions throughout the world, includes 307 videos (American students in Germany, native German interviews, vocabulary and culture presentation videos) recorded vocabulary lists, phonetic lessons, online grammar lessons (600 pages) with self-correcting exercises and audio dialogues, online grammar tools, and diagnostic grammar tests. The accompanying textbook of classroom activities and homework is downloadable from the website in pdf format and available from the online publisher, *qoop.com*.

Deutsch im Blick was developed at the University of Texas Austin in the German Department. It has been funded and created by Liberal Arts Instructional Technology Services at the University of Texas, and is currently supported by U.S. Department of Education Fund for the Improvement of Post-Secondary Education (FIPSE Grant P116B070251 & P116Y090057) as an example of the open access initiative. Open access sites require neither password nor fees. They are free and open multimedia resources which promote learning and scholarship for everyone, everywhere!

Second Edition
ISBN: 978-1-937963-01-9

Library of Congress Control Number: 2012943410
Manufactured in the United States of America.

Contributors

German Department
The University of Texas at Austin

Zsuzsanna Abrams, Primary Author
Karen Kelton, Editor in Chief

Developers:
Zsuzsanna Abrams
Karen Kelton

Web, Layout Design, Multimedia:
Eric Eubank
Nathalie Steinfeld
Rachael Gilg
Trey Cartwright

Illustrations/ Cartoons
Walter Moore
Trey Cartwright

Audio-artist:
Mike Heidenreich

Chapter Authors/Co-authors (primary authors):
Chapters 3, 4, 8 and 10:
Sarah Schuchard
Chapter 6 and 10:
Jasmin Weilbacher
Chapter 7:
Sarah Schuchard, Carla Ghanem
Chapter 8:
Carla Ghanem
Chapter 9:
Vince VanderHeijden

Summer 2009 (significant) revisions:
Judith Atzler
Anke J Zwietasch Sanders

Fall 2012/Spring 2013 (significant) revisions:
Anke J Zwietasch Sanders

Grimm Grammar Editing:
Sebastian Heiduschke
(proof-reading Eng & Ger)
Karen Kelton (proof-reading Eng)
Julia Flachenecker (proof-reading Ger)

Webquest & Interactive Polls:
Sebastian Heiduschke, Ph.D.

Phonology:
Sarah Schuchard & Guido Halder

Support
Liberal Arts ITS, Director:
Joe TenBarge

Video assistants (interviews with):
Judith Atzler (Hassan)
Björn Freitag (Peter and Harald)
Carla Ghanem (Berna and Jan)
Carla Ghanem (Berna and Jan)
Jansen Harris (Christian)
Mindy Maul (Sophia and Adan)
Anke J Zwietasch Sanders (Eisdiele)

Interviewees
Harald Becker
Sophia Clark
Sara Cottingham
Erin Covert
Susan Dietz
Adan Gallardo
Vincenzo Gaico
Berna Güneli
Florian Flachenecker
Josh Froemming
Peter Hess
Stephan Kempf
Mario Klammer
Andrew Kulha
Andrea Klusch
Eva Kunkel
Doug Marshall
Stephan "Stevie" Liedtke
Vanessa Martinez
Adam McElwee
Hassan Mojtabaeezamani

Peter Müller
Kersten Horn

Interviewees cont.
Frau Roswitha Paul
Austin Pierce
Kerstin Somerholter
Rika, Christine, Brigitte
Tobias Rotter
Jan Ülzmann
Verkäuferin
Kathrin Zöller
Anke J Zwietasch Sanders

Grimm Grammar Characters audio:
Zsuzsanna Abrams
Caroline Ahlemann
Kit Belgum
Gary Dickerson
Helmut Flachenecker
Julia Flachenecker
Carla Ghanem
Berna Güneli
Sabine Hake
Guido Halder
Judith Hammer
Martin Kley
Werner Krauss
Marc Rathmann
Daniela Richter
Karen Roesch
Jan Ülzmann
Jasmin Weilbacher
Julia Zerger

Photos
Zsuzsanna Abrams
Marion Eisenschmied
Judith Atzler
Anke J Zwietasch Sanders
Vince VanderHeijden
Joseph Steinfeld

Creative Commons License

 This work is licensed under the Creative Commons Attribution-Noncommercial-No Derivative Works 3.0 United States License. To view a copy of this license, visit http://creativecommons.org/licenses/by-nc-nd/3.0/us/ or send a letter to Creative Commons, 171 Second Street, Suite 300, San Francisco, California, 94105, USA.

You are free:

> **to Share** — to copy, distribute and transmit the work

Under the following conditions:

 Attribution — You must attribute the work in the manner specified by the author or licensor (but not in any way that suggests that they endorse you or your use of the work).

 Noncommercial — You may not use this work for commercial purposes.

 No Derivative Works — You may not alter, transform, or build upon this work.

Glossary of Symbols
How to use Deutsch im Blick

Aussprache (pronunciation)
These exercises, found at the end of each chapter, guide you through different areas of the German sound system. From tricky German sounds to regional dialects in Europe and the US.

Grimm Grammar
This symbol indicates where the materials in Deutsch im Blick connect to relevant grammar points in Grimm Grammar. Complete the exercises online before coming to class.

Gruppenarbeit (group activity)
Group activities ask students to work with 3-4 of their peers to survey cultural and personal preferences, to collaborate on written and oral presentations and benefit from student-to-student learning.

Kultur (cultural information)
In culture activities, students explore similarities and differences between their own culture(s) and those of the German-speaking world. The purpose is to help learners analyze cultural phenomena, and recognize individual versus societal patterns.

Lesen und Forschung im Internet (research on line)
These activities guide students in research on the Internet and provide literacy skills in German, as well as real-life examples of the language presented in Deutsch im Blick .

Leseverständnis (reading tasks)
There are different types of reading we do every day: scan texts, read for specific information, read different types of texts The activities in Deutsch im Blick aim to help you develop reading strategies to cope with these diverse reading demands in German.

Lieder, Musik, Dichtung (songs, music, poetry)
Deutsch im Blick brings you music in each chapter, so you get to know groups and music that your German contemporaries like to listen to. These are fun portals to German youth-culture and a playful way to reinforce the language you are learning.

Meinungsumfragen (polls)
Interactive polls online provide a foundation for in-class discussions about cultural preferences regarding topics covered in Deutsch im Blick. The (highly unscientific) statistics are fun to analyze.

Partnerarbeit (pair activity)

Pair activities ask you to work together with one partner, asking each other questions, solving problems, or creating short pieces of writing. It is helpful to work with different partners throughout the semester.

Schreiben (writing activity)

These activities ask you to use ideas and phrases you have learned to express your own thoughts or create with the language. There are different genres of writing: poetry, dialogs, screen plays, position papers, to help you prepare for 2nd-year German.

Spiele (games)

Games, as the name suggests, focus on playful group interaction (small or large groups of students) using German. They typically involve social activities that Germans themselves learn / play during childhood or as young adults.

Videoclips

Clips with native and non-native speakers of German are the main organizational framework for all materials in Deutsch im Blick. They provide examples for lexical and grammatical concepts and ideas for cultural exploration.

WebQuests

Longer on-line research projects (two-three per chapter) help students immerse themselves in the topics covered by each chapter, using mostly websites relevant for college students in the German-speaking countries.

Wortschatz (vocabulary)

One of the most crucial components of effective communication is vocabulary. Vocabulary exercises help you build strategies for learning expressions, phrases (in context) that you need to be able to communicate in German.

Zum Nachdenken (something to think about)

Language exists in a sociocultural context. These little mental exercises in each chapter ask you to stop and reflect on what you just learned, to analyze the language or concepts in the Deutsch im Blick materials. They help you locate the pedagogical tasks in a broader sociocultural environment, and understand that German is not merely a university subject but a language spoken in the real world by real people (a concept students who go study abroad sometimes find amusingly surprising :))

Authentisch

This symbol indicates that the material is authentic. Authentic material is not or only minimally edited by DIB. The idea is to represent language as it appears in every day interactions, where editing would not be an option. These are great sources to discuss errors, when they are spotted by students/teachers. A scavenger hunt could be integrated in the course, allowing students to gain points for spotting an error and providing an explanation of how it should be in proper German.

Einführung

Deutsch im Blick is an online, non-traditional language learning program for beginning and early intermediate students of German. It is quite different from your traditional language textbooks, so it might take some getting used to. However, you'll enjoy learning German as long as you like to play with language, explore how vocabulary and grammar work together to create meaning, and are curious about the cultures of the German-speaking countries.

The main premise of Deutsch im Blick is that learning a foreign language should focus on learning language in use. Thus, all activities are guided by real-life, plausible language situations: How would native and non-native speakers use the vocabulary, grammar and sociolinguistic rules in everyday contexts to make sense of what others tell them and to make meaning themselves?

Deutsch im Blick and grimm grammar

There are two components to this online program: the video-based learning materials online Deutsch im Blick and the zany, irreverent exploration of German . Your textbook introduces you to life in the German-speaking countries, with the assistance of several native speakers of German and students from the University of Texas:

> The Germans & The Swiss:
> Berna, Eva, Harald, Jan and Peter.
>
> The American students:
> Adan, Erin, Hassan, Sara and Sophia

Through their experiences and voices, you will get to know life in Germany and the US, and will learn how to use German the way native- and non-natives speakers use it in everyday, real-life conversations. Through their interviews they share with you how they talk about themselves, their interests, school and free time, friends and family, and in general, how to have fun with the German language (yes, it is possible!).

Before you begin working with each chapter, you should watch the introductory video to get an idea about the chapter's contents. Then to learn the material of the chapter, you will:

1. work with the interviews with the native and non-native speakers,
2. develop your vocabulary,
3. learn to understand vocabulary in cultural situations presented in Sprache im Kontext videos,
4. learn how to use the structures presented in to talk about your own life,
5. practice pronunciation,
6. complete WebQuests that take you to the German-speaking countries (at least virtually), and
7. explore cultural practices via interactive polls.

Deutsch im Blick emphasizes the building of vocabulary as a primary pillar of the ability to communicate. In the experience of many students, knowing grammar (a component of language emphasized in most other textbooks) is not sufficient to interact with other people. The idea for this book developed from the experiences of several students on study abroad programs. These students had learned German grammar, but had not emphasized vocabulary enough to communicate successfully.

Deutsch im Blick also recycles lexical and grammatical information through the different chapters to help reinforce meaningful semantic, structural and cultural connections. Grammatical accuracy is important. There is a life and death difference between saying "I could kill that frustrating person!" and "I have killed that frustrating person!" (the life and death difference: death penalty v. not, in Texas). Yet, as you will see, there are no simple grammar exercises in the workbook asking learners to manipulate pronouns or verb tenses in 6-10 isolated sentences. Instead, grammatical sophistication and accuracy are fostered through listening, speaking, reading and writing tasks that reflect how grammatical structures work – along with relevant vocabulary – in real language use contexts. If the user looks carefully, many exercises focus on how to use grammar for effective meaningful communication. To recap, in order to help learners prepare for real-life interactions in German, Deutsch im Blick develops:

- vocabulary as the key component of language at beginning levels of instruction. Without vocabulary, grammar has no meaning. Each chapter provides suggestions for learning important lexical items in the Core vocabulary list at the beginning of each chapter. There is also an expanded list at the end of each chapter to provide an additional resource. Each chapter also offers a number of exercises that help practice, reinforce and illustrate the real-life uses of German words, phrases, collocations (how words are used together) and idiomatic expressions.
- listening skills with the help of extensive video clips (both guided interviews and authentic footage);
- writing skills that focus on fun, interpersonal and academic genres our college-age learner population needs;
- reading skills that help learners understand a variety of types of texts they would encounter in a study abroad situation and in later academic work if they pursue a major in German. These activities focus on building vocabulary, developing cultural literacy and preparing for independent reading beyond the classroom;
- cultural analytic skills through regular authentic materials and tasks – through the listening, reading, writing and speaking tasks – that foster reflection, comparison and articulation of findings. There are web-quests that guide students to immersion in cultural and language topics and lots of music that offer a fun portal to German youth-culture(s). Culture, in this program, is understood as both literary and historical knowledge (Culture) as well as everyday concepts in the workings of a society (culture). Language is very much seen as integrally embedded and reflective of culture.

Authentic texts

You will work intensively with authentic materials throughout the program. It is by design that we provide you with products and perspectives which were produced for a German-speaking audience. We made sure that the tasks we built around the texts are appropriate for your level of German learning throughout the chapters. You will find that from the very beginning you can derive understanding from a variety of materials.

Culture

It is our understanding that culture and language are fundamentally intertwined and that culture is not a separate skill set to acquire, but rather the foundation of all language use. We also believe that there is no one "target" culture, but rather that communities have a variety of subcultures, with different practices and preferences. Therefore, we expect that the process of "learning German" involves discovery about ourselves, our own cultures and assumptions as well. Throughout the chapters you will find multiple opportunities to reflect on your own perspectives as you strive to understand the viewpoints reflected in the Austrian, German and Swiss examples you encounter.

Deutsch im Blick: http://www.coerll.utexas.edu/dib/

is the grammar component of this learning program. Most fortunately, several Grimm fairy tale characters volunteered to teach you all kinds of exciting and intricate things about German grammar.

Snow White and the seven dwarfs - among many other characters - tirelessly present grammatical concepts from adjectives (very exciting!) to verbs (to fascinate you). They model these concepts through – what they consider – witty dialogs and poignant narratives, which are supported by audio-files and illustrations that help make each grammar point a bit more memorable (the audio-recordings were done with the help of over 30 guest artists).

Each part of speech (e.g., adjectives, adverbs, nouns, verbs) is introduced in an overview, which provides a portal to more detailed information about relevant sub-topics (e.g., articles, the past tense of regular verbs, etc.). The grammar descriptions are provided in English and German to foster in-depth understanding and autonomous work by beginning language learners. The fill-in-the-blank, slash-sentence, multiple-choice and other types of self-correcting exercises that follow each grammar point also aim to promote understanding grammar in plausible communicative contexts (i.e., what someone might actually say in real life).

Using the Textbook with the Website

Wortschatz
- *Begrüßungen*
- *Persönliche Informationen*
- *Jemanden kennenlernen*
- *Herkunft*
- *Zahlen*
- *Mehr persönliche Informationen*
- *Die Farben*
- *Wie geht's?*
- *Geld, Handy, usw.*
- *An der Uni studieren*
- *Studienfächer*
- *Die Woche*

Aussprache
- *Kapitel Eins: Das Alphabet*

Grammatik
Focus
- *Nouns gender*
- *Verbs overview*
- *Haben*
- *Sein*
- *Nominative pronouns*
- *Question words*

Recommended
- *Nouns overview*
- *Nouns plural*
- *Nominative case*
- *Articles*
- *Present regular verbs*
- *Pronouns overview*

Videos
Sprache im Kontext
- *Mit dem Bus zur Uni*
- *Der Studentenausweis*
- *Das Handy*

◇ Kapitel Eins

◇ Einführung ins Kapitel
Willkommen in Würzburg! . In this chapter you are introduced to city of Würzburg, the University, and to the native and non-native speakers of German who will be your guides during your journey of learning German!

📄 Kurspaket
Kapitel Eins [pdf, 7.25 MB]

▣ Interviews

Deutsche und Schweizer

Wer bin ich?	*Berna, Eva, Harald, Jan, Peter*
Studium & Wohnen	*Berna, Eva, Jan*
Freunde & Weiteres	*Berna, Eva, Jan*
Hobbys & Interessen	*Eva*

Amerikanische Studenten

Wer bin ich?	*Adan, Hassan, Erin, Sara, Sophia*
Studium & Wohnen	*Adan, Hassan, Erin, Sara, Sophia*
Freunde & Weiteres	*Hassan, Erin, Sara*
Hobbys & Interessen	*Adan*

▣ Sprache im Kontext
Mit dem Bus zur Uni . With the bus to the university
Der Studentenausweis . The student ID
Das Handy . The cell phone

◀) Wortschatz
Begrüßungen . Greetings
Persönliche Informationen . Personal information
Jemanden kennenlernen . To meet someone
Herkunft . Origin/Nationality
Zahlen . Numbers
Mehr persönliche Informationen . More personal information
Die Farben . The colors
Wie geht's? . How are you? (informal)
Geld, Handy, usw. . Money, cell phone, etc.
An der Uni studieren . Studying at the University
Studienfächer . Field of study
Die Woche . The week

◀) Aussprache
Kapitel Eins: Das Alphabet

✎ Grammatik
◇ Focus
Nouns gender
Verbs overview
Haben
Sein
Nominative pronouns
Question words

◇ Recommended
Nouns overview
Nouns plural
Nominative case
Articles
Present regular verbs
Pronouns overview

@ Webquests
1.1 Webquest: Deutschland, Österreich und die Schweiz
1.2 Willkommen in Würzburg!
1.3 Deutschland-Portal: *Einfach. Besser. Informiert.*

◎ Meinungsumfragen
Kapitel Eins: Meinungsumfragen . Ergebnisse

▦ Diashow
Kapitel Eins

© 2008 · Germanic Studies · UT Austin · Kontakt

1 ANKUNFT IN WÜRZBURG

Mit dem Bus zur Uni . With the bus to the university
Der Studentenausweis . The student ID
Das Handy . The cell phone

☑ Meinungsumfragen

    Kapitel Eins: Meinungsumfragen . Ergebni

◀» Wortschatz

Begrüßungen . Greetings
Persönliche Informationen
Jemanden kennenlerne
Herkunft . Origin/Natio
Zahlen . Numbers
Mehr persönliche Infor
information
Die Farben . The color
Wie geht's? . How are
Geld, Handy, usw. . M
An der Uni studieren .
Studienfächer . Field
Die Woche . The week

🖿 Diashow

    Kapitel Eins

⟐ Wortschatz

✧ Kapitel 1: Willkommen in Würzburg!

This chapter's vocabulary: Arrival in Würzburg (public transportation, alone or in a group, being picked up by host family, being jetlagged); extensive greeting and introduction scenarios (beyond 'hello' and 'good-bye').

Sections

- Begrüßungen . Greetings
- Persönliche Informationen . Personal information
- Jemanden kennenlernen . To meet someone
- Herkunft . Origin/Nationality
- Zahlen . Numbers
- Mehr persönliche Informationen . More personal information
- Die Farben . The colors
- Wie geht's? . How are you? (informal)
- Geld, Handy, usw. . Money, cell phone, etc.
- An der Uni studieren . Studying at the University
- Studienfächer . Field of study
- Die Woche . The week

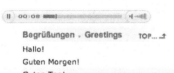

   ❚❚ 00:08 ▰▰▰▮▮▯▯▯▯▯▯▯▯▯▯▯▯▯▯▯ ◀·ıllıllıl

Begrüßungen . Greetings   TOP... ⬆

Hallo!	Hello!
Guten Morgen!	Good morning.
Guten Tag!	Hello ("good day").
Guten Abend!	Good evening.
Gute Nacht.	Good night.
Tschüss!	Bye!
Auf Wiedersehen!	Goodbye! (Formal)
Mach's gut!	Take care!
Bis bald!	See you soon!

Wortschatz
Vorbereitung

✎ Grammatik

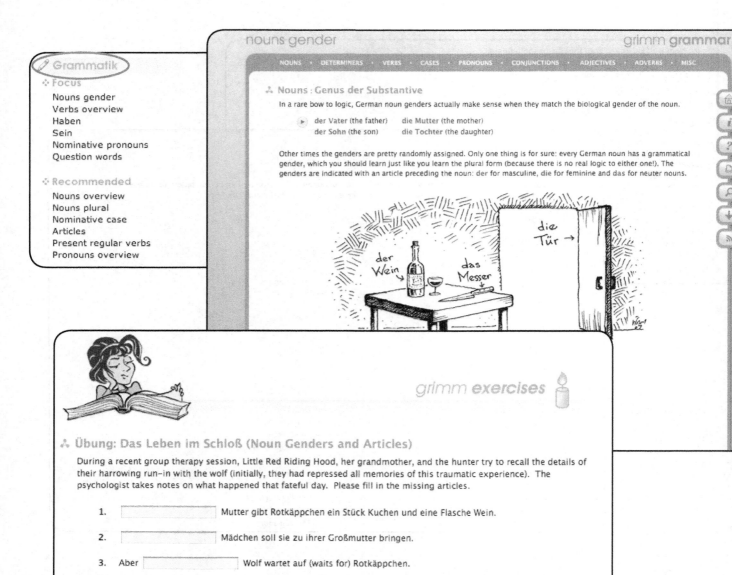

Grammatik

Focus
- Nouns gender
- Verbs overview
- Haben
- Sein
- Nominative pronouns
- Question words

Recommended
- Nouns overview
- Nouns plural
- Nominative case
- Articles
- Present regular verbs
- Pronouns overview

nouns gender   grimm **grammar**

NOUNS · DETERMINERS · VERBS · CASES · PRONOUNS · CONJUNCTIONS · ADJECTIVES · ADVERBS · MISC

♣ Nouns : Genus der Substantive

In a rare bow to logic, German noun genders actually make sense when they match the biological gender of the noun.

> der Vater (the father)   die Mutter (the mother)
> der Sohn (the son)   die Tochter (the daughter)

Other times the genders are pretty randomly assigned. Only one thing is for sure: every German noun has a grammatical gender, which you should learn just like you learn the plural form (because there is no real logic to either one!). The genders are indicated with an article preceding the noun: der for masculine, die for feminine and das for neuter nouns.

grimm **exercises**

♣ Übung: Das Leben im Schloß (Noun Genders and Articles)

During a recent group therapy session, Little Red Riding Hood, her grandmother, and the hunter try to recall the details of their harrowing run-in with the wolf (initially, they had repressed all memories of this traumatic experience). The psychologist takes notes on what happened that fateful day. Please fill in the missing articles.

1. _____ Mutter gibt Rotkäppchen ein Stück Kuchen und eine Flasche Wein.

2. _____ Mädchen soll sie zu ihrer Großmutter bringen.

3. Aber _____ Wolf wartet auf (waits for) Rotkäppchen.

4. Er sagt: " _____ Blumen riechen sehr gut. Du solltest einige sammeln (gather)!"

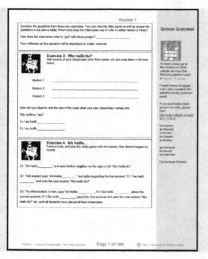

Grimm Grammar
At home please read the following grammar point on the *Grimm Grammar* website.

Entering accented characters

character	Macintosh	PC	character	Macintosh	PC
à	opt ` + a	alt + 0224	ñ	opt n + n	alt + 0241
á	opt e + a	alt + 0225	ò	opt ` + o	alt + 0242
â	opt i + a	alt + 0226	ó	opt e + o	alt + 0243
ä	opt u + a	alt + 0228	ô	opt i + o	alt + 0244
ç	opt + c	alt + 0231	ö	opt u + o	alt + 0245
è	opt ` + e	alt + 0232	ß	opt + s	alt + 0223
é	opt e + e	alt + 0233	ù	opt ` + u	alt + 0249
ê	opt i + e	alt + 0234	ú	opt e + u	alt + 0250
ë	opt u + e	alt + 0235	û	opt i + u	alt + 0251
ì	opt ` + i	alt + 0236	ü	opt u + u	alt + 0252
í	opt e + i	alt + 0237	¡	opt + 1	alt + 0161
î	opt i + i	alt + 0238	¿	opt shift ?	alt + 0191

Technology

The Deutsch im Blick textbook provides all the audio files and chapters of the textbooks in electronic format on the Deutsch im Blick website at the following link:

  http://coerll.utexas.edu/dib/

The Deutsch im Blick textbook is using a new technology that quickly delivers the audio for this textbook to the reader's camera-enabled cell phone using programmed quick response (QR) codes. The index number of the QR codes are placed in this textbook with every vocabulary and video. The QR code picture for the index number can be found at the end of each chapter.

What is a QR code?

A QR code is a type of barcode programmed with information that a camera-enabled smart phone can read. Originally introduced in Japan in 1994 as a tracking method for packages, QR codes have evolved into a diverse range of uses.

How does it work?

By far the best way to read QR codes is to use a smart phone with a barcode reader app (there are many in the app store or marketplace). But what if you don't have a smart phone? Most readers require need to be positioned quite far away from the QR code. Try to cover up adjacent QR codes to enhance readabilty.

If you don't have a smart phone, you will need at least a phone or a computer with a camera and an adequate zoom. Take a clear, crisp picture of the QR code. Then, email or text the picture to x@snpmy.com. You'll get an instant email or text back. Once you send or scan the QR code you will get a link for the audio file through the app, text message, or email on your electronic device. Click the link and it will take you straight to the audio player on the website.

DEUTSCH IM BLICK INTERVIEWEES

Deutsche und Schweizer

Berna

Eva

Harald

Jan

Peter

Amerikanische Studenten

Adan

Erin

Hassan

Sara

Sophia

Wortschatz

- *Begrüßungen*
- *Persönliche Informationen*
- *Jemanden kennenlernen*
- *Herkunft*
- *Zahlen*
- *Weitere persönliche Informationen*
- *Die Farben*
- *Wie geht's?*
- *Geld, Handy, usw.*
- *An der Uni sudieren*
- *Studienfächer*
- *Die Woche*

Aussprache

- *Kapitel 1: Das Alphabet*

Grammatik

Focus
- *Nouns gender*
- *Verbs overview*
- *Haben*
- *Sein*
- *Nominative pronouns*
- *Question words*

Recommended
- *Nouns overview*
- *Nouns plural*
- *Nominative case*
- *Articles*
- *Present regular verbs*
- *Pronouns overview*

Videos

Sprache im Kontext
- *Mit dem Bus zur Uni*
- *Der Studentenausweis*
- *Das Handy*

1 ANKUNFT IN WÜRZBURG

This chapter offers your first introduction to life in Würzburg, Germany. With the help of your native and non-native tour-guides, you will learn how to introduce yourself and provide some basic information about yourself. Your guides are:

The Germans and the Swiss:
Berna, Eva, Harald, Jan and Peter

The American students:
Adan, Andrew, Erin, Sara and Sophia

Online Book links

You can find a list of QR codes to access the videos directly from your smart device at the end of all chapters or you can go to the *Deutsch im Blick* website http://coerll.utexas.edu/dib/toc.php?k=1 to select your clip from the „Interviews" or „Sprache im Kontext" sectionsj.

You can find the vocabulary at:
http://coerll.utexas.edu/dib/voc.php?k=1

Sections
Begrüßungen • Greetings
Wer bist du? • Who are you?
Zahlen • Numbers
Die Farben • The colors
Wie geht's? • How are you? (informal)
Herkunft • Origin/nationality
An der Uni studieren • Studying at the university
An die Uni fahren • Getting to the university
Studienfächer • Majors
Die Woche • The week

You can find the grammar topics covered in this chapter at:
During the chapter exercises, you are regularly referred to *Grimm Grammar* at the *Deutsch im Blick* website. These are the grammar points the chapter covers, and you need to complete all online exercises in order to get the most benefit from the exercises in this workbook. The points on the left are necessary for completing the exercises in this course packet. The points on the right are recommended if you need some refreshers on parts of speech or what the present tense actually is ☺.

- Present tense of regular verbs — http://coerll.utexas.edu/gg/gr/v_02.htm

- If you need background information on verbs — http://coerll.utexas.edu/gg/gr/v_01.html

- Present tense verbs - sein — http://coerll.utexas.edu/gg/gr/vi_11.html

- Nouns - gender — http://coerll.utexas.edu/gg/gr/no_02.html

- If you need some background information on nouns — http://coerll.utexas.edu/gg/gr/no_01.html
  http://coerll.utexas.edu/gg/gr/det_01.html

- Personal pronouns - nominative case — http://coerll.utexas.edu/gg/gr/pro_02.html

- If you need background information on personal pronouns — http://coerll.utexas.edu/gg/gr/pro_01.html

- Question words (interrogatives) — http://coerll.utexas.edu/gg/gr/con_05.html

- Present tense verbs - haben — http://coerll.utexas.edu/gg/gr/vi_05.htm

Wortschatz
Vorbereitung

A. **LISTEN**

Listen carefully to the pronunciation of each word or phrase in the vocabulary list.

B. **REPEAT**

Repeat each word or phrase OUT LOUD several times until you remember it well and can recognize it as well as produce it. Make a list of the words in this chapter which you find difficult to pronounce. Your teacher may ask you to compare your list with other students in your class. Make sure to learn nouns with their correct gender!

> **Beispiel:**
> die Sprache
> fünf

These ideas are suggestions only. Different learners have different preferences and needs for learning and reviewing vocabulary. Try several of these suggestions until you find ones that work for you. Keep in mind, though, that knowing many words – and knowing them well, both to recognize and to produce – makes you a more effective user of the new language.

C. **WRITE**

Write key words from the vocabulary list so that you can spell them correctly (remember that it makes a big difference whether you cross the Atlantic by ship or by sheep). You may want to listen to the vocabulary list again and write the words as they are spoken for extra practice.

D. **TRANSLATION**

Learn the English translation of each word or phrase. Cover the German column and practice giving the German equivalent for each English word or phrase. Next cover the English column and give the translation of each.

E. **ASSOCIATIONS**

Think of word associations for each category of vocabulary. (What words, both English and German, do you associate with each word or phrase on the list?) Write down ten (10) associations with the vocabulary from the chapter.

> **Beispiel:**
> der Student/die Universität
> das Flugticket/das Flugzeug

F. **COGNATES**

Which words are *cognates*? (Cognates are words which look or sound like English words.) Watch out for *false friends*!!! Write down several cognates and all the false friends from the chapter, create fun sentences that illustrate similarities and differences between the English and German meanings of these words.

> **Beispiel:**
> Nacht/night
> grün/green
> False Friends: hell = light, bright vs. Hölle = hell

G. **WORD FAMILIES**

Which words come from word families in German that you recognize (noun, adjective, verb, adverb)? Write down as many as you find in the chapter.

> **Beispiel:**
> das Studium (noun; studies)
> der Student (noun; person)
> studieren (verb)

H. **EXERCISES**

Write out three (3) „Was passt nicht?" ('Odd one out') exercises. List four words, three of which are related and one that does not fit the same category. Categories can be linked to meaning, grammar, gender, parts of speech (noun, verb, adjective), etc. USE YOUR IMAGINATION! Give the reason for why the odd word does not fit. Your classmates will have to solve the puzzles you provide!

> **Beispiel:**
> grün – blau – gelb – neun
> Here *neun* does not fit, because it is a
> number and all the others are colors.

Kapitel 1

Basiswortschatz
Core Vocabulary

The following presents a list of core vocabulary. Consider this list as the absolute minimum to focus on. As you work through the chapter you will need more vocabulary to help you talk about your own experience. To that end, a more complete vocabulary list can be found at the end of the chapter. Likewise, knowing your numbers, colors and fields of study will greatly aid your achievement of Chapter 1's objectives.

(QR 1.1 p.50)

Begrüßungen	Greetings
Hallo!	Hello!
Guten Morgen!	Good morning.
Guten Tag!	Hello! (Good Day)
Auf Wiedersehen!	Goodbye! (formal)
Bis morgen!	See you tomorrow.
Bis Samstag!	See you Saturday.

Persönliche Informationen	Personal information
Wie heißt du?/Wie ist dein Name?	What's your name?
Wie heißen Sie?/Wie ist Ihr Name?	What's our name? (formal)
Ich heiße …	My name is …
Ich bin …	I am …
Ich bin Student/Studentin.	I am a student (m/f).
heißen	to be called
sein	to be
haben	to have
wohnen	to live (reside)
gehen	to go or walk
bleiben	to stay or remain
finden	to find

Jemanden kennenlernen	To meet someone
Wer ist das?	Who is that?
vorstellen	to introduce
Freut mich!	Nice to meet you.
Angenehm.	(here) Pleased to meet you.
Es freut mich, dich/Sie kennen zu lernen.	It is nice to meet you (informal/formal).
Danke.	Thank you.
Bitte.	Please / You are welcome.
Entschuldigung.	Excuse me
(Es) tut mir leid.	I am sorry.
Ja, bitte.	Yes, please.
Nein, danke.	No, thank you.

Herkunft	Origin/Nationality
kommen aus	to come from
Woher kommst du?	Where do you come from? (informal)
die USA	the US
Deutschland	Germany
Österreich	Austria
die Schweiz	Switzerland
Amerika (Nord-, Mittel-, Südamerika)	America (North, Central, South America)
Europa	Europe

Weitere persönliche Informationen	More personal information
das Jahr (Jahre)	the year
Wie alt bist du?	How old are you?
Wie alt sind Sie?	How old are you? (formal)
Ich bin achtzehn Jahre alt.	I am 18 years old.
Was ist Ihre Adresse?	What is your address?
die Hausnummer (-nummern)	house number
die Postleitzahl (-zahlen)	zip code

Wie geht's?	**How are you? (informal)**
Wie geht es Ihnen?	How are you? (formal)
Sehr gut, danke!	Very well, thanks.
Es geht mir gut.	I'm doing great!
Ausgezeichnet!	Excellent!
Es geht mir nicht so gut.	I'm not feeling well.
Ich bin müde.	I'm tired.

An der Uni studieren	**Studying at the University**
das Hauptfach (-fächer)	major
das Nebenfach (-fächer)	minor
lernen	to learn, to study (homework, for a test, etc.)
studieren	to study (major in; study at university)
der Studentenausweis (-ausweise)	student ID card
das Studentenwohnheim (-heime)	dormitory
die Toilette (Toiletten)	restrooms
das Studienfach (-fächer)	fields of study

Die Woche	**The week**
Montag	Monday
Dienstag	Tuesday
Mittwoch	Wednesday
Donnerstag	Thursday
Freitag	Friday
Samstag/Sonnabend	Saturday
Sonntag	Sunday
das Wochenende (-enden)	the weekend

Sich vorstellen

Aktivität 1. Harald und Peter: Wer bin ich?

Listen to the interviews with Harald and Peter. Circle the correct answers to the questions as they introduce themselves.

(QR 1.22 p.50)

HARALD

	Münster	München	Mainz
Herkunft? Er kommt aus	Münster	München	Mainz
Alter? Er ist	15 Jahre alt	25 Jahre alt	50 Jahre alt
Lieblingsfarbe? Seine Lieblingsfarbe ist	Rot	Blau	Braun
Warum? Warum ist das seine Lieblingsfarbe?	Sie ist wie Bayern und der Himmel (sky).	Er weiß es nicht.	Diese Farbe ist energisch.

(QR 1.26 p.50)

PETER

	der Schweiz	Texas	Stuttgart
Herkunft? Er kommt aus	der Schweiz	Texas	Stuttgart
Nummer? Welche Nummer sagt er?	seine Telefonnummer	seine Hausnummer	
Lieblingsfarbe? Seine Lieblingsfarbe ist	Rot	Blau	Braun
Warum? Warum ist das seine Lieblingsfarbe?	Sie ist ruhig (peaceful).	Sie ist intensiv.	Sie ist die Farbe der Liebe (love).

Aktivität 2. Wer bin ich?

What are the questions? Listen to the clips with Harald and Peter again. What questions does the interviewer ask, and what do the questions mean?

(QR 1.22 p.50)
(QR 1.26 p.50)

Wie heißen Sie?	What's your telephone number?
Woher kommen Sie?	What's your favorite color?
Wie alt sind Sie?	Where are you from?
Wie lautet Ihre Telefonnummer?	How old are you?
Was ist Ihre Lieblingsfarbe?	What's your name?
Warum?	Why?

Consider the questions from these two interviews. You can view the clips again as well as review the questions in *Aktivität 2*. What word does the interviewer use to refer to either Harald or Peter?

How does the interviewer refer to "you" with these people? _____

Your reflection on this question will be important for a later exercise.

Aktivität 3. Wie heißt du?

Ask several of your classmates what their names are and write them in the box below

Student 1 _____

Student 2 _____

Student 3 _____

Now tell your teacher and the rest of the class what your new classmates' names are:

Wie heißt er/sie?

Er/sie heißt _____.

Er/sie heißt _____.

Aktivität 4. Ich heiße …

Form a circle, and play the chain-game with the names: One student begins by saying

S1: „Ich heiße_____" and asks his/her neighbor on the right or left "Wie heißt du?"

S2: That student says „Ich heiße_____" and adds (regarding the first student) „Er/sie heißt _____" and asks the next student „Wie heißt du?".

S3: The third student, in turn, says „Ich heiße _____", „Er/Sie heißt _____" (about the second student), „Er/Sie heißt _____" (about the first student) and asks the next student „Wie heißt du?" etc. until all students have named all their classmates.

Grimm Gramma

At home please read the following grammar point on the *Grimm Gramma* website.

Present tense of regular verbs (also complete the activities for this grammar point)

If you need some background on verbs, please read http://coerll.utexas.edu/gg/gr/v_01.html

ich komm • e
du komm • st
er komm • t
sie komm • t
es komm • t

wir komm • en
ihr komm • t
sie komm • en

Sie komm • en (formal)

Die Zahlen

Aktivität 5. Wie lautet deine Telefonnummer?
Die Zahlen

0	1	2	3	4	5	6	7	8	9	10
null	eins	zwei	drei	vier	fünf	sechs	sieben	acht	neun	zehn

A. Ask two of your classmates what their phone numbers are:
Wie lautet deine Telefonnummer?

Meine Telefonnummer ist: _____

B. Now report back to your instructor: Seine/Ihre Telefonnummer ist…

Aktivität 6. Wichtige Adressen & Telefonnummern in Deutschland

When you go to German-speaking countries, you will likely need to call someone at some point (e.g., your school, a pizzeria, etc.). Contact information is often presented differently in various cultures, so it helps to familiarize yourself with how to glean phone numbers, addresses, opening times abroad. As a first step, read the following information and answer the questions below.

Amerikanische Botschaft Berlin
Neustädtische Kirchstr. 4-5
10117 Berlin
Tel.: (030) 2385 174

American Citizen Services
Tel.: (030) 832-9233, 14-16 Uhr, Montag bis Freitag
Tel. in Notfällen außerhalb der Öffnungszeiten:
(030) 8305-0,   Fax: (030) 8305-1215
Öffnungszeiten: 8:30-12:00 Uhr, Montag bis Freitag
Geschlossen an deutschen und amerikanischen Feiertagen

Notrufnummern

Feuer	112
Polizei	110
Rettungsleitstelle	19222

International Office
Partnerhochschulen
Internationale Netzwerke

Pizza Station | Heisenbergstr. 1 | 97076 Würzburg

So finden Sie das International Office:

Postadresse:

Universität Würzburg
International Office
Sanderring 2
D-97070 Würzburg

Kontakt

www.international.uni-wuerzburg.de

international@uni-wuerzburg.de

Tel.: Ansprechpartner/innen
Fax: +49/ (0)931/ 31 82603

1. What are the address and the telephone number of the American Embassy? When is its office for citizenship services open? Which days and what time? What is the phone number and what is the fax number?

2. What is the address of the *Uni Würzburg*'s international student office? Where could you get more information about the office?

3. What is the address of the pizza delivery service? What is the zip code? What is the phone number?

4. What do you think **Notrufnummern** means? What does **Feuer** mean and who do you call with the number **112**?

Aktivität 7. Zahlen und Nummern
Although you can list the individual digits of your phone number (and many Germans do), a lot of people use double or triple digits like in English, or as you would state your age.

So, your friend's phone number can be 0-1-7-5-6-1-8-0-6-7-0

null-eins-sieben-fünf-sechs-eins-acht-null-sechs-sieben-null

or   0-1-7-5-61-80-670 null-eins-sieben-fünf-einundsechzig-achtzig-sechshundertsiebzig

Similarly, your age is not 1-9 (eins neun) but rather 19 (neunzehn).

11	elf	40	vierzig
12	zwölf	50	fünfzig
13	dreizehn	60	sechzig
14	vierzehn	70	siebzig
15	fünfzehn	80	achtzig
16	sechzehn	90	neunzig
17	siebzehn	100	(ein)hundert
18	achtzehn	200	zweihundert
19	neunzehn	252	zweihundertzweiundfünfzig
20	zwanzig	500	fünfhundert
21	einundzwanzig	1000	(ein)tausend
22	zweiundzwanzig	1982	(ein)tausendneunhundertzweiundachtzig *or* neunzehnhundertzweiundachtzig (if it's a date)
30	dreißig	2008	zweitausendacht
31	einunddreißig	2012	zweitausendzwölf
32	zweiunddreißig	10000	zehntausend
33	dreiunddreißig	1000000	eine Million
34	vierunddreißig		

Aktivität 8. Das Alter
Ask the two classmates you've been working with how old they are.

S1: Wie alt bist du?

  S2: Ich bin _____ Jahre alt.

S2: Und du? Wie alt bist du?

  S1: Ich bin _____ Jahre alt.

When you report back to your instructor, use

  Er/sie ist _____ Jahre alt.

„Zum Geburtstag viel Glück!
Zum Geburtstag viel Glück!
Zum Geburtstag, lieber/liebe _____,
zum Geburtstag viel Glück!"

Aktivität 9. Wie viel kostet es?
You use double and triple digits for expressing how much something costs as well. Look at the following *Rechnung* and identify how much we paid for the Pizza Margherita, the „Quo Vadis" house salad, the coke, the Pellegrino mineral water, and the espresso. Write the prices out with words; some of the items have already been modeled for you.
http://www.r-quovadis.de/html/karte.html

Die Pizza Margherita _____ .

Der Salat _____ .

Die Cola _____ .

Das Mineralwasser _____ .

Ein Espresso _____ .

Insgesamt bezahlen wir _____ .

Das Eis (der Schneemann) kostet zwei Euro fünfzig. ⇨

Die Pizza Molto Forte kostet sechs Euro achtzig. ⇨

Ein Glas Apfelschorle kostet ein Euro neunzig. ⇨

Die Mehrwertsteuer beträgt sechs Euro fünfundsiebzig.

```
         RISTORANTE PIZZERIA CAFE
            QUO VADIS
             DOMSTRASSE 24
AUTHENTISCH  97070 WÜRZBURG
         TEL.: 0931/4605330

#0000                    18-07-200

    RECHNUNG             1821

        TISCHNR. 60

2   327 SCHNEEMANN   2.50    *5.00
1   151 MARGHERITA   4.50    *4.50
1   121 SAL.QUO VADI 7.00    *7.00
1   162 MOLTO FORTE  6.80    *6.80
1  x0.5 COLA         3.00    *3.00
3  x0.5 SAN PELLEGRI 2.30    *6.90
2  x0.3 A-SCHORLE    1.90    *3.80
1   141 TROMBINI     2.50    *2.50
2   ESPRESSO         1.40    *2.80
SUMME                       *42.30

BAR-EURO             *42.30
NETTO-MWST 19%              *35.55
MWST 19% EURO               *6.75

  Vielen Dank für Ihren Besuch.
Wir freuen uns auf ein Wiedersehen.
Es bediente Sie .Bedienung 2
```

Aktivität 10. Sprache im Kontext:
Mit dem Bus zur Uni
Knowing your numbers comes in very handy when you want to travel by bus, too.

(QR 1.28 p.50)

A. Watch the Sprache im Kontext clip with Tobias, and write down what the clip is about:
What do you notice? Who is in the clip? Where does it take place? etc.

B. Watch the clip again and check all words that you hear.

❑ Busticket
❑ Universität
❑ Bargeld
❑ Studenten
❑ Studentenausweis
❑ bezahlen
❑ kosten
❑ fahren
❑ Fahrplan

C. Watch the clip again and answer the questions below.

1. Which three buses go *in die Stadt* and to the *Hubland*?

    1   10   14   40   114   1400

2. What do you need to get to the Hubland campus by bus?

    1. A bus pass, which you can buy on any bus or tram in Würzburg

    2. Cash (*Bargeld*); at least 10 Euro

    3. Your student ID card, which lets you travel free on any public transportation in Würzburg

D. Listen to the clip one more time. What article does Tobias use in front of the key nouns in his message? What does the article indicate about the gender of these nouns?

_____ Tobias   _____ Hubland (Campus)

_____ Bushaltestelle   _____ Nummer

_____ Linie   _____ Studentenausweis

Grimm Grammar

At home please read the following grammar point on the *Grimm Grammar* website.

• Verbs – *sein*
(and complete the exercise, too)

ich bin – I am
du bist – you are
er ist – he is
sie ist – she is
es ist – it is

wir sind – we are
ihr seid – you all are
sie sind – they are

Sie sind – you are (formal)

Aktivität 11. Würzburg entdecken

You just arrived in Würzburg and even though it is not the biggest city as you will see in the next exercise it is different than what you are used to in the US. Answer the questions on the next page using the map below.

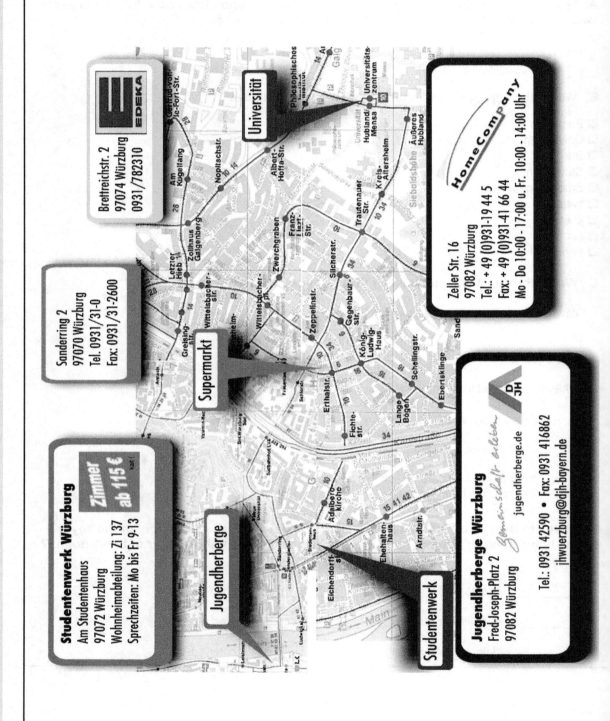

1. Wie lautet die Adresse des Studentenwerks? (Write out the numbers of the zip code.)

2. Wie lautet die Telefonnummer der Jugendherberge in Würzburg?

3. In welcher Straße liegt die Universität in Würzburg und welche Hausnummer hat sie?

4. Deine Wohnung liegt „Am Kugelfang". Welchen Bus/welche Busse musst du zur Uni nehmen?

Aktivität 12. Und wer wohnt in Würzburg?

Here are statistical information about the city of Würzburg from their website. Practice your *Zahlen* and try to match the nouns on the right hand side with the corresponding German terms in the table. You may use a dictionary. Then check with your classmates and the teacher.

Bevölkerung

	2010	2000	1990
Einwohner	133799	127966	127777
Männer	62401	59038	58376
Frauen	71398	68928	69401
ausländische Mitbürger	16977	15544	9241
Einwohner je km²	1528	1461	1459
Zuzüge	11192	12596	-
Fortzüge	10253	11522	-
Geburten	1014	1051	1329
Sterbefälle	1355	1509	1553

A. Match

moves away from

births • women

moves to • citizens

men • foreign citizens

population • deaths

Altersstruktur
im Jahr 2009 bzw. 2029

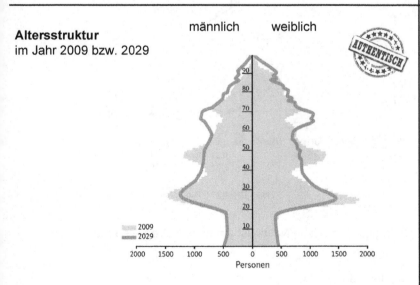

B. Answer & discuss

What do you call this type of graph?

What does it tell us about the city of Würzburg?

Do you know how this graph would look like for your city?

Weitere Informationen
Stadt Würzburg **www.wuerzburg.de**

Aktivität 13. Wüzburg versus Deutschland

In the following you will engage with more statistical data about Würzburg and Germany. The *Bundesinstitut für Bevölkerungsforschung* (federal institute for population research) offers a variety of tables, maps, graphs and other visualized statistics along with explanations. Visit any of the following websites for more facts about Germany: http://www.bib-demografie.de (go to the Download-Center), http://www.tatsachen-ueber-deutschand.de or http://www.auswaertiges-amt.de.

A. Compare and discuss the information about Würzburg and Germany

Infobox	Würzburg	Deutschland
Einwohner	135.212	82.002.400
Ausländeranteil	12,8%	8,8%
Bevölkerung mit Migrationshintergrund	Keine Angaben	19,3%
Arbeitslosenquote	5%	7%
Bruttoeinkommen	26.319€	27.493€
Sozialhilfeempfänger	2,6%	3,5%
Kita-Quote	55,25%	50,25%

1. What does *Bevölkerung mit Migrationshintergrund* mean? How is it different to *Ausländeranteil*?

2. What is a *Kita-Quote*? Do you have that in your city or country?

3. Which information surprise/confuse/shock you?

B. What does the following statistic tell you?

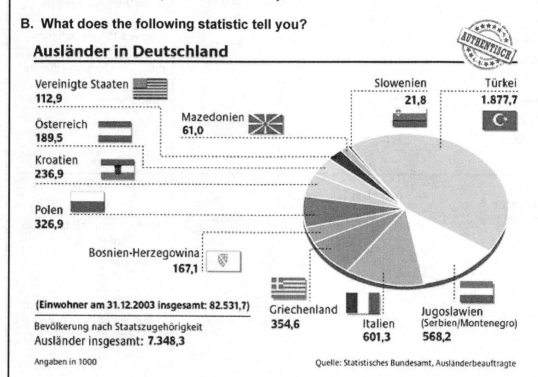

1. Wie heißen die Nationen auf Englisch? Welche Nation ist am meisten vertreten (most represented)? Warum?

2. Wie heißen die Personen aus den Ländern? Complete below and pick two more.

die Türkei	Österreich	Italien		
der Türke die Türkin	der Österreicher die	der d		

WER BIN ICH?

Aktivität 14. Wer sind sie?

Watch the „Wer bin ich?" set of video clips and take notes about the native speakers of German. Wie heißen sie? Woher kommen sie? Wie alt sind sie? Was erzählen (*tell*) sie uns noch?

	(QR 1.15 p.50)	(QR 1.18 p.50)	(QR 1.23 p.50)
Name			
Kommt aus			
Alter			
Telefonnummer			
Lieblingsfarbe (warum?)			

You may want to use http://maps.google.de to find out where their home towns are in Germany!

Aktivität 15. Was ist die Antwort?

Listen to Berna's clip again. Connect the correct questions with the correct answers.
(QR 1.15 p.50)

Wie heißt du?	Rot, weil es temperamentvoll ist.
Woher kommst du?	(512) 749-8940
Wie alt bist du?	Ich heiße Berna.
Was ist deine Telefonnummer?	Aus Kiel.
Was ist deine Lieblingsfarbe?	30.

Aktivität 16. Woher kommst du und was ist deine Lieblingsfarbe?
Find out where your two classmates are from and what their favorite colors are and why.

Name		
Woher kommst du?		
Was ist deine Lieblingsfarbe?		
Warum?		

Woher kommst du?

Ich komme aus _____ (Er/Sie kommt aus …)

Was ist deine Lieblingsfarbe?

Meine Lieblingsfarbe ist _____ (Seine/Ihre Lieblingsfarbe ist …)

Warum?

_____ ist meine Lieblingsfarbe, weil es _____ ist.

Nota bene:
When colors are used as adjectives to describe something, they are **not** capitalized: *Das Haus ist rot.*

Ich komme aus …
Amerika
Texas
Kalifornien
Großbritannien
England
der Türkei
dem Irak
Ungarn
den Niederlanden
Russland
Houston
Kanada
Mexiko
Australien
Schweden
Norwegen
Südafrika
Indien

Rot Blau Grün
Braun Schwarz
Grau Lila
Rosa Orange
Weiß
hell ◁□□□□□□■■▶dunkel

ruhig/beruhigend (calm/calming)
energisch/intensiv/temperamentvoll/dynamisch
schön (pretty)
ungewöhnlich (unusual)
warm/freundlich/gemütlich (friendly)
glücklich/fröhlich (happy)

Aktivität 17. Wer sind die Amerikaner?

Below is a similar table to the one you filled out in *Aktivität* 13. Go to the Internet site again and watch the „Wer bin ich?" video clips of the American students and fill out the information based on what they say.

	(QR 1.2 p.50)	(QR 1.5 p.50)	(QR 1.7 p.50)	(QR 1.10 p.50)	(QR 1.13 p.50)
Name					
Herkunft					
Alter					
Telefonnummer					
Lieblingsfarbe (warum?)					

Now, consider the questions posed to both the American and German speakers in Aktivität 13 and 16. What word is used to refer to "you" with these people? _____

Consider now your answer to the question as it refered to Harald and Peter in *Aktivität* 1 and 2. What has changed? How do those two men differ from the people interviewed in *Aktivität* 13 and 16? Write down your thoughts and discuss them with your classmates.

Aktivität 18. Kurze Beschreibungen

Select any one of the interview subjects (either from the native or the non-native speaker group) and write a brief paragraph that introduces that person. Mention their N*ame, Herkunft, Alter, Telefonnummer* and *Lieblingsfarbe*.

Er/Sie heißt _____ . _____ kommt aus _____

_____

_____

_____

Aktivität 19. Meine Kommilitonen

Collect the information you jotted down about one of your classmates, and write a paragraph that introduces him or her, using the same information as listed in the previous *Aktivitäten*.

_____

_____

_____

_____

Grimm Grammar

At home please read the following grammar point on the *Grimm Grammar* website.

• nouns – gender

If you need background information, please see

• nouns – overview
• determiners – articles

• personal pronouns in the nominative case

If you need background information, please read

• personal pronouns overview

ich – I
du – you
er – he
sie – she
es – it

wir – we
ihr – you guys (y'all)
sie – they

Sie – you (formal)

Aktivität 20. Sprache im Kontext: Der Studentenausweis

Watch the „Sprache im Kontext" clip entitled „Studentenausweis - Student ID"
What information you can find on a German University ID according to Mario?

((QR 1.29 p.50))

A. Watch the video and check all the words you hear

❑ Name	❑ Bibliothek	❑ Vorlesung
❑ Universität	❑ lesen	❑ ausgehen
❑ Studienfach	❑ Barcode	❑ offen
❑ Monate	❑ Studiengang	❑ Verkehrssystem

B. What purposes does the Studentenausweis serve? Circle the numbers of all the sentences that apply

1.   It's proof of one's status as student.
2.   It lets students take a vacation in Germany.
3.   Students can use the public transportation system (for free).
4.   It allows students to borrow books from the library.
5.   It allows students to find a course of study.
6.   It provides information about one's course of study.

C. Watch the clip again and fill in the blanks with the missing words
(they are provided on the left, out of order).

studiere
Deutschland
Student
Name
geht
Bücher
Semester
Ticket

Der Studentenausweis. Damit können wir jedem zeigen, dass wir

_____ sind. Es ist zum Beispiel die Universität vermerkt.
Universität Würzburg. Studentenausweis. Und das Semesterticket.

Semesterticket bedeutet, _____ einfach, ja, es gibt zwei Semester
im Jahr und dazwischen jeweils 2 oder 3 Monate Pause in _____.

Und mit diesem _____ können wir im öffentlichen
Verkehrsnahsystem herumfahren.

Der _____ ist darauf gemerkt, in dem wievielten Semester ich mich
befinde.

Und ein Barcode, damit man in der Bibliothek _____ ausleihen
kann.

Zudem ist vermerkt, welchen Studiengang ich belege und was ich

_____.

Und die Vorlesungsdauer, wie lang eben das Semester _____.

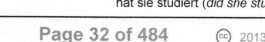

Das ist ein Studentenausweis von einer Studentin. Wie heißt sie? Was ist ihre
Matrikelnummer? Was ist eine Matrikelnummer überhaupt? Wann, wo und was
hat sie studiert (*did she study*)?

Aktivität 21. Die Uni Würzburg

Here is an authentic excerpt from the actual registration form for the Julius-Maximilians-Universität in Würzburg. Fill it out according to the prompts, and you are ready to study there next summer! Keep in mind: Germans dates are written differently from American English: Day/Month/Year (e.g., 10. Mai 2013).

JULIUS-MAXIMILIANS-UNIVERSITÄT WÜRZBURG

Matrikelnummer/*matriculation number*
(wird vom Studentensekretariat ausgefüllt/ *filled out by the Registrar's Office*)

Antrag auf Einschreibung / *application for matriculation*

zum WINTER - / SOMMER – Semester   *(winter term / summer term)*   ....

für Studiengang/Studiengangkombination / *for Course of Studies/Combination of Study Courses*
....

Bitte beachten Sie beim Ausfüllen dieses Antrags die **ERLÄUTERUNGEN** und verwenden Sie Groß- und Klein-schreibung sowie Umlaute (ä, ö, ü). Schreiben Sie **bitte leserlich in Druckbuchstaben**. *To fill out this form, please notice the* ***ELUCIDATIONS*** *and* ***print legibly***.

Angaben zur Person / *Personal Data*

Name/*Surname*: ....   Geb.-Datum/*Date of Birth*:............................

Vorname/*Christian name*: ....   Geburtsort/*Place of Birth*: ....

Namenszusatz/*Name Affix*: .... (z.B. Dr,./*e.g. Dr.*)   Geburtsname/*Name of Birth*:.................

Geschlecht/*Gender*:   ☐ männlich/*male*   ☐ weiblich/*female*

Staatsangehörigkeit/*Citizenship*:

bitte **internationales Kfz-Kennzeichen** (z.B. D, F, GB)   ....
angeben oder falls nicht bekannt, Staat ausschreiben'
please specify ***international licence plate number*** *(e.g. F, GB, IR for Iran)*

Name und Vorname der Eltern
Surname an Christian name of Parents   Vater/*Father*   ....
(freiwillige Angaben/*voluntary data*)   Mutter/*Mother*   ....

Heimatanschrift / *Home Adress:*

Str., Nr./*Adress Line 1*   ....   Zusätze/*Adress Line 2*
....
PLZ, Ort/*Postal code, City*   ....
....
bitte **internationales Kfz-Kennzeichen** (z.B. D, F, GB)
angeben oder falls nicht bekannt, Staat ausschreiben
please specify ***international licence plate number***
....

Semesteranschrift / *Address during Semester:*

Str., Nr./*Address Line 1*   ....   Zusätze/*Address Line 2*............................
PLZ, Ort/*Postal code, City*   ....
....

Korrespondenzanschrift soll sein   ☐ Heimatanschrift/*Home Address*   ☐ Semesteranschrift/*Address*
during Semester
Address of correspondence shall be:

E-Mail-Adresse/ *Email Adress:* ....@...
(soweit vorhanden und regelmässig genutzt/*as far as available and regularly used*)
(freiwillige Angaben/*voluntary data*)

Angaben zum gewünschten Studiengang / Data for the desired Course of Studies

Ich beantrage die Einschreibung in folgenden Studiengang:
I apply for study in the following discipline:

1.Studiengang / *1. Course of Studies* **(i.e., major)**

angestrebter Abschluss/*aspired Certificate*: ....
    1.   Studienfach/*1. subject* ....
    2.   Studienfach/*2. subject* ....

2.Studiengang / *2. Course of Studies* **(i.e., second major—there is no minor)**

angestrebter Abschluss/*aspired Certificate*: ....
    1.   Studienfach/*1. Field of Study* ....
    2.   Studienfach/*2. Field of Study* ....

Sind Sie außer an der Universität Würzburg auch an einer anderen Hochschule eingeschrieben? Falls ja,
Are you matriculated at another univerisity or academia ? If so,

an welcher Hochschule/*at which university*? ....
angestrebter Abschluss/*aspired Certificate*: ....
    1.   Studienfach/*1. subject* ....
    2.   Studienfach/*2. subject* ....

Haben Sie bereits im Heimatland oder in einem anderen Land außerhalb Deutschlands studiert? / *Did you study*
abroad (outside Germany)?   (Mehrfachnennungen möglich/*multiple answers permitted*)

Falls ja, geben Sie bitte an/*If so, please specify:*

1. Staat / *Country*

bitte **internationales Kfz-Kennzeichen**

(z.B. D, F, GB) angeben oder falls nicht
bekannt, bitte **Namen des Staates** ausschreiben
please specify **international licence plate number**

.... ☐ ☐

Anzahl der Monate/*Number of Months*   ☐ ☐

....
Ort, Datum / *Place, Date*   Unterschrift / *Signature*

Amerikanistik	Französisch	Ökonomie/Wirtschaft
Anglistik	Geographie	Philosophie
Anthropologie	Geologie	Physik
Archäologie	Geschichte (Europas, Asiens usw.)	Psychologie
Architektur	Ingenieurwissenschaften	Sonderpädagogik
Astronomie	Italienisch	Spanisch
Biologie	Jura	Sportwissenschaften
Chemie	Kunst	Medizin
Computerwissenschaften/Informatik	Kunstgeschichte	Pädagogik
Deutsch	Linguistik/Philologie	Politologie/Politikwissenschaft
Englisch	Mathematik	Soziologie
Film	Musikwissenschaft	Theologie

You can explore the other areas of study at Würzburg at http://www.uni-wuerzburg.de/ueber/fakultaeten/

Aktivität 22. Was machen sie gern?

Listen to the videoclips from Eva, Sara and Adan. The titles of the videos are the column headings in the table. Take notes about what information they give you about themselves. Use the words in the word-bank to help you listen better.

Gymnasium • Kulturwissenschaften • Eltern • Wohnung
Sportverein • Freunde • turnen • Weindorf • Fluss • Grundschule
Hauptfach • Studentenwohnheim • viele Bekannte • Ruderklub • verstehen • schwer
auf Deutsch denken • Lieblingsfarbe • neutral • Deutsch als Fremdsprache
Musik • ins Konzert gehen • teuer • Haustiere

	Studium & Wohnen	Hobbys & Interessen	Freunde & Weiteres
	(QR 1.16 p.50)		(QR 1.17 p.50)
	(QR 1.19 p.50)	(QR 1.21 p.50)	(QR 1.20 p.50)
	(QR 1.24 p.50)		(QR 1.25 p.50)

Aktivität 23. Ein bisschen Journalismus

Using the notes you took above, try to re-create Eva's, Berna's and Jan's comments. For this exercise, you'll need to review the regular verbs in the present tense in *Grimm Grammar*.

Aktivität 24. Interview

Generate some questions with your classmates that would elicit the kinds of answers the interviewees gave. Select 5-7 questions and conduct an interview with a partner you haven't worked with yet.

A. Fragen

B. Ein kurzes Interview

Frage	Antwort

C. Die Reportage

Write a short paragraph describing your partner's interests. Feel free to include the previously learned materials regarding his/her name, heritage, studies, etc.

Aktivität 25. Wer macht was?

Watch the „Studium & Wohnen" video clips from Hassan, Erin and Sophia. Then put H, E and/or S next to each statement to indicate who said it.

(QR 1.6 p.50)

(QR 1.8 p.50)

(QR 1.14 p.50)

Ich wohne in der Nähe der Universität.		Ich studierte Philosophie, Altgriechisch und Latein.	
Ich wohne in der Nähe von der Autobahn.		Ich wohne im Europahaus 1.	
Ich studiere Deutsch und Kunstgeschichte.		Jetzt wohne ich in Würzburg.	
In der ersten Woche ist es schwer [in Deutschland] Deutsch zu verstehen.		Ich wohne in Austin.	

Aktivität 26. Erin und Hassan – „Freunde & Weiteres"

Richtig oder falsch? Watch Erin's and Hassan's clip „Freunde & Weiteres" and decide which of the following statements are correct, and which are not. Correct those that are false.

A. Erin

Ich habe viele deutsche Freunde.	R	F		
Ich habe in Würzburg ein Praktikum gemacht.	R	F		
In Bayern kann ich Deutsch nicht verstehen.	R	F		(QR 1.9 p.50)
Nach ein paar Tagen versteht man viel Deutsch.	R	F		

B. Hassan

Ich war letzten Sommer in Würzburg.	R	F		
Ich habe viele Freunde getroffen.	R	F		
Meine Freunde heißen Alfred und Tina.	R	F		(QR 1.27 p.50)
Meine Freunde wollen, dass ich ihnen mit ihrem Englisch helfe.	R	F		
Es ist leicht in Würzburg Deutsch zu verstehen.	R	F		

Aktivität 27. Berna

View Berna's videos, „Studium & Wohnen" and „Freunde & Weiteres" and find out more about her by answering the following questions.

Studieren & Wohnen   (QR 1.16 p.50)

What does Berna study at the university?	
Which languages does Berna know?	
In which city does Berna live now?	
When did Berna move there?	

Freunde & Weiteres   (QR 1.17 p.50)

What are Berna's best friends called?	
Where are her friends from?	
Did she find it difficult to learn English?	
How long did she study English in Germany?	

Aktivität 28. Jan

You would like to get to know Berna's housemate, Jan. Fill in the blanks with the missing information after you watch the following clips of him.

Grimm Gramma

Studieren & Wohnen   (QR 1.24
                                p.50)

Ich studiere _____ .

Ich wohne in _____, _____ .

Ich bin im Jahre _____ in Amerika angekommen.

Ich habe hier schon in _____ gelebt und ich habe in

Austin gelebt.

Freunde & Weiteres   (QR 1.25
                                p.50)

Meine besten Freunde in Austin sind _____ .

Sie kommen beide aus _____ .

Wir haben schon im deutschen Gymnasium _____ gelernt, ab

der _____ten Klasse.

Und ich habe in _____ auch schon etwas Englisch studiert.

At home please read the following grammar point on the *Grimm Grammar* website.

question words
(Interrogatives)

Wann? – When?
Warum? – Why?
Was? – What?
Wer? – Who?
Wie? – How?
Wo? – Where?

Review also the personal pronouns in nominative.

Zum Nachdenken:

In clip 3, Berna emphasizes the word **studieren**. She says she had English classes at school, then studied English afterwards. Jan also separates learning English in high school and afterwards. First of all, what do you think **Schule** and **Gymnasium** refer to? Second, what do you think the word **studieren** means for German speakers? How is it used differently from the English word **to study**?

Aktivität 29. Fragen, Fragen, noch mehr Fragen

You learned the question words and a lot of other things that are useful when meeting new people. You are participating in the exchange program with Würzburg. With a partner collect keywords that can help you generate questions to ask people you meet in your courses.

A. Keywords for personal questions

Beispiel: *Herkunft*		
		Woher?

B. Generate questions using question words and the keywords above.

Persönliche Fragen

C. Interview one of your classmates using some of the questions you generated.
Jot down their answers and then write a short report about their answers. Present your report to the class.

Aktivität 30. Sprache im Kontext: Das Handy
Now that you got to know new people in Würzburg you need a way to contact them. Therefore, one of the first things you will need (ok, want) to buy right away in Würzburg is a Handy. Listen to Adam to learn what a Handy actually is (since you will want it so soon, you might as well find out what it is!), how to get it, and what phrases you will need to be able to purchase it.

A. Watch the „Sprache im Kontext" clip with Adam and and write down what the clip is about:

What do you notice? Who is in the video? Where does it take place? What do you think is it about?

(QR 1.30 p.<?>)

B. Watch the clip again, jot down all the words you recognize:

C. Watch the clip a third time, and figure out what a *Handy* is: _____

D. When you watch the clip the forth time, answer these more detailed questions:

What is the name of the *Handy*-store?		What is the special offer?	
What kind of a *Konto* does he recommend opening?		How much does it cost to use the *Handy* in Germany?	
What kind of *Handy* can you buy?		How much does it cost when someone calls you?	
How much is a *Handy* without a *SIM-Karte*?		How much is it to send and receive an *SMS*?	

E. Watch the clip one more time and bring the following statements in the right order:

_____ Der Verkäufer kann das Geld auf Ihr Handy laden.

_____ Sie bekommen eine Karte mit einem PIN-Code darauf.

_____ Sie bezahlen 30 Euro.

_____ Sie sagen: „Ich brauche 30 Euro Guthaben, bitte."

Grimm Grammar

At home please read the following grammar point on the *Grimm Grammar* website.

present tense verbs **haben**

ich habe – I have
du hast – you have
er hat – he has
sie hat – she has
es hat – it has

wir haben – we have
ihr habt – you all have
sie haben – they have

Sie haben – you have (formal)

review also:

present tense regular verbs

personal pronouns nominative

Aktivität 31. Lieder & Musik

Annett Louisan – Drück die 1. Listen to this song by German singer Annett Louisan, then complete the activities in the pdf available on the *Deutsch im Blick* website (*Kapitel 1*: „Lieder & Musik").

Aktivität 32. Sprechen Sie Deutsch?

You already learned different greetings throughout the chapter, but there are many other forms depending where you are. The following text describes the different greetings used in the German speaking countries on the European continent. Read the text below and answer the questions.

In Deutschland, Österreich und der Schweiz sprechen die Menschen zwar alle Deutsch, aber es hört sich teilweise ganz unterschiedlich an. In dem Text lernen Sie, wie man sich in den drei Ländern begrüßt und verabschiedet.

In den deutschsprachigen Ländern hört man verschiedene Dialekte. In Norddeutschland zum Beispiel spricht man Plattdütsch und begrüßt sich mit „Moin moin". Im Süden (zum Beispiel in Bayern oder in Baden-Württemberg) sagen die Menschen „Grüß Gott", wenn sie andere Leute treffen. In Deutschland spricht man auch Hochdeutsch und benutzt Begrüßungsformeln wie „Guten Morgen", „Guten Tag", oder „Guten Abend". In Österreich hören wir auch „Servus" und „Grüß dich". In der Schweiz hört man „Grüezi" (Grüß Sie). Die hochdeutschen Begrüßungen und die Verabschiedung „Auf Wiedersehen" versteht man natürlich auch in der Schweiz.

Wichtig ist auch, dass man unbekannte oder fremde Leute mit „Sie" anspricht (siezen). Normalerweise spricht man nur gute Freunde oder Familienmitglieder mit „du" an (duzen). Freunde begrüßen sich mit „Hallo", „Hi" oder in Bayern auch „Servus". Zur Verabschiedung sagt man unter Freunden „Tschüss", „Mach's gut" oder „Ciao". Speziell in Mittel- und Norddeutschland sagt man „Tschüss" und im Rheinland „Tschö". Standarddeutsch für Verabschiedungen ist „Auf Wiedersehen". In Baden-Württemberg sagt man zur Verabschiedung „Ade".

Fragen zum Text

1. Write down all the greetings for the three countries: which terms are used for greeting and taking leave?

Deutschland		Österreich		die Schweiz	
Begrüßung	Verabschiedung	Begrüßung	Verabschiedung	Begrüßung	Verabschiedung

2. According to the text which of these greetings are formal and which are informal?

3. How do you understand „*duzen*" and „*siezen*" based on this text? With whom do you think you would use each of these? Is there any similar distinction in formality in your own language?

4. Do you have German-speaking family or friends? If yes, find out from them, what greetings they use with various people (either in writing or in spoken interactions).

Aktivität 33. Kennenlernspiel

In this chapter you learned how to introduce yourself and get to know others. You already talked to a couple of your peers during this chapter, and now it's time to get to know everyone else in class as well.

First, write three questions that you would need in order to find the information the boxes ask for. Try the rest as you go. Remember, instead of using a question word simply use and conjugate the verb of the sentence. Place it in the very beginning (the place a question word would have taken) of the sentence. *Tada!*
Some of the verbs might look strange, those are irregular forms, just recognize it for now.

For example: „Reist du in die Schweiz?"

- _____

- _____

- _____

Then, talk to your classmates. Ask the questions and write down the student's name who can answer each question with "yes".

Finde mindestens eine Person, die …

in die Schweiz reist. (reisen = to travel)	kaltes Wetter liebt. (lieben = to love)	eine Katze als Haustier hat.	Yoga macht.
keinen Kaffee trinkt. (trinken = to drink)	Schokolade mag. (mögen = to like)	aus Austin kommt.	Tennis spielt.
kein Fleisch (meat) mag.	Ski fährt. (fahren = ride)	warmes Wetter liebt.	21 Jahre alt ist.
die Lieblingsfarbe Gelb hat.	Hunde gern hat. (gern haben = to like)	mehr als drei Sprachen spricht. (sprechen = to speak)	Allergien hat.

Please go to the Deutsch im Blick website, Kapitel 1

Aussprache

The „Aussprache" (pronunciation) section of each chapter will introduce you to the amazing (or bizarre) sound system and dialects of the German language. The German language is incredibly rich in local and regional varieties, and it is actually quite difficult to settle on what basic sound-system to present to the beginning language learner. We settled on the high-German variety spoken in Germany because it is the most flexible and the most natural choice for non-native speakers, until they establish a cultural link to a specific region of the German-speaking countries and adopt the dialect spoken there (there is a standard high German in Austria and a standard high German in Switzerland, which later chapters will explore). The German standard variety is spoken by most people in official settings (e.g., television, travel, in education).

Das Alphabet

The German alphabet consists of 26 (plus 4) letters: 8 vowels and 22 consonants
While this is a longer list than the English alphabet, you should most definitely not despair. Once you learn the sound-symbol associations (how each letter or compound letter is pronounced), you will know how any and all German words are pronounced because German is very consistent. For example, in English, the letter "i" can be pronounced in different ways (consider: ice, igloo, girl, just to name a few). In German an "i" stays "i" (ist, immer, Blitz, even if there are long vs. short versions: finden vs. Isar).

A, Ä, B, C, D, E, F, G, H, I, J, K, L, M, N, O, Ö, P, Q, R, S, ß, T, U, Ü, V, W, X, Y, Z

Please go to the *Deutsch im Blick* website, Kapitel 1, and listen to the alphabet, as well as sample vocabulary to hear how these letters are pronounced.

a	das Ausland, der Autobus, das Alphabet, die Alpen	foreign country, motor coach, alphabet, the Alps
b	die Bevölkerung, Berlin, die Bahn, das Bundesland	population, Berlin, train, state
c	campen, ICE, der (Video-)Clip, checken	to camp, ICE (bullet train), video-clip, to check
d	Deutschland, Döner, drei, Donnerwetter	Germany, kabobs, three, thunderstorm
e	der Einwohner, eben, essen, erfahren	inhabitant, flat, to eat, to experience
f	der Flughafen, die Fantasie, Rad fahren, das Formular	airport, fantasy, to ride a bike, form
g	die Gastfamilie, geben, gastfreundlich, das Gemüse	host family, to give, hospitable, vegetable
h	das Heimweh, historisch, die Hälfte, das Haus	homesickness, historical, half, house
i	das Inland, die Insel, insgesamt, der Ingenieur	home country, island, altogether, engineer
j	jetzt, das Jahr, joggen, die Jugendherberge	now, year, to jog, youth hostel
k	die Kreuzfahrt, der Käse, der Kurs, kommunizieren	cruise, cheese, course, to communicate
l	das Land, leben, laufen, leer	country, to live, to walk or run, empty
m	das Meer, meinen, die Minderheit, München	ocean, to mean, minority, Munich
n	die Nationalität, nehmen, nachfragen, nein	nationality, to take, to ask about, no
o	offen, die Oper, oberflächlich, das Ohr	open, opera, superficial, ear
p	der Pass, pfeifen, die Post, die Pause	passport, to whistle, mail, break
q	das Quartier, der Quadratmeter, der Quatsch, das Quiz	accommodation, square meter, nonsense, quiz
r	reisen, der Reporter, Regensburg, das Ruhrgebiet	to travel, reporter, Regensburg, the Ruhr
s	die Schweiz, das Salz, schreiben, singen	Switzerland, salt, to write, to sing
t	der Tourismus, die Technologie, bitte, trainieren	tourism, technology, please, to train
u	der Urlaub, untersuchen, die U-Bahn, unbequem	vacation, to investigate, subway, uncomfortable
v	die Verkehrsmittel, vierzig, vorstellen, verbringen	means of transportation, 40, introduce, spend
w	wandern, die Wolke, wir, Würzburg	to hike, cloud, we, Würzburg
x	x-Achse, x-fach, das Xylofon, die Existenz	x-axis, ever so often, xylophone, existence
y	y-Achse, die Yacht, der Typ	y-axis, yacht, type
z	der Zug, das Zimmer, zurück, ziehen	train, room, back, to haul

There are also a handful of "strange-looking" letters in German, with which the following chapters will deal in detail. Here is a very brief overview of them as an appetizer:

Ä, ä	ähnlich, die Anwältin, ärgern, die Ästhetik	similar, attorney, to anger, aesthetic
Ö, ö	Österreich, öffnen, das Öl, ökologisch	Austria, to open, oil, ecological
Ü, ü	die Übung, überzeugen, kühl, amüsieren	practice, to convince, cool, to amuse
ß	die Straße, spaßen, heißen, außen	street, to joke, to be called, outside

WebQuests

In the first chapter, there are three WebQuests that introduce you to a variety of cultural issues in German-speaking countries. Go to "WebQuests" on the website and choose between:

1. An Introduction to the three primary German-speaking countries (Austria, Germany and Switzerland).
2. Your first trip (again, virtual) to Würzburg.
3. A virtual visit to Germany through the *Deutschland-Portal*.

Meinungsumfragen

In the first chapter, the interactive poll focuses on what countries you've been to, how you get around, what languages you speak, your favorite color and whether you are athletic or not. You can participate in them by going to „Meinungsumfragen" on the website.

Begrüßungen	Greetings
Hallo!	Hello!
Guten Morgen!	Good morning.
Guten Tag!	Hello! (Good Day)
Guten Abend!	Good evening.
Gute Nacht!	Good night.
Tschüss!	Bye!
Auf Wiedersehen!	Goodbye! (formal)
Mach's gut!	Take care!
Bis bald!	See you soon!
Bis morgen!	See you tomorrow.
Bis nächste Woche!	See you next week.
Bis Samstag!	See you Saturday.
Bis dann!/Bis später!	See you later!

Persönliche Informationen	Personal information
Wie heißt du?/Wie ist dein Name?	What's your name?
Wie heißen Sie?/Wie ist Ihr Name?	What's your name (formal)?
Ich heiße …	My name is …
Ich bin …	I am …
Ich bin Student/Studentin.	I am a student (m/f).
heißen	to be called
sein	to be
haben	to have
wohnen	to live (reside)
gehen	to go or walk
bleiben	to stay or remain
finden	to find
unterschreiben	to sign
die Unterschrift	signature

Wortschatz

(QR 1.1 p.50)

Jemanden kennenlernen	To meet someone
Wer ist das?	Who is that?
vorstellen	to introduce
Darf ich vorstellen?	May I introduce?
Das ist mein Freund, Udo.	This is my friend, Udo.
Freut mich!	Nice to meet you.
Angenehm.	(here) Pleased to meet you.
Es freut mich, dich/Sie kennen zu lernen.	It is nice to meet you (informal/formal).
Danke.	Thank you.
Bitte.	Please/You are welcome.
Entschuldigung.	Excuse me.
(Es) tut mir leid.	I am sorry.
ja	yes
nein	no
Ja, bitte.	Yes, please.
Nein, danke.	No, thank you.

Herkunft	Origin/Nationality
kommen aus	to come from
Woher kommst du?	Where do you come from?(informal)
Woher kommen Sie?	Where do you come from? (formal)
das Land (die Länder)	country (countries)
Ich komme aus Texas.	I come from Texas.
die USA	the U.S.
Ich komme aus den USA.	I come from the U.S.

Belgien	Belgium
Deutschland	Germany
Frankreich	France
Italien	Italy
Kanada	Canada
Luxemburg	Luxemburg

Mexiko	Mexico
die Niederlande (Holland)	the Netherlands (Holland)
Österreich	Austria
Polen	Poland
die Schweiz	Switzerland
Spanien	Spain
die Türkei	Turkey
Ungarn	Hungary
der Irak	Iraq

Afrika	Africa
Amerika (Nord-, Mittel-, Südamerika)	America (North, Central, South America)
Asien	Asia
Australien	Australia
Europa	Europe

Zahlen

		Numbers	
die Zahl (Zahlen)		number	
die Nummer (Nummern)		specific number (phone, house)	

null	zero	dreißig	thirty
eins	one	vierzig	forty
zwei	two	fünfzig	fifty
drei	three	sechzig	sixty
vier	four	siebzig	seventy
fünf	five	achtzig	eighty
sechs	six	neunzig	ninety
sieben	seven	hundert	one hundred
acht	eight	zweihundert	two hundred
neun	nine		
zehn	ten		
elf	eleven	zweiunddreißig	thirty-two
zwölf	twelve	vierundvierzig	forty-four
dreizehn	thirteen	fünfundfünfzig	fifty-five
vierzehn	fourteen	sechsundsechzig	sixty-six
fünfzehn	fifteen	siebenundsiebzig	seventy-seven
sechzehn	sixteen	achtundachtzig	eighty-eight
siebzehn	seventeen	neunundneunzig	ninety-nine
achtzehn	eighteen	hundert(und)eins	one-hundred-and-one
neunzehn	nineteen	tausend	one thousand
zwanzig	twenty		
einundzwanzig	twenty-one		

Weitere persönliche Informationen

	More personal information
das Jahr (Jahre)	the year
Wie alt bist du?	How old are you?
Wie alt sind Sie?	How old are you? (formal)
Ich bin achtzehn Jahre alt.	I am 18 years old.
Was ist Ihre Adresse?	What is your address?
die Hausnummer (-nummern)	house number
die Postleitzahl (-zahlen)	zip code

Die Farben	The colors
beige	beige
blau	blue
braun	brown
gelb	yellow
grau	gray
grün	green
lila	purple
rosa	pink
rot	red
schwarz	black
weiß	white
dunkel	dark
hell	light
bunt	color full
Welche Farbe hat dein Auto?	What color is your car? (informal)
Mein Auto ist schwarz.	My car is black. (color used as an adjective)
die Lieblingsfarbe (-farben)	favorite color
Was ist deine Lieblingsfarbe?	What is your favorite color?
Meine Lieblingsfarbe ist Rosa.	My favorite color is pink. (color used as a noun)

Wie geht's?	How are you? (informal)
Wie geht es Ihnen?	How are you? (formal)
Positive Reaktionen	**Positive Reactions**
Sehr gut, danke!	Very well, thanks.
Es geht mir gut.	I'm doing great!
Ausgezeichnet!	Excellent!
Toll!	Great!
Wunderbar!	Wonderful!
Negative Reaktionen	**Negative reactions**
Was ist los mit dir?	What's the matter?
Es geht mir nicht so gut.	I'm not feeling well.
Es geht mir schlecht.	I'm feeling bad.
Ich fühle mich schlecht.	I don't feel well.
Ich bin müde.	I'm tired.
Ich bin krank.	I'm sick.
Ich habe Kopfschmerzen.	I have a headache.

Geld, Handy usw.	Money, cell phone, etc.
anrufen	to call someone on the phone
aufladen	to upload (e.g., on a computer)/add money on cell phone
bezahlen	to pay
brauchen	to need
die EC-Karte (EC-Karten)	European bank card
das Geld (no plural)	money
der Geldautomat (-automaten)	the automatic teller machine (ATM)
Geld wechseln	to exchange money
das Handy (Handys)	cell phone
(Was ist/) wie lautet deine Handynummer?	What is your cellphone number?
das Konto (Konten)	account (also for cell phone)
kosten	to cost
Wie viel kostet ...?	How much does ... cost?
die Kreditkarte (-karten)	credit card
der PIN-Code (PIN-Codes)	PIN number
das Sonderangebot (-angebote)	special offer/sale
telefonieren	to talk to someone on the phone
die Telefonkarte (-karten)	calling card
das Telefon (Telefone)	telephone
die Telefonnummer (-nummern)	telephone number
(Was ist/) wie lautet deine Telefonnummer?	What is your phone number?

An der Uni studieren	Studying at the University
das Studienfach (-fächer)	field of study
das Hauptfach (-fächer)	major
das Nebenfach (-fächer)	minor
lernen	to learn, to study (homework, for a test, etc.)
studieren	to study (major in; study at university)
der Studentenausweis (-ausweise)	student ID card
das Studentenwohnheim (-heime)	dormitory
die Toilette (Toiletten)	restrooms
Wo ist die Toilette, (bitte)?	Where are the restrooms?

Studienfächer	Fields of study
Amerikanistik	American studies
Anglistik	British studies
Anthropologie	Anthropology
Architektur	Architecture
Biologie	Biology
Chemie	Chemistry
Computerwissenschaften	Computer Sciences
Deutsch	German
Englisch	English
Ethnologie/Volkskunde	Cultural anthropology
Film	Film/Film studies
Französisch	French
Geographie	Geography
Geschichte (von Europa, Asien usw.)	History
Germanistik	German studies
Ingenieurwissenschaften	Engineering
Italienisch	Italian
Jura	Law
Kunst	Art
Kunstgeschichte	Art history
Linguistik/Philologie	Linguistics/Philology
Mathematik	Math
Medizin	Medicine
Musikwissenschaft	Music
Ökonomie/Wirtschaft	Economics
Pädagogik	Pedagogy/Education
Philosophie	Philosophy
Physik	Physics
Politologie/Politikwissenschaft	Political science
Psychologie	Pscyhology
Soziologie	Sociology
Spanisch	Spanish
Theologie	Theology/Religious studies

Die Woche	The week
der Tag (Tage)	day
Montag	Monday
Dienstag	Tuesday
Mittwoch	Wednesday
Donnerstag	Thursday
Freitag	Friday
Samstag/Sonnabend	Saturday
Sonntag	Sunday
das Wochenende (-enden)	the weekend
die Woche (Wochen)	week
während der Woche	during the week
jede Woche	each week (e.g., how many times each week?)
am Wochenende	on the weekend
diese/nächste Woche	this/next week

QR Codes

1.1	1.2	1.3	1.4	1.5	1.6
Wortschatz	01_02_int_ag_ who	01_03_int_ag_ studies-home	01_04_int_ag_ interests	01_05_int_hm_ who	01_06_int_hm_ studies-home

1.7	1.8	1.9	1.10	1.11	1.12
01_07_int_ec_ who	01_08_int_ec_ studies-home	01_09_int_ec_ friends	01_10_int_sco_ who	01_11_int_sco_ studies-home	01_12_int_sco_ friends

1.13	1.14	1.15	1.16	1.17	1.18
01_13_int_scl_ who	01_14_int_scl_ studies-home	01_15_int_bg_ who	01_16_int_bg_ studies-home	01_17_int_bg_ friends	01_18_int_ek_ who

1.19	1.20	1.21	1.22	1.23	1.24
01_19_int_ek_ studies-home	01_20_int_ek_ friends	01_21_int_ek_ interests	01_22_int_hb_ who	01_23_int_ju_ who	01_24_int_ju_ studies-home

1.25	1.26	1.27	1.28	1.29	1.30
01_25_int_ju_ friends	01_26_int_ph_ who	01_27_int_hm_ friends	01_28_sik_bus-to-uni	01_29_sik_ student-id	01_30_sik_cell-phone

2 AN DER UNI

As the first step, you will be asked to view the introductory video to get an idea about the chapter's contents. In this chapter, you will learn more about University life. Specifically, by the end of this chapter, you will be able to describe your courses in terms of when they take place, whether you like them or not and why, and the types of homework assignments and exams you have.

Furher you will learn how to describe what you have in your dorm room and what you might still want or need and become skilled in using computers and the Internet in German!

Wortschatz
- *An der Uni*
- *Das Studium*
- *Im Kurs*
- *Auf dem Schreibtisch*
- *Alles über den Computer*
- *Es ist Zeit!*
- *In der Wohnung*
- *In der Küche*
- *Im Badezimmer*
- *Das Wohnzimmer*
- *Das Arbeitszimmer*
- *Das Schlafzimmer*

Aussprache
- *Kapitel 2*

Grammatik
Focus
- *die Uhrzeiten (telling time)*
- *die Tage der Woche (days of the week)*
- *der Akkusativ (accusative case)*
- *sehen*

Recommended
- *cases overview*
- *present regular verbs*
- *word order (in declarative sentences and after weil)*

Videos
Sprache im Kontext
- *Katrins Studiengang*
- *Katrin: Anforderungen*
- *Rikes, Christines & Brigitt Semester*
- *Katrin: Im Ausland studier*
- *Bernas Wohnung*
- *Tobe: Der Computer*
- *Tobe: Das Internet*
- *Vanessa: Im Ausland studieren*
- *Tobias: Die Bibliothek*
- *Saras Küche*
- *Saras Bad*
- *Saras Schlafzimmer*

Online Book links

You can find video clips at:
http://coerll.utexas.edu/dib/toc.php?k=2

You can find the vocabulary at:
http://coerll.utexas.edu/dib/voc.php?k=2

Sections
An der Uni • At the university
Das Studium • Course of Study
Im Unterricht • In class
Auf dem Schreibtisch • On the desk
Alles über den Computer • All about the computer
Es ist Zeit! • It's time!
In der Wohnung • In the apartment
In der Küche • In the kitchen
Im Badezimmer • In the bathroom
Das Wohnzimmer • The living room
Das Arbeitszimmer • The study
Das Schlafzimmer • The bedroom

You can find the grammar topics covered in this chapter at:
During the chapter exercises, you are regularly referred to *Grimm Grammar* at the *Deutsch im Blick* website. These are the grammar points the chapter covers, and you need to complete all online exercises in order to get the most benefit from the exercises in this workbook. The points on the left are necessary for completing the exercises in this course packet. The points on the right are recommended if you need some refreshers on parts of speech or what the present tense actually is ☺.

• Conjunctions: Coordinating Conjunctions	http://coerll.utexas.edu/gg/gr/con_03.html
• Conjunctions: Overview	http://coerll.utexas.edu/gg/gr/con_01.html
• Telling time	http://coerll.utexas.edu/gg/gr/cas_04.html
• Days of the week	http://coerll.utexas.edu/gg/gr/cas_05.html
• Accusative Case	http://coerll.utexas.edu/gg/gr/cas_03.html
• Present tense verbs – sehen	http://coerll.utexas.edu/gg/gr/vi_10.html

Wortschatz
Vorbereitung

A. LISTEN

Listen carefully to the pronunciation of each word or phrase in the vocabulary list.

B. REPEAT

Repeat each word or phrase *out loud* as many times as necessary until you remember it well and can recognize it as well as produce it. Make a list of the words in this chapter which you find difficult to pronounce. Your teacher may ask you to compare your list with other students in your class. Make sure to learn nouns with their correct gender!

> **Beispiel:**
> die Sprache
> fünf

Always learn nouns with the article!!!

These ideas are sugges-
tions only. Different learner
have different preference
and needs for learning an
reviewing vocabulary. Tr
several of these sugges-
tions until you find ones tha
work for you. Keep in minc
though, that knowing man
words – and knowing ther
well, both to recognize ar
to produce – makes you
more effective user of th
new language.

C. WRITE

Write key words from the vocabulary list so that you can spell them correctly (remember that it makes a big difference whether you cross the Atlantic by ship or by sheep). You may want to listen to the vocabulary list again and write the words as they are spoken for extra practice.

D. TRANSLATION

Learn the English translation of each word or phrase. Cover the German column and practice giving the German equivalent for each English word or phrase. Next cover the English column and give the translation of each.

E. ASSOCIATIONS

Think of word associations for each category of vocabulary. (What words, both English and German, do you associate with each word or phrase on the list?) Write down ten (10) associations with the vocabulary from the chapter.

> **Beispiel:**
> der Student/die Universität
> das Flugticket/das Flugzeug

F. COGNATES

Which words are *cognates?* (Cognates are words which look or sound like English words.) Watch out for *false friends*! Write down several cognates and all the false friends from the chapter, create fun sentences that illustrate similarities and differences between the English and German meanings of these words.

> **Beispiel:**
> Nacht/night
> grün/green
> → False Friends: *hell* = light, bright vs. *Hölle* = hell

G. WORD FAMILIES

Which words come from word families in German that you recognize (noun, adjective, verb, adverb)? Write down as many as you find in the chapter.

> **Beispiel:**
> das Studium (noun; studies)
> der Student (noun; person)
> studieren (verb)

H. EXERCISES

Write out three (3) „Was passt nicht?" ('Odd one out') exercises. List four words, three of which are related and one that does not fit the same category. Categories can be linked to meaning, grammar, gender, parts of speech (noun, verb, adjective), etc. USE YOUR IMAGINATION! Give the reason for why the odd word does not fit. Your classmates will have to solve the puzzles you provide!

> **Beispiel:**
> grün – blau – gelb – neun
> Here *neun* does not fit, because it is a
> number and all the others are colors.

Basiswortschatz
Core Vocabulary

The following presents a list of core vocabulary. Consider this list as the absolute minimum to focus on. As you work through the chapter you will need more vocabulary to help you talk about your own experience. To that end, a more complete vocabulary list can be found at the end of the chapter. This reference list will aid your attainment of Chapter 2's objectives.

(QR 2.1 p.103)

Im Unterricht	**In class**
die Hausaufgabe (-aufgaben)	homework
das Klassenzimmer (-zimmer)	the classroom
die Klausur (Klausuren)	exam (written during a course)
der Kurs (Kurse)	course
lesen	to read
das Referat (Referate)	oral presentation
sagen	to say
schreiben	to write
sprechen	to speak
die Übung (Übungen)	exercise

Auf dem Schreibtisch	**On the desk**
das Arbeitsheft (-hefte)	the workbook
der Bleistift (-stifte)	pencil
das Buch (Bücher)	the (text)book
der Kugelschreiber/der Kuli (-schreiber/Kulis)	pen
das Kurspaket (-pakete)	course packet

Alles über den Computer	**All about the computer**
anmachen/anschalten	to turn on
ausmachen/ausschalten	to turn off (the light or TV)
der Computer (Computer)	computer
das Dokument (Dokumente)	document (word document, for example)
der Drucker (Drucker)	printer
speichern	to save files
die E-Mail (E-Mails)	e-mail
die Maus (Mäuse)	mouse

Es ist Zeit!	**It's time!**
der Abend (Abende)	evening
am Abend	in the evening
abends	evenings (usually in the evening)
der Mittag (Mittage)	noon
um/gegen Mittag	at/around noon
die Mitternacht (no plural)	midnight
um Mitternacht	at midnight
der Morgen (Morgen)	morning
am Morgen	during the morning
morgens	mornings
der Nachmittag (Nachmittage)	afternoon
am Nachmittag	in the afternoon
nachmittags	afternoons (usually)
die Nacht (Nächte)	night
in der Nacht	at night
der Tag (Tage)	day
die Uhr (Uhren)	clock, time
der Vormittag (Vormittage)	morning
am Vormittag	during/in the morning
vormittags	mornings
die Woche (Wochen)	week

In der Wohnung	**In the apartment**
die Wohnung (Wohnungen)	apartment
die Wohngemeinschaft (-gemeinschaften)	student co-op

Die Küche/In der Küche	**The kitchen/In the kitchen**
Dinge zum Kochen und Essen	**Things for cooking and eating**
die Gabel (Gabeln)	fork
das Glas (Gläser)	glass
der Löffel (Löffel)	spoon
das Messer (Messer)	knife
der Teller (Teller)	plate

Das Badezimmer/Im Badezimmer	The bathroom/In the bathroom
baden	to take a bath
die Badewanne (-wannen)	bathtub
die Dusche (Duschen)	shower
duschen	to shower
der Spiegel (Spiegel)	mirror
das Waschbecken (-becken)	sink

Das Wohnzimmer	The living room
der Couchtisch (-tische)	coffee table
der Fernseher (Fernseher)	TV
das Sofa/die Couch (Sofas/Couchen)	sofa
der Teppich (Teppiche)	rug

Das Arbeitszimmer	The study
das Bücherregal (-regale)	bookshelf
der Papierkorb (-körbe)	waste basket
der Schreibtisch (-tische)	desk
der Stuhl (Stühle)	chair

Das Schlafzimmer	The bedroom
das Bett (Betten)	bed
der Kleiderschrank (-schränke)	armoir (for clothes)
die Lampe (Lampen)	lamp
der Nachttisch (-tische)	nightstand

Aktivität 1. Was studieren Sie?

As you already learned in the last chapter, the verb *studieren* refers specifically to one's area of study, his or her major. As a class collect as many words that you associate with the term *das Studium*.

(QR 2.2 p.103)

Deutsch studieren ← **das STUDIUM**

Aktivität 2. Evas Studium

What are some other important components of studying at the university: when you have classes, where you have classes, when you are finally done, and what exams you have to take … Watch Eva's first video clip „Mein Studium", and find out what she says about her studies. Check off the correct responses to the questions below. There may be more than one correct answer to each question!

(QR 2.3 p.103)

Was studierst du?
- ❏ Amerikanistik.
- ❏ Englisch und Geographie.
- ❏ Geographie.

Wann bist du (mit dem Studium) fertig?
- ❏ Nächstes Jahr im Frühjahr.
- ❏ Nächsten Februar.

Wie findest du dein Studium?
- ❏ Sehr interessant, weil ich gerne reise.
- ❏ Ich möchte in Kanada leben.
- ❏ Ich mag die englische Sprache.

Sind deine Kurse auf Englisch oder auf Deutsch?
- ❏ Teils-teils (*half and half*), es ist nicht typisch.
- ❏ Meine Grammatikkurse sind manchmal (*sometimes*) auf Englisch.
- ❏ Geographie ist manchmal auf Englisch.

Aktivität 3. Wer studiert was?

Watch Adan's, Sara's and Sophia's first clips „Mein Studium" and identify which details match which person. Connect the picture to the correct info-bubble.

(QR 2.4
p.103)
(QR 2.5
p.103)
(QR 2.6
p.103)

- Ich studiere Geographie.
- Ich liebe Fremdsprachen, weil sie mir viel Spass machen.
- Ich studiere an der Universität von Texas und jezt an der Universität in Würzburg

- Ich studiere Deutsch als Fremdsprache und europäische Kunstgeschichte in Heidelberg.

- Ich studiere in Heidelberg.
- Ich studiere Deutsch als Fremdsprache, weil ich mein Deutsch verbessern möchte.
- In Long Beach studiere ich Deutsch und Wilderness Studies.

Aktivität 4. Berna und Jan: Mein Studium

Watch the first clips „Mein Studium" with Berna and Jan.

A. Watch the video twice. Take notes the first time. Answer the questions the second time you watch it.

What is their major? Where are they studying? How do they like their studies? You will need to listen to these clips several times in order to find out the answers! Feel free to take notes either in English or in German – or a combination of both!

(QR 2.7 p.103)

(QR 2.9 p.103)

Was studiert sie/er?		
Wo studiert sie/er?		
Wie findet sie/er das Studium?		

Grimm Grammar

At home please read the following grammar point on the *Grimm Grammar* website.

Conjunctions: Coordinating Conjunctions

Quick overview:
In a regular German statement (also called a declarative sentence), you start the sentence with a subject or an adverb of time, or perhaps another part of the sentence. Then in the second position, you must have the conjugated verb:

Harald ist *ein guter Student. In der Unibibliothek* schaut *er sich hübsche Mädhcen* an.

When you use *weil* (which is a subordinating conjunction), the verb in the part of the sentence in which *weil* is, goes to the end of the clause whether that clause starts the sentence or ends it:

Harald ist nostalgisch, weil er gerne Student war.

Weil er sich gute Notizen macht, *bekommt er immer gute Noten.*

B. Auf Deutsch!
How do you say the following phrases in German? Listen carefully to the expressions Berna and Jan use, and match up the English and German equivalents:

1. Es ist schon manchmal sehr viel Arbeit.

2. Ich mag mein Studium sehr.

3. Ich bin sehr zufrieden damit.

4. Ich studiere an der Universität von...

a. I am studying at the University of...

b. I really like my studies.

c. Sometimes it's a lot of work.

d. I'm quite happy with it (i.e., my studies).

Aktivität 5. Hassans Studium
Watch Hassans clip „Mein Studium". Circle the correct answers below.

(QR 2.10 p.103)

a) Was studiert Hassan an UT?   Philosophie • Psychologie • Philharmonie

b) Was studiert Hassan nächstes Jahr?   Flora • Matura • Jura • Algebra

c) Wo studiert Hassan nächstes Jahr?   in New York • in York • in New Jersey • in Nürnberg

d) Was war Hassans Lieblingskurs?   Quatsch • Französisch • Deutsch

e) Warum will Hassan Jura studieren?   Geld • Ansehen • Menschen helfen

Zusatzfrage: Warum war Deutsch sein Lieblingskurs?

_____

Aktivität 6. Haralds Studium
Listen to Harald's description of his life as a student – „Mein Studium". What did he like about his student experience? What did he dislike? What kind of a student was he?

(QR 2.8 p.103)

A. Beim ersten Schauen
Watch the clip and identify the *Stimmung (atmosphere, mood)* in Harald's narrative. Does he have fond or unhappy memories? How can you tell? Take notes on words that support your claim.

Stimmung	Beweise (*evidence*) aus dem Text:
Harald ist nostalgisch; er war sehr gerne Student.	
Harald ist sehr glücklich, dass er nicht mehr Student ist; er hasste das Studentenleben.	

B. Beim zweiten Schauen

Watch the video clip a second time, and listen for the characteristics Harald relates about his life as a student. What details does he provide about these characteristics.

Charakteristiken	Details
das Unileben	Bücher, Literatur, Musik
Hauptfach	
Dauer (*length*) des Studiums	
Notizen machen	
Anwesenheit (*attendance*)	
die Unibibliothek	
die (Uhr-)Zeiten	

What joke does the interviewer completely miss towards the end?

_____

Aktivität 7. Ihr Studium

To what extent are Harald's memories similiar to your current experience?

A. Answer the questions below

1. Was ist das Wichtigste am Unileben für Sie?
   - das Studium
   - lernen
   - mein Deutschkurs
   - Parties
   - meine Freunde
   - die Wohngemeinschaft

   _____

   _____

2. Was studieren Sie?

   _____

3. Wie lange dauert Ihr Studium?
   - Noch ein Jahr.
   - Noch zwei Jahre.
   - Wer weiß?

4. Machen Sie sorgfältige Notizen in der Vorlesung?
   - JA! Natürlich!
   - Nein.

5. Sind Sie immer im Unterricht oder fehlen Sie ab und zu?
   - Ich bin immer im Unterricht.
   - Ich fehle ab und zu, weil ich krank bin.
   - Ich fehle ab und zu, weil ich verschlafe.
   - Ich fehle manchmal, weil ich gern auf Partys gehe.

6. Gehen Sie in die Bibliothek? Wenn ja, was machen Sie dort? Wenn nein, warum nicht?

   _____

   _____

7. Wann stehen Sie auf, essen Sie zu Mittag, gehen Sie ins Bett?

   _____

   _____

   _____

   _____

B. Compare your answers with two classmates
Are your experiences and habits the same or do they differ?

Nützliche Ausdrücke

- ☐ *Ich studiere an einer Universität/ High School/an einem Gymnasium.*
- ☐ *Ich studiere _____.*
- ☐ *Ich mag mein Studium.*
- ☐ *Ich hasse mein Studium.*
- ☐ *Ich mag Fremdsprachen (zum Beispiel Deutsch, Englisch, Französisch).*

- ☐ *Mein Studium macht sehr viel Arbeit.*
- ☐ *Mein Studium ist zu einfach (easy) für mich.*
- ☐ *Ich möchte ewig (forever) Student bleiben.*
- ☐ *Ich finde meine Kurse meistens sehr interessant.*
- ☐ *Meine Lehrer und Kurse sind ziemlich langweilig.*
- ☐ *Für mich ist _____ am wichtigsten.*

Student 1	Student 2

C. Tell the class about your experiences, focusing on one or more of the topics mentioned in (A) and (B).
Have someone take notes and create a class chart. Who share similar experiences and who breaks the ranks *(aus der Reihe tanzen: Er/Sie tanzt aus der Reihe)*?

1. _____ Studenten finden ihre Kurse sehr interessant.	2. _____ Studenten finden ihre Kurse ziemlich langweilig.	3. _____ Studenten finden manche (some) Kurse interessant.

Aktivität 8. Meine Lieblingskurse

Watch Sophia's video clip „Lieblingskurse" and circle the correct information she provides about courses she liked and courses she really didn't like. There may be more than one correct answer in each sentence!

(QR 2.11 p.103)

Mein Lieblingskurs ist ein ...	a) Literaturkurs. b) Seminar für Internationale Beziehungen.
Wir lesen Goethes ...	a) „Die Leiden des Jungen Werthers". b) Gedicht „Prometheus".
Ich mag Grammatikkurse normalerweise nicht. Ich finde sie zu ...	a) trocken. b) langweilig.
Es macht mir Spass, wenn die Lehrer ... sind.	a) unterhaltend b) witzig c) intelligent

Aktivität 9. Weitere Lieblingskurse ... oder auch nicht

Watch the „Lieblingskurse" videoclips by Berna, Eva, Jan, Adan, Erin and Sara, and identify their most and least favorite courses, as well as the reasons they give for liking/disliking these courses.

| Berna
 (QR 2.12 p.103) | Eva
 (QR 2.13 p.103) | Jan
 (QR 2.14 p.103) | Adan
 (QR 2.15 p.103) | Erin
 (QR 2.16 p.103) | Sara
 (QR 2.18 p.103) |

A. Indicate in the lines after each course, whose favorite it is.

1. Phonetik und Klettern (*climbing*), weil sie anders sind als meine Kurse [zu Hause] _____

2. Kultur/Literatur/Film des 20. Jahrhunderts _____

3. Literaturkurse (die mit Büchern und Romanen zu tun haben) _____

4. Französisch (weil der Lehrer einfach Spitze war!) und Geographie _____

5. Film und Kunst, wo ich mit anderen Studenten zusammen lernen und schreiben kann _____

6. Englische Literaturwissenschaft (weil ich gerne lese) und Wirtschaftsgeographie (weil der Zusammenhang [*connection*] zwischen Wirtschaft und Geographie mich sehr interessiert) _____

B. Indicate in the lines after each course, who does not like it. Do you agree with their opinion?

1. Deutsch, weil wir gar nicht gesprochen haben (*spoke*). _____

2. Kurse, die nur am Text arbeiten. _____

3. Langweilige Kurse, wo man sinnlose Sachen machen muss. _____

4. Ökonomie, weil sie nur mit Nummern zu tun hat. _____

5. Mathematik finde ich sehr schlecht. _____

6. Physische Geographie (z.B. bodenbildende Prozesse), weil es zu viel Chemie ist. _____

Aktivität 10. Positiv/Negativ

Identify the following expressions: which group is positive, which is negative? What courses are you taking this semester? Which expressions would apply to which of your courses?

positiv/negativ	**positiv/negativ**
mein Kurs ist langweilig der Professor hat keine Ahnung, was mich interessiert der Unterricht dauert zu lang die Bücher sind schwer zu verstehen es gibt zu viel sinnlose Arbeit der Lehrer ist zu streng	mein Kurs ist sehr interessant der Professor weiß genau, was mich interessiert die Stunde ist viel zu schnell vorbei die Bücher sind einfach faszinierend wir schreiben eine bedeutungsvolle Seminararbeit die Professorin ist ausgezeichnet, ein Genie!

A. Mein Lieblingskurs

Was ist Ihr Lieblingskurs? Warum finden Sie diesen Kurs so gut? Welchen Kurs finden Sie gar nicht gut? Warum?

> Mathe · Biologie · Chemie
> Deutsch · Französisch · Spanisch · Rhetorik
> Informatik · Anthropologie · Musik · Psychologie
> Geschichte · Soziologie · Betriebswirtschaft · Archäologie
> Philosophie · Geographie · Astronomie · Kunstgeschichte
> Ökonomie · Englisch · Geologie · Griechisch
> Politologie · Linguistik · Physik

Before you talk about your favorite and least favorite course think about more reasons why you like or dislike a course.

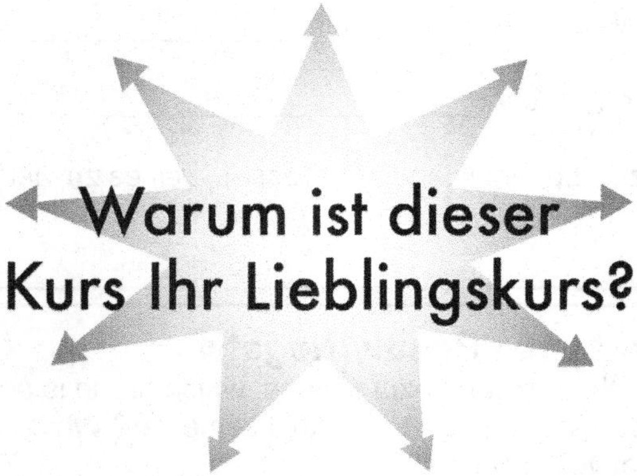

Warum ist dieser Kurs Ihr Lieblingskurs?

Der Kurs ist am Nachmittag.

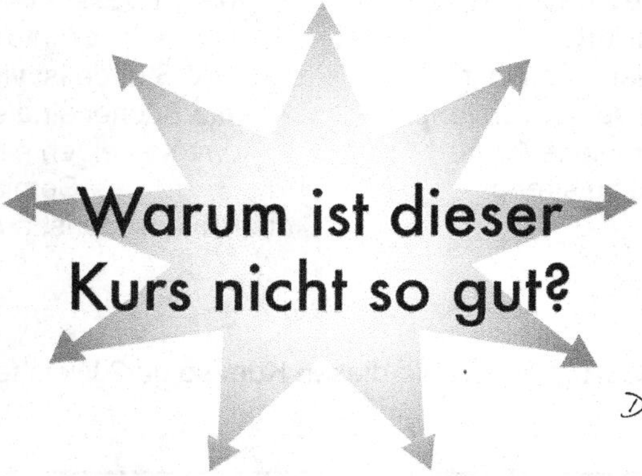

Warum ist dieser Kurs nicht so gut?

Der Kurs beginnt um 8 Uhr.

Now it's your turn: Write down your favorite and least favorite course and give reasons for your choice.

Mein Lieblingskurs ist _____,

weil   ich gerne lese.
           ich Fremdsprachen sehr interessant finde.
           wir viele Filme sehen

Ich finde _____ uninteressant/gar nicht gut,

weil   wir zu viel sinnlose Arbeit machen.
            ich den Kurs zu schwierig finde.
            der Kurs/der Lehrer zu langweilig ist.

Aktivität 11. Ein kleines Interview

Ask two of your classmates what their favorite courses are and why, and which course(s) they don't like and why not. Note their answers.

A.   **Student A:**
     Was ist dein Lieblingskurs?
     Warum?
     Welchen Kurs findest du nicht so gut?

     Student B:
     Mein Lieblingskurs ist _____.
     Weil ...
     Ich finde _____ nicht so gut, weil ...

NAME		
Sein/ihr Lieblingskurs		
weil ...		
Er/sie mag _____ nicht,		
weil ...		

Nota Bene: Instead of „Ich finde ..." you can use „Ich mag ...". It is one of the modal verbs that you will learn in *Kapitel 4* but it comes in handy when expressing likes and dislikes.

Grimm Gramma

At home you can read about *mögen* on the *Grimm Grammar* website. But for now the conjugation and negation of it is more relevant.

For preview:
Verbs: <u>Modalverben</u>

mögen (to like)
ich mag
du magst
er/sie/es mag

wir mögen
ihr mögt
sie mögen

Sie mögen

Negation: To negate, you need to use *kein/keine* with a noun and *nicht* if you are negating the *mögen* itself.

Do not confuse ***mögen*** with ***möchten.***
The two are closely related but used quite differently.

Consider these examples:

Ich mag Mathe.

→ *I like math.*

versus

Er möchte Mathe studieren.

→ *He would like to study math.*

Grimm Grammar

At home please read the following grammar points on the *Grimm Grammar* website.

Die Uhrzeiten
(telling time)

um 9 Uhr
um Viertel nach 9
20 (Minuten) nach 9
um halb 10 (9:30)
5 (Minuten) nach halb 10
um Viertel vor 10
um Mittag
um Mitternacht
am Morgen
am Nachmittag
am Abend

Die Tage der Woche
(days of the week)

am Montag	*(on Monday)*
am Dienstag	*(on Tuesday)*
am Mittwoch	*(on Wednesday)*
am Donnerstag	*(on Thursday)*
am Freitag	*(on Friday)*
am Samstag	*(on Saturday)*
am Sonntag	*(on Sunday)*

B. Ein kleiner Bericht

Write a short description about each of your interviews. Tell the class 1) who they are, 2) what their favorite course is, and why, and 3) what their least favorite course is.

Beispiel:

Das ist _____.
Sein/ihr Chemiekurs ist ziemlich langweilig, weil der Lehrer zu streng ist.

_____

_____

_____

_____

_____

_____

_____

Aktivität 12. Wann haben sie Unterricht?

When are Hassan's, Eva's and Jan's classes? Watch their clips „Im Unterricht" and select the correct answers from the choices provided. It usually helps with listening comprehension to read the text provided below before you actually watch the video clips!

Ich hatte	**jeden Tag** **jeden Montag** **jeden Donnerstag**	Unterricht.
Wagner ist das	**Politologie-** **Philharmonie-** **Philosophie-**	Gebäude.

Hassan
(QR 2.19
p.103)

Dreimal die Woche beginnen die Kurse	**um 8 Uhr** **gegen Mittag.**	
Sie enden	**gegen 2-3 Uhr am Nachmittag.** **erst spät am Abend.**	
Freitags habe ich	**nur zwei Kurse.** **leider (*unfortunately*) viele Kurse.**	

Eva
(QR 2.21
p.103)

Meistens habe ich	**morgens** **nachmittags**	Unterricht.
Die Kurse fangen	**um 9 Uhr an.** **zwischen 2 und 3 Uhr an.**	

Jan
(QR 2.22
p.103)

Zum Nachdenken:

- What do you think the difference is between „um 9 Uhr" and „gegen 9 Uhr"? Hint: one is precise („at"), the other is approximate („around").
- Telling time in German is often referred to as „military time." That is actually incorrect. While German formal time is expressed on a 24-hour basis (e.g., „It is 18 hour 22 minutes" for 18:22), nobody would say 0 – 600 (oh-sixhundred) for 6 am.

Aktivität 13. Sara

When does Sara have class while she is in Würzburg during her summer Study Abroad program? Watch her clip titled „Im Unterricht". Check the *richtig* (*true*) and *falsch* (*false*) boxes below.

(QR 2.23 p.103)

	richtig	falsch
a) Sara hat jeden Tag Unterricht.	R	F
b) Sara hat nur zwei Tage pro Woche Unterricht.	R	F
c) Sara hat am Dienstag, am Mittwoch und am Donnerstag Unterricht.	R	F
d) Ihre Kurse beginnen um acht Uhr.	R	F
e) Am Dienstag hat Sara einen Ökonomiekurs.	R	F
f) Am Donnerstag hat Sara einen Deutschkurs.	R	F

Aktivität 14. Ihr Studium

Wann haben Sie Unterricht (Vorlesungen/Seminare)? Wann hat ihr Partner/ihre Partnerin Unterricht? First, fill out your own course schedule, then ask a classmate about his/her schedule. Use these helpful phrases to describe your and your partner's schedules in the following activities.

---

um Viertel vor acht • von halb zehn bis zwölf • um ein Uhr • kurz nach halb drei • nie
jeden Tag um neun Uhr • um Viertel nach fünf • zehn (Minuten) nach elf
von zwei bis vier Uhr • von fünf Minuten vor vier bis Viertel nach sechs
nachmittags • morgens • gegen Mittag • gegen sechs Uhr • am Abend • am nächsten Tag
zweimal am Tag • jeden Tag • oft • selten

A. Meine Kurse dieses Semester

Fill in the table with the courses you have each day, zum Beispiel:

Montag	Dienstag
Deutsch 8–9	Geographie 8:30–10

Montag	Dienstag	Mittwoch	Donnerstag	Freitag

B. Und Ihr/e PartnerIn?

Ask a classmate what his/her schedule is like, using the questions and possible answer prompts below. Naturally, you need to change the information (e.g., day, course) to reflect your own schedule ☺.

       am Montag
       am Dienstag

Welche Vorlesungen/Seminare hast du   am Mittwoch   ?
       am Donnerstag
       am Freitag

Mögliche Antworten:

• Am Montag um 9.30 (neun Uhr dreißig/halb zehn) habe ich _____Chemie_____.

• Mein _____Deutschkurs_____ ist jeden Tag von 11 bis 12.

• Ich habe am Dienstag von 11 bis 12.15 (elf bis Viertel nach zwölf) _Geschichte_.

• Am Freitag habe ich keine Vorlesungen oder Seminare.

Der Stundenplan meines Partners: _____

Montag	Dienstag	Mittwoch	Donnerstag	Freitag

Aktivität 15. Eine Verabredung

You are trying to set up an appointment with a classmate. You will need at least three hours during the week to watch a German movie and write a report for class. Compare your schedules and find a time when you can meet for the three hours. Write down your dialog, and feel free to use the following question and answer prompts. Your teacher might ask you to perform your discussion as a skit.

Mögliche Fragen:
Wann hast du diese Woche Zeit?
Hast du am Montag Zeit?
Hast du Dienstagvormittag oder -nachmittag Zeit?
Um wie viel Uhr bist du am Donnerstag fertig?
Hast du am Mittwoch zwischen neun Uhr und zwei Uhr Zeit?

Mögliche Antworten:
Leider habe ich am Montag keine Zeit!
Ja, ich habe Dienstagnachmittag zwei Stunden frei.
Ich bin erst gegen Mittag fertig.
Nein, aber ich habe am Donnerstag ein bisschen Zeit.
Diese Woche kann ich mich nur abends mit dir/euch treffen.

Weitere Ausdrücke:
Wir müssen diese Woche einen deutschen Film sehen.
Wo treffen wir uns?
Den Film können wir in der Bibliothek ausleihen.
Also, bis dann!
Ich rufe dich dann Donnerstagabend an!

Grimm Gramma

At home please read the following grammar point on the *Grimm Grammar* website.

Coordinating Conjunctions

Nota bene: As you may notice in exercise 14B each example sentence starts with a different part of speech. The first and last ones with an adverb of time (*Am Montag um 9:30* and *Am Freitag*) while the two middle ones with the subject (*Mein Deutschkurs* and *Ich*). German word order allows you to start a sentence with just about anything, as long as you place the conjugated verb (e.g., *habe* and *ist* above) right after the introductory phrase (in basic declarative sentences). This variability helps you diversify your sentences; try to play around with different introductory phrases, just remember to keep the conjugated verb in the second position!

Der Dialog:

_____

_____

_____

_____

_____

_____

_____

_____

_____

_____

_____

Aktivität 16. Sprache im Kontext: Katrins Studiengang

The *Studiengang* is one's course of study, the required and elective courses one has to take to complete a degree. Watch Katrin's video to learn more about different course types in Germany.

A. Listen to the clip. What is it about? What do you think Katrin talks about?

(QR 2.17 p.103)

B. Listen to the clip again and check all the words that you hear.

❏ Einführungskurse
❏ Universität
❏ Bargeld
❏ Mensa
❏ Grundstudium

❏ Proseminar
❏ Staat
❏ Kursangebote
❏ Hauptseminare
❏ Masters

C. Listen to the clip again and pay attention to the kind of courses she describes.

The course of study is separated into two major parts. What are those?

1. _____

2. _____

What are the names of classes you take during the first and second part of the course of study?

1. _____ 2. _____

☐ _____   ☐ _____

☐ _____   ☐ _____

What is the difference between the course you listed above and the _Vorlesung_ Katrin mentions? Additionally, what do you think _Anwesenheitspflicht_ means?

D. Genauer zuhören

Listen to the clip again (you may have to listen to the clip a few times), and decide whether the following statements are *richtig* or *falsch*.

1. Katrin ist Professorin für Amerikanistik an der Uni Würzburg.	**richtig**	**falsch**
2. Sie spricht über den Aufbau des Studiums an der Uni Würzburg.	**richtig**	**falsch**
3. Das Studium hat zwei Teile: Grund- und Hauptstudium.	**richtig**	**falsch**
4. Im Grundstudium belegen die Studenten nur Vorlesungen.	**richtig**	**falsch**
5. Im Hauptstudium belegen die Studenten Haupt- und Oberseminare.	**richtig**	**falsch**
6. Bei Vorlesungen müssen alle Studenten anwesend sein.	**richtig**	**falsch**
7. Am Ende des Studiums machen alle Studenten das gleiche Examen.	**richtig**	**falsch**
8. Das Staatsexamen ist eine Prüfung für spätere (*future*) Lehrer.	**richtig**	**falsch**

Aktivität 17. Studieren in Deutschland: Vorlesungverzeichnis in Würzburg

Have a look at the *Vorlesungsverzeichnis* (course schedules) for the College of Humanities & Social Sciences at the Uni Würzburg. Go online to search for „Vorlesungsverzeichnis & Würzburg" or enter http://www.uni-wuerzburg.de/fuer/studierende/vorlesungsverzeichnis/ directly, and select *Online-Vorlesungsverzeichnis*. Then chose *Philosophische Fakultät I* from the list of possible areas of study.

Vorlesungsverzeichnis (WS 2012/13)
Seitenansicht wählen: › **kurz** › mittel › lang

ⓘ Vorlesungsverzeichnis der Universität Würzburg
→ ⓘ Philosophische Fakultät I

Vst.-Nr.	Vst.-Kürzel	Veranstaltung	Vst.-Art	Aktion
0409388		Intensive refresher course - Blockveranstaltung - Waltie , Zöller , Harris , O'Connor , Tunwell , Großer	Übung	Zur Zeit keine Online-Belegung möglich
		Antrittsvorlesung Prof. Steinhart - Steinhart	Vorlesung	

→ ⓘ Allgemeine und Angewandte Sprachwissenschaft
→ ⓘ Englischsprachiges Kursprogramm / Würzburg English Language Program (Allgemeine Schlüsselqualifikationen für alle BA-Studiengänge)
→ ⓘ Studierwerkstatt
→ ⓘ Mittelalter und Frühe Neuzeit
→ ⓘ Klassische Philologie
→ ⓘ Lehrstuhl für klassische Archäologie
→ ⓘ Lehrstuhl für Vor- und Frühgeschichtliche Archäologie
→ ⓘ Altorientalistik (Assyriologie, Kleinasiatische Philologie, Semitistik)
→ ⓘ Vergleichende Indogermanische Sprachwissenschaft
→ ⓘ Ägyptologie
→ ⓘ Sinologie
→ ⓘ Indologie
→ ⓘ Slavische Philologie
→ ⓘ Russicum
→ ⓘ Musikwissenschaft
→ ⓘ Musikpädagogik
→ ⓘ Deutsche Philologie
→ ⓘ Anglistik und Amerikanistik
→ ⓘ Romanische Philologie
→ ⓘ Geschichte
→ ⓘ Kunstgeschichte
→ ⓘ Geographie

A. Die Lehrveranstaltung

Select a "department" that is particularly interesting to you. Then, pick two courses you might want to take. When you click on a specific class, you will see all the details about this class.

	Kurs 1	Kurs 2
Name of the course		
Name of the professor		
When and where does the class meet?		
What other details are provided (e.g., reading list, course assignments, etc.?		

Aktivität 18. Bernas und Jans Anforderungen

Watch Berna's and Jan's videos „Anforderungen", and note what kinds of assignments each of them have to complete this semester. Pay attention to the phrases they use for talking about their studies.

> Klausur · Examen · ein Forschungsprojekt
> Seminararbeiten · Essays · Referate
> Tests · Quiz · kurze Papers

A. Berna

Hat Berna viele Klausuren und Seminarbeiten oder wenige?

Was muss sie im Laufe (*during*) des Semesters erledigen (here: *complete*)?

Was muss sie am Ende des Semesters machen?

(QR 2.25 p.103)

B. Jan

Welche Anforderungen hat Jan dieses Semester in seinen Kursen (z.B. Tests, Hausarbeiten usw.)?

Muss er während (= im Laufe) des Semesters viel arbeiten?

(QR 2.26 p.103)

C. Anforderungen

Re-listen to Berna and Jan's clips and answer the following questions:

1. What do you think Berna's „jede Menge" means?

    lots of   sometimes

2. Which of the following do you think mean "exams?" Circle all that apply. How do you know?

    Examen   Prüfungen   Aufgaben   Klausuren   Hausarbeiten

3. Which of the following do you think mean "term paper?" Circle all that apply. How do you know?

    Papier   Semesterarbeit   Hausarbeit   Aufgabe

4. Match the correct German and English phrases in the following columns:

    im ganzen Semester verteilt   different things
    ständig viel zu tun   spread out over the semester
    verschiedene Sachen   constantly having a lot to do

Guido says an *Examen* T F
is the same as a *Prü-*
ung.

An *Abschluss-* T F
xamen/Ab-
chlussprüfung is the
ast exam beore gradu-
ating.

A *Seminararbeit* is a T F
erm paper written for a
course.

Many courses have T F
Quizze.

The test for a driver's T F
cence is a *Fahrprü-*
ung, an eye exam is a
Sehtest.

Aktivität 19. Guido erklärt alles ...

Just what is the difference between an *Examen*, a *Klausur*, a *Seminararbeit*
or a *Prüfung* at German universities? Can you tell from Guido's letter below?
Be prepared that depending on whom you ask, the answer might be different;
different universities use different assessments. Read the following *E-Mail* from
Guido, in which he explains the difference between various types of tests he took
at a Swiss university.

Hallo Susi,

Für mich besteht kein Unterschied zwischen Examen und Prüfung. Examen ist das lateinische Wort für Prüfung. Normalerweise schreibt man ein Examen ganz am Ende des Studiums, also ein Abschluss (wie das Magisterexamen). Diese "Arbeit" kann auch Abschlusspruefung heissen. Prüfungen gibt es während des Schuljahrs. Universitäten haben normalerweise eine Klausur (wie ein Examen). Quizze gibt es nicht wie ihr es in Amerika kennt. Ein Quiz ist normalerweise eine Quiz-Show. Eine Semesterarbeit schreiben wir am Ende des Semesters.

NB: Um den Führerschein zu bekommen macht meine eine Fahrprüfung und nicht Fahrexamen und beim Optiker gibt es den Sehtest und nicht die Sehprüfung oder das Sehexamen :-)

Ich hoffe das hat ein bisschen geholfen.

Liebe Grüße, Guido

Aktivität 20. Ihre Anforderungen und die Anforderungen von Ihren Mitstudenten

A. Welche Anforderungen gibt es für Sie in diesem Semester?

Are you going to have a stressful exam period? Or a relatively easy one? Think
of the courses you are taking this semester. What requirements do you have in
those courses? Fill out the mind-maps and than finish the sentences.

Merk's Dir: „Es gibt ..." is th German way to say "There is/are ..."
Someone might ask you „Gibt es viele Tests?" and you can reply by saying „Ja, es gibt drei Tests!"

Dieses Semester	*habe ich keine Prüfungen, nur ein Projekt.*
	habe ich _____ *Prüfungen: in*
	_____ , _____ ,
	_____ *und* _____ .
	habe ich zu viele Prüfungen!

Am Ende des Semesters	*muss ich eine Semesterarbeit für meinen*
	_____ *-kurs schreiben.*
	muss ich zwei Semesterarbeiten schreiben.
	muss ich für jeden Kurs eine Semesterarbeit schreiben!

In meinem Deutschkurs	*muss ich viele Essays, aber keine Examen schreiben.*
	habe ich viel zu viele Hausaufgaben!
	kann ich ruhig schlafen; es gibt keine Anforderungen

B. Welche Anforderungen haben Sie?

Ask one of your classmates what s/he is studying (i.e., major), what courses s/he is taking this semester, how s/he likes them, and what types of assignments s/he has this semester.

Wie heißt du?

Welche Kurse belegst du dieses Semester?

Wie findest du deine Kurse?

Was ist dein Lieblingskurs? Warum?

Welche Anforderungen gibt es in deinem Lieblingskurs?

Wieviel Zeit verbringst du mit Hausaufgaben?

C. Ein bisschen Journalismus

Now write a brief paragraph about your interviewee: Studienfach, Universität, Kurse, wie er/sie seine/ihre Kurse findet, und seine/ihre Lieblingskurse. What kinds of Examen or Semesterarbeiten does this person have this semester?

Ein Bericht

_____ studiert _____ an der Uni

_____.

Dieses Semester belegt er/sie Kurse: _____,

_____, und _____.

Seine/ihre Kurse findet er/ sie _____.

Sein/ihr Lieblingskurs ist _____ , weil

_____.

Dieses Semester _____

_____.

Survey: Now the reports are presented in class. Everyone needs to listen carefully and write down the *Anforderungen* of their peers as well as their *Lieblingskurse*. What is the most common *Anforderung* and what is the top *Lieblingskurs*?

Anforderungen	Lieblingskurse
	Beispiel: Deutsch ⊪⊪ ⊪⊪

Now view Katrin's Sprache im Kontext video clip „Anforderungen"
Katrin works at the Universität Würzburg. What types of *Anforderungen* does she mention?

Katrin also mentions two types of courses: *Einführungskurse* and *Seminare*. Which *Anforderungen* are typically used in which course type?

Einführungskurse

Seminare

Are there differences in the way Katrin and Jan and Berna talk about *Anforderungen*?

What questions would you have for Katrin (or Berna or Jan) in order to come to understand better the way students at German Universities are evaluated? How would you explain the different types of assignments you do to a visiting German, Austrian or Swiss friend?

Aktivität 21. Erfahrungsbericht
You agreed to help the international office by responding to e-mails and telling students about your University. Many of the students would like to know what it takes to get a degree at your university, how hard they would have to study, how much homework they would have, and whether they would still have a life... In order to prepare your response, first you need to collect some information from your classmates about their practices (you would not want to give somebody advice of this magnitude based only on your experience, would you?).

A. Interview a partner about his/her study practices (feel free to ask additional questions!):

> Wie viele Kurse belegst du dieses Semester?
> Wann musst du zur Uni?
> Wie viele Stunden sitzt du im Hörsaal?
> Wann lernst du und wie viele Stunden?
> Arbeitest du neben dem Studium?
> Wie viele Stunden arbeitest du jede Woche?
> Wie viele Klausuren hast du dieses Semester?
> In welchem Kurs?
> Hast du Zeit für ein Hobby?
> ...?

Interviewnotizen:

B. With 2-3 classmates write an *E-Mail* to a student in Germany who contacted you about your University for further information.
How many courses do people typically take at your university? How many classes each day? How many hours do people study/do homework? How many exams do they have each semester? Do they work? Is there any time left for fun?

Make sure to proofread your entry afterwards so it's comprehensible to your audience. In addition, make sure you start and end the *E-Mail* in a polite manner!

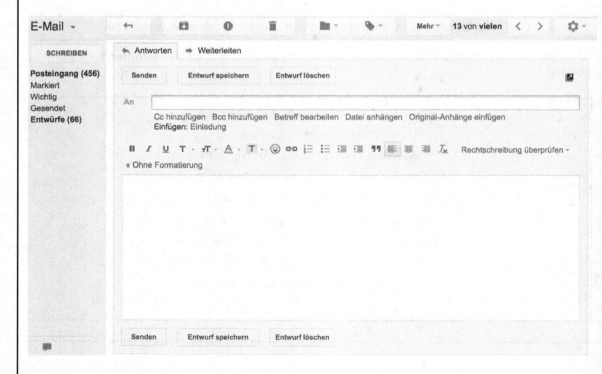

Studi-Tipp: When browsing the internet, make sure you set the language of the traget website to German to practice navigating the world wide web *auf Deutsch*! Also, try and use your email account or social media (Facebook, Pinterest etc.) in German.

Zum Nachdenken:

In Germany, the grading is a bit "backwards" for American learners. '1' (*eins*) is *sehr gut*; '2' (*zwei*) is *gut*; '3' (*drei*) is *befriedigend*; '4' is *ausreichend*; '5' (*fünf*) is *mangelhaft*; and '6' (*sechs*) is *ungenügend*. Austria has grades 1–5 (*fünf* is *nicht ausreichend*). Switzerland also has the 1–6 scale where 6 is the best grade (except in the *Kanton* Waadt, where it goes all the way to 10, 10 being the best). What would your grades have been like last semester according to the German grading system? What *Durchschnittsnote* (average grade, ca. GPA) would you have gotten?

Aktivität 22. Sprache im Kontext: Katrin und Vanessa: Im Ausland studieren

While it is true that most Germans speak English quite well, it is essential to learn a foreign language if you want to study abroad. Watch Katrin and Vanessa's clips and answer the questions below.

A. Watch the clip and check all words that you hear.

(QR 2.27 p.103)

(QR 2.28 p.103)

❑ Ausland	❑ Doktorat
❑ Englisch	❑ Oktober
❑ Anforderungen	❑ Universität
❑ Noten	❑ Sportwissenschaft
❑ Semester	❑ Münster
❑ Tage	❑ Studentenausweis
❑ Seminararbeit	❑ Hauptwache

B. Watch the clip again and answer the *richtig–falsch* questions below.

	richtig	falsch		richtig	falsch
1) Katrin hat dreimal im Ausland studiert.	❑	❑	1) Vanessa beginnt im Oktober mit ihrem Doktorat.	❑	❑
2) Sie hat von 2004 bis 2005 in den USA studiert.	❑	❑	2) Sie studiert Sportmedizin in München.	❑	❑
3) Sie hat Englisch unterrichtet.	❑	❑	3) Ihre Uni ist in Mingen.	❑	❑
4) Das Studium in Deutschland ist nicht so streng geregelt wie in Amerika.	❑	❑	4) Ihr Hauptfach ist Sportwissenschaft.	❑	❑

C. Listen to the clips one more time and answer the questions below.

Fragen zu Katrins Video:

1. Wann hat Katrin in den USA studiert?

_____

2. Wo hat Katrin studiert?

_____

3. Was ist in Deutschland die wichtigste Anforderung?

_____

Fragen zu Vanessas Video:

1. In welcher Stadt liegt Vanessas Universität?

_____

2. Auf welches Fach will sich Vanessa spezialisieren?

_____

3. Wo möchte Vanessa vielleicht arbeiten?

_____

Zum Nachdenken:

What differences does Katrin mention about the American and German course requirements? What are the *Vorteile* (*advantages*) and *Nachteile* (*disadvantages*) of each system? Why do you think Vanessa is doing her Ph.D. in Germany (as opposed to the U.S., Canada or Mexico)?

Aktivität 23. Ein kleines Interview

Work with a partner and ask each other the following questions. Write down your partner's answers. Ask follow-up questions whenever possible.

Möchtest du einmal im Ausland studieren? Wo?   **Notizen:**

Findest du Fremdsprachen wichtig für dein Studium? Und für deine Karriere? Warum/ warum nicht?

Welche Fremdsprachen sprichst du schon? Welche möchtest du noch lernen?

Sollten (*should*) – deiner Meinung nach (*in your opinion*) – alle Studenten eine Fremdsprache lernen? Wenn ja, warum? Wenn nein, warum nicht?

...?

Aktivität 24. Das schwarze Brett

Very common in universities is the giant column in the middle of the hallway, with layer upon layer of student advertisements: students seeking books, lecture notes, bikes, others offering these or letting you know about a new adventure club. This is „das schwarze Brett", the campus bulletin board still found at every German university. „Das schwarze Brett" is a gold-mine for the inexpensive furniture you need for your dorm room or the new conversation partner who will swap English lessons with you for German lessons. Take a look at the following advertisements students posted and find out what they were looking for or what they were trying to sell.

A. Anzeigen: verkaufen/suchen/anbieten/informieren.

Look at the ads the students put up on *das schwarze Brett* (see next page). Which ones are selling/offering something, which are seeking something? Which ones are just presenting information?

	advertisement number:	selling/seeking what?
zu verkaufen:		
suchen:		
informieren:		

B. Wie sagt man?

Read the advertisements carefully and note important phrases and expressions the authors of these ads used. *Wie sagt man auf Deutsch?*

seeking = _____

wanted = _____

to trade = _____

subletting = _____

from (+ date) = _____

if you have questions, you can call us at ... = _____

1 LATEIN GRUNDKURS!!!!!
22.08 – 09.09.07
TAUSCHPARTNER GESUCHT

ICH NEHME AN DEM LATEINKURS BEI HERR
LUKAS (14:00–17:15 UHR) TEIL!!!
WÜRDE ABER GERNE IN DEN KURS VON HERR
LANGE (08:15–12:45 UHR) WECHSELN!!!!
IST JEMAND BEREIT DEN KURS MIT MIR ZU
TAUSCHEN ???
BITTE MELDET EUCH UNTER: 0160/99713661
(ANNE)

2 zur
Zwischenmiete (m

ab Sept./Okt. 07
bis voraussichtlich Mai 08

• **16 m²** mit schönen Möbeln
• 2 sehr nette Mitbewohner (w, 25 · 26)
• große Wohnung mit schöner Küche, Balkon, grün
  Innenhof, DSL-Flatrate, Fahrradkeller und u
• Straßenbahnhaltestelle, Einkaufsmöglichkeiten
  gleich ums Eck

In der Zellerau (Denklerblock)

für 220,– warm !!!

Wir freuen uns auf Anne!

3 AN ALLE FRAUEN + MÄDELS,
(ausnahmsweise mal nicht an die Männer)

Habt Ihr bzw. Du Lust
__Fußball__
zu spielen?
Dann kommt einfach mal
vorbei!

Mittwochs ab 17:30 Uhr (Mädels)
ab 18:30 Uhr (Frauen)
→ in den Pfingstferien findet KEIN Training
statt!!

WO...?? → Am Sportgelände des
TSV Prosselsheim!

Falls Ihr Fragen habt, könnt Ihr euch auch bei
Anita Bielek melden (Tel. 09386/1376)

Mitbewohnerin gesucht
für 2er-WG in der Sanderau

• Zimmer ca 14 m²
• Miete 180 Euro+NK(Strom,Gas)
• 5 Minuten zu Stadtmensa, Sanderuni, FH
• 10 Minuten zu Fuß in die Stadt
• 10er Haltestelle zum Hubland vor der Haustür
• frei ab 1.8.

Wohnung Sanderau, 14m² 180€+NK
Anne - 0170/4613584

Zum Nachdenken:
Looking at the language that the students used, what values are expressed?
What is important in a room (e.g., lightness , air, heating?)? In a roommate?

C. Noch einmal lesen

Now it's time to explore these ads a bit more deeply. Read 2 of the *Anzeigen* that look interesting to you, and fill in the table below.

	Anzeige 1	Anzeige 2
Title/Name		
Is this ad from someone offering a service or looking for one?		
What is the service that is being offered or sought?		
What is the contact information of the person who posted this ad?		
What other information is provided that seems particularly useful?		
What are 2-3 useful phrases in this ad?		

D. Antworten

Of the *Anzeigen* you just read, pick one to respond to. In the space provided below, write a script for a phone call you would make to respond to the author of the ad. Express your interest in what the person has to offer. Use as many of the useful phrases as you can from the ads you read. Make sure you include the information that is provided in the given advertisements!

E. Meine Anzeige

Unfortunately, the person tells you immediately (or calls you back to tell you) that whatever he/she had for sale is no longer available! *Wie schade!* Now you have to write your own advertisement seeking/selling what you need or have for sale. Make sure that you make your advertisement effective, funny, concise, with all the necessary information on the ad! Feel free to decorate it too – that always helps catch the reader's eye!

Aktivität 25. Im Studentenwohnheim

Now you know a lot about the university in Germany, but you still need to know where to live and other important things you need to be aware of. Read the message Jackie received from her German friend, and answer the questions below.

Hi Jackie,

Alles klar bei dir? Ich habe wenig Zeit, also hier nur eine kurze Antwort: Studentenwohnheime sind ein Teil des Studentenlebens - so wie das Essen in der Mensa, das Einschlafen in einer Vorlesungen und das Feiern nach einem Examen... Manche Wohnheime haben WGs! Das macht meistens besonders viel Spaß! Oft organisieren Tutoren ein Freizeitprogramm für die Bewohner und viele Wohnheime haben auch große Gemeinschaftsräume, Fitnessgeräte, Tischtennisplatten oder sogar Volleyballfelder. Ich habe in Bonn studiert, aber die Wohnheime sind, glaub' ich, ähnlich an den deutschen Unis. Google mal den Begriff „Studentenwerk" oder geh' direkt auf www.studentenwerk.de. Es gibt bestimmt eine englische Version und du bekommst noch mehr Infos.

Ich hoffe das hilft dir bei deinen Plänen für das nächste Semester in Würzburg.

Bis bald, Anke

P.S.: Übrigens, wenn man in Würzburg in ein Haus, eine Wohnung, eine WG oder ein Wohnheim zieht, muss man sich (sein Auto, seinen Hund) innerhalb einer Woche beim Einwohnermeldamt anmelden - auch als Amerikaner :) ! Ich glaub'das geht auch online!

A. Wohnheime

1. What is a part of the *Studentenleben* in Anke's opinion?

2. What kind of sport can you do at the dorms?

3. What do you think „WG" means?

4. What does Anke suggest, where can Jackie get more information?

B. Meldepflicht

1. According to Anke´s postscript, who has to register at the local municipality?

2. When do you have to register?

3. What does Anke think, how can you register?

4. What do you think might be some reasons for requiring people to register?

5. Is there something similar people in your home state/country have to do?

6. Go to the following website:
http://www.wuerzburg.de/media/www.wuerzburg.de/org/med_4567/26794_4091501004404_0832.pdf
You will find the form to register in Würzburg. What information do they require from you? What do you think about this law?

C. Haushaltspaket

Since you are an exchange student, and you will only be in Germany for one or two semesters, you don't want to buy all the stuff you need for your apartment or dorm. Thankfully, the „Studentenwerk" (*student union*) offers a package with all the basic things you need.
Source: http://www.studentenwerk-wuerzburg.de/international/haushaltspaket.html

Das Studentenwerk Würzburg bietet seinen ausländischen Studenten/-innen an:

DAS HAUSHALTSPAKET

AUTHENTISCH

Was ist das Haushaltspaket?
Im Haushaltspaket findet ihr eine Bettdecke mit Kopfkissen, Bettbezüge und Bettlaken sowie Essgeschirr, Besteck und Gläser für zwei Personen, Kochgeschirr (Töpfe, Pfanne) und noch andere diverse Kochutensilien.

Für wen ist das Haushaltspaket?
Das Haushaltspaket ist gedacht für ausländische Studenten/-innen, die nur für ein oder zwei Semester zum Studium nach Würzburg kommen und nicht immer die Möglichkeit haben, Geschirr und Kochutensilien oder auch Bettwäsche mit zu bringen.

Wieviel kostet das Haushaltspaket?
Für das Haushaltspaket ist eine Leihgebühr in Höhe von 10,00 Euro pro Monat zu bezahlen. Es muss eine Kaution in Höhe von 50,00 Euro hinterlegt werden, die bei ordnungsgemäßer Rückgabe (das heißt vollzählig, ohne Beschädigungen und sauber) wieder ausbezahlt wird.

Von wem bekomme ich das Haushaltspaket?
Das Haushaltspaket könnt ihr bei eurem Einzug von eurem zuständigen Hausmeister bekommen. Vorher müsst ihr bei ihm eine Vereinbarung unterschreiben. Der Hausmeister gibt die Vereinbarung weiter an die Verwaltung im Studentenwerk. Die Leihgebühr sowie die Kaution für das Paket werden dann anschließend von eurem Bankkonto, welches ihr vorher bei einer deutschen Bank eröffnen müsst, abgebucht. Bei eurem Auszug müsst ihr das Paket auch wieder bei dem Hausmeister abgeben.

Wer ist für die Reinigung zuständig?
Für die Reinigung des Geschirrs sowie der Bettbezüge ist der Mieter selbst verantwortlich.

1. To whom are *Haushaltspakete* offered?

2. What things are included in the *Haushaltspaket*?

3. How much does the *Haushaltspaket* cost?

4. What is a *Kaution*?

5. Who is responsible for cleaning the items included in the *Haushaltspaket*?

6. What do you think is missing? What should also be included in the *Haushaltspaket*? Alternately, what is in the *Haushaltspaket* which you didn't expect to see?

Aktivität 26. Im Studentenwohnheim

Knowing a foreign language can lead you to exciting and wonderful new places. While you are on a study abroad program, you are staying with a host family whose house you can see in the picture on the next page. Next to the labels for the different rooms and items in these rooms, write down what your host family has. Make sure that you use the correct accusative form (and with the correct gender!). We have already furnished the bathroom for you and bought you some essential toiletries as well! ☺

Beispiel:

Im Bad/Zimmer gibt es ... (+Akk.)

Note that we use „**im**" (a contraction of the preposition "in" and the dative article "dem") for the masculine and neuter nouns and „**in der**" for the feminine nouns. When talking about rooms in our house only the kitchen is feminine and we use „**in der**"to say what we find in it.

das Wohnzimmer

1. der Fernseher → *den Fernseher*
2. die Couch → *die Couch*
3. die Stereoanlage →
4. die Zimmerpflanze →

das Arbeitszimmer

5. der Schreibtisch →
6. das Bücherregal →
7. der Computer →

das Schlafzimmer

8. das Bett →
9. die Kommode →

das Dachgeschoss

10. der Kleiderschrank →

(few German houses have closets like in the US, they are freestanding pieces of furniture instead)

das Bad

11. die Badewanne →
12. die Toilette →
13. das Waschbecken →
14. der Spiegel →

die Küche

15. der Herd →
16. der Kühlschrank →
17. die Schränke →

das Esszimmer

18. der Esstisch →
19. die Stühle →

der Garten

20. die Bäume →

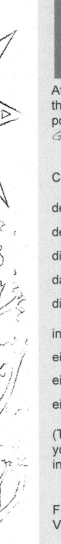

At home please read the following grammar point on the *Grimm Grammar* website.

Cases: <u>accusative case</u>

definite articles (= the):

der → den (m.)

die → die (f.)

das → das (n.)

die → die (pl.)

indefinite articles (= a/an):

ein → einen (m.)

eine → eine (f.)

ein → ein (n.)

(There is no plural for *ein*; you can't say "an apples" in English either.)

For review:
Verbs: <u>haben</u>

ich habe
du hast
er/sie/es hat

wir haben
ihr habt
sie haben

Sie haben

Aktivität 27. Sprache im Kontext: Bernas Wohnung

Watch Berna's *Sprache im Kontext* video and identify what rooms she has in her house and what items she has in her own room. Where does she like to buy things for her house?

A. Listen to Berna and write down all the rooms she has in her house.

Sie hat _____ (#) Zimmer in ihrem Haus.

(QR 2.29 p.103)

B. Listen to the clip again and check all the things Berna has in her room.

In ihrem Zimmer hat sie ...

❑ ein Bett mit ganz viel Bettzeug ❑ einen (Kleider-) Schrank ❑ einen Wecker

❑ einen Fernseher ❑ einen Computer ❑ einen Teppich

❑ einen Schreibtisch ❑ ein Telefon ❑ ein Poster an der Wand

❑ viele Postkarten und Photos an der Wand von Familie und Freunden ❑ ein Bücherregal mit ganz vielen Büchern dadrin (*in it*) ❑ eine Stehlampe (*a tall standing lamp*)

C. Listen to the clip a third time and answer the questions below.

Warum hat Berna drei Zimmer in ihrem Haus?

Auf welchem Möbelstück steht Bernas Computer?

Wo kaufen Sie Sachen für Ihr Zimmer? Warum?

Aktivität 28. Sprache im Kontext: Was hat Sara in ihrer Wohnung?
The title of each activity below indicates the name of the video you should view.

A. Saras Küche
Watch and listen as Sara describes some of the items she has in her kitchen. Jot down some of the kitchen items she specifically mentions in the spaces below. Remember to include the accusative article for each word

(QR 2.30 p.103)

Beispiel:

Sie hat einen Ofen

1	5
2	6
3	7
4	8

Note these useful verbs:

brauchen (to need)
ich brauche
du brauchst
er/sie/es braucht

wir brauchen
ihr braucht
sie brauchen

Sie brauchen

möchten (would like)
ich möchte
du möchtest
er/sie/es möchte

wir möchten
ihr möchtet
sie möchten

Sie möchten

B. Saras Bad
"I spy ..." Which items do you see in Sara's bathroom(s)? Watch the video a second time if you need to and write down the German names of at least six items she mentions. Again, remember to include the accusative indefinite (*eine, ein, einen*) article for each word.

Beispiel:

In Saras Badezimmer gibt es einen ...

1	4
2	5
3	6

Zum Nachdenken:
Is there anything "different" you notice about Sara's dorm room compared to how American houses/apartments/dorms are set up? If yes, what did you notice? (Suggestions: think of color, use of space, light, look of furniture etc.)

Grimm Grammar

At home please read the following grammar point on the *Grimm Grammar* website.

Negation: *Kein*

Kein = nicht ein

Kein will always precede nouns.

Consider these pairs of sentences. Which show nominative and which show accusative use?

masculine
Kein Tisch steht da.
Ich habe keinen Tisch.

feminine
Keine Lampe steht da.
Ich habe keine Lampe.

neuter
Kein Bett steht da.
Ich habe kein Bett.

plural
Keine Bücher sind da.
Ich habe keine Bücher.

C. Saras Schlafzimmer

Watch as Sara talks about her dormroom in Würzburg. In the space below, list as many of the items she mentions as possible (there are 13 items all together), and use the correct accusative article for each noun!

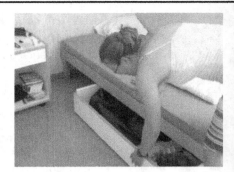

Im Schlafzimmer hat Sara ...

Aktivität 29. Viel Spaß in der Wohnung!

Now that you've listed all of the bedroom items Sara mentions, find these 13 words in the word search below (the articles are omitted). The words may be forward or backward, horizontal, vertical or diagonal. This activity will help your spelling!

```
X S T U V Ö B E T T W Ä S C H E P E Ü H U A M C
P I Ä N Y K F K R A D S R I Ü ß D M N Q G D T N
Z V O P S D N O Ü K ß K A D K A W K S T Z I Y Ö
F I Ä Z B H M J L P K N X U L T A Ö R S S W Z L
F E N S T E R T ß R O K I A L B W Y M E K C R I
I O K N S Ü W P K R Ö C U I M T F H H Z W M Ü D
S R I O P K C T M A D H K N ß H G U Q U Ö R Y W
C J N ß C Y V T P O Q T C T W A Q U Ü H T W M O
H Z O T J A E J T S V T X R T W C C P K S L Ö R
R F Z Y W J B Q O Ä B I B I E M O S K C V L C Q
A T K V O A K E C Y Z S N O H Ü A Ö T D G X I U
N B I O T R E F T I W C I ß O Z Q N U I S A Ö A
K U O E S C K Y G T N H Ä J W V P C Ö N E Q V D
L C I B J R C W Q X O P I C O M P U T E R Z M K
S U X Z H O Ä Y W I K L U T I E B R A L U H C S
B N Y O P W S Z Ü Z R S Z Z M N O Ü Q X Z H D F
```

Aktivität 30. Mein Zimmer
Jetzt sind Sie dran! What do you have in your own room?

A. Make a list
Write all the items that you already have (*haben*; column 1), what you really need (*brauchen*; column 2) and what of these items you would really like to have (*möchten*; column 3). Let a classmate know what these items are. Make sure you use the correct direct object article (einen, ein, eine, den, das, die, die, etc.) to describe what you have, need or would really like!

Ich habe schon einen Tisch. Ich brauche noch einen Wecker. Und ich möchte sehr gerne einen großen Fernseher haben!

Ich habe schon ...	Ich brauche ...	Ich möchte auch ...
_____	_____	_____
_____	_____	_____
_____	_____	_____
_____	_____	_____

B. Go Shopping
Now that you know what it is that you don't have (and would like), go shopping at a swedish furniture store that is very popular in Germany: *Gehen wir bei IKEA einkaufen! Sie haben ein Budget von 250 Euro: Welche Objekte auf Ihrer Liste oben wollen Sie kaufen? Sie finden die Preise hier:* http://www.ikea.com/de/de/

Was ich kaufe:	Preis:
_____	_____
_____	_____
_____	_____
_____	_____
_____	_____

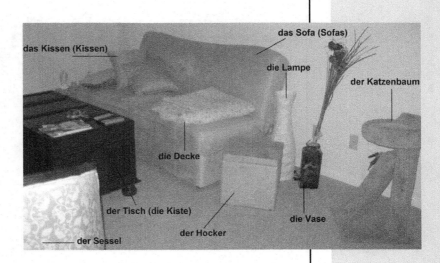

Oh nein! Es fehlen Pluralfomen.
Wie lauten sie?

Grimm Grammar

At home please read the following grammar point on the *Grimm Grammar* website.

Review: Accusative case (nouns)

Es gibt:
Where you use "there is/ there are" in English, you use *„es gibt"* in German.

Note, that in German the noun that follows takes the accusative case:

Zum Beispiel

Es gibt einen Schreibtisch. There is a desk.

Aktivität 31. Mein Traumhaus

On a sheet of paper draw a picture of your dream house. Label the different rooms and the items in each room. Remember, this is your dream home, so go wild and be creative! Label at least 15-20 items. Present your Traumhaus to the class! Remember: „es gibt" and „ich habe" take the accusative! Use the accusative form of the words in the boxes for exercise 27 (i.e., the words in the second column).

In meinem Traumhaus gibt es ein Schlafzimmer. Dort habe ich einen Schreibtisch, ein Bett, einen Computer und einen Stuhl.

Aktivität 32. Geschmäcker sind verschieden

Talk with a partner. First label the pictures with the correct words and articles. Then talk to your partner. Ask each other how you like the furniture pieces and electronics. Watch out for the accusative case!

Beispiel:

S1: *Wie findest du den Sessel?*
S2: *Ich finde den Sessel unbequem.*

Eigenschaften:
praktisch • hässlich • klein • modern • alt
schön • bequem • groß • interessant
elegant • unpraktisch • unbequem • genial
altmodisch • ganz toll • super

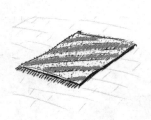   

_____

_____

_____

_____

Aktivität 33. Sprache im Kontext: Tobe: Der Computer

In this video Tobe explains the computer and some of the accessories.

(QR 2.35
p.103)

A. Watch the clip and circle all the words that you hear

Drucker • Tischplatte • Festplatte • Drücker • Scanner • Brenner • Bildschirm • Regenschirm

Laptop • Maus • Haus • Tastatur • Taschenuhr • USB-Stick • Geschick • Geschirr

B. Watch the clip again and listen carefully to Tobe as he explains the different parts of his computer and accessories.

After watching try to match the words with the computer parts and accessories. Don't forget to write down the correct article.

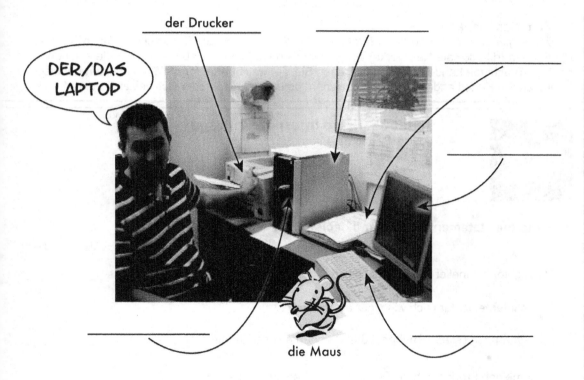

C. Der Scanner scannt ...

Watch Tobe's clip again, and match the correct computer parts with the expressions Tobe uses with them.

1. die Festplatte   a. Hier muss man Papier einlegen, wenn man Dokumente ausdrucken möchte.

2. die Maus   b. Hier kann man Dokumente einscannen und sie vom Blatt auf den Computer übertragen.

3. der Drucker   c. Wo man den Computer ein- und ausschalten kann; hier kann man den USB-Stick anschließen.

4. der Scanner   d. Was den Zeiger auf dem Bildschirm bewegt und womit man auf verschiedene Symbole klicken kann.

Aktivität 34. Interviews: E-Mails schreiben: ja oder nein?

Although for many people, and in many instances computers make our lives much easier, there are some stressful aspects to e-mail as well. Listen to what Harald has to say about e-mails:

A. Watch Harald's clip

Wie findet er E-Mails? Circle all that apply!

(QR 2.34 p.103)

1. Er findet E-Mails toll.
2. Er schreibt jeden Tag ungefähr zwei Stunden lang E-Mails.
3. Er hasst die modernen Kommunikationsmethoden, wie E-Mail.
4. In einem Jahr verschwendet (*waste*) man ungefähr zwei Wochen mit E-Mails.
5. Er liest gern echte, altmodische Briefe.
6. Er ruft Leute sehr gern an.

B. Zum Nachdenken

Wie wichtig sind E-Mails und das Internet für Sie? Wie oft benutzen Sie solche sozialen Online-Plattformen (d.h. soziale Netzwerke) wie *Facebook* oder *Twitter*? Haben Sie Freunde aus den deutschsprachigen Ländern? Wenn ja, fragen Sie sie, welche Plattform sie am meisten benutzen. Benutzen Sie E-Mail anders als Ihre deutschen, österreichischen oder Schweizer Freunde?

Aktivität 35. Eine Internet-Umfrage

Are you *really* into the Internet?

A. Read the statements below and decide if they apply to you or not

	Ja	Nein
1. Ein guter, schneller Internetanschluss ist für mich sehr wichtig.	____	____
2. Das Internet ist für mich wichtiger als Kaffee.	____	____
3. Ich verbringe (*spend*) mehr als drei Stunden pro Tag im Internet.	____	____
4. Mit meinen Freunden spreche ich nur per Facebook oder SMS.	____	____
5. Ich checke meine E-Mails mindestens (*at least*) jede halbe Stunde.	____	____
6. Wenn ich mit einem Freund spreche, lese ich SMS-Nachrichten im Handy.	____	____
7. Ich kriege mehr als 20-25 E-mails bzw. SMS-Nachrichten pro Tag.	____	____

B. Klassenumfrage

Use the statements above to create questions, and ask your peers whether the statements apply to them. If their answer is "yes," have them initial your questionnaire. How many students answered positively to each of the questions? Is your class addicted to the Internet?

1. Ist ein guter, schneller Internetanschluss sehr wichtig für dich?

2. Ist das Internet für dich wichtiger als Kaffee?

3. _____

4. _____

5. _____

6. _____

	Ja	Nein
1. Ein guter, schneller Internetanschluss ist für mich sehr wichtig.	____	____
2. Das Internet ist für mich wichtiger als Kaffee.	____	____
3. Ich verbringe (*spend*) mehr als drei Stunden pro Tag im Internet.	____	____
4. Mit meinen Freunden spreche ich nur per Facebook oder SMS.	____	____
5. Ich checke meine E-Mails mindestens (*at least*) jede halbe Stunde.	____	____
6. Wenn ich mit einem Freund spreche, lese ich SMS-Nachrichten im Handy.	____	____
7. Ich kriege mehr als 20-25 E-mails bzw. SMS-Nachrichten pro Tag.	____	____

Aktivität 36. Ein Interview

Ask one of your classmates about his/her use of *Technik* (technology). You can use the questions below or pose your own questions. When you are done, present your findings to the rest of the class.

Wofür (*for what*) benutzt du den Computer?

Hast du ein Laptop oder einen Computer?

Magst du lieber PCs oder MACs?

Spielst du Videospiele? Wie oft? Wie viele Stunden pro Woche?

Hast du ein Lieblingsvideospielsystem (Xbox, Wii usw.)?

Hast du eine Homepage? Wenn ja, was ist auf deiner Homepage?

Hast du ein Handy oder Smartphone?

Wie viele SMS bekommst du und verschickst du jeden Tag?

Hast du einen großen Fernseher? Und einen DVD-Player?

Wie viele Stunden in der Woche siehst du fern?

Wie viel Zeit verbringst du auf Facebook?

> Ich spiele sehr gerne Computerspiele, besonders *World of Warcraft*.

> Auf meiner Homepage ist ein Link zu *Spiegel.de*.

> Ich schreibe täglich fast 50 SMS-Nachrichten!

Aktivität 37. Das Technoleben

With your classmates (or a small group of friends), write a short story – using dialogs or narration, prompts and "voice-overs" – that illustrates the effect of technology on your life. Be creative and humorous. You have a lot of language resources in this chapter to help you: phrases to talk about courses, exams, and technology, for example. All that's needed is your imagination!

_____

_____

_____

_____

_____

_____

_____

_____

_____

_____

Aussprache
Der Umlaut

Please go to the *Deutsch im Blick* website, Kapitel 2

In the last chapter, we briefly mentioned four "strange-looking" letters in German. These letters represent sounds that are distinct from the sounds represented by the 26 letters of the alphabet – hence their unusual appearance! In this chapter, we discuss three of these letters.

Ä/ä	anhängen, beschäftigt, die Gläser, die Universität	to attach, busy, glasses, university
Ö/ö	der Dosenöffner, die Körbe, um zwölf Uhr, ich möchte	the can opener, the baskets, at twelve o'clock, I would like
Ü/ü	die Bücher, die Küche, die Prüfung, üben	books, kitchen, exam, to practice

On the *Deutsch im Blick* website („Aussprache") click on each pair of words below, and pay close attention to the differences in pronunciation between the original sound and the „*umlauted*" version.

der Anhang (attachment)	anhängen (to attach)	schon (already)	schön (pretty)	das Buch (book)	die Bücher (book)
der Saal (hall)	die Säle (halls)	mochte (wanted)	möchte (would like)	der Kuchen (cake)	die Küchen (kitchens)
ich wasche (I wash)	die Wäsche (laundry)	der Topf (pot)	die Töpfe (pots)	cool (cool: hip)	kühl (cool: temperature)

UMLAUT AND THE UMLAUT MARK

The letters above have undergone what is known as **umlaut**. Umlaut is the technical term for the process of transforming a *back* vowel (i.e., a vowel articulated in the back part of your mouth) to its corresponding *front* vowel (i.e., a vowel articulated in the front part of your mouth).

And here is how you can form them on your computer:

1. One possibility is to go to the Menu bar and under INSERT, select SYMBOL and insert the correct lower- or upper-case letters.
2. Second, you can create short-cuts (also under the INSERT, SYMBOL short-cut key) for the different letters.
3. Third, you can use some pre-set control functions on your keyboard as listed below:

	PCs	Macs
Ä/ä	CTRL+SHIFT+: then A or a	ALT + u then A or a
Ö/ö	CTRL+SHIFT+: then O or o	ALT + u then O or o
Ü/ü	CTRL+SHIFT+: then U or u	ALT + u then U or u

But what if your computer program or e-mail server does not recognize the umlaut marks? No problem. Simply write the letters as Ae/ae, Oe/oe, or Ue/ue. Long ago, the umlaut process was actually indicated in a similar way.

A superscript lowercase *"e"* was written above the base letter (i.e., "A"). Over time, the superscript lowercase e became *two dashes*, which became *two dots*, and the modern-day *Umlaut* mark was born!

Because these *umlauted* letters represent sounds distinct from the sounds of the alphabet, you need to be careful to pronounce them correctly. Many words actually change meaning if there is an umlauted letter!

die Affen (monkeys)	nachäffen (to mimic)
der Bruder (brother)	die Brüder (brothers)
der Donner (thunder)	der Döner (Kebap)
schon (already)	schön (pretty)
schwul (gay)	schwül (muggy)
die Toten pl. (dead people)	töten (to kill)
tuten (to hoot)	Tüten (bags)
[ich] wusste (I knew)	die Wüste (desert)
zahlen (to pay)	zählen (to count)

Now it's time to practice, so here are some tongue-twisters for you to have fun with!

Bäcker Braun bäckt braune Brezeln.
Braune Brezeln bäckt Bäcker Braun.
"Baker Brown bakes brown pretzels.
Brown pretzels bakes baker Brown."

Es grünt so grün, wenn Spaniens Blüten blühen.
"It turns so green when the flowers in Spain flower."

Tongue-twisters taken from:
http://german.about.com/od/pronunciation/a/tonguetwisters.htm

WebQuests

If you recall from *Kapitel 1*, the "WebQuests" help you get to know the social contexts in which German is used. In *Kapitel 2*, in particular, you will explore:

1. Looking for an apartment through an online roommate–finding service.
2. Getting to know *Young Germany* (a website, and a way of life ☺).

Meinungsumfragen

Just for fun, there are several Interactive Polls in this chapter too! There are zany questions again that you are asked to answer, then before you hit submit, you also need to select your nationality. These polls, obviously not scientific, are a fun way to examine how cross-cultural practices are different – or not!

In this chapter, the Interactive Polls focus on where you live, what you study and how you furnish your humble abode.

Just go to this chapter's *Deutsch im Blick* website and select „Meinungsumfragen".

Wortschatz
Vorbereitung

(QR 2.1 p.103)

An der Uni — At the university

die Unibibliothek (die UB)	university library
das Gebäude (Gebäude)	building
lernen	to study (for an exam)
der Professor (Professoren)	male professor
die Professorin (Professorinnen)	female professor
das Schwarze Brett	university bulletin board
der Student (Studenten)	male university student
die Studentin (Studentinnen)	female university student
der Studentenausweis (Studentenausweise)	student I.D.
studieren	to study (as a major, specialization)
Was studierst du?	what is your major?
die Universität (Universitäten)	university
An welcher Uni studierst du?	Which university do you go to?

Das Studium — Course of Study

der Abschluss (die Abschlüsse)	diploma
Er macht gerade seinen Abschluss.	He's working on his diploma.
die Hochschule	university
die Note (Noten)	grade
das Praktikum (Praktika)	internship
ein Praktikum machen	to do an internship
das Seminar (die Seminare)	advanced level university course
die Vorlesung (die Vorlesungen)	lecture course (a type of introductory course)
der Vorlesungssaal (Vorlesungssäle)	the lecture hall
das Vorlesungsverzeichnis (Vorlesungsverzeichnisse)	course catalogue

Im Unterricht — In class

das Examen (Examen)	exam (usually final exam at the end of one's studies)
die Hausaufgabe (Hausaufgaben)	homework
die Hausaufgaben machen	to do homework
die Hausaufgaben abgeben/einreichen	to turn in the homework
die Klasse (Klassen)	class (as in group of students)
das Klassenzimmer (Klassenzimmer)	the classroom
die Klausur (Klausuren)	exam (written during a course)
der Kreis (Kreise)	circle
Bilden wir einen Kreis!	let's make a circle!
der Kurs (Kurse)	course
lesen	to read
das Projekt (Projekte)	project
das Quiz (Quizze)	quizzes
das Referat (Referate)	oral presentation
ein Referat vorbereiten/halten	to prepare/give a presentation
sagen	to say
schreiben	to write
die Seminararbeit (also: die Hausarbeit)	term-paper
sprechen	to speak
eine Fremdsprache sprechen	to speak a foreign language
die Übung (Übungen)	exercise
eine mündliche/schriftliche Übung	oral/written excercise
der Unterricht	class, instruction
Kommst du zum Unterricht?	Are you coming to class?

Auf dem Schreibtisch — On the desk

das Arbeitsheft (Arbeitshefte)	the workbook
der Bleistift (Bleistifte)	pencil
das Buch (Bücher)	the (text)book
die Kreide (Kreiden)	chalk
der Kugelschreiber/der Kuli (Kugelschreiber/Kulis)	pen
das Kurspaket (Kurspakete)	course packet

Alles über den Computer	**All about the computer**
der Anhang (Anhänge)	attachment (to an e-mail)
anhängen/beifügen	to attach
anmachen/anschalten	to turn on
ausdrucken	to print
ausmachen/ausschalten	to turn off (the light or TV)
der Computer (Computer)	computer
der Bildschirm (-schirme)	monitor
die Digitalkamera (-kameras)	digital camera
das Dokument (Dokumente)	document (word document, for example)
der Drucker (Drucker)	printer
speichern	to save files
der Eintrag (Einträge)	entry (e.g., in a chat)
die E-Mail (E-Mails)	e-mail
hochladen/uploaden	upload
herunterladen/downloaden	download
das Internet (no plural)	the Internet
im Internet surfen/suchen	to surf/search the Internet
der/das Laptop (Laptops)	laptop computer
der Lautsprecher (Lautsprecher)	speaker
die Maus (Mäuse)	mouse
das Programm (Programme)	program/application
der Scanner (Scanner)	scanner
einscannen	to scan in
der Speicher/der USB-Stick	memory drive (flash drive, USB drive)
die Tastatur (Tastaturen)	keyboard
die Tintenpatrone (-patronen)	ink cartridge
das Verbindungskabel (-kabel)	connecting cable

Es ist Zeit!	**It's time!**
der Abend (Abende)	evening
am Abend	in the evening
abends	evenings (usually in the evening)
der Augenblick (Augenblicke)	minute
im Augenblick	at this moment
immer	always
das Jahr (Jahre)	year
dieses/nächstes Jahr	this/next year
das erste Mal	the first time
zweimal	twice
niemals	never
die Minute (Minuten)	minute
der Mittag (Mittage)	noon
um/gegen Mittag	at/around noon
die Mitternacht (no plural)	midnight
um Mitternacht	at midnight
der Morgen (Morgen)	morning
am Morgen	during the morning
morgens	mornings
der Nachmittag (Nachmittage)	afternoon
am Nachmittag	in the afternoon
nachmittags	afternoons (usually)
die Nacht (Nächte)	night
in der Nacht	at night
nie	never
oft	often
die Sekunde (Sekunden)	second
selten	rarely, seldom
die Stunde (Stunden)	hour
der Tag (Tage)	day

jeden Tag	every day
an welchem Tag?	on which day?
täglich	every day, daily
die Uhr (Uhren)	clock, time
Um wie viel Uhr?	at what time?
Viertel vor/nach 10	a quarter before/after 10
von ... bis ...	from ... to ... (time)
vor Kurzem	recently
der Vormittag (Vormittage)	morning
am Vormittag	during/in the morning
vormittags	mornings
die Woche (Wochen)	week
in der Woche	during the week
viermal die Woche	four times a week
die Zeit (Zeiten, but typically, no plural)	time
Ich habe keine Zeit.	I have no time.

In der Wohnung — In the apartment

das Bad (Bäder)	bathroom
der Balkon (Balkone)	balcony
die Garage (Garagen)	garage
der Garten (Gärten)	garden
das Klo (Klos)	colloquial for toilet
Ich muss auf's Klo.	I have to go to the bathroom.
die Küche (Küchen)	kitchen
das Schlafzimmer (-zimmer)	bedroom
die Toilette (Toiletten)	toilet
Ich muss auf die Toilette.	I have to go to the bathroom.
die Treppe (Treppen)	stairs (pl)
die Wohnung (Wohnungen)	apartment
die Wohngemeinschaft (-gemeinschaften)	student co-op
die WG (WGs)	abbrev. for student co-op
in einer WG wohnen	in a student co-op
das Wohnzimmer (-zimmer)	living room
das Zimmer (Zimmer)	room

In der Küche — In the kitchen
Dinge zum Kochen und Essen — Things for cooking and eating

der Becher (Becher)	plastic cup
das Besteck (Bestecke)	silverware
die Dose (Dosen)	can, tin
der Dosenöffner (-öffner)	can opener
die Flasche (Flaschen)	bottle
der Flaschenöffner (-öffner)	bottle opener
die Gabel (Gabeln)	fork
das Glas (Gläser)	glass
der Herd (Herde)	stove
die Kaffeemaschine (Kaffeemaschinen)	coffee maker
der Korkenzieher (Korkenzieher)	cork screw
der Küchenschrank (Küchenschränke)	kitchen cabinet, cupboard
der Kühlschrank (Kühlschränke)	fridge
der Löffel (Löffel)	spoon
das Messer (Messer)	knife
der Ofen (Öfen)	oven
die Pfanne (Pfannen)	pan
die Schüssel (Schüsseln)	bowl
die Tasse (Tassen)	cup
der Teller (Teller)	plate
die Serviette (Servietten)	napkin
der Topf (Töpfe)	pot

Dinge zum Saubermachen	Things for tidying up
aufräumen	clean up/tidy up
das Spülmittel (Spülmittel)	dishwashing detergent
Geschirr spülen	to do the dishes
das Papiertuch (Papiertücher)	paper towel
das Zewa (Zewas)	paper towel (brand name, like Kleenex)
der Schwamm (Schwämme)	sponge

Im Badezimmer	In the bathroom
baden	to take a bath
die Badeschlappen (already in plural)	bathroom slippers
das Badetuch (Badetücher)	towel
die Badewanne (Badewannen)	bathtub
die Dusche (Duschen)	shower
duschen	to shower
der Duschvorhang (Duschvorhänge)	shower curtain
der Spiegel (Spiegel)	mirror
das Toilettenpapier/das Klopapier (no plural)	toiletpaper
das Waschbecken (Waschbecken)	sink
der Wasserhahn (Wasserhähne)	faucet

Das Wohnzimmer	The living room
das Bild (Bilder)	picture
die CD (CDs)	CD
der CD-Spieler/Player (CD-Spieler)	CD-player
der Couchtisch (Couchtische)	coffee table
die DVD (DVDs)	DVD
der DVD-Spieler/Player (DVD-Spieler)	DVD-player
der Fernseher (Fernseher)	TV
fernsehen	to watch TV
das Poster (Poster)	poster
das Radio (Radios)	radio
das Sofa/die Couch (Sofas/Couchen)	sofa
die Stereoanlage (Stereoanlagen)	stereo system
der Teppich (Teppiche)	rug
der Tisch (Tische)	table
die Vase (Vasen)	vase

Das Arbeitszimmer	The study
das Bücherregal (Bücherregale)	book shelf
der Papierkorb (Papierkörbe)	waste basket
der Schreibtisch (Schreibtische)	desk
der Stuhl (Stühle)	chair

Das Schlafzimmer	The bedroom
das Bett (Betten)	bed
die Bettwäsche (no plural)	bedding (sheets, pillowcases, etc.)
die Decke (Decken)	blanket
der Kleiderschrank (Kleiderschränke)	armoir (for clothes)
die Kommode (Kommoden)	dresser
das Kopfkissen (Kopfkissen)	pillow
das Bettlaken (Bettlaken; Laken)	sheet
die Lampe (Lampen)	lamp
der Nachttisch (Nachttische)	nightstand
der Wecker (Wecker)	alarm clock
der Wecker klingelt	the alarm clock goes off
den Wecker stellen	to set the alarm clock
auf die Schlummertaste drücken	to press the snooze button

QR Codes

2.1	2.2	2.3	2.4	2.5	2.6

Wortschatz	01_01_intro_ arrival	02_02_int_ek_ studies	02_03_int_ag_ studies	02_04_int_sco_ studies	02_05_int_scl_ studies

2.7	2.8	2.9	2.10	2.11	2.12

02_06_int_bg_ studies	02_07_int_hb_ studies	02_08_int_ju_ studies	02_09_int_hm_ studies	02_10_int_scl_ favorite	02_11_int_bg_ favorite

2.13	2.14	2.15	2.16	2.17	2.18

02_12_int_ek_ favorite	02_13_int_ju_ favorite	02_14_int_ag_ favorite	02_15_int_ec_ favorite	02_16_sik_katrin- studies	02_17_int_sco_ favorite

2.19	2.20	2.21	2.22	2.23	2.24

02_18_int_hm_ class	02_19_sik_katrin- requirements	02_20_int_ek_ class	02_21_int_ju_ class	02_22_int_sco_ class	02_23_sik_r-c-b- semester

2.25	2.26	2.27	2.28	2.29	2.30

02_24_int_bg_ requirements	02_25_int_ju_ requirements	02_26_sik_katrin- abroad	02_27_sik_ vanessa-abroad	02_29_sik_ bernas-house	02_30_sik_sara- kitchen

2.31	2.32	2.33	2.34	2.35	2.36

02_31_sik_sara- bath	02_32_sik_sara- bedrm	02_33_int_ph_ email	02_34_int_hb_ email	02_35_sik_tobe- computer	02_36_sik_ tobias-library

Page 104 of 484

3 DER ALLTAG UND DAS STUDENTENLEBEN

Getting ready in the morning, heading to class, running errands, eating at the cafeteria, doing homework, and going shopping for groceries. All of these activities are part of your everyday life as a student, so it's essential you learn how to talk about them. In this chapter, you'll do just that by taking a chronological tour through einen typischen Tag (a typical day).

By the end of this chapter, you will be able to talk about many aspects of your day. You will have a good command of separable prefix verbs and negation, as well as the irregular verbs essen (to eat), fahren (to drive), laufen (to walk), nehmen (to take) and schlafen (to sleep). In addition, you will be familiar with a wealth of cultural information relating to shopping and eating in the German-speaking countries.

Online Book links

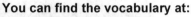

You can find video clips at:
http://coerll.utexas.edu/dib/toc.php?k=3

You can find the vocabulary at:
http://coerll.utexas.edu/dib/voc.php?k=3

Sections
Der Tagesablauf • Daily routine
Das Frühstück • Breakfast
Das Mittagessen • Lunch
Das Abendessen • Dinner
Diese Geschäfte gibt es in der Stadt • A town has these stores
Im Supermarkt • At the supermarket
Beim Gemüseladen • At the green grocer
In der Drogerie • At the drug store
In der Schreibwarenhandlung • At the stationery store
Eine Pause machen • To take a break
Zurück zum Campus fahren • to return (go back) to campus

You can find the grammar topics covered in this chapter at:
During the chapter exercises, you are regularly referred to *Grimm Grammar* at the *Deutsch im Blick* website. These are the grammar points the chapter covers, and you need to complete all online exercises in order to get the most benefit from the exercises in this workbook. The points on the left are necessary for completing the exercises in this course packet. The points on the right are recommended if you need some refreshers on parts of speech or what the present tense actually is ☺.

• Present tense verbs	- essen	http://coerll.utexas.edu/gg/gr/vi_01.html
	- fahren	http://coerll.utexas.edu/gg/gr/vi_02.html
	- laufen	http://coerll.utexas.edu/gg/gr/vi_06.html
	- nehmen	http://coerll.utexas.edu/gg/gr/vi_08.html
	- schlafen	http://coerll.utexas.edu/gg/gr/vi_09.html
• Review: present tense of regular verbs		http://coerll.utexas.edu/gg/gr/v_02.html
• Present tense verbs – separable prefix		http://coerll.utexas.edu/gg/gr/v_04.html
• Conjunctions – negation		http://coerll.utexas.edu/gg/gr/con_02.html
• Review: telling time		http://coerll.utexas.edu/gg/gr/cas_04.html

A. LISTEN

Listen carefully to the pronunciation of each word or phrase in the vocabulary list.

B. REPEAT

Repeat each word or phrase *out loud* as many times as necessary until you remember it well and can recognize it as well as produce it. Make a list of the words in this chapter which you find difficult to pronounce. Your teacher may ask you to compare your list with other students in your class. Make sure to learn nouns with their correct gender!

> **Beispiel:**
> die Sprache
> fünf

C. WRITE

Write key words from the vocabulary list so that you can spell them correctly (remember that it makes a big difference whether you cross the Atlantic by ship or by sheep). You may want to listen to the vocabulary list again and write the words as they are spoken for extra practice.

D. TRANSLATION

Learn the English translation of each word or phrase. Cover the German column and practice giving the German equivalent for each English word or phrase. Next cover the English column and give the translation of each.

E. ASSOCIATIONS

Think of word associations for each category of vocabulary. (What words, both English and German, do you associate with each word or phrase on the list? Write down ten (10) associations with the vocabulary from the chapter.

> **Beispiel:**
> der Student/die Universität
> das Flugticket/das Flugzeug

F. COGNATES

Which words are *cognates?* (Cognates are words which look or sound like English words.) Watch out for *false friends*! Write down several cognates and all the false friends from the chapter, create fun sentences that illustrate similarities and differences between the English and German meanings of these words.

> **Beispiel:**
> Nacht/night
> grün/green
> False Friends: *hell* = light, bright vs. *Hölle* = hell

G. WORD FAMILIES

Which words come from word families in German that you recognize (noun, adjective, verb, adverb)? Write down as many as you find in the chapter.

> **Beispiel:**
> das Studium (noun; studies)
> der Student (noun; person)
> studieren (verb)

H. EXERCISES

Write out three (3) „Was passt nicht?" ('Odd one out') exercises. List four words, three of which are related and one that does not fit the same category. Categories can be linked to meaning, grammar, gender, parts of speech (noun, verb, adjective), etc. USE YOUR IMAGINATION! Give the reason for why the odd word does not fit. Your classmates will have to solve the puzzles you provide!

> **Beispiel:**
> grün – blau – gelb – neun
> Here *neun* does not fit, because it is a
> number and all the others are colors.

Wortschatz
Vorbereitung

Always learn nouns with the article!!!

These ideas are sugges tions only. Different learners have different preference and needs for learning an reviewing vocabulary. Tr several of these sugges tions until you find ones tha work for you. Keep in mind though, that knowing man words – and knowing then well, both to recognize an to produce – makes you more effective user of the new language.

Basiswortschatz
Core Vocabulary

The following presents a list of core vocabulary. Consider this list as the absolute minimum to focus on. As you work through the chapter you will need more vocabulary to help you talk about your own experience. To that end, a more complete vocabulary list can be found at the end of the chapter. This reference list will aid your attainment of Chapter 3's objectives.

(QR 3.1 p.152)

Der Tagesablauf	Daily routine
zu Abend essen	to eat dinner
sich anziehen	to get dressed
sich ausziehen	to get undressed
aufwachen	to wake up
aufstehen	to get up
ins Bett gehen	to go to bed
(sich) duschen	to shower
das Essen	meal
frühstücken	to eat breakfast
sich die Haare kämmen	to comb one's hair
zu Mittag essen	to eat lunch
sich rasieren	to shave
schlafen	to sleep
zur Uni gehen	to go to (travel to) the university
sich die Zähne putzen	to brush one's teeth

Das Frühstück	Breakfast
das Brot (Brote)	bread
das Brötchen, die Semmel (Brötchen, Semmeln)	bread rolls
die Butter (no plural)	butter
das Ei (Eier)	egg
essen	to eat
das Getränk (Getränke)	beverage
der Joghurt (Joghurts)	yogurt
der Kaffee (Kaffees)	coffee
der Kakao (no plural)	hot chocolate
der Käse (Käse)	cheese
die Milch (no plural)	milk
das Obst	fruit
der Saft (Säfte)	juice
der Tee (Tees)	tea
trinken	to drink

Zur Uni fahren	To go to (travel to) the university
das Auto (Autos)	car
der Bus (Busse)	bus
fahren	to drive, to travel
das Fahrrad (Fahrräder)	bicycle
zu Fuß gehen	to go by foot (to walk)
laufen	to walk
nehmen	to take

Das Mittagessen	Lunch
das Gericht (Gerichte)	dish, meal
die Mensa (Mensen)	cafeteria
die Nudeln (used in plural)	pasta
die Pommes/die Fritten (used in plural)	french fries
der Salat (Salate)	salad
das Sandwich (Sandwiche/Sandwiches)	sandwich
der Schnellimbiss/der Imbiss (Schnellimbisse)	fastfood place
der Speiseplan (Speisepläne)	menu at the cafeteria
die Speisekarte (Speisekarten)	menu at a restaurant

In der Drogerie	At the drug store
das Duschgel (Duschgels)	shower gel
die Seife (Seifen)	soap
das Shampoo (Shampoos)	shampoo
das Taschentuch (Taschentücher)	tissue, handkerchief
die Zahnbürste (Zahnbürsten)	toothbrush
die Zahnpasta (Zahnpasten)	toothpaste

In der Schreibwarenhandlung	At the stationery store
der Bleistift (Bleistifte)	pencil
der Kugelschreiber (die -schreiber)	pen
das Heft (Hefte)	notebook
der Ordner (Ordner)	binder
das Papier (Papiere)	paper

Im Gemüseladen	At the green grocer
der Apfel (Äpfel)	apple
die Apfelsine (Apfelsinen)/die Orange (Orangen)	orange
die Banane (Bananen)	banana
der Brokkoli (no plural)	broccoli
die Erdbeere (Erdbeeren)	strawberry
die Gurke (Gurken)	cucumber
die Kartoffel (Kartoffeln)	potato
die Kirsche (Kirschen)	cherry

Aktivität 1. Der Alltag

Now that you already now how to talk about *das Studium let's expand and learn how to describe your every day routine - der Alltag. Was machst du? Wo bist du? Mit wem machst du was? Wann hast du Uni und wann hast du Freizeit?*

(QR 3.34
p.152)

Aktivität 2. Erins typischer Tag

What are typical days for Erin? Watch her video clip and determine which of the following statements are *richtig* and which are *falsch*. Make sure to correct the *falsche Aussagen!*

(QR 3.2
p.152)

Ich stehe gegen 7 Uhr auf.	R	F
Dann mache ich meinen Kaffee und ich spiel' mit der Katze (*cat*) 'rum.	R	F
Ich schrei' meinen Freund an: „Steh auf, du fauler Sack!"	R	F
Wir essen normalerweise kein Frühstück.	R	F
Nachmittags kommt meine Freundin Louisa vorbei und manchmal spielen wir ein bisschen Racquetball oder so was oder wir backen auch.	R	F
Abends entspanne ich mich und schaue "The Simpsons" oder "Family Guy" an oder ich guck' (*to watch*) einen Film.	R	F
Dann gehe ich ins Bett.	R	F

Watch Erin's clip a second time and match the German expressions with their English equivalents.

Ich stehe gegen 8 Uhr auf.	I shout at my boyfriend: "Get up, you lazy bum!"
Ich spiel' mit der Katze 'rum.	Then in the evenings I continue to work.
Ich schrei' meinen Freund an: „Steh auf, du fauler Sack!"	I watch "The Simpsons" or "Family Guy".
Nachmittags kommt Louise vorbei.	I get up around 8 o'clock.
Dann abends arbeite ich weiter.	I play around with my cat.
Ich schaue "The Simpsons" oder "Family Guy" an.	In the afternoons Louise comes by.

Aktivität 3. Bernas typischer Tag

What is a typical day like for Berna? View her „Ein typischer Tag" video and number her daily routines in the order in which she describes them. How is Berna's typical day different from Erin's?

(QR 3.3 p.152)

Dann muss ich erst mal essen, weil ich meistens sehr ausgehungert (*starved*) bin.

Wenn die Kurse fertig (*finished*) sind, komme ich dann nach Hause.

Dann trinke ich eine Tasse Kaffee, ich dusche mich, mache mich fertig.

Vormittags bin ich damit beschäftigt zu unterrichten, vorbereiten, Tests korrigieren...

Dann lese ich wieder weiter für den nächsten Tag.

Ich stehe morgens relativ früh auf, so um sieben.

Dann gehe ich zur Universität.

Nachmittags muss ich dann in meine Kurse reingehen. Dann wird da viel diskutiert.

Grimm Grammar

At home please read the following grammar point on the *Grimm Grammar* website.

Separable prefix verbs – present tense
(Please also complete the exercises at the end.)

Some examples are verbs with *an, auf, aus, ein, mit, nach*, etc.

The prefix is separated from the stem and moved to the end of the clause/sentence:

einkaufen (shop)
ich kaufe ein
du kaufst ein
er/sie/es kauft ein

wir kaufen ein
ihr kauft ein
sie/Sie kaufen ein

Telling Time (review)

Grimm Grammar

Note: Many German verbs dealing with one's Tagesablauf are reflexive verbs (i.e., sich rasieren, sich entspannen, etc.). There is a shift (informal, slang and youth-initiated, of course) to make them non-reflexive. If you are interested in more information about these verbs, check out the *Grimm Grammar* website. In the meantime: briefly, a reflexive verb is a verb in which the subject directs an action at itself.

Ich rasiere mich
= I shave [myself].

Ich entspanne mich
= I relax.

You will learn much more about reflexive verbs next semester in Chapter 7.

Aktivität 4. Und was macht Hassan an einem typischen Tag?

Finally, watch as Hassan describes a typical day in his life and answer the following questions based on his responses.

(QR 3.5 p.152)

1. Wann steht Hassan morgens auf? _____

2. Was macht er am Morgen? _____

3. Wie lange arbeitet er? _____

4. Was macht er am Nachmittag? _____

5. Warum ist Hassan momentan nicht an der Universität? _____

_____

Aktivität 5. Der Tagesablauf

Below are some common activities for each part of the day (i.e., mornings, afternoons, evenings, nights). What other common activities can you think of to add to the list? Circle the ones that describe your daily routine.

morgens
vormittags

aufwachen
aufstehen
duschen   (Ich dusche.)
anziehen   (Ich ziehe meine Kleidung an.)
die Zähne putzen   (Ich putze meine Zähne.)
die Haare bürsten   (Ich bürste meine Haare.)
die Haare kämmen   (Ich kämme meine Haare.)
rasieren   (Ich rasiere mich.)
frühstücken

_____

_____

mittags
nachmittags

zur Universität gehen
in die Kurse gehen/zum Unterricht gehen
zu Mittag essen
Besorgungen machen/etwas erledigen
mit Freunden Kaffee trinken gehen/ausgehen
nach Hause gehen

_____

_____

abends/nachts

Hausaufgaben machen
sich entspannen   (Ich entspanne mich.)
zu Abend essen
ausziehen   (Ich ziehe meine Kleidung aus.)
ins Bett gehen

_____

_____

Aktivität 6. Und was machst du denn den ganzen Tag?

What is a typischer Tag in your life and the life of one of your classmates? In the left column check all the activities that you do and add anything that may apply to you on a typical day. Afterwards ask your partner what s/he goes throughout the day.

Du: *Was machst du an einem typischen Tag?*

Dein Partner: *Ich stehe um 11 Uhr auf, trinke Kaffee, aber komme pünktlich zu meinem Deutschkurs!*

Mein typischer Tag	**Mein Partner:**
❑ Ich wache früh auf.	❑ Ich wache früh auf.
❑ Ich schlafe lange.	❑ Ich schlafe lange.
❑ Ich dusche (jeden Tag/manchmal).	❑ Ich dusche (jeden Tag/manchmal).
❑ Ich schminke mich (nicht).	❑ Ich schminke mich (nicht).
❑ Ich trinke zwei Tassen Kaffee.	❑ Ich trinke zwei Tassen Kaffee.
❑ Ich gehe pünktlich zu meinen Kursen.	❑ Ich gehe pünktlich zu meinen Kursen.
❑ Ich komme oft zu spät zu meinen Kursen.	❑ Ich komme oft zu spät zu meinen Kursen.
❑ Ich esse zu Mittag.	❑ Ich esse zu Mittag.
❑ Ich telefoniere mit Freunden.	❑ Ich telefoniere mit Freunden.
❑ Ich sehe (vier Stunden) fern.	❑ Ich sehe (vier Stunden) fern.
❑ Ich mache Sport.	❑ Ich mache Sport.
❑ Ich mache (zu viele) Hausaufgaben.	❑ Ich mache (zu viele) Hausaufgaben.
❑ Ich esse zu Abend.	❑ Ich esse zu Abend.
❑ Ich gehe ziemlich früh ins Bett.	❑ Ich gehe ziemlich früh ins Bett.
❑ Ich schlafe sehr spät ein!	❑ Ich schlafe sehr spät ein!
❑ Ich entspanne mich.	❑ Ich entspanne mich.
❑ _____	❑ _____
❑ _____	❑ _____
❑ _____	❑ _____

Grimm Grammar

At home please read the following grammar point on the *Grimm Grammar* website.

Verb: schlafen
(Please also complete the exercise).

ich schlafe
du schläfst
er/sie/es schläft

wir schlafen
ihr schlaft
sie/Sie schlafen

Aktivität 7. Ein typischer Tag im Leben von meinem Lieblingsstar

You may not be able to conduct an interview with your favorite star about their daily routine, but who needs facts nowadays! Brainstorm what you think a typischer Tag for your favorite star looks like and create a fictional interview between you and that star.

Sie:	*Hallo! Schön, Sie kennenzulernen. Ich bin ein großer Fan!*
Ihr Lieblingsstar:	*Danke schön.*
Sie:	*Ok, meine erste Frage ... wie sieht Ihr typischer Tag aus?*
Ihr Lieblingsstar:	

_____

_____

_____

_____

_____

_____

_____

Aktivität 8. Lieder & Musik

Jürgen von der Lippe – Guten Morgen, liebe Sorgen. Listen to this song by Jürgen von der Lippe, who – in a parody of a popular children's song – describes a less than desirable day in his imaginary life, and complete the activities in the pdf on the *Deutsch im Blick* website in *Kapitel* 3 under „Lieder & Musik".

Aktivität 9. Alexander und der mistige Tag (von Judith Viorst)

Do you know the story of Alexander, who at one point had a terrible, horrible, no-good, very bad day? Well, he did. Have you ever had one of those? If yes, describe what happened (if not, make something up, and consider yourself very fortunate). For now, describe this event as if you were watching it in a movie, using the present tense.

Aktivität 10. Eine Schlaf-Umfrage

Ich gehe schlafen.
Hopefully, at the end of any day comes some well-deserved sleep! Read the statements below about sleeping habits and decide if they apply to you or not.

	Ja	Nein
1. Ich brauche acht Stunden Schlaf, um zu funktionieren.		
2. Ich bekomme jede Nacht acht Stunden Schlaf.		
3. Ich schlafe immer vor (*before*) Mitternacht ein.		
4. Ich verschlafe oft, obwohl (*although*) ich meinen Wecker stelle.		
5. Ich habe meistens schöne Träume (*sweet dreams*).		
6. Ich schnarche (*snore*) sehr laut.		
7. Ich bin ein großer Fan von Schläfchen (*naps*).		

Aktivität 11. Morgenmenschen vs. Nachtmenschen

Do these speakers like to get up early or sleep in? Watch the „Sind Sie ein Morgenmensch" videos as these people discuss whether they consider themselves to be "morning people," "night people," neither of the two, or both. After watching, put the speaker's name in the appropriate column in the table.

Berna
(QR 3.16 p.152)

Eva
(QR 3.17 p.152)

Harald
(QR 3.18 p.152)

Jan
(QR 3.20 p.152)

Adan
(QR 3.21 p.152)

Hassan
(QR 3.12 p.152)

Erin
(QR 3.23 p.152)

Sara
(QR 3.25 p.152)

Morgenmenschen	Weder ... noch (*neither ... nor*) Beides (*both*)	Nachtmenschen

Aktivität 12. Sind Sie selber ein Morgenmensch oder ein Nachtmensch?

How about you? Do you like to get up early or sleep in? Why? What can you or can't you do in the mornings or at night that make you a *Morgenmensch* or *Nachtmensch*? Write a paragraph of 6-7 sentences explaining your reasons. Look at the example from Anke.

Ich bin Beides. Am Wochenende bin ich ein Nachtmensch. Nachts kann ich mich sehr gut konzentrieren. Am Wochenende schreibe ich nachts immer meine Essays. Im Rheinland sagen wir daher auch „Ich bin eine Nachteule". Am Samstag und Sonntag schlafe ich auch gerne lange. Das geht in der Woche nicht. Montag bis Freitag stehe ich früh auf. Ich gehe zum Unterricht, und arbeite viel. Ich brauche dazu morgens sehr viel Koffein. Also hole ich unterwegs mindestens einen großen Kaffee. Nachts kann ich gut schlafen, wenn ich viel gearbeitet und gelernt habe, aber ich freue mich trotzdem immer auf das Wochenende ...

Helpful expressions:
Ich bin ein Morgenmensch • Ich bin ein Nachtmensch.
Morgens kann ich gut ... • Morgens kann ich nicht so gut ...
Nachts kann ich ... • Nachts kann ich nicht so gut ...

MANN, JETZT HAB' ICH ABER HUNGER!

The daily routine includes a variety of meals, the first of which is Frühstück, followed by ein Mittagessen, and finally concluded by either ein Abendessen or a small Abendbrot. In the next sections, you will learn lots of new information about the types of foods from your native- and non-native-speaking guides.

Grimm Gramma

At home please read the following grammar point on the *Grimm Grammar* website.

Aktivität 13. Frühstücken sie?

Breakfast is the first meal of the day, and as such, nutritionists say it is also the most important meal of the day. Do these speakers agree? Watch as they discuss eating breakfast and take notes on their responses to each question. *Essen sie Frühstück? Wenn ja (if so), wo und was essen sie?* Use the words in the word bank as a guide.

hungrig – Eier – Schinken – zu Hause – Müsli – Nussschnecke mit Zimt und Nüssen – Hunger haben – Haferflocken – Brot

<u>verbs: essen</u>
ich esse
du isst
er/sie/es isst

wir essen
ihr esst
sie/Sie essen

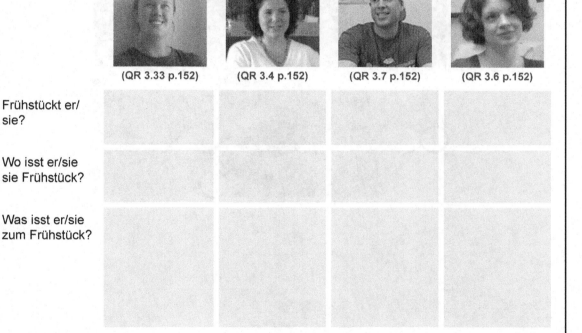

	(QR 3.33 p.152)	(QR 3.4 p.152)	(QR 3.7 p.152)	(QR 3.6 p.152)
Frühstückt er/sie?				
Wo isst er/sie sie Frühstück?				
Was isst er/sie zum Frühstück?				

Nota Bene: Many German speakers say that they eat „XYZ zum Frühstück", however, feel free to use the verb *frühstücken* to imply eating the early meal :) Just watch for the difference in sentence structure if you use the first form:

Ich **frühstücke** ein Eibrot. vs. Ich **esse** ein Eibrot **zum Frühstück**.

Aktivität 14. Ein typisch deutsches Frühstück

A. Take a good look at the image below.
How many of the items can you identify and spell correctly in German? Write down as many items (with the correct article) as you can in 2 minutes – than compare your results with the rest of the class.

1.	6.
2.	7.
3.	8.
4.	9.
5.	10.

Nota Bene: There may be regional differences in breakfast preferences, as well as personal ones. *Mamorkuchen mit Coca-Cola,* anyone?
Some of the terms also differ: *Semmel* (*rolls*) in Bavaria and Austria, *Brötchen* in the northern parts of Germany.

B. Frage zur Diskussion
How does the "typical" German breakfast differ from the "typical" American breakfast?
Discuss with your classmates what everyone eats and explore whether there is such a thing as "typical" American breakfast food.

Aktivität 15. Ein kleines Interview

Ask two of your classmates whether they eat breakfast, and if so, when, where and what they eat. Be ready to share their answers with the rest of the class! If you usually don't eat breakfast pretent you do - because you get the best breakfast in the world ☺.

	Name:	Name:
Frühstückst du?		
Wann frühstückst du?		
Wo frühstückst du? ... in der Cafeteria/Mensa. ... zu Hause. ... im Restaurant. ... ?		
Was isst du zum Frühstück? (at least 5 items) ... Eier ... Müsli ... Obst ... Pfannkuchen ... Speck ... Toast ... ?		
Was trinkst du zum Frühstück? (at least 2 items)		

Aktivität 16. Landbäckerei Köhler

Many bakeries in Germany offer a variety of tasty breakfast menus. Below you can read such a menu from the *Landbäckerei Köhler* and decide what three items you might want to try out – note also how much your breakfast would cost and what is included in the price. After you are done, check with your class: what was the most popular breakfast choice?

Source: http://www.baeckerei-koehler.de/downloads/Fruehstueckskarte_2010.pdf

FRÜHSTÜCK

Frühstücken können Sie bei uns den ganzen Tag!

AUTHENTISCH

French Kiss 1 Tasse Milchkaffee und 1 Croissant	2,90
Schnellstarter 1 Heißgetränk nach Wahl, 1 Scheibe Käse, 1 Scheibe Wurst, 1 Scheibe Salami[4,7,8] 2 Brötchen, Butter und Marmelade	4,10
Bäcker Frühstück 1 Heißgetränk nach Wahl, Rühreier mit zarten Schinkenstreifen[4,7,8] bunt gemischter Brötchenkorb, Butter, Marmelade und Honig	6,80
Handwerker Frühstück 1 Heißgetränk nach Wahl, kross gebratene Bratkartoffeln mit herzhaften Speckwürfeln[4,7,8] und Zwiebeln, 2 Spiegeleier, bunt gemischter Brötchenkorb, Butter, Marmelade und Honig	8,50
Deutsches Frühstück 1 Heißgetränk nach Wahl, 1 frischer Orangensaft, verschiedene Wurstspezialitäten[4,7,8,9] und Käsespezialitäten, 2 Spiegeleier, bunt gemischter Brötchenkorb, Butter, Marmelade und Honig	8,90
American Style 1 Heißgetränk nach Wahl, 1 frischer Orangensaft, 2 doppelseitig gebratene Spiegeleier mit knusprigem Bacon[4,7,8], bunt gemischter Brötchenkorb, Butter, Marmelade und Honig	7,20
Sportler Frühstück 1 Heißgetränk nach Wahl, 1 frischer Orangensaft, Rührei mit Kürbiskernen und Paprika, Hüttenkäse natur, fettarmer Putenschinken, Naturjoghurt mit zarten Haferflocken und Ahornsirup, bunt gemischter Brötchenkorb, Butter, Marmelade und Honig	9,20
Seemanns Frühstück 1 Heißgetränk nach Wahl, 1 frischer Orangensaft, locker geschlagene Kräuterrühreier, Räucherlachs, geräuchertes Forellenfilet mit Sahnemeerrettich, Shrimpscocktail, bunt gemischter Brötchenkorb, Butter, Marmelade und Honig	12,50
Napoli Frühstück 1 Heißgetränk nach Wahl, 1 frischer Orangensaft, Rührei mit würzigen Salamistreifen[4,7,8] Mozzarella mit saftigen Tomaten an Kräuterdressing, Zabaione-Quark mit Amarettini und Schokostreuseln, bunt gemischter Brötchenkorb, Butter, Marmelade und Honig	11,50
Big Ben 1 Heißgetränk nach Wahl, 1 frischer Orangensaft, Rührei mit kräftig gebackenem Bacon[4,7,8] und Champignons dazu Rostbratwürstchen[3], knusprige Cornflakes mit Milch, bunt gemischter Brötchenkorb, Butter, Marmelade und Honig	9,50
El Greco 1 Heißgetränk nach Wahl, 1 frischer Orangensaft, Rührei mit Schafskäsewürfeln, Oliven und milden Peperoni, bunt gemischter Brötchenkorb, Butter, Marmelade und Honig	7,50
Süßschnabel 1 Heißgetränk nach Wahl, 1 frischer Orangensaft, süßer French Toast mit Ahornsirup	4,80

1 = mit Farbstoff	4 = mit Konservierungsstoffen	7 = mit Antioxidationsmittel	10 = mit Chinin
2 = mit Koffein	5 = mit Süßungsmitteln	8 = mit weiteren Zusatzstoffen	
3 = mit Phosphat	6 = mit Aspartam	9 = mit Geschmacksverstärker	

Erste Wahl

Zweite Wahl

Dritte Wahl

Aktivität 17. Was essen Berna und Jan zu Mittag?

After a good *Frühstück* and searching *Das schwarze Brett* for hours you worked up an appetite. Watch the „Zu Mittag essen" clips from Berna and Jan and answer the following questions (in complete sentences) about their lunch-time preferences.

(QR 3.8 p.152)

(QR 3.9 p.152)

1. Wo isst Berna gern?

_____

2. Was isst Jan, wenn (*when*) er in ein Schnellrestaurant geht?

_____

3. Isst Jan manchmal in der Cafeteria auf dem Campus?

_____

4. Wo isst Jan, wenn er sein Essen mitbringt?

_____

Aktivität 18. Ein Speiseplan

Below, you'll find a *Speiseplan* (menu) for an *Uni-Mensa*. As you can see, there are two main meals that you can choose from (*Hauptgericht* 1 & 2) and sides (*Beilagen*). Select for each day (Monday through Thursday) which menu you'd like to order, what sides you want with your meal and how much your lunch will cost. Then work with a partner and tell him or her why you chose those meals.

Beispiel:

S1: *Was isst du am Montag?*
S2: *Am Montag esse ich Schnitzel mit Salat.*
S1: *Warum isst du Schnitzel?*
S2: *Weil es gut schmeckt. / Weil es billig ist.*

Weitere Fragen:

_____

_____

_____

_____

_____

PRISKA gGmbH, Ernstkirchen 4, 63825 Schöllkrippen

Speiseplan KW 19

Diese Woche (05.05. - 09.05.2008) empfehlen wir:

	Hauptgericht 1 **Preis: 3,10 €**	**Hauptgericht 2** **Preis: 3,10 €**	**Beilagen - Preise:** Suppe: 0,80 € Dessert: 0,80 € Kleiner Salat: 1,50 € Großer Salat: 2,80 € Salat mit Putenstreifen und Baguette: 3,80 €
Montag	Schnitzel "Wiener Art" Pommes Salat	Kartoffeltasche mit Frischkäsefüllung Kräuterdipp	Tagessuppe bunter Salat Dessert
Dienstag	gebratenes Hähnchenbrustfilet Rahmgemüse Kroketten	Gemüse-Nudelauflauf Salat	Tagessuppe bunter Salat Dessert
Mittwoch	Erbserneintopf mit Bärlauch	Eierpfannkuchen mit Heidelbeerfüllung Vanillesauce	Tagessuppe bunter Salat Dessert
Donnerstag	Kesselgulasch Nudeln Salat	Spiegelei Spinate Kartoffelpüree	Tagessuppe bunter Salat Dessert
Freitag	Pausenverpflegung	Pausenverpflegung	Tagessuppe bunter Salat Dessert

Heiße Theke: wechselnde Angebote, z. B. Pizzataschen, Flammkuchen verschieden belegt, heiße Leberkäs
Im Sommer werden neben Suppen auch Früchte- und Gemüsekaltschalen angeboten
Änderungen vorbehalten

Aktivität 19. Sprache im Kontext: Döner

If going to the Mensa is not your thing, you can head out for a quick lunch at a *Schnellimbiss* (*fast-food place*). One of the most beloved *Schnellimbisse* in the German-speaking countries is the *Dönerbude*, where you can feast on a delicious Turkish specialty called *Döner*.

A. Watch the video "Döner" and write down what you think the man talks about.

What does he describe?

What things does he mention/explain?

(QR 3.30 p.152)

B. Was für Garnierungen (*toppings*) gibt es für Döner?

Watch the video again an check all items you hear. Afterwards write down the English word below the German word for the possible toppings.

Beispiel:

☑ *Cobansalat: diced tomato, onion, green pepper and cucumber salad*

☐ Krautsalat   ☐ Aubergine

_____   _____

☐ Pilze   ☐ Gurken

_____   _____

☐ Eis[berg]salat   ☐ Oliven

_____   _____

☐ Zwiebeln   ☐ Mais

_____   _____

☐ Bohnen   ☐ Käse

_____   _____

☐ Tomaten   ☐ Soße mit Knoblauch

_____   _____

☐ Soße ohne Knoblauch   ☐ Rettiche

_____   _____

C. Watch the clip again and complete the prompts:

1. Wie heißt der Mann?

2. Woher kommt er?

3. Welches Fleisch brät (*roasts*) er für die Döner?

4. Welche Garnierungen essen Sie gern und welche essen Sie gar nicht gern?

There are lots of different kinds of *Döner* at *Dönerbuden*: beef (*Rindfleisch*), chicken (*Hähnchen*) and lamb (*Lammfleisch*), for example

Grimm Grammar

At home please read the following grammar point on the *Grimm Grammar* website.

<u>Conjunctions: Negation</u>

Nicht is used with verbs, adjectives, adverbs and definite articles in front of nouns:

e.g., Kaspar isst *nicht*. Am Anfang ist er *nicht* so dünn.
"Ich esse nicht" war *nicht* die richtige Antwort!

Kein is used with nouns that are preceded by an indefinite article or ones that have no article before them:

e.g., Kaspar isst *keine* Suppe. Er hat *keinen* Hunger. Er hat *keine* roten, frischen Backen mehr. Er hat *kein* Glück!

Aktivität 20. Sprache im Kontext: Andrew und Austin: Döner kaufen

Watch the video „Andrew/Austin: Döner kaufen" several times and answer as many of these questions as you can.

1. Welche Garnierungen bestellen (*to order*) die Studenten?

Andrew bestellt einen Döner mit _____.

Austin bestellt einen Döner mit _____.

(QR 3.35 p.152)

2. Bezahlen sie zusammen (*together*) oder getrennt (*separate*)? _____.

3. Wie oft essen sie Döner?

Andrew sagt: _____

Austin sagt: _____

Another *Döner* topping frequently served at *Dönerbuden* is a spicy red pepper sauce. When ordering at a *Dönerbude* which serves this sauce, you'll be asked if you'd like yours „*mit scharf*" (*with heat*) or „*ohne scharf*" (*without heat*).

You can try *Döner* with a variety of toppings (including this spicy red sauce) right here in Austin (where this book has its origin) at a *Döner* stand called "Kebabalicious". Check out their location and opening hours on the "Kebabalicious" website http://www.austinkebab.com.

Is there one in your town?

Aktivität 21. Das Mittagessen nicht verpassen!

If you're thinking about skipping lunch today, you might want to think again. The story below – „Die Geschichte vom Suppen-Kaspar" – is a cautionary tale, one of ten stories in Heinrich Hoffmann's famous *Struwwelpeter* (1845) collection, which chronicles the horrifying consequences of children's mischief.
Source: http://gutenberg.spiegel.de/buch/3070/17

A. Vor dem Lesen
Look at the illustrations accompanying the story. What do they tell you about the main character and what happens to him?

_____

_____

B. Nach dem Lesen – Fragen zur Diskussion
1. Summarize the story in your own words: who does what when, and what happens to him?
2. This is clearly a story with a moral. What is it?
3. What do you think the target age-group is? What do you base your response on?
4. How could you tweak the story for a contemporary child audience?

war: was
kerngesund: as fit as a fiddle
ein dicker Bub: a plump boy
kugelrund: round as a ball
hatte: had
Backen: cheeks
aß: ate
fing er an zu schrei'n: he began to shout
eß': esse

sieh nur her!: just see here!
schon: already
magerer: thinner
wieder: again

o weh und ach!: oh, pain and sorrow!
dünn und schwach: thin and weak
kam herein: came in

endlich: finally
ein Fädchen: a little thread
wog: weighed
ein halbes Lot: equivalent to 7.5 grams
tot: dead

Die Geschichte vom Suppen-Kaspar

Der Kaspar, der war kerngesund,
Ein dicker Bub und kugelrund.
Er hatte Backen rot und frisch;
Die Suppe aß er hübsch bei Tisch.
Doch einmal fing er an zu schrein:
„Ich esse keine Suppe! Nein!
Ich esse meine Suppe nicht!
Nein, meine Suppe eß ich nicht!"

Am nächsten Tag – ja sieh nur her!
Da war er schon viel magerer.
Da fing er wieder an zu schrein:
„Ich esse keine Suppe! Nein!
Ich esse meine Suppe nicht!
Nein, meine Suppe eß ich nicht!"

Am dritten Tag, o weh und ach!
Wie ist der Kaspar dünn und schwach!
Doch als die Suppe kam herein,
Gleich fing er wieder an zu schrein:
„Ich esse keine Suppe! Nein!
Ich esse meine Suppe nicht!
Nein, meine Suppe eß ich nicht!"

Am vierten Tage endlich gar
Der Kaspar wie ein Fädchen war.
Er wog vielleicht ein halbes Lot –
Und war am fünften Tage tot.

Aktivität 22. Was essen Sie nicht?

Ich esse's nicht! In „Die Geschichte vom Suppen-Kaspar", Kaspar's stubborn refusal to eat soup is highlighted in the story's refrain: „Ich esse keine Suppe! Nein!/Ich esse meine Suppe nicht!/Nein, meine Suppe eß' ich nicht!" Is there something you would refuse to eat if it were served to you? Personalize the refrain by adding your own despised food item. (Don't forget to use the *Akkusativ* case!)

„Ich esse kein _____ _____ ! Nein!

Ich esse mein _____ _____ nicht!

Nein, mein _____ _____ eß' ich nicht!"

Aktivität 23. Essgewohnheiten

What kinds of eating habits do your classmates have? Ask your classmates questions about what they like to eat, what not, who is a vegetarian, and so forth. Before asking your classmates, generate the specific questions you will need. If you find someone who matches the description, have them sign their name on the line. Make sure to ask and answer in German!

Du:	Isst du gern Pizza?
Student:	Nein, ich mag keine Pizza.
Du:	Ach, unterschreib hier, bitte!

Finden Sie jemanden, der ...

1. Pizza nicht gern ißt.

2. Vegetarier/Vegetarierin ist.

3. nie Frühstück ißt.

4. keine Milch trinken kann.

5. zu viel Schokolade ißt.

6. mehr als fünf Tassen Kaffee am Tag trinkt.

7. gerne Fisch ißt.

8. schon Döner probiert hat.

9. sehr gut kocht.

10. jede Woche zum Essen ausgeht.

Aktivität 24. Ein kurzer Bericht

On a separate sheet of paper, describe your own eating habits based on the above survey (i.e., *Ich esse Pizza nicht gern. Ich bin Vegetarier/Vegetarierin*). IMPORTANT: Do not put your name down! Your instructor will collect the reports and read them; the whole class will try to guess whose eating habits are being described!

Aktivität 25. Kaffee trinken

Some type of caffeine is essential for many people, especially students! In the morning, students often rely on caffeine to wake up for their classes; in the afternoon and evenings, they need it to stay awake to get all their work done.

A. Brauchen sie Kaffee, um zu funktionieren?

Watch each speaker's video clip, „Brauchen Sie Kaffee?" and decide whether the following statements are true or false. Then correct the false statements to make them true.

1. **Adan:** Fast gar nicht. Vielleicht [trinke ich] eine Cola oder etwas, aber nichts anderes.　　T　F

(QR 3.11 p.152)

2. **Eva:** Ich trinke ganz gern Kaffee. Es ist lebensnotwendig (*vital*).　　T　F

(QR 3.13 p.152)

3. **Harald:** Ich trinke zwei große Tassen Espresso jeden Morgen.　　T　F

(QR 3.14 p.152)

B. Trinken Sie Kaffee, um zu funktionieren?

Do you drink coffee to remain a functioning individual? What about your partner? Discuss the following questions with him/her:

Trinken Sie Kaffee?

Ja

Warum trinkst du keinen Kaffee?
Trinkst du Tee?
Was für Tee trinkst du?
Trinkst du Cola, Redbull oder etwas Ähnliches?
Wie kannst du ohne Kaffee wach bleiben?

Nein

Welchen Kaffee trinkst du?
Was ist dein Lieblingskaffee?
Wie viel Kaffee trinkst du am Tag?
Wann trinkst du Kaffee?
Wo kaufst du Kaffee?
Wie viel Geld gibst du für Kaffee aus?

KULTURTIPP

Tipping – *Trinkgeld* – in Germany is done differently than in the US.

Instead of giving 15-20% of the total as a tip, you round up.

For example, if your Eis was 2 Euro 70, you can give the waiter 3 Euros (i.e., a 30-cent tip). Or you can give him a 5-Euro Schein (bill) and say „(Auf) drei, bitte!" (i.e., give me 2 Euros back) or only take 2 Euros from the tray.

The larger the bill, the more you round up (e.g., for a 76 Euro bill, you would leave "only" about 4 Euros.

However, if you just buy ice cream or something at an Imbiss you don't have to leave a tip, although it will be appreciated if you do.

Aktivität 26. Sprache im Kontext: Eis!

A very popular dessert, especially in the summer heat, is *Eis* (ice cream), which comes in lots of creamy flavors and can be served in a *Waffel* (cone) or a *Becher* (cup). It can be served by itself or with amazing toppings and decorations. At roughly .70 – 1.50 Euro per *Kugel* (scoop; lit: *ball*), it is a pricey treat, but the taste and the experience are worth every cent! Keep in mind that the German ice cream is like gelato and not like American ice cream.

(QR 3.24 p.152)

A. Die Eisdiele

Many *Eisdielen* in Germany are family businesses run by German-Italian families. In the following you will meet Vincenzo, a German-Italian (*surprise*) who runs a *Eisdiele* in Brühl, a town close to Cologne. The following paragraph is taken from http://www.inbruehl.com/ about his ice cream parlor. Then complete the exercises below and discuss in pairs or/and with your teacher, what you understand and what you do not understand.

Eiscafe il Gelato da Vincenzo – Uhlstraße 59

Wer die Eiskarte des Ehepaars Petra und Vincenzo Caico liest, erfährt sehr schnell die Philosophie des Eiscafe il Gelato da Vincenzo. Hier steht die Herstellung eines qualitativ höchstwertigen Lebensmittels im Mittelpunkt, das wertvolle Vitamine und Proteine enthält. Die Verwendung von Frischmilch, natürlicher Süße, frischem Obst und pflanzlicher Fette garantiert neben der besonderen Cremigkeit des Speiseeis einen hervorragenden Geschmack und auch eine sehr gute Bekömmlichkeit. Auf Farbstoffe, Eier, Sahne und Butter wird ganz bewusst verzichtet. Eine genau festgelegte Rezeptur und die zügige Verarbeitung sorgen für einen gleichbleibend hohen Qualitätsstandard des Eis', den der Eisgenießer sofort schmeckt. Auch die Wahl der Kaffeebohnen-Sorten entspricht diesem Anspruchsdenken. Ihre privaten Einstellung, bewusst und konsequent gesund zu leben, führte zum Entschluss, ihr Café zum Nichtraucher-Café zu erklären. Ihr Grundsatz "Eis, ein edler Genuss, statt Masse bei uns Klasse!" erfreut sich in Brühl großer Beliebtheit.

Öffnungszeiten: täglich 9 - 22 Uhr, Montag Ruhetag   Telefon: 02232 - 94 37 38

List 2 words you know: List 2 words you look up: List 2 words your partner knows:

_____   _____   _____

_____   _____   _____

What makes *das Esicafe il Gelato da Vincenzo* special?

_____

_____

_____

B. Ice Cream Flavors

Watch the video „Sprache im Kontext: Eis". What ice cream flavors are mentioned in the clip?

Chili-Schokolade	Pfefferminz	Vanille	**Rotwein**
Schokolade	**Kiwi**	**Erdbeer**	Zitrone
Kirsch	**Kaffee**	Stracciatella	Kokos
Ananas	Pfirsich	Cappuccino	Joghurt
Haselnuss	**Zimt**	Banane	**Walnuss**
Mandel	**Himbeer**	Grapefruit	Melone

C. Bei *Da Vincenzo*

Watch the video „Sprache im Kontext: Eis" to put the following statements in the correct order.

Was macht das?	
Milchspeiseeis ist sehr lecker.	
Aber nur eine Kugel.	
Danke auch.	
Apfelmus-Zitrone hört sich gut an.	
Siebzig Cent.	
Was haben Sie denn? Was würden Sie denn empfehlen?	
Danke schoen.	
Wir haben leckeres Fruchteis, wenn es zu warm ist!?	
Tschüss.	
Ich hätte gerne ein Eis.	
Was darf es denn sein?	

D. Milch oder Frucht?

What is the difference between *Milcheis* and *Fruchteis*? List three *Milcheis* and two *Fruchteis* flavors (use the vocabulary you have learned in this chapter!) that are not mentioned in the clip.

Milcheis ist _____ .

Fruchteis ist _____ .

Milcheis	Fruchteis

E. Jetzt sind Sie dran!

With a partner, act out an ice-cream buying event. First, the sales person typically asks what the customer wants, and the customer chooses one ore more flavors (more than 4 *Kugeln* and you should get a *Becher* or lots of *Servietten*!). Then the sales person lets you know how much to pay. After you pay, he/she gives you back your change. Fill in the dialog, and practice asking/answering these questions. FYI: These are phrases our students learned *very quickly* in Germany! ☺

VerkäuferIn:	Was darf`s sein?
Sie:	Ich möchte/Ich hätte gerne _____ (eine Kugel, zwei Kugeln ...)
VerkäuferIn:	In einer Waffel oder im Becher?
Sie:	_____ , bitte.
VerkäuferIn:	Bitte schön. _____ Euro _____ .
Sie:	_____

Image source: www.villa-vanilla.de

Aktivität 27. Zu Abend essen

It's time to take a little break from your work and get a bite to eat. In German there are two words that are used to talk about an evening meal: *das Abendbrot* and *das Abendessen*. In groups of three, brainstorm some ideas about why there are two words and what the difference between them might be. (Do not look on the next page, unless you want to spoil the fun!)

das Abendbrot	**das Abendessen**

Aktivität 28. Das Abendbrot – Die wichtigste Familienmahlzeit Deutschlands

The following article appeared in the *Berliner Zeitung* on March 26, 2008.

A. Vor dem Lesen

1. Look at the title („Allein am Frühstückstisch") and subheading („Umfrage zu Essverhalten") of the passage below. Based on these clues, what do you think the focus of the passage is?

_____

_____

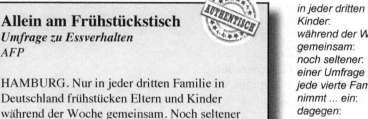

Allein am Frühstückstisch
Umfrage zu Essverhalten
AFP

HAMBURG. Nur in jeder dritten Familie in Deutschland frühstücken Eltern und Kinder während der Woche gemeinsam. Noch seltener ist ein gemeinsames Mittagessen. Einer Umfrage nach nimmt nur jede vierte Familie das Mittagessen ein. Zum Abendbrot sitzen dagegen meist Eltern und Kinder zusammen am Tisch - mit 73 Prozent in der Woche und sogar 81 Prozent am Wochenende. Es ist "die wichtigste Familienmahlzeit der Deutschen" laut dem Bericht. Mehr als die Hälfte (53 Prozent) der Eltern gab an, mindestens einmal pro Woche mit ihren Kindern zu kochen. Am häufigsten stehen junge Familien gemeinsam am Herd.
Drei Viertel der Eltern legen Wert darauf, das Essen gemeinsam zu beginnen und zu beenden. Aufessen, was auf den Teller kommt, müssen die Kinder in jeder sechsten Familie. (AFP)

in jeder dritten Familie:	in every third family
Kinder:	children
während der Woche:	during the week
gemeinsam:	together
noch seltener:	even more seldom
einer Umfrage nach:	according to a survey
jede vierte Familie:	every fourth family
nimmt ... ein:	to take in (i.e., food)
dagegen:	in contrast
gab ... an:	indicated
mindestens:	at least
am häufigsten:	most frequently
drei Viertel:	three-fourths
Wert darauf legen:	to make a point of doing something
aufessen:	to eat up
müssen:	to have to

B. Fragen zur Diskussion

From what you just learned about family *Essverhalten* (*eating practices*) in Germany, and based on your own experience, would you say that they are the same in the US? In your family? For example, is dinner the most important meal for your family? Lunch? Breakfast? Why/why not? Before discussing take a few notes, that are helpful to bring your points across.

vs.

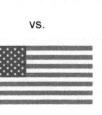

Das Essverhalten in Deutschland	Das Essverhalten in den USA

Aktivität 29. Einkaufen gehen

Unless you go to a restaurant, you need to buy groceries before you can eat. Just as you need to purchase other items for your everyday life.

Where do you need to go and what will you buy?

Geschäfte/Läden		Ich gehe ...
die Apotheke	→	zur Apotheke.
die Bäckerei	→	zur Bäckerei.
die Bank	→	zur Bank.
die Buchhandlung		zur Buchhandlung.
die Drogerie	→	zur Drogerie.
die Post	→	zur Post.
der Friseur	→	zum Friseur.
der Gemüseladen	→	zum Gemüseladen.
der Papierladen	→	zum Papierladen.
der Supermarkt	→	zum Supermarkt.
das Schuhgeschäft	→	zum Schuhgeschäft.

To talk about running errands, you can use any of the following phrases:

- etwas besorgen *(to go get something)* Ich gehe zur Post und **besorge** Briefmarken.
- etwas einkaufen *(to go get something)* Ich gehe zum Supermarkt und **kaufe** Butter ein.
- etwas holen *(to go get something)* Ich gehe zum Bäcker und **hole** Brot.

For each location in the left column below, write the letter of the description, that most closely fits it.

die Apotheke	_____	a. Wo man frisches Obst und Gemüse kauft.
die Bäckerei	_____	b. Wo man einen Haarschnitt bekommt.
die Bank	_____	c. Wo man Briefmarken kauft.
die Buchhandlung	_____	d. Wo man Papier und Schreibwaren kauft.
die Post	_____	e. Wo man Sandalen, Stiefel und Tennisschuhe kauft.
die Drogerie	_____	f. Wo man alles kauft, was man isst.
der Friseur	_____	g. Wo man Geld holt.
der Gemüseladen	_____	h. Wo man Bücher kauft.
das Lebensmittelgeschäft	_____	i. Wo man verschreibungspflichtige Arzneimittel *(prescription drugs)* kauft.
der Schreibwarenladen	_____	j. Wo man frisches Brot und Gebäck kauft.
das Schuhgeschäft	_____	k. Wo man allerlei Waren *(all kinds of goods)* kauft, zum Beispiel Kosmetik, Zahnpasta und Schulsachen.

Aktivität 30. Sprache im Kontext: Sophia im Supermarkt

Watch the video clip „Sophia im Supermarkt".

(QR 3.19
p.152)

A. Write down what you notice in the clip.

What is Sophia talking about? What items does she mention?

B. Watch the clip again.

Sophia discusses what she needs at the *Supermarkt* every week. Fill in the items she mentions that are missing from her *wöchentlichen Einkaufszettel* (*weekly grocery list*) below.

EINKAUFSZETTEL
- ❑ Hackfleisch für Frühlngsrollen (*spring rolls*)
- ❑ _____
- ❑ _____
- ❑ _____
- ❑ Weizenmehl für Crepes

Welche Lebensmittel kann man im Supermarkt kaufen? Feel free to add your favorties, if they are not on the list.

der Aufschnitt, -	das Gemüse, -	das Obst, -
das Brot, Brote	das Gewürz, Gewürze	der Reis, -
die Butter, -	der Joghurt, Joghurts	der Saft, Säfte
die Cola, Colas	der Kaffee, Kaffees	die Suppe, Suppen
das Ei, Eier	die Kartoffel, Kartoffeln	die Schokolade, Schokoladen
das Eis, -	die Kartoffelchips	die Süßigkeit, Süßigkeiten
der Fisch, Fische	der Käse, -	der Tee, Tees
das Fleisch, -	der Keks, Kekse	die Tiefkühl-Pizza, Tiefkühl-Pizzas
- das Hackfleisch	das Mehl, -	die Tomatensoße, Tomatensoßen
- das Kotelett, -s	die Milch, -	die Wurst, Würste
- das Rindfleisch	das Müsli, die Müslis	der Zucker, -
- das Schweinefleisch	die Nudeln	

Aktivität 31. Sprache im Kontext: Obst und Gemüse

Watch the two videos of a Würzburg green grocer and her prized *Obst (fruits)* and *Gemüse (vegetables)*. Write down what each item listed below costs and (if she mentions it) the origin. Use the words in the word bank to help you! Can you figure out from the videos which fruit and/or vegetable is which?

teilweise • kilogrammweise

schälchenweise • pro Stück • Klima

aus dem Ausland • einheimisch

unbehandelt • Saison

(QR 3.31 p.152)
(QR 3.32 p.152)

Das Obst

	Obstart	Preis	Woher kommt das Obst?
1.	Äpfel		Aus …
2.	Birnen		
3.	Ananas		
4.	Bananen		
5.	Trauben		
6.	Wassermelonen		
7.	Zitronen		
8.	Pfirsiche		
9.	Kirschen		
10.	Erdbeeren		

Das Gemüse

	Gemüseart	Preis	Woher kommt das Gemüse?
1.	Gurken		
2.	Champignons		
3.	Karotten		
4.	Paprika		
5.	Bohnen		
6.	Blumenkohl		
7.	Salat		
8.	Tomaten		

Aktivität 32. Obst und Gemüse essen

Now that you know the names of the different *Obst und Gemüse*, how many of these do you actually eat? Which ones do you not like? Ask a partner and jot down his/her response. Be prepared to share your partner's answers with the class!

1. Was für Obst isst du?

2. Was für Obst isst du nicht (gern)?

3. Was für Gemüse isst du?

4. Was für Gemüse isst du nicht (gern)?

Aktivität 33. Sprache im Kontext: Austin kauft ein

Watch the Video entitled „Austin beim Einkaufen" and see what you can understand after each viewing of the clip.

A. During the first viewing, write down what you see.
What do you notice about in the video? Who is in it?
Where does it take place? What do you think is it about?

B. Watch the clip again and write down all the groceries you hear in the clip.

(QR 3.28 p.152)

C. Watch the clip a third time and answer the questions below.

1. Was brauchen Austin und Andrew nicht?

2. Was für *Cereals* kaufen Sie?

D. Watch the clip one more time and write down all the adjectives you hear in the video (the adjectives that are used to describe the products).

Aktivität 34. Milka-Schokolade – Werbung und Recherche im Internet

In a previous *Sprache im Kontext* video you saw Andrew and Austin expressing their love of *Milka-Schokolade*, a popular brand of chocolate in the German-speaking countries. In the following you will do a *Recherche* (*research*) on the brand and its *Werbung* (*advertisement*). To get you started, the name *Milka* is an acronym of *Milch* and *Kakao*, chocolate's two primary ingredients.

A. Vor der Inernetrecherche – Fragen zur Diskussion

- Have you ever tried German or Swiss chocolate (for example, *Kinderschokolade, Lindt, Ritter Sport,* etc.)?
- Did it taste different from American chocolate?
- Have you ever tried *Milka-Schokolade* before? If so, how did it taste?

> Nützliche Wörter:
>
> die Luft • die Alpenmilch • nah • die Marke
> das Produkt • der Himmel • die Versuchung
> zart • lila • die Kuh

B. Die Internetrecherche

Go to www.milka.de. What can you do on the *Milka* website? What are the categories on the top of the page? Which category would you like to explore more? What do you learn about *Milka*?

Notizen:

C. Die Werbung

On the *Milka* website and click *Marke*, and then *TV-Spots*. Chose a clip or alternatively, search for „Milka TV Werbung 1996" on youtube. We transcribed the dialogue for this commercial.

das Mädchen:	Omi, wieso ist die Milka so zart?
die Omi:	Viele glauben, es liegt am klaren Wasser und der frischen Luft, oder man sagt, es ist wegen der cremigen Alpenmilch. Aber wenn du mich fragst, Herzel, liegt's daran, weil es hier oben, wo die Milch herkommt, ganz nah am Himmel ist.

D. Nach dem Schauen/Lesen – Fragen zur Diskussion

1. How would you describe each person, the setting and the *Milka* itself? Take notes in the table:

The girl/ character 1	The grandmother/ character 2	The setting	*Milka*-Schokolade

2. How does the commercial try to "lure" you in? Is it successful? Does the commercial make you want to eat *Milka-Schokolade*? Why or why not?

E. Jetzt sind Sie dran!

How would you market *Milka-Schokolade*? In groups of three, create your own commercial, app or website content for the product. Before you begin, you might want to consider the following questions:

- Will there be "characters"? If so, who will they be? If not, why not?
- Where and when will the dialogue and/or action take place?
- Are you going for a comedic effect, a dramatic effect, or something else entirely?
- How will you place the purple *Milkakuh*, a mandatory element of all *Milka* commercials?

Marions Kochbuch

Aktivität 35. Mein Lieblingsrezept
Go online to the following webpage: http://www.marions-kochbuch.de/

A. Search for a recipe that you like to try.
You can search by name or by category on the left side of the screen (e.g. *Suppen, Gemüse, Eierspeisen, Fleisch, Salate*, etc.). After you found your dish write down the name of the dish and all the *Zutaten* (*ingredients*) you would need to get for it (don't forget the quantities). Make sure you know what those ingredients are.

Beispiel:

Das will ich kochen:
        Schweinebraten mit Blaukraut
        Zutaten: 900 g Schweinebraten
            600 g Rotkohl ...

Das will ich kochen: _____

B. Go to http://www.aldi-sued.de, www.lidl.de or www.kaisers.de
All three links will bring you to popular discount grocery stores. Search one of the websites for their grocery products (*das Sortiment*) and create an *Einkaufszettel* (*grocery shopping list*). Since you still need practice with the *Euro* and *Zahlen*, also write down how much each ingredient/item would cost.

MEIN EINKAUFSZETTEL

_____

_____

_____

_____

_____

_____

_____

_____

_____

Aktivität 36. Sprache im Kontext: In der Drogerie

In addition to food items, you also need a variety of personal hygiene products. Listen as Florian explains what kinds of things one can buy at a *Drogerie*. All the items he mentions are in the left column below.

A. Can you match these German terms with their English equivalents in the right column?

Shampoo	vitamins
Duschgel	makeup
Seife	toilet paper
Vitamintabletten	toothbrushes
Schminke	tissues
Cremesorten	soap
Nagellack	toothpaste
Kondome	shampoo
Zahnbürste	condoms
Zahnpasta	types of creams
Taschentücher	shower gel
Klopapier	nail polish

(QR 3.26 p.152)

Watch the video a second time. Which additional items do you see in the store that Florian does not specifically mention?

_____

_____

B. Im Schreibwarengeschäft

As a university student, you will need notebooks, paper, pens and other school items. While watching Florian's clip about the *Papierladen*, write down the items he mentions. As a guide, the first letters of the words he mentions are provided to you. (Note: one complicated word is provided to you in its entirety ☺). This exercise will help refine your sound-symbol association (i.e., how something sounds and the way it is written). Don't consult your dictionary until you've given it the ol' college try!

B _ _ _ ◯ _ _ _ _ _   = pencil

K _ _ _ _ ◯◯ _ _ _ _ _   = ball-point pens

B◯ _ _ _ _ _ _ _   = colored pencil

K (L) A R S I C H (T) S H (Ü) L L E N   = clear plastic sheet protectors

(T) _ _ _ _ _ _   = stapler

K _ _ _ ◯ _   = glue

Das Lösungswort. If you spelled the above words correctly, you should be able to figure out the name of the item to the right. Take the letters you wrote in the ovals above and enter them (in the order in which they appeared) in the spaces below.

_ _ _ _ _ _ _ _ _ _

Aktivität 37. Der erste Schultag

You may be wondering just what exactly the *Lösungswort* and the image of the item on the previous page is. In Germany, elementary school children receive one of these on the first day of school (see the image below, the girl is holding a *Schultüte*). They are filled with different kinds of *Süßigkeiten* and *Schulsachen* for the children to enjoy. The tradition dates back to the early 19th century! Now, flash forward to today; your German friend is starting his/her first day at your university, and you want to welcome him/her with a university-level version of the classic *Schultüte – eine Unitüte!* What do you put in your German friend's *Unitüte*? Include at least 6-8 items.

Für die Unitüte kaufe ich ... (+ Akk.)

_____

_____

_____

_____

_____

_____

Now draw a picture of this *Unitüte* with all the goodies inside. Use the space below, and label the items in the *Tüte* (using the nominative case)!

Studi-Tipp: You may use your *Unitüte* as a Vocabbox. Write all relevant vocab on slips of paper (English on the front, German on the back) and put them in your *Unitüte*. Each day test yourself. Whenever you know a card, you can leave it out - once your *Unitüte* is empty restock it with new words. But dont forget to reward yourself with some *Milka, Kinderschokolade* or *Gummibärchen.*

Aktivität 38. Zur Uni fahren (zurück zum Campus)

After having done all your shopping, you need to return to your dorm room at the end of the day. How can you get to your shopping and then home? Do you ride your bike or take the bus?

A. Match the names of the different modes of transportation on the left with the appropriate pictures on the right.

das Auto

der Bus

das Einrad

das Skateboard/das Rollbrett (Switzerland)

das Fahrrad

das Motorrad

die Inlineskates (pl.)

To say that you travel via one of these modes of transportation, use the verb *fahren* :

Die Verkehrsmittel		Ich fahre ...
das Auto	→	mit dem Auto.
der Bus	→	mit dem Bus.
das Einrad	→	mit dem Einrad.
das Fahrrad	→	mit dem Fahrrad.
das Motorrad	→	mit dem Motorrad.
die Inlineskates	→	mit den Inlineskates.
das Skateboard	→	mit dem Skateboard.

If you simply walk to school, you can either use the verbs *gehen* or *laufen*:

Ich gehe zu Fuß.　　　(OR)　　　　　Ich laufe.

Grimm Gramma

At home please read the following grammar point on the *Grimm Grammar* website.

Verbs: fahren
ich fahre
du fährst
er/sie/es fährt

wir fahren
ihr fahrt
sie/Sie fahren

Verbs: laufen
ich laufe
du läufst
er/sie/es läuft

wir laufen
ihr lauft
sie/Sie laufen

Verbs: nehmen
ich nehme
du nimmst
er/sie/es nimmt

wir nehmen
ihr nehmt
sie/Sie nehmen

B. Wie wir an die Uni gehen

Which modes of transportation do you and your classmates use? A student or the teacher should ask the class how many students travel by each mode of transportation and note the number of responses on the board. Follow along by marking the numbers in the column on the right. When the poll is done, discuss as a class why these particular modes of transportation are the most common.

Wer fährt mit dem Auto zur Uni?	
Wer fährt mit dem Bus zur Uni?	
Wer fährt mit dem Einrad zur Uni?	
Wer fährt mit dem Fahrrad zur Uni?	
Wer fährt mit dem Motorrad zur Uni?	
Wer fährt mit den Rollschuhen zur Uni?	
Wer fährt mit dem Skateboard zur Uni?	
Wer geht zu Fuß/läuft zur Uni?	

Nota Bene: Another verb you can use to talk about your means of transportation is the verb *nehmen* (*to take*). Just as you can say in English "I take the bus," in German you say „Ich nehme den Bus".

Aktivität 39. Neue Studenten in Austin!

A. Brainstorming

You've worked with a lot of information in this chapter which will help you during your study abroad in Würzburg. What if the international studies office approached you to generate material to help German-speaking students in your city? Below is a table with a number of topics which were featured in the chapter. Write down information you think should be included for new students.

As you write, consider that these students will have certain expectations about where and how to do what and those expectations might or might not coincide with what is available here. For example, if you are used to going to a *Schreibwarenladen* for pens and paper, what are you going to do if you live on or near campus? The following questions might help you get started.

- Wo frühstückt man?
- Wie sieht ein "typisches" Studentenfrühstück aus?
- Gibt es eine Bäckerei in der Nähe vom Campus? Wo findet man frische Backwaren?
- Wenn man Kulis oder mehr Schreib- oder Druckpapier braucht, wo kauft man das alles?
- Wo kauft man Lebensmittel ein? Machen Studenten das überhaupt (*at all*) oder isst man immer in der Mensa oder in einem Restaurant?
- Wie kommt man meist zur Uni?

Frühstück Mittagessen Abendessen/Abendbrot	
Beschäftigungen und Einkaufen	
Tagesablauf	

B. A Handout

Now, work in a group and design an informational pamphlet to be included with other welcome material for these new students. You may make it of general focus or you can concentrate on one specific topic. Pool your resources and think about how best to help transition into life in your town!

Aussprache
Beachtenswerte deutsche Konsonanten

There are quite a few noteworthy German consonants which pride themselves on tripping up English speaking guests in their language:

single consonants: **ß, s, z, v, w, j**

consonant clusters: **kn, pn, ps**

We will try to elucidate these sounds on the next few pages, or at least provide some articulatory fun for you – and possibly your friends who are listening to you learn German.

1. DAS ESZETT/SCHARFES S

The German **ß** looks pretty funny to most learners, who often mis-read it as a capital 'B'. It is not a capital 'B'! It's what is called an **Eszett**, or **scharfes S** (sharp s), and it's pronounced a lot like the English 's' in words like sweet, curious or strange.

ß	die Straßenbahn, zu Fuß, die Süßigkeit, ißt*	streetcar, on foot, sweets, eats

*This word is now written as *isst* instead of *ißt* because of the 1996 spelling reform (http://www. coerll.utexas.edu/gg/gr/mis_05.html). But you will see it spelled with an ß in many written texts, so you need to be familiar with both forms.

Notice that none of the examples above start with ß. That's because ß is a letter that exists only in the lower case! The *Eszett* has a long and rather complicated history dating back to the Middle Ages. It first appears in Gothic writing towards the end of the 13th century. While some linguists believe the letter was initially a ligature of ʃ and z, others believe it was a ligature of ʃ and s. The name *Eszett* reflects the former combination. Either way, the letters morphed over time into a new and unique German letter.

It is not at all surprising that the independent-spirited Swiss broke tradition a while ago already and abolished the use of the *Eszett* in the 1930s when *Kantone* decided not to teach it anymore, and the postal service stopped using it in place names. Thus, in Switzerland you write *ss* instead of ß.

And here is how you can form the **ß** on your computer:

1. You can insert the *Eszett* by clicking on the Menu bar and under INSERT, select SYMBOL.
2. Second, you can create a short-cut (also under the INSERT, SYMBOL short-cut key)
3. Third, you can use key combination on your keyboard as listed below

PCs	Macs
CTRL+SHIFT+7 then s	Option + s

2. DAS S

The letter **s** can be pronounced as an /s/ or a /z/ or like 'sh' in English (called allophones) depending on the other sounds in the word, where it is in the word or even depending on where the speaker is from (see chapters 7-10 for regional variation). *S* is pronounced as 'sh' after word initial 'st' and 'sp' combinations (or when the combination is at the beginning of a compound in a compound word).
It is also pronounced as 'sh' in the trigraph 'sch' as in *die Schule* (not like 'sk' in English *school, schooner*, etc.!)

s	pronounced as English	z	/z/	rasieren, die Kurse, der Saft, die Suppe
s	pronounced as English	s	/s/	das Essen, das Obst, der Toast, etwas
s	pronounced as English	sh	/ʃ/	der Speck, der Student, der Bleistift, die Vorspeise
s	pronounced as English	sh	/ʃ/	schlafen, die Schokolade, die Schlagsahne, schwarz

3. DAS Z

The letter **z** in German is pronounced like the 'ts' combination in the "English" tse-tse fly. It is easy to forget what the German letter *z* represents and pronounce it like the English *z* (as in zebra), but try to avoid doing so. This is one sound that will definitely leave you – ahem – sounding foreign!

zu Abend essen	to have dinner
anziehen	to put on (clothes)
die Mahlzeit	meal
die Zähne	teeth
Notizen machen	take notes
die Zitrone	lemon

the pronunciation is the same for the 'tz' letter combination (digraph)

putzen	to clean
das Schnitzel	a pork or veal cutlet
sitzen	to sit

4. V AND W

As native speakers of English, the letters **v** and **w** are particularly exciting in German. This is because the German *w* is pronounced like the English 'v' and the German *v* is pronounced like the English 'f' (in most cases, although, of course, there are exceptions to this rule...)

v = /f/	vier, verschlafen, die Vorlesung, verbringen	four, oversleep, lecture, to spend (time)
w= /v/	etwas, die Wurst, die Wassermelone, aufwachen	something, sausage, watermelon, to wake up

v vs. w

Here are some "minimal" pairs (words where there is only one difference in sound) that can help you train your ears and eyes:

Vieh (cattle)	-	wie (how)
volle (full)	-	Wolle (wool) as in Wolljacke (wool jacket)
Veilchen (violet)	-	Weilchen (a little time)
Vetter (cousin)	-	Wetter (weather)

Exceptions:

1) some words starting with V are pronounced with an initial /v/ and not /f/:

Vase (vase)   Vibration (vibration)   Vokal (vowel)

2) Words starting with *vu* are generally pronounced as /v/ + /u/ and not /f/ + /u/ :

Vulkan (volcano)   vulgär (vulgar)

Although *v* and *f* look different, they are phonetically the same. As a matter of fact, in German they are homophones (exceptions mentioned above: *Vase, Vogel,* etc.) because they sound the same. Compare the initial sounds in the following sets of words:

Vogel (bird)	are pronounced the same as	**F**lugzeug (plane)
Vater (father)		**F**rühling (spring)

5. DAS J

This letter represents a semi-vowel in German, and is pronounced like the 'y' in the English "young," "yesterday" or "yikes." German speakers will look at you rather funny if you pronounce it like you would the 'j' in the English "jester" or "jovial." And you do not want people to look at you any funnier than absolutely necessary. So, practice with the following words:

der Joghurt	yogurt
die Johannisbeeren	currants
jung	young
der Jägermeister	you don't need any explanation, do you???
jodeln	to yodel

6. DIE KN KOMBINATION

In English, the 'k' has become silent, resulting in 'knobby knee' being pronounced like 'nobby nee'. German has, in contrast, merrily retained the distinct sounds of both k and n.

die Kneipe	bar, pub
der Knoblauch	garlic
knubbelig	knobby
das Knie	knee

7. PS and PN

Now this is fun! These combinations typically occur at the beginning of words, and only in the rarest cases, in borrowed words like "Psychologe" or "Pneumonie" (psychologist and pneumonia). You have to tackle each letter separately because in German the 'p' is very decidedly pronounced:

der P – s – ychologe	die P – n – eumonie
die P – s – yche	p – n – eumatisch
das P – s – eudonym	

Here are some tongue-twisters to help you practice and unravel the mysteries of these sounds!

Acht alte Ameisen aßen am Abend Ananas.
Eight old ants ate pineapple in the evening.

Esel essen Nesseln nicht, Nesseln essen Esel nicht.
Donkeys don't eat nettles, nettles don't eat donkeys.

Fischers Fritz isst frische Fische, frische Fische isst Fischers Fritz.

Sechs sächsische Säufer zahlen zehn tschechische Zechen.
Six Saxon drinkers pay ten Czech checks (bills).

Selten ess ich Essig. Ess ich Essig, ess ich Essig nur im Salat.
Seldom do I eat vinegar. If I eat vinegar, I eat vinegar only in salad.

Wer nichts weiß und weiß, dass er nichts weiß, weiß mehr als der, der nichts weiß und nicht weiß, dass er nichts weiß.
He who knows nothing & knows that he knows nothing, knows more than he who knows nothing & doesn't know that he knows nothing.

Zehn Ziegen zogen zehn Zentner Zucker zum Zoo, zum Zoo zogen zehn Ziegen zehn Zentner Zucker.
Ten goats pulled ten centners of sugar to the zoo, to the zoo pulled ten goats ten centners of sugar.
(A 'hundredweight," der Zentner, equals 50 kg, 100 Pfund or 110 US pounds)

Am zehnten zehnten um zehn Uhr zehn zogen zehn zahme Ziegen zehn Zentner Zucker zum Zoo.
On Oct. 10 at 10:10 then tame goats pulled ten centners of sugar to the zoo.

Zwanzig Zwerge zeigen Handstand, zehn im Wandschrank, zehn am Sandstrand.
Twenty dwarfs are doing handstands, ten in the closet, ten on the sandy beach.

Vier Vampire trafen sich bei Vollmond vor einem Vulkan.
Four vampires met in front of a volcano during full moon.

Weiß Werner, wie wenig die Violetten in der Valentinstagsvase wiegen?
Does Werner know, how little the violets in the Valentine's day vase weigh?

WebQuests

This time there are two "Webquests" on the website. Simply choose between:

1. Das schwarze Brett
2. Lebensmittel einkaufen

Meinungsumfragen

Go to the *Deutsch im Blick* website to access the „Meinungsumfragen" on the subject of *der Alltag* und *das Studentenleben*.

Wortschatz

(QR 3.1 p.152)

Der Tagesablauf	Daily routine
zu Abend essen	to eat dinner
das Abendbrot	light evening meal, e.g., cold cuts
das Abendessen	dinner
sich anziehen	to get dressed
sich ausziehen	to get undressed
aufwachen	to wake up
aufstehen	to get up
Besorgungen machen	to run errands, to do some shopping
ins Bett gehen	to go to bed
(sich) duschen	to shower
einschlafen	to fall asleep
sich entspannen	to relax
das Essen	meal
Das Essen ist fertig.	Lunch/Dinner is ready.
frühstücken	to eat breakfast
sich die Haare bürsten	to brush one's hair
sich die Haare kämmen	to comb one's hair
in die Kurse gehen	to go to one's classes
zu Mittag essen	to eat lunch
das Mittagessen	lunch
sich rasieren	to shave
schlafen	to sleep
ausschlafen/lange schlafen/verschlafen	to sleep in/sleep long/oversleep
zur Uni gehen	to go to (travel to) the university
sich die Zähne putzen	to brush one's teeth

Das Frühstück	Breakfast
der Aufstrich (Aufstriche)	spread
der Aufschnitt (Aufschnitte)	cold cuts
die Backwaren (primarily used in plural)	baked goods
das Brot (Brote)	bread
das Brötchen/die Semmel (Brötchen/Semmeln)	bread rolls
die Butter (no plural)	butter
das Ei (Eier)	egg
essen	to eat
das Getränk (Getränke)	beverage
der Honig (no plural)	honey
der Joghurt (Joghurts)	yogurt
der Kaffee (Kaffees)	coffee
der Kakao (no plural)	hot chocolate
der Käse (Käse)	cheese
die Margarine (Margarinen)	margarine
die Milch (no plural)	milk
das Mü(e)sli (Mü(e)sli)	cereal
die/das Nutella (no plural)	Nutella (gender depends on region!)
das Obst (no plural)	fruit
der Quark (no plural)	cheese curd
der Saft (Säfte)	juice
der Speck	bacon
der Tee (Tees)	tea
der Toast (Toasts)	toast
trinken	to drink

Zur Uni fahren	**To go to (travel to) the university**
ankommen	to arrive
das Auto (Autos)	car
mit dem Auto fahren	to travel by car
der Bus (Busse)	bus
mit dem Bus fahren	to travel by bus
das Einrad (Einräder)	unicycle
mit dem Einrad fahren	to travel by unicycle
fahren	to drive, to travel
die Fahrgemeinschaft (-gemeinschaften)	carpool
gemeinsam fahren	to carpool
das Fahrrad (Fahrräder)	bicycle
mit dem Fahrrad fahren	to ride a bicycle
zu Fuß gehen	to go on foot (to walk)
laufen	to walk
das Motorrad (Motorräder)	motorcycle
mit dem Motorrad fahren	to ride a motorcycle
nehmen	to take
Er nimmt den Bus.	He takes the bus.
die Inlineskates (used in plural)	rollerblades
mit den Inlineskates fahren	to rollerblade
Ich gehe inlineskaten.	I go rollerblading
das Skateboard (Skateboards)	skateboard
mit dem Skateboard fahren	to skateboard

In die Kurse gehen	**Going to class**
das Arbeitsblatt (-blätter)	worksheet
diskutieren	to discuss
Etwas ist fällig	something is due
der Laborbericht (-berichte)	lab report
Notizen machen	to take notes
mit einem Partner arbeiten	to work with a partner
eine Vorlesung anhören	to listen to a lecture

Das Mittagessen	**Lunch**
die Beilage (Beilagen)	side dish
der Döner (Döner)	Turkish specialty similar to a gyro
die Dönerbude (-buden)	Turkish fastfood place serving Döner
das Gemüse (no plural)	vegetable(s)
das Gericht (Gerichte)	dish, meal
der Hamburger (Hamburger)	hamburger
die Mensa (Mensen)	cafeteria
die Nudeln (used in plural)	pasta
die Pommes/die Fritten (used in plural)	french fries
der Salat (Salate)	salad
das Sandwich (Sandwiche/Sandwiches)	sandwich
der Schnellimbiss/der Imbiss (-imbisse)	fastfood place
das Wiener Schnitzel	cutlet of meat (authentic is veal)
der Speiseplan (-pläne)	menu at the mensa or canteen
die Speisekarte (-karten)	menu at a restaurant
die Suppe (Suppen)	soup

Diese Geschäfte gibt es in der Stadt	A town has these stores
die Apotheke (Apotheken)	pharmacy
die Bäckerei (Bäckereien)	bakery
die Bank (Banken)	bank
die Buchhandlung (-handlungen)	bookstore
die Drogerie (Drogerien)	drug store
etwas (ein)kaufen	to buy something or go shopping
der Gemüseladen (-läden)	green grocer
das Geschäft (Geschäfte)	store
der Friseur (Friseure)	hairdresser
das Lebensmittelgeschäft (-geschäfte)	grocery store
der Schreibwarenladen (-läden)	stationery store
die Post (-ämter)	post office
das Schuhgeschäft (-geschäfte)	shoe store
der Supermarkt (-märkte)	supermarket
die Tankstelle (-stellen)	gas station
der Tante-Emma-Laden (-Läden)	small grocery (convenience) store

In der Drogerie	At the drug store
die Creme (Cremes)	cream
das Duschgel (-gels)	shower gel
die Haarbürste (-bürsten)	hair brush
der Kamm (Kämme)	comb
das Kondom (Kondome)	condom
der Nagellack (-lacke)	nail polish
die Schminke/das Makeup (no plural)	makeup
die Seife (Seifen)	soap
das Shampoo (Shampoos)	shampoo
das Taschentuch (-tücher)	tissue, handkerchief
das Tempo (Tempos)	name of a tissue brand, used to refer to it
die Zahnbürste (-bürsten)	toothbrush
die Zahnpasta (-pasten)	toothpaste

In der Schreibwarenhandlung	At the stationery store
die Büroklammer (-klammern)	paper clip
der Bleistift (-stifte)	pencil
der Buntstift (-stifte)	crayon
die Klarsichthülle (-hüllen)	clear plastic sheet protector
das Klebeband (-bänder)	tape
der Klebstoff (Klebstoffe)/Kleber (Kleber)	glue
die Kreide (Kreiden)	chalk
der Kugelschreiber/Kuli (-schreiber/Kulis)	pen
das Heft (Hefte)	notebook
der Locher (Locher)	hole puncher
die Mappe (Mappen)	folder
der Ordner (Ordner)	binder
das Papier (Papiere)	paper
die Schere (Scheren)	scissors
der Tacker (Tacker)/der Hefter (Hefter)	stapler
zusammenheften	to staple together
der Taschenrechner (-rechner)	calculator

Im Gemüseladen	At the green grocer
die Ananas (Ananas or Ananasse)	pineapple
der Apfel (Äpfel)	apple
die Apfelsine (Apfelsinen)/die Orange (Orangen)	orange
die Aprikose (Aprikosen)	apricot
die Aubergine (Auberginen)	eggplant
die Banane (Bananen)	banana
die Birne (Birnen)	pear
der Brokkoli (no plural)	broccoli
der Blumenkohl (no plural)	cauliflower
die grünen Bohnen	green bean
die Erdbeere (Erdbeeren)	strawberry
die Gurke (Gurken)	cucumber
die Johannisbeere (-beeren)	currant
die Karotte (Karotten)	carrot
die Kartoffel (Kartoffeln)	potato
die Kirsche (Kirschen)	cherry
der Knoblauch (no plural)	garlic
der Lauch (no plural)	leek
die Paprika (Paprikas)	bell pepper
die Pflaume (Pflaumen)	plum
der Pfirsich (Pfirsiche)	peach
der Pilz (Pilze)	mushroom
der Salat (no plural)	lettuce
die Tomate (Tomaten)	tomato
die Traube (Trauben)	grape
die Wassermelone (-melonen)	watermelon
die Zitrone (Zitronen)	lemon
die Zwiebel (Zwiebeln)	onion

Im Supermarkt	At the supermarket
das Bonbon (Bonbons)	candy
die Cola (Colas)	soda pop
das Eis (no plural)	ice cream
Eine Kugel Vanilleeis, bitte!	One scoop of vanilla, please!
der Fisch (Fische)	fish
das Fleisch (typically, no plural)	meat
das Hackfleisch	ground meat
das Hühnerfleisch	chicken meat
das Putenfleisch	turkey hen meat
das Rindfleisch	beef
das Schweinefleisch	pork
das Gewürz (Gewürze)	spice
die Kartoffelchips	potato chips
der Keks (Kekse)	cookie
das Mineralwasser	mineral water
der Reis (no plural)	rice
der Schinken (typically, no plural)	ham
die Schokolade (Schokoladen)	chocolate
die Süßigkeit (Süßigkeiten)	sweets
die Tiefkühlpizza (-pizzas/-pizzen)	frozen pizza
die Wurst (Würste)	sausage
der Zucker (no plural)	sugar

QR Codes

3.1 Wortschatz	3.2 03_01_int_ec_ typischertag	3.3 03_03_int_bg_ typischertag	3.4 03_04_int_ek_ fruhstuck	3.5 03_05_int_hm_ typischertag	3.6 03_06_int_ec_ fruhstuck
3.7 03_07_int_hm_ fruhstuck	3.8 03_08_int_bg_ mittag	3.9 03_09_int_ju_ mittag	3.10 03_14_sik_ indermensa	3.11 03_19_int_ag_ kaffee	3.12 03_20_int_hm_ morgenmensch
3.13 03_21_int_ek_ kaffee	3.14 03_22_int_hb_ kaffee	3.15 03_23_int_sco_ kaffee	3.16 03_24_int_bg_ morgenmensch	3.17 03_25_int_ek_ morgenmensch	3.18 03_26_int_hb_ morgenmensch
3.19 03_26_sik_ sophiaimsupermarkt	3.20 03_27_int_ju_ morgenmensch	3.21 03_28_int_ag_ morgenmensch	3.22 03_29_int_hm_ kaffee	3.23 03_30_int_ec_ morgenmensch	3.24 03_30_sik_ icecream
3.25 03_31_int_sco_ morgenmensch	3.26 03_44_sik_ drogerie	3.27 03_45_sik_ anategutdairy	3.28 03_46_sik_ anafood	3.29 03_47_sik_ ananderkasse	3.30 03_50_sik_ donerowner
3.31 03_51_sik_obst	3.32 03_52_sik_ gemuse	3.33 03_53_int_sco_ fruhstuck	3.34 03_54_intro_ alltag	3.35 03_55_sik_ doeneraanda	3.36 03_56_sik_ schoolsuppliesstore

Wortschatz

- *Verschiedene Freizeitaktivitäten*
- *Wohin man gehen kann*
- *Kleidung kaufen/tragen*
- *Spiele spielen*
- *Kreative Beschäftigungen*
- *Musik und Instrumente*
- *Verschiedene Sportarten*
- *Wo man essen gehen kann*
- *Ins Kino gehen*
- *Hobbys beschreiben*

Aussprache

- *Kapitel 4:*
  Three more exciting sounds
  /r/ /ç/ and /χ/

Grammatik

Focus
- *Modal Verbs – present tense*
- *Coordinating conjunctions*
- *tragen*

Recommended
- *Regular verbs – present tense*
- *die Uhrzeiten (telling time)*
- *die Tage der Woche (days of the week)*
- *Cases: accusative case*
- *Interrogatives*

Videos

Sprache im Kontext
- *Harald: im Kino*
- *Peter Süß gibt Trinkgeld*
- *Brigitte: Ausgehen in Würzburg*

4 FREIZEIT UND AUSGEHEN

You've now completed Chapter 3, in which you learned how to talk about daily routines and life as a student. But as students well know, when you work hard, you've got to play hard. Thus in Chapter 4, you'll learn how to talk about free time and the weekend: hobbies such as shopping for clothes, listening to music and playing sports, eating out and going to the movies.

By the end of this chapter, you will be able to talk about a wide range of free-time and weekend activities, asking questions, giving advice and defending your ideas pertaining to these topics. You will also become familiar with cultural information relating to shopping and eating out, among other topics.

Online Book links

You can find video clips at:
http://coerll.utexas.edu/dib/toc.php?k=4

You can find the vocabulary at:
http://coerll.utexas.edu/dib/voc.php?k=4

Sections
Verschiedene Freizeitaktivitäten • Different freetime activities
Wohin man gehen kann • Where one can go
Kleidung kaufen/tragen • Buying/wearing clothing
Spiele spielen • Playing games
Kreative Beschäftigungen • Creative activities
Musik und Instrumente • Music and instruments
Verschiedene Sportarten • Different kinds of sports
Wo man essen gehen kann • Where one can go eat
Ins Kino gehen • Going to the movies
Hobbys beschreiben • Describing Hobbies

You can find the grammar topics covered in this chapter at:
During the chapter exercises, you are regularly referred to *Grimm Grammar* at the **Deutsch im Blick** website. These are the grammar points the chapter covers, and you need to complete all online exercises in order to get the most benefit from the exercises in this workbook. The points on the left are necessary for completing the exercises in this course packet. The points on the right are recommended if you need some refreshers on parts of speech or what the present tense actually is ☺.

- Present tense verbs – modals   http://coerll.utexas.edu/gg/gr/vm_01.html
- Coordinating Conjunctions   http://coerll.utexas.edu/gg/gr/con_03.html
- Present tense verbs – tragen   http://coerll.utexas.edu/gg/gr/vi_13.html

Wortschatz
Vorbereitung

Always learn nouns with the article!!!

These ideas are sugges‐
tions only. Different learner
have different preference‐
and needs for learning an‐
reviewing vocabulary. Tr
several of these sugges‐
tions until you find ones tha
work for you. Keep in mind
though, that knowing man‐
words – and knowing then‐
well, both to recognize an‐
to produce – makes you ‐
more effective user of the
new language.

A. LISTEN Listen carefully to the pronunciation of each word or phrase in the vocabulary list.

B. REPEAT Repeat each word or phrase *out loud* as many times as necessary until you remember it well and can recognize it as well as produce it. Make a list of the words in this chapter which you find difficult to pronounce. Your teacher may ask you to compare your list with other students in your class. Make sure to learn nouns with their correct gender!

> **Beispiel:**
> die Sprache
> fünf

C. WRITE Write key words from the vocabulary list so that you can spell them correctly (remember that it makes a big difference whether you cross the Atlantic by ship or by sheep). You may want to listen to the vocabulary list again and write the words as they are spoken for extra practice.

D. TRANSLATION Learn the English translation of each word or phrase. Cover the German column and practice giving the German equivalent for each English word or phrase. Next cover the English column and give the translation of each.

E. ASSOCIATIONS Think of word associations for each category of vocabulary. (What words, both English and German, do you associate with each word or phrase on the list? Write down ten (10) associations with the vocabulary from the chapter.

> **Beispiel:**
> der Student/die Universität
> das Flugticket/das Flugzeug

F. COGNATES Which words are *cognates?* (Cognates are words which look or sound like English words.) Watch out for *false friends*! Write down several cognates and all the false friends from the chapter, create fun sentences that illustrate similarities and differences between the English and German meanings of these words.

> **Beispiel:**
> Nacht/night
> grün/green
> → False Friends: *hell* = light, bright vs. *Hölle* = hell

G. WORD FAMILIES Which words come from word families in German that you recognize (noun, adjective, verb, adverb)? Write down as many as you find in the chapter.

> **Beispiel:**
> das Studium (noun; studies)
> der Student (noun; person)
> studieren (verb)

H. EXERCISES Write out three (3) „Was passt nicht?" ('Odd one out') exercises. List four words, three of which are related and one that does not fit the same category. Categories can be linked to meaning, grammar, gender, parts of speech (noun, verb, adjective), etc. USE YOUR IMAGINATION! Give the reason for why the odd word does not fit. Your classmates will have to solve the puzzles you provide!

> **Beispiel:**
> grün – blau – gelb – neun
> *Neun* does not fit, because it is a number and all the others are colors.

Basiswortschatz
Core Vocabulary

The following presents a list of core vocabulary. Consider this list as the absolute minimum to focus on. As you work through the chapter you will need more vocabulary to help you talk about your own experience. To that end, a more complete vocabulary list can be found at the end of the chapter. This reference list will aid your attainment of Chapter 4's objectives.

(QR 4.1 p.203)

Verschiedene Freizeitaktivitäten	Different freetime activities
Computerspiele spielen	to play computer games
fernsehen	to watch television
die Freizeit	free time
mit Freunden ausgehen	to go out with friends
malen	to paint
Musik hören	to listen to music
schwimmen	to swim
spazieren gehen	to go walking
tanzen	to dance

Wohin man gehen kann	Where one can go
sich amüsieren	to amuse oneself
in die Kneipe gehen (Kneipen)	go to a bar
einen netten Abend haben	to have a nice evening
das Restaurant (Restaurants)	restaurant

Kleidung kaufen/tragen	Buying/wearing clothing
der Anzug (Anzüge)	suit
der Badeanzug (Badeanzüge)	bathing suit
die Bluse (Blusen)	blouse
das Hemd (Hemden)	shirt
die Hose (Hosen)	pants
die Jeans (plural only)	jeans
das Kleid (Kleider)	dress
der Mantel (Mäntel)	coat
der Pullover/der Pulli (Pullover/Pullis)	sweater
der Rock (Röcke)	skirt
die Sandalen	sandals
der Schuh (Schuhe)	shoes
die Socke (Socken)	sock
der Stiefel (Stiefel)	boot
tragen	to wear

Musik und Instrumente	Music and instruments
Flöte spielen	to play flute
Gitarre spielen	to play guitar
das Instrument (Instrumente)	musical instrument
Klavier spielen	to play piano
Musik machen	to play music
singen (sang, habe gesungen)	to sing

Verschiedene Sportarten	Different kinds of sports
angeln	to fish
Fußball spielen	to play soccer
reiten	to ride horseback
Sport treiben	to do sports
der Sportler (Sportler)	athlete
sportlich	athletic
Tennis spielen	to play tennis

Wo man essen gehen kann	Where one can go eat
der Chinese	Chinese restaurant
zum Chinesen gehen (zum... gehen)	to go to a Chinese restaurant
essen gehen	to go out to eat
das Gasthaus (Gasthäuser)	traditional restaurant
der Italiener	Italian restaurant

Ins Kino gehen	Going to the movies
die Eintrittskarte (Eintrittskarten)	ticket
der Film (Filme)	film, movie
der/die Schauspieler/in (Schauspieler/innen)	actor/actress

Hobbys beschreiben	Describing Hobbies
entspannend	relaxing
gefährlich	dangerous
gesund	healthy
interessant	interesting
spannend	exciting, thrilling
teuer	expensive
ungewöhnlich	unusual

Aktivität 1. Was machst du gern in deiner Freizeit?

You already talked a little bit about „Hobbys und Interessen". Think back and collect as many hobbies and leisure time activities you can think of.

Aktivität 2. Freizeitaktivitäten

A. What do the native speakers and American students like to do in their free time?

Do they have any? A little? A lot? You can find some helpful expressions in the box below. Watch the videos „In der Freizeit" and note which activities each speaker enjoys.

in die Disco gehen – Fahrrad fahren – mit Freunden ausgehen

Freunde besuchen oder treffen – Gitarre spielen – schlafen

Kaffee – trinken gehen – mit den Katzen spielen – klettern gehen

in die Kneipen gehen – lesen – Musik hören – in die Natur gehen – reisen – rudern

spazieren gehen – Sport machen – tanzen – in den Berge wandern

Die Deutschen und der Schweizer		Die amerikanischen Studenten
Berna (QR 4.2 p.203)		**Adan** (QR 4.7 p.203)
Eva (QR 4.3 p.203)		**Hassan** (QR 4.8 p.203)
Harald (QR 4.4 p.203)		**Erin** (QR 4.9 p.203)
Jan (QR 4.5 p.203)		**Sara** (QR 4.10 p.203)
Peter (QR 4.6 p.203)		**Sophia** (QR 4.11 p.203)

Grimm Grammar

At home please read the following grammar point on the *Grimm Grammar* website.

Present tense of regular verbs (review)

gehen
ich gehe
du gehst
er/sie/es geht

wir gehen
ihr geht
sie/Sie gehen

B. Weitere Aktivitäten

You are already familiar with a handful of the free-time activities mentioned by the speakers from earlier chapters:

Rad fahren   Kaffee trinken gehen   turnen   lesen   tanzen   mit der Katze spielen

However, there's also a lot of new vocabulary. Use your best guessing skills to see if you can figure out what this new vocabulary refers to. Write the letter of each English term in the right column below next to its corresponding German term in the left column.

in die Disco gehen	_____	a. to play guitar
mit Freunden ausgehen	_____	b. to do sports
Freunde besuchen oder treffen	_____	c. to travel
Gitarre spielen	_____	d. to listen to music
klettern gehen	_____	e. to go to a club
in die Kneipe gehen	_____	f. to row
Musik hören	_____	g. to go to a bar
in die Natur gehen	_____	h. to hike in the mountains
reisen	_____	i. to visit or meet friends
rudern	_____	j. to go climbing
spazieren gehen	_____	k. to go out with friends
Sport machen	_____	l. to go into nature
tanzen	_____	m. to go walking
in den Berge wandern	_____	n. to dance

Grimm Gramma

Zum Nachdenken:

In the last exercise, Eva mentions **Kaffee trinken gehen** as one of her free-time activities. What is the difference between **Kaffee trinken gehen** and just plain **Kaffee trinken**? When would you use each of these? As you may have noticed, when using **Kaffee trinken gehen**, the verb *gehen* is conjugated rather than the verb *trinken*. Keep this rule in mind as you progress through this chapter – it will come in handy, especially when we talk about the different sports!

At home please read the following grammar point on the *Grimm Grammar* website.

Cases: Die Uhrzeiten (review)

Cases: Die Tage der Woche (review)

Fragewörter (review)

Aktivität 3. Jetzt bist du dran!

How much free time do YOU have at the moment? When do you have free time? How do you spend it?

Wie viel Freizeit hast du?

Im Moment habe ich _____ Freizeit.

←--→

(sehr viel)   (viel)   (ein wenig)   (wenig)   (gar keine)

Wann hast du Freizeit?

Ich habe _____ Freizeit.

... morgens/nachmittags/nachts
... montags/dienstags/mittwochs/donnerstags/freitags/samstags/sonntags
... freitagabends
... am Wochenende
... um 3 Uhr

Was machst du gern in deiner Freizeit?

In meiner Freizeit ...

_____

_____

_____

_____

Weitere populäre Freizeitaktivitäten:

Computerspiele spielen • Kleidung kaufen • fernsehen • Football spielen • jagen • Karten spielen • ins Kino gehen • kochen • ins Konzert gehen • malen • schwimmen • ins Theater gehen • zeichnen

Aktivität 4. Eine kleine Reportage: Das Wochenende

One of the greatest sources of free time is the weekend! In this activity, you will be conducting a survey with your classmates, but you need to devise some questions beforehand.

Montag	Dienstag	Mittwoch	Donnerstag	Freitag	Samstag	Sonntag

<--> <------------------------------->
(Arbeit, Schularbeit usw.) (Freizeit!)

A. Was machst du am Wochenende?

Work together with a partner to find out what s/he usually does on the weekend. Before you interview him/her, you'll of course need some questions to ask! With your partner, develop five questions you could ask each other about what you usually do on the weekends. These w-words should be useful:

Wann? · Was? · Wie lange? · Woher? · Wo? · Wohin?
Warum? · Wessen? · Wie viel? · Wieso? · Wie viele?

Beispiele:

Wie lange schläfst du am Samstagmorgen?
Wohin gehst du am Wochenende essen?

Fragen zum Interview:

Frage #1:

Frage #2:

Frage #3:

Frage #4:

Frage #5:

B. Ein kleines Interview

Now turn your interview questions on each other (after all, you and your partner count as subjects too!). Jot down your partner's responses in the space below.

Antworten zum Interview:

Antwort #1:

Antwort #2:

Antwort #3:

Antwort #4:

Antwort #5:

C. Reportage

Now report back to your instructor what you've learned about your partner.

Mein Partner/meine Partnerin schläft bis 10 Uhr samstags morgens.
Mein Partner/meine Partnerin geht jedes Wochenende ins Sportzentrum.

Aktivität 5. Was machen Studenten am Wochenende?

A. Die Ergebnisse

Based upon *Aktivität 4* above, collect (as a class) a list of the most common responses. Then decide which responses deserve to be in the Top-10 list (à la David Letterman) of activities students do on the weekend. Rank them from 10 to 1, with 1 (the last item) being the "best" response, of course.

(Auf der zenten Stelle steht ...)
10.

9.

8.

7.

6.

5.

4.

3.

2.

(Und auf der ersten Stelle steht ...)
1.

Grimm Grammar

At home please read the following grammar point on the *Grimm Grammar* website.

Verben: Modalverben

dürfen (may, allowed to)
ich darf
du darfst
er/sie/es darf

wir dürfen
ihr dürft
sie/Sie dürfen

können (can, be able to)
ich kann
du kannst
er/sie/es kann

wir können
ihr könnt
sie/Sie können

mögen (like + noun)
ich mag
du magst
er/sie/es mag

wir mögen
ihr mögt
sie/Sie mögen

müssen (must, have to)
ich muss
du musst
er/sie/es muss

wir müssen
ihr müsst
sie/Sie müssen

sollen (supposed to)
ich soll
du sollst
er/sie/es soll

wir sollen
ihr sollt
sie/Sie sollen

wollen (want to)
ich will
du willst
er/sie/es will

wir wollen
ihr wollt
sie/Sie wollen

B. Studenten am Wochenende
What do typical students do on the weekend? Write 4-5 statements describing what they do.

Beispiel:

Typische UT-Studenten sehen am Wochenende viel fern.

Aktivität 6. Während der Woche *versus* am Wochenende
How does your lifestyle during the week differ from your lifestyle on the weekend?

A. Look at the word bank below and write each activity into the column that best reflects your schedule:
Which activity do you do *während der Woche* and which *am Wochenende*?

ausgehen – Besorgungen machen – fernsehen – Freunde treffen

Hausaufgaben machen – ins Internet gehen – Bücher lesen – in den

Bergen wandern – viel schlafen – Sport machen – in die Stadt fahren

zum Unterricht gehen

	während der Woche	am Wochenende
Was ich machen möchte:	• •	• •
Was ich machen muss:	• •	• •
Was ich (nicht) machen kann:	• •	• •
Was ich (nicht) machen will:	• •	• •
Was ich machen soll:	• •	• •
Was ich (nicht) machen darf:	• •	• •

B. Now ask a partner what they are (not) doing on the weekend, using the same questions you answered above.

Write down the questions you need to ask him/her. It is your friend/classmate – what form do you use to address friends?

Was musst du am Wochenende tun?

Was sollst du am Wochenende tun?   _____?

_____?   _____?

_____?   _____?

ICH   MEIN PARTNER

WIR
BEIDE

Aktivität 7. Eine perfekte Woche

What would you do if you could plan the perfect week for yourself? Jot down ideas of all the activities you would want to do.

A. What activities do you want to do?
Select the answers given below or write down your own ideas. Choose at least eight activities.

- schwimmen
- einkaufen gehen
- faulenzen
- Hausaufgaben machen

- _____

- _____

- _____

- _____

- _____

Freizeit
Arbeit
Spaß
Stress

B. When do you want to do what?

Create a plan for your perfect week. Write down the activities and the time you plan to do them.

Montag	Dienstag	Mittwoch	Donnerstag	Freitag	Samstag	Sonntag

C. Your perfect week is just about to get even more perfect

A friend of yours wants to spend some time with you. Talk with a partner and find out what activities the other person is doing when (do not look at each other's schedules, try to talk through this exercise). See if there is an activity you both would like to do, and find a time when you can both do it (you might need to compromise).

First, think about the questions you need to ask your partner and write them down.

Beispiel:

„Was willst du machen?" oder „Wann möchtest du das machen?" oder „Was willst du am Montag machen?" usw.

D. Was mein Partner machen möchte

Take notes on your partner's schedule, then circle the activity you want to do together.

Montag	Dienstag	Mittwoch	Donnerstag	Freitag	Samstag	Sonntag

Aktivität 8. Wohin kann man gehen?

Where can one go to do the following activities? Some possible destinations are provided below in the word bank. (There is certainly more than one possible destination for each activity, and of course each destination may be used more than once).

(zum) Biergarten	(auf die) Kirmes	(in den) Park
(ins) Café	(in die) Kneipe	(ins) Restaurant
(zur) Dönerbude	(ins) Konzert	(ins) Theater
(ins) Einkaufszentrum	(ins) Museum	(zur) Vorlesung
(ins) Kino	(in die) Oper	

Beispiel:

Wenn man spazieren gehen möchte, kann man ...

_____ in den Park gehen _____.

1. Wenn man ein Bier trinken möchte, kann man ...

_____.

2. Wenn man gute Musik hören möchte, kann man ...

_____.

3. Wenn man einen Film sehen möchte, kann man ...

_____.

4. Wenn man einen Döner essen möchte, kann man ...

_____.

5. Wenn man eine Pizza essen möchte, kann man ...

_____.

6. Wenn man Kleidung kaufen möchte, kann man ...

_____.

Aktivität 9. Was magst du lieber?

What is your *Vorliebe* (preference), American Football or *deutschen Fußball* (soccer)? Opera or hard rock? Why? Find all the answers to these questions below:

A. Partnerarbeit

With a partner, take turns asking which of the items below you prefer. Jot down some notes on your partner's responses and be prepared to share them with the class.

Beispiel:

S1: *Magst du lieber Rap oder Rock?*
S2: *Ich mag lieber Rock. Und du?*
S1: *Ich mag lieber Rap.*

Magst du lieber ...

1. Tee oder Kaffee?

2. Basketball oder Football?

3. Filme oder Theaterstücke?

4. Schach (*chess*) oder Poker (oder weder ... noch ...)?

5. Pizza oder Hamburger?

6. Bücher oder Zeitschriften (*magazines*)?

7. wandern (*hiking*) oder spazieren gehen (*going on walks*)?

> Do you and your partner have things in common or do you like mostly different things?
>
> Wir sind total verschieden! Wir haben die gleichen Vorlieben!

B. Warum?

Why do you prefer certain things over others? Think about reasons for your decisions:

Vorliebe	Grund	Vorliebe	Grund
Tee	*schmeckt gut ...*	Kaffee	*Koffein ...*
Basketball		Football	
Filme		Theaterstücke	
Schach		Poker	
Pizza		Hamburger	
Bücher		Zeitschriften	
wandern		spazieren gehen	

C. We have now collected many reasons why you might prefer one thing over the other.

How did you respond to these questions above? Now use the coordinating conjunction *denn* to explain why you responded as you did. Write complete sentences. Explain at least 4 *Vorlieben*.

Beispiel:

Ich mag lieber Kaffee, denn ich brauche immer viel Koffein (caffeine).
Ich gehe lieber spazieren, weil es ruhiger ist.

1. _____ .

2. _____ .

3. _____ .

4. _____ .

Aktivität 10. Eine Verbesserung

Now revisit *Aktivität* 6 about what you have to/like to do during the week and on the weekend. Read your paragraph and decide where it might be possible to incorporate coordinating conjunctions: *aber, denn, oder, sondern, und.*

A. In the space provided below, rewrite your paragraph using these conjunctions

This will make your writing sound more sophisticated!

B. Help your peers

Share your paragraph with a partner. Read each other's paragraph and give suggestions on how to improve the writing. This will not only benefit your partner but will also help you because you have to think about how to communicate your ideas for an actual audience! In the space below write down some of the suggestions.

Grimm Gramma

At home please read the following grammar point on the *Grimm Grammar* website.

coordinating conjunctions

aber – but

denn – because

oder – or

sondern – but rather

und – and

The verb usually stays in the second position in each clause with a coordinating conjunction.

Beispiel:

Er isst gern Pizza, aber e isst nur selten Hamburger

In Kapitel 2 you already learned to use *weil* to express reasons.

Notice the difference in word-order: with *weil*, the conjugated verb goes to the end of clause in which the *weil* is (otherwise known as the subordinate clause ☺).

With *denn* the conjugated verb stays in its original location: second place.

Aktivität 11. Kleidung kaufen

In *Kapitel* 3, we discussed shopping for groceries and other odds and ends. Now we discuss a kind of shopping which, for many people, is quite a hobby! Watch the following „Kleidung kaufen" video clips and take notes about how Berna, Eva, Harald, Erin and Sara go shopping for clothes and answer the questions below.

(QR 4.12 p.203)   (QR 4.13 p.203)   (QR 4.14 p.203)   (QR 4.15 p.203)   (QR 4.16 p.203)

1. Wie oft geht Berna Kleidung kaufen?

_____

2. Wohin fährt Eva, wenn sie Kleidung kaufen möchte?

_____

3. Wer kauft Kleidung im Internet?

_____

4. Wo kauft Harald seine Kleidung? (use the preposition *bei*)

_____

5. Was kaufte (*bought*) Erin das letzte Mal?

_____

6. Wessen Lieblingsläden sind *Galeria Kaufhof* und *H&M*?

_____

Aktivität 12. Einkaufsgewohnheiten – Ein kleines Interview

Ask two of your classmates about their shopping habits – how often they buy clothes, how much money they spend each month on clothing, where they go and what their favorite store is.

Name

Wie oft gehst du Kleidung kaufen?

... jede Woche, natürlich!
... einmal im Monat.
... zweimal im Jahr.
... nur wenn ich absolut muss.

Wie viel Geld gibst du jeden Monat für Kleidung aus?

... meinen ganzen Gehaltsscheck (paycheck).
... nicht sehr viel.
... höchstens $20 im Jahr.

Wo kaufst du am liebsten Kleidung?

... in der Stadt.
... im Einkaufszentrum.
... im Internet.

Was ist dein Lieblingsgeschäft?

Grimm Grammar

At home please read the following grammar point on the *Grimm Grammar* website.

Verbs: tragen

ich trage
du trägst
er/sie/es trägt

wir tragen
ihr tragt
sie/Sie tragen

Accusative case (review)

Aktivität 13. Wie heißen die Kleidungsstücke?

A popular place to shop for clothes in the German-speaking countries is *H&M*, the Swedish department store which prides itself on its fashionable clothing and affordable prices. Do you know it?

Ein H&M-Geschäft in Hamburg.

A. Die Umkleidekabine

Go tot the interactive "Dressing Room" (*Umkleidekabine*) on the *H&M* Germany website at http://www.hm.com/de/ to dress a virtual model. Pay attention to new vocabulary. Then look at the drawings below and try to find similar items on the website. Does H&M sell what you would need to dress like this?

Zeichnung von Megan A. (UT Austin)

Zeichnung von Brittany S. (UT Austin)

B. Sonstige Kleidung

Can you guess the meaning of some other common items of clothing? Match each clothing item on the left with its English equivalent on the right. Then go to the next page and try to fill in the blanks on the last student drawing. You can also draw your own fanatsay outfit and label the items you will need. In case your class loves fashion, have a contest for the best drawing/laebling work!

der Anzug	dress
der Badeanzug	hat
der Gürtel	bathing suit
der Hut	coat
das Kleid	socks
der Mantel	boots
der Pullover/Pulli	underwear
die Socken	belt
die Stiefel	suit
die Unterhose	sweater

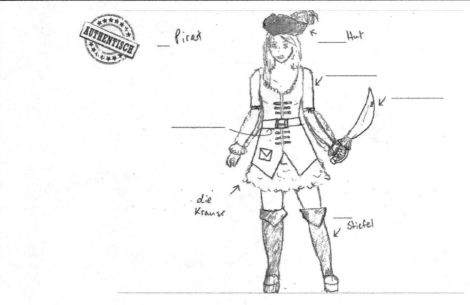

Pirat   _Hut_

die Krause

Stiefel

Zeichnung von Erica H. (UT Austin)

Aktivität 14. Alles durcheinander!

You are an exchange student in Germany and you need more money. You decide to take on a part time job at a department store. As you get to work today everything is a big mess and you need to sort it out. What clothing item does not belong with the others? Write down the correct word for each clothing item, mark the one that does not fit, and explain why that item is different.

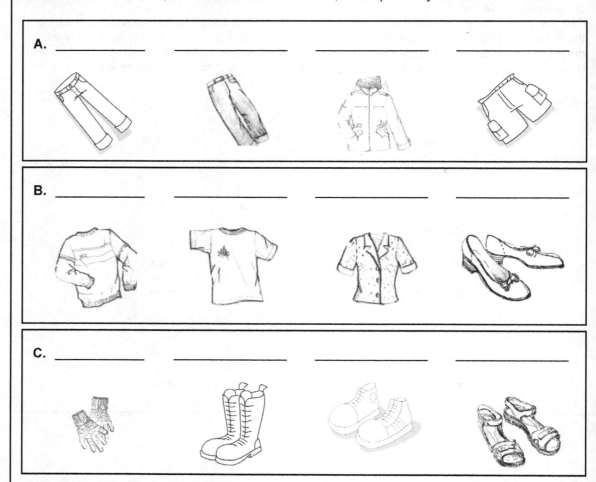

A. _____ _____ _____ _____

B. _____ _____ _____ _____

C. _____ _____ _____ _____

Aktivität 15. Was trägt mein Lieblingsstar?

Find a picture of your favorite movie or music star. Label the articles of clothing they wear, and write one sentence about each item. Is her hat *altmodisch* (old-fashioned), *hässlich* (ugly) or *nicht modisch* (unfashionable)? Or is it *modisch* (fashionable), *schick* (chic) or *schön* (nice, pretty)? Present your star to the rest of your class.

Aktivität 16. Ratespiel

On a small sheet of paper, describe your own outfit. Be as specific as possible: mention articles of clothing, their colors and whether they are *schick* or *bunt*. Afterwards your teacher or a student can read off the descriptions all the students wrote, and the rest of the class has to guess who is being described.

Beispiel:

Ich trage einen Pullover. Der Pullover ist grün und sehr bequem ...

_____

_____

_____

_____

Aktivität 17. Was trägst du wo?

What would you wear at the following locations or take with you?. Be as specific as possible.

Zum Wandern trage ich ...

Beim Camping trage ich ...

Zum Strandurlaub nehme ich ... mit.

Im Skiurlaub trage ich ...

Auf einem Rockkonzert trage ich ...

Aktivität 18. Einkaufen online

At home, log onto the Internet and visit Peek/Cloppenburg (http://www.peek-cloppenburg.de) oder H&M (http://shop.hm.com/de/). Imagine that you received a 250 Euro Gutschein (*gift card*) zum Geburtstag. You need to buy some new clothing. *Was kaufst du? Wie sehen diese Kleidungsstücke aus?*
Take notes and present your items to a partner. He/She draws your items. Did she/he get it right?

Aktivität 19. Interviews: Die beste Musik

Begin by reading the different musical preferences in the left column below. Then watch as the native and non-native speakers of German discuss the types of music they like to listen to. Can you identify which musical preferences belong to each speaker? (The preferences are listed out of order, of course ☺) You may need to watch each video a second time to complete the activity.

Berna
(QR 4.17 p.203)

Eva
(QR 4.18 p.203)

Harald
(QR 4.19 p.203)

Jan
(QR 4.20 p.203)

Peter
(QR 4.21 p.203)

Erin
(QR 4.22 p.203)

Hassan
(QR 4.23 p.203)

Sophia
(QR 4.24 p.203)

Sara
(QR 4.25 p.203)

Adan
(QR 4.26 p.203)

Er mag Rap-Musik und deutschsprachige Musik. _____

Er mag amerikanischen Rock, Folkmusik, Jazz und Blues. Er mag aber auch deutsche Musik, zum Beispiel deutschen Rock und Hip-Hop. _____

Sie mag besonders gern Musik aus den 70er Jahren, zum Beispiel Disco, denn sie tanzt sehr gern. _____

Sie mag viel Musik, aber kein bestimmtes Genre. _____

Er mag klassische Musik und klassischen Rock 'n' Roll, zum Beispiel die „Rolling Stones", die „Beatles", Eric Clapton und Beethoven. _____

Sie mag klassische Musik, aber sie hört alles gern. _____

Er mag jede Musik, aber am besten gefallen ihm klassische Musik und Hip/Hop. _____

Sie mag alles außer (*except for*) Techno. Sie ist ein großer Fan von Country. _____

Sie mag fast jede Musik, aber sie hört meistens Bluegrass, denn sie spielt Banjo. Sie mag auch klassische Musik, Jazz und Blues. _____

Er hört gern klassische Musik, zum Beispiel Bach und Beethoven. Er liebt aber auch neue Musik wie Jazz oder Rhythm and Blues. _____

Aktivität 20. Welche Musik hörst du gern?

Now that you know the names of the different musical categories, take turns asking your partners (two other students) questions about his/her musical tastes. Ask at least one additional question of your own!

Namen der Partner: S2:   S3:

S1: Welche Musik hörst du gern?
S2: Ich höre gern ...
S3: ...

S1: Wer ist dein Lieblingssänger/deine Lieblingssängerin/deine Lieblingsgruppe?
S2: Mein Lieblingssänger/meine Lieblingssängerin/meine Lieblingsgruppe ist ...
S3: ...

S1: Welche Musik hörst du nicht gern?
S2: Ich höre nicht gern ...
S3: ...

S1: _____?

S2: _____.

S3: _____.

Aktivität 21. Musik machen – Eine Umfrage

Most people have played music at some point in their lives, and many people continue to play music on a regular basis. Go around the room and interview your classmates as to whether they play or used to play an instrument. Have them sign their names next to the appropriate line(s) below. Who knows – maybe you'll find the members of your new band right here in German class!

Beispiel:

S1: Spielst du ein Instrument, oder hast du früher ein Instrument gespielt?
S2: Ja, ich habe früher Klarinette und Klavier gespielt.

Wer spielt **Posaune** (oder hat Posaune gespielt)?   _____

Wer spielt **Flöte** (oder hat Flöte gespielt)?   _____

Wer spielt **Geige** (oder hat Geige gespielt)?   _____

Wer spielt **Gitarre** (oder hat Gitarre gespielt)?   _____

Wer spielt **Klarinette** (oder hat Klarinette gespielt)?   _____

Wer spielt **Klavier** (oder hat Klavier gespielt)?   _____

Wer spielt **Schlagzeug** (oder hat Schlagzeug gespielt)?   _____

Wer singt (oder hat gesungen)?   _____

Wer spielt **Trompete** (oder hat Trompete gespielt)?   _____

Aktivität 22. Ein kleines Musik-Referat

Pick one of your favorite singers, bands, composers, or instruments. Prepare a short oral report (2-3 minutes) to give in class on this topic. Be sure to bring pictures and/or short clips of music to spice up your talk! (You'll have access to a stereo and/or the Internet.) For your presentation, you should only use index cards with facts and prompts, but do not read the entire speech (booooring!).

Mein Thema:

Wichtige Details:

Aktivität 23. Lieder & Musik

Die Sportfreunde Stiller – 54, 74, 90, 2006/10. Read the lyrics and/or listen to this song by the German Indie-Rockband *Sportfreunde Stiller* about *Deutschlands Hobby #1 - Fußball.* Then complete the activities in the pdf available on the *Deutsch im Blick* website (Kapitel 4: Lieder & Musik).

Aktivität 24. Die Sportarten

For the more active among us, sports are a great hobby! When it comes to the German names of some common sports, you're in luck – you already know half of them, whether because they are exactly the same as they are in English, or because you learned them earlier in the chapter!

These sports include:

> **Baseball • Basketball • Football**
> **Golf • Jogging • Karate • Mountainbike fahren • Rudern**
> **Turnen • Volleyball • Wandern**

Some other common sports are:

Angeln

Kegeln

Fußball

Schwimmen

Billard

Leichtathletik

Judo

Segeln

Aktivität 25. Ein Kreuzworträtsel

Practice using your new sports vocabulary by completing the crossword puzzle below! The across words are numbered 1-7 from top to bottom, and the down words are numbered 1-7 from left to right. Also, you will need to write out the letter ß as *ss*. Viel Spaß!

Waagerecht:

2. Man braucht ein Paar gute Schuhe, um diesen Sport zu treiben; in den Alpen besonders beliebt!
3. Man geht in das Wasser, um diesen Sport zu treiben.
6. Der berühmteste (*most famous*) Sportler dieses Sports ist Tiger Woods.
8. In diesem Sport gibt es fünf Sportler pro Mannschaft.
10. Dieser Sport ist nicht für Leute, die sich vor großen Höhen (*heights*) fürchten.
13. Ein Synonym von Fischen.
14. Man hört oft Musik (zum Beispiel auf einem iPod), wenn man diesen Sport treibt.

Senkrecht:

1. Man braucht ein besonderes (*special*) Boot, um diesen Sport zu treiben.
4. In diesem Sport darf man nur die Hände benutzen.
5. Die deutsche Version von Bowling.
7. Der beliebteste (*most beloved*) Sport Deutschlands.
9. In diesem Sport gibt es verschiedene Geräte (*apparatuses*).
11. Steffi Graf hat diesen Sport getrieben (here: *played sport*).
12. Oft bringt man einen Hund mit, wenn man diesen Sport treibt.

Aktivität 26. Treiben Jan und Eva Sport?

Jan and Eva represent two opposite ends of a spectrum when it comes to doing sports. Watch the video clips, "Sport treiben" and fill in the blanks with the missing information to learn about their exercise habits.

(QR 4.30 p.203)

Ich treibe im Moment _____ Sport, und ich bin sehr

unzufrieden (*dissatisfied*) damit.

Eigentlich würde ich gerne _____ Sport treiben.

Zum Beispiel _____ würde ich gerne machen oder

auch mal _____ spielen oder _____.

Aber es ist im Moment für mich schwer, das irgendwie in meinen

_____ einzubringen.

Aber in der Zukunft (*future*) würde ich gerne _____ machen.

(QR 4.31 p.203)

Ich gehe _____ die Woche _____ zum Sport.

Montag bis Mittwoch ist das eineinhalb Stunden.

Donnerstags sind's _____ bis _____ Stunden.

Ich _____ selbst, ich gebe Kinderturnen.

Das heißt, wir _____ mit denen in der Turnhalle 'rum, über

die Kästen (*boxes*), über die Pferde (*horses*), auf den Matten, Trampolin

springen, solche Sachen ...

Aktivität 27. Über Sport sprechen

A. Treibt dein Partner Sport?

Ask a partner the following questions about what sports they like, and circle the responses he/she gives you. Write down any additional information they give you, too!

Treibst du Sport? Ja/Nein.

Was für Sport treibst du? Ich <u>spiele</u> ...
Baseball • Basketball • Billard • Football • Fußball • Golf • Tennis • Volleyball

Ich <u>mache</u> ...
Karate • Leichtathletik

Ich <u>gehe</u> ...
joggen

Ich angele.	ODER	Ich gehe angeln.
Ich fahre Mountainbike.	ODER	Ich gehe Mountainbike fahren.
Ich kegele.	ODER	Ich gehe kegeln.
Ich klettere.	ODER	Ich gehe klettern.
Ich rudere.	ODER	Ich gehe rudern.
Ich schwimme.	ODER	Ich gehe schwimmen.
Ich segele.	ODER	Ich gehe segeln.
Ich turne.		
Ich wandere.	ODER	Ich gehe wandern.

Wie oft treibst du Sport? Wie oft __gehst du joggen__?

<-->

jeden Tag   fast jeden Tag   einmal die Woche   manchmal   selten   nie

B. Ein kurzer Bericht
Using the notes you took on your partner's responses, write a paragraph of 5-6 sentences that discusses his or her involvement in sports (including what kind of sports he or she participates in and how often).

Aktivität 28. Wie findest du ...?

Now that you've learned all about the different hobbies, how do you really feel about them? For each sentence below, select the adjective(s) which, in your opinion, best describe the hobby. You may, of course, use each adjective more than once!

eher positiv	kann positiv oder negativ sein	eher negativ
entspannend	interessant	gefährlich
gesund	langsam	langweilig
kreativ	verrückt	schwierig
lustig		teuer
spannend		
unterhaltsam		

Beispiel:

Fussball spielen finde ich spannend. *Einen Marathon laufen finde ich verrückt.*

1. Ins Museum gehen finde ich _____ .

2. Moutainbike fahren finde ich _____ .

3. Monopoly spielen finde ich _____ .

4. Zeichnen finde ich _____ .

5. Briefmarken sammeln (*stamp collecting*) finde ich _____ .

6. Musik hören finde ich _____ .

Web-Tipp: Go to Yahoo's Eurosport report at
http://de.eurosport.yahoo.com/

1. What are today's featured sports-stories in the news?

2. Are there similar websites available in your own country?

3. What are some similarities and differences between those websites and the Eurosport one?

Spaß am Abend!

Aktivität 29. Ins Restaurant gehen

Surely one of the most enjoyable uses of evening free time is going out to eat. You don't have to cook, and you get to have exactly what you want! Or so you think. It can be very difficult to satisfy an entire group of people when deciding on a location – you may not get what you want!

A. Wohin gehen wir heute Abend?

Your instructor will divide the class into groups of three to four. Imagine that your group will be going out to dinner tonight, and create a 4-5 minute dialogue in which you are trying to decide where to go so that it makes everyone happy. The following notes can help you get started with your dialogue.

Name			
Wo gehst du gerne essen? ... in den Biergarten. ... ins Café. ... zum Chinesen. ... zur Dönerbude. ... zum Gasthaus. ... zum Grieche. ... zum Inder. ... zum Italiener. ... zum Japaner. ... zum Mexikaner. ... zur Pizzeria. ... zur Pommesbude.			
Wo gehst du nicht gerne essen?			
Bist du Vegetarier oder Vegetarierin?			
Wie viel Geld möchtest du ausgeben (*to spend*)?			

Ideen zum Dialog (instead of writing out the entire dialogue, just jot down prompts and ideas):

B. Wohin gehen die anderen?
After all groups have finished planning their dialogues, your instructor will call each group up to perform it in front of the class. Take notes on all the groups: *Wohin gehen sie? Wie viel Geld möchten/wollen/können sie ausgeben?*

geht zum/zur/ins/in den …   **weitere Details:**

Gruppe 1

Gruppe 2

Gruppe 3

.

.

.

Aktivität 30. Auswärts essen.
The following passage is taken from a manual published by the Deutscher Akademischer Austauschdienst (DAAD) in Germany. Can you figure out what it's about?

A. Vor dem Lesen
Look at the title „Kulinarisches" and subheading „Auswärts essen" of the passage below.

1. What do you think the passage is about? Write down your ideas.

_____

_____

_____

B. Bei dem Lesen
Begin by reading the first two sentences of the passage (starting with „Es stimmt schon …").

1. Who might be the intended audience of this passage?

_____

2. Where might you find this passage (i.e., in what kind of materials)?

_____

3. Now read the rest of the passage, using the vocabulary gloss as necessary!

Kulinarisches

Es stimmt schon: In Deutschland essen viele
Menschen gerne deftig. Aber keine Angst,
Sie müssen sich während des Studiums nicht
ausschließlich von Sauerkraut, Bratwürsten und
Grünkohl ernähren.

deftig: hearty
sich... ernähren: to subsist (on)

Auswärts essen

Es gibt kaum eine Landesküche, die Sie in
größeren Städten nicht finden. Ob persisch,
thailändisch, russisch, mexikanisch oder
koreanisch – das Angebot an Restaurants in
Deutschland ist groß. Sehr beliebt sind bei
Studierenden auch die italienischen, griechischen
und türkischen Lokale, weil man hier oft für
wenig Geld satt wird. Andere schwören auf den
Lieferservice, den viele Pizzerien, chinesische,
indische und mexikanische Restaurants anbieten.

Landesküche: national cuisine

das Angebot: the choice, range

satt: full
schwören auf: to swear by
Lieferservice: delivery service

In den Städten werden Sie heutzutage
Schwierigkeiten haben, Restaurants zu finden,
die eine rein deutsche Küche haben. Bedingt
durch die steigenden Lohnkosten und auch die
hohen Mieten in den Innenstädten mussten
viele Gastronomiebetriebe aufgeben und
wurden von ausländischen Pächtern – meist als
Familienbetriebe – oder von Restaurantketten
übernommen.

eine rein deutsche Küche: an all-German cuisine
bedingt durch: limited by
die steigenden Lohnkosten: the rising costs of labor
mussten viele Gastronomiebetriebe aufgeben: many
    eating establishments had to give up
und wurden von ausländischen
Pächtern – meist als Familienbetriebe – oder von
Restaurantketten übernommen:
    and were taken over by foreign entrepreneurs –
    mostly as family businesses – or by restaurant
    chains

Die typischen deutschen „Gasthöfe", auch
„Gasthäuser" oder „Gastwirtschaften" genannt,
die deutsche und regionale Gerichte anbieten,
begegnen Ihnen daher vor allem in ländlichen
Gegenden. Mit etwas Glück erleben Sie hier die
„deutsche Gemütlichkeit" und hervorragende
Kochkunst. Sie werden sehen: Auch in der
deutschen Küche setzt sich leicht bekömmliche
Kost mehr und mehr durch. Einige Köche haben
die Kochkunst ihrer Urgroßmütter wiederentdeckt,
vor allem, was Gemüse und Kräuter angeht.
Kombiniert mit „moderner" Kochkunst erzielen sie
oft überraschende und vor allem schmackhafte
Effekte.

Gerichte: dishes (food)
begegnen Ihnen: you will come across
ländlichen Gegenden: rural areas
„deutsche Gemütlichkeit":
    German coziness, friendliness, welcoming
    atmosphere (no English term for this concept)
leicht bekömmliche Kost: easily digestible food
setzt sich ... durch: to become accepted
wiederentdeckt: rediscover
erzielen: to achieve

C. Nach dem Lesen

Stimmt das oder stimmt das nicht? Based on the passage above, are the following statements true?

	Das stimmt.	Das stimmt nicht.
Many Germans like to eat hearty dishes such as sauerkraut, Bratwurst, and green cabbage.		
In Germany's big cities, there is a wide selection of national cuisines from which to choose.		
The majority of restaurants that serve traditional German fare can be found in these big cities.		
German cooks have not tried to lighten up and modernize traditional German fare.		

D. Fragen zur Diskussion

Read the questions below and answer them for yourself. Then talk to your partner. Do you have similar ideas? Then share your thoughts in an open class discussion.

- Were you surprised by anything you read about eating out in Germany? If so, what surprised you and why?
- Is eating out in Germany similar to eating out in America? How would you compare the two?
- What kinds of national cuisines are available at restaurants in Austin? Which ones are your favorites, and why?
- The article uses the phrase "rein deutsche Küche" but doesn't elaborate on what that might entail. What do you think?
- What might "rein amerikanische Küche" include? How might that differ from "regionale Gerichte"?

Aktivität 31. Sprache im Kontext: Trinkgeld

Now that you've read the main passage, take a look at the *Tipp* you overlooked earlier (reprinted again below). This *Tipp* (i.e., hint) discusses the subject of *Trinkgeld* (i.e., gratuity, tip) when eating out at restaurants in Germany.

A. Sprache im Kontext: Peter Süß gibt Trinkgeld

Watch Dr. Peter Süß (who teaches Art and Art History in Würzburg, as well as fascinating mini-lessons on etiquette) handle the tipping after lunch at a restaurant in Rothenburg. Put the following statements in order, and note whether Dr. Süß made them or the Kellner (the waiter, not seen in the video).

(QR 4.32 p.203)

PS/K

		PS/K
_____	17 Euro bitte.	_____
_____	Danke schön.	_____
1	Ein Spezi und ein Schnitzel.	K
_____	Geben Sie mir bitte auf 18 heraus.	_____
_____	Zwei Euro zurück, vielen Dank.	_____

Do a quick search on the internet and find out what a Spezi is. Would you want to try it?

How does this exchange differ from paying in an American restaurant/café?

B. Tipp: Das Trinkgeld

Read the short text below about tipping customs in the German-speaking countries. How are tipping customs in the U.S. compare to those in Germany. For example, is a service charge generally included in the bill in the U.S.? What percentage of the total bill is appropriate for a tip in the U.S.? In Germany? Use the vocabulary gloss to the right if necessary.

Tipp

Trinkgeld: Eigentlich sind die Mehrwertsteuer und das Bediennungsgeld in der Rechnung schon enthalten. Trotzdem wird in Restaurants, Cafés und überall dort, wo jemand die Bestellung an den Tisch bringt, ein Trinkgeld erwartet. Als Faustregel gilt: Man gibt etwa 5 bis 10% des Rechnungsbetrages als Trinkgeld.

die Mehrwertsteuer: federal sales tax

das Bedienungsgeld: service charge (tip)
die Rechnung: bill, check
schon enthalten: already included
trotzdem: nevertheless, even so

die Bestellung: order (of food)
die Faustregel: rule of thumb
wird ... erwartet: (passive voice) is expected
als Faustregel gilt: as a rule of thumb

des Rechnungsbetrages: of the balance

Aktivität 32. Wir gehen ins Kino!

After a hearty evening meal, you may not want to do much but sit down and relax! If that's the case, the movies are the perfect place to go. What do you associate with going to the movies? Jot down some ideas (in English or German) in the space provided below.

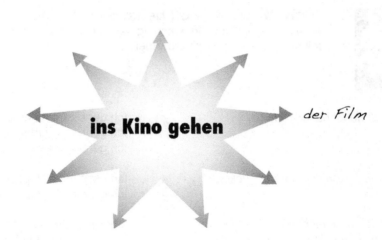

ins Kino gehen   *der Film*

Aktivität 33. Sprache im Kontext: Harald im Kino (oder vielleicht auch nicht?)

Watch as Harald answers the following three questions about his movie-going habits and fill out the blanks below with his responses. (Hint: There may be more than one word per blank!)

(QR 4.33 p.203)

Wie oft gehst du ins Kino?

> Leider Gottes, _____
> _____. Ich bin früher _____
> _____ ins Kino gegangen, und ich war (*was*), glaube ich, letztes Jahr
> _____ im Kino.

Popcorn: gesalzen oder gezuckert?

> Oh nein, _____, ja. Ich kann mich an das gezuckerte
> erinnern (*to remember*), im Tierpark in München, aber das ist schon lange
> her. _____ ganz bestimmt gesalzen.

Hast du einen Lieblingsschauspieler oder eine Lieblingsschauspielerin?

> Ich verliebe mich immer in _____.
> _____ ist immer noch ganz oben.
> Unter den Schauspielern gibt es einige (*some*), aber _____
> _____ war (*was*) mir immer sehr ... ja, _____
> _____ vielleicht.

Aktivität 34. Wie oft gehst du ins Kino?

How do Harald's movie-watching habits compare to those of yours? Answer the following questions with a partner.

Wie oft gehst du ins Kino?	Ich gehe **oft** ins Kino.
	Ich gehe **manchmal** ins Kino.
	Ich gehe **nie** ins Kino.
Popcorn: gesalzen oder gezuckert?	Ich esse mein Popcorn **gesalzen**.
	Ich esse mein Popcorn **gezuckert**.
Hast du einen Lieblingsschauspieler oder eine Lieblingsschauspielerin?	**Mein Lieblingsschauspieler** ist ...
	Meine Lieblingsschauspielerin ist ...

Aktivität 35. Interviews: Lieblingsfilme & -bücher

Watch Berna's, Harald's and Jan's video clips, and find out what their favorite books and movies are. Have you heard of these books, authors, movies and directors? Which ones are your favorites?

A. Bernas, Haralds und Jans Lieblingsfilme & Lieblingsbücher

(QR 4.27 p.203)

Bernas Lieblingsfilm ist:

Wer spielt in diesem Film? _____ &
_____ sind die Hauptdarsteller, die Stars.

Bernas Lieblingsbuch ist:

Sie findet in diesem Buch die Idee faszinierend, dass …

(QR 4.29 p.203)

Harald schaut gern im Fernsehen:

Über Schauspielerinnen sagt er, dass …

Sein Lieblingsschauspieler ist:

Er findet diesen Schauspieler besonders im Film _____
_____ gut, weil der Schauspieler …

Im Moment liest Harald alles, was _____ je
publiziert hat und

ein Buch von _____. Das Buch heißt …

Ein <u>Roman</u> ist
       a) a junky romance book
       b) a novel
       c) classical Roman writings (e.g. Virgil)

Jans Lieblingsfilme sind:

Er hat diese Filme gern, weil …

Jans Lieblingsbuch ist:

Er hat dieses Buch gern, weil …

(QR 4.28 p.203)

B. Jetzt bist du dran! Was sind deine Lieblingsfilme & Lieblingsbücher?

- Was ist <u>dein</u> Lieblingsfilm?
- Wer sind <u>deine</u> Lieblingsschauspieler?
- Warum findest <u>du</u> diesen Film/diese Filme besonders bemerkenswert (*worthy of mentioning*)?
- Was ist <u>dein</u> Lieblingsbuch? Wer ist <u>dein/e</u> Lieblingsautor/in? Warum liest <u>du</u> dieses Buch am liebsten?
- Welche Themen in der Literatur oder in Filmen findest <u>du</u> besonders faszinierend?

C. Eine kleine Umfrage

Ask your classmates about their favorite movies, books, authors, directors, and why they like these the best.

Name des Partners			
Lieblingsbuch oder -autor			
Warum?			
Lieblingsfilm oder -regisseur			
Warum?			

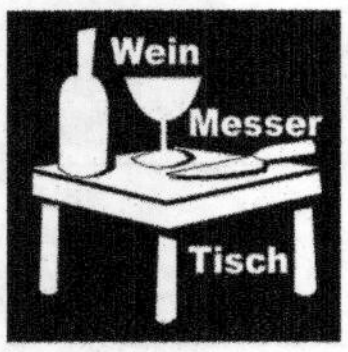

Aktivität 36. Alles über das Kino

First, try to figure out which genre each of the following terms refers to. Then write down the name of a movie that fits each genre.

A. Filmgenres.

Write at least two titles for each type of film. Go to amazon.de and see if you can find the German title for them! Which three are your favorite from among these films?

Abenteuerfilm _____

Drama _____

Horrorfilm _____

Kinderfilm _____

Komödie _____

Krimi _____

Liebesfilm _____

Science-Fiction-Film _____

Zeichentrickfilm _____

B. Kurzbeschreibungen

Write a brief plot summary in German (a paragraph of 6-8 sentences) for one of your favorite movies! <u>HOWEVER</u>: Leave out the actual name of the movie and the characters in your summary (you'll see why in the next exercise ☺).

Mein Lieblingsfilm:

C. Raten Sie mal!

Your instructor will ask for volunteers to read their plot summaries out loud to the class. The rest of the class will guess which film is being described in each summary! Take notes on your classmates' reports, following this or a similar pattern.

Machen Sie sich Notizen!	*Raten Sie, wie der Film heißt!*
Student 1: Details:	Der Film heißt:
Student 2: Details:	Der Film heißt:
Student 3: Details:	Der Film heißt:

Aktivität 37. Ein Theaterstück

Do you prefer to spend your evening free time doing something a bit more cultural than a movie and popcorn? Then going to the theater is probably right up your alley...

The city of Würzburg has several theaters to explore. To the right is an entry from the Theater am Neunerplatz. The whole program can be downloaded as a pdf as well under http://www.neunerplatz.de/Downloads. Skim and/or scan the entry to answer the questions below.

1. Wie heißt das Theaterstück?

_____

2. Wo kann man das Theaterstück sehen?

_____

3. Wer sind die Hauptfiguren im Stück?

_____

4. An welchen Tagen kann man das Theaterstück sehen?

_____

5. Um wie viel Uhr ist das Theaterstück?

_____

6. Was machen Peterchen, Anneliese und der Maikäfer?

_____

_____

7. Für wen ist das Theaterstück geeignet (*suitable*)?

_____

KINDERTHEATER / EIGENPRODUKTION

PETERCHENS MONDFAHRT
EINE FANTASTISCHE REISE FÜR KINDER AB 5 JAHREN

Es war einmal ... und könnte wieder sein. Peter und Anneliese können einfach nicht einschlafen. Der Mond scheint so hell. Aber was ist das? Weint der Mond etwa? Sogar sein Schnurrbart wird ganz nass. Sein Schnurrbart? Nein, das ist doch das Bein eines Käfers. Aber wie kam das dahin? Und bevor sie sich den Kopf darüber zerbrechen können, mischt sich ein Maikäfer ein. Er heißt Sumsemann, kann sprechen und erzählt den beiden eine wirklich wunderliche Geschichte. Der Maikäfer Sumsemann ist der letzte Sprössling einer berühmten Familie. Vor vielen hundert Jahren verlor der Ur-Ur-Ur-Ur-Ur-Großvater Sumsemann auf traurige Weise eines seiner sechs Beinchen auf dem Mond. Seit dieser Zeit leben alle Sumsemänner mit nur fünf Beinchen. Um wieder komplett zu sein, braucht der Maikäfer sein Bein zurück. Und so beschließen Peter und Anneliese, dem Maikäfer zu helfen und mit ihm das Beinchen vom Mond herunterzuholen. Es beginnt eine abenteuerliche Reise über die Sternenwiese mit den Sternenkindern und dem Sandmann, zu den Naturgewalten bei der Nachtfee und zum Mond mit dem gefährlichen Mondmann, der überwunden werden muss. Erst dann bekommt der Maikäfer sein Bein zurück.

Gerdt von Bassewitz' Kinderbuchklassiker Peterchens Mondfahrt wurde 1912 am Stadttheater Leipzig mit großem Erfolg uraufgeführt und ist aus dem Schatz unserer Tradition nicht mehr wegzudenken. Bis heute genießt die fantastische und zugleich romantische Reise von Peterchen, Anneliese und dem Maikäfer Sumsemann ungebrochene Popularität. Denn wen berührt und verführt dieses Abenteuer nicht? Seien wir doch ehrlich:

Wer träumt nicht im Geheimen von einem Flug zum Mond?

Premiere: Freitag, 25. November 2011, 19 Uhr
Weitere Termine: 26., 27. und 30. November, 16 Uhr
         2. bis 4., 7. bis 11., 17., 18.,
         21. und 23. Dezember 2011, 16 Uhr
Eintritt: 9,- / 6,- erm.

Aktivität 38. Ausgehen

A. Wie verbringen Sie Ihre Freizeit?

Read the statements below and mark down whether you and your friends ever do these Austin activities when you go out. If you are not familiar with Austin, look the places up online or just find alternatives from your area.

	Ja	Nein
1. Wir fahren zu Mount Bonnell. _____		
2. Wir gehen ins Alamo Drafthouse. _____		
3. Wir feiern auf Sixth Street. _____		
4. Wir essen bei Rudy's. _____		
5. Wir schwimmen bei Barton Springs. _____		

B. Warum? Warum nicht?

Now explain your reasons for responding to these statements the way you did.

Beispiel:

Wir fahren zu Mount Bonnell, denn die Aussicht (view) ist abends sehr schön.

1. _____

_____

2. _____

_____

3. _____

_____

4. _____

_____

5. _____

Aktivität 39. Ausgehen in Würzburg

You already looked at some menus from restaurants in Würzburg. You have eaten, but the night is still young. Go to the following website: http://www.wuerzburg.de/. and click on „Veranstaltungskalender" (Events). Here you'll be able to search for activities to do after dinner. FYI: Set the website language to German.

A. To the left you see the navigation bar. Answer the questions below about what you see.

1. What elements does the navigation provide?

2. What can you search for?

3. What categories can you choose from?

4. What categories are most useful to search for evening/night activities only?

B. At home or in the lab

Go to the website http://www.wuerzburg.de/ and create your own *Nachtprogramm*. Write down your *Nachtprogramm* on a separate sheet of paper. Where are you going to go? What are you going to do? Explore the categories and what events, shows, groups, etc. are offered in Würzburg. For each thing you'd like to do/see, write down the appropriate information:

> Was für ein Event/eine Veranstaltung ist es?
> Wo in der Stadt ist es? Wie heißt der Ort/die Kneipe/das Theater …?
> Wie viel soll es kosten?
> Warum wollen Sie hin?

C. In class

Was machst du? Talk to your partner and find out what he/she has planned. Whose *Nachtprogramm* is better, more fun, etc.? Or do you have the same plans?

=> Before you start the interview collect a few questions you can ask your partner.

_____

_____

_____

Mein Nachtprogramm	Das Nachtprogramm von meinem Partner/meiner Partnerin

Aktivität 40. Ein Dokumentarfilm: Ein langes Wochenende

Wir gratulieren!

You have been selected as a participant in a new German Reality-TV shoot-off of *Deutschland sucht den Superstar* (the German version of *American Idol ...*) called *Deutschland sucht die Superstudis*! You have to create a 5-10-minute screenplay documentary for your audition. The topic: "*How do American students at your university spend their weekend*". If you want to win, you better not limit your comments to "ich schlafe" and "ich mache meine Hausaufgaben" – not only won't you get to remain in the contest, but just imagine the scathing comments you'd get from the show's judges! Be creative, use as much of the new vocabulary you learned in this chapter as possible. Feel free to perform this skit to your classmates (or even make the movie)!

Please go to the Deutsch
im Blick website, Kapitel 4

Aussprache
Three more exciting sounds – /r/ /ç/ and /χ/

After being introduced to some 'interesting' consonants in Kapitel 3, we continue here
with a discussion of the German 'r' sound and the sounds made by the 'ch' digraph.

1. DAS R

The German *r* is one of the most challenging consonants for native speakers of English to master.
Its pronunciation depends on a number of factors, including its position within a word, how fast
the speaker is talking, and where the speaker is from. In this chapter, we'll focus on how the first
two factors affect the pronunciation of *r* in Standard German (for regional variations, see chapters
7, 8 and 9). By itself, the German *r* sounds a lot like the word "err" in English as if you're gargling
mouthwash. But what happens when it's placed in words? When you are online and click on each
German word below, pay close attention to the differences you hear between the *r* sounds!

die Reise	the trip
die Karten	cards
der Computer	the computer

Could you hear the differences? These three sounds are called **allophones** of /r/. Allophones are
different ways of pronouncing a particular sound in a language.

When the letter *r* appears at the beginning of a word, as in *Reise*, or immediately after another
consonant as in *Freizeit*, it is pronounced deep in the throat, almost as if you're gargling mouthwash.

die Reise

When it appears between a vowel and a consonant, as in *Karten*, it tends to take on the qualities of
the vowel that precedes it, thereby losing its "husky" quality. In rapid speech, it can be difficult to tell
that the *r* is actually there (think of the South Boston accent or British English where the Queen's *r* is
RRRolled, thank you veRRRy much.)!

Karten

A similar phenomenon occurs when the letter *r* is at the end of a word, as in *Computer*. Technically,
the last two letters *e* and *r* could be pronounced separately to create a sound similar to the English
word "err," but when you speak quickly, the *r* sound usually disappears. In its place, you have
something that sounds a little like the German letter *a*. This sound is known in linguistics as *schwa*.

Computer

Here are some more examples to help train your ears:

gargle r	husky r	schwa r
die Freizeit (free time)	der Garten (garden)	klettern (to climb)
die Freunde (friends)	[ihr] fahrt (you guys travel)	das Theater (theater)
das Restaurant (restaurant)	das Konzert (concert)	die Oper (opera)
spazieren (to walk)	der Park (park)	die Kleider (clothes)
der Rock (skirt)	die Shorts (shorts)	der Pullover (sweater)
hören (to listen, hear)	die Sportjacke (sport coat)	der Sportler (athlete)

Now try these tongue-twisters:

Der dicke Dachdecker deckte das dicke Dach.
Dann trug der dicke Dachdecker die dicke Dame durch den dicken Dreck.
Dann dankte die dicke Dame dem dicken Dachdecker,
dass der dicke Dachdecker die dicke Dame durch den dicken Dreck trug.
The fat roofer roofed the thick roof.
Then the fat roofer carried the fat lady through the thick mud.
Then the fat lady thanked the fat roofer
for (the fat roofer) carrying the fat lady through the thick mud.

> **Es sprach der Herr von Rubenstein:**
> **„Mein Hund, der ist nicht stubenrein."**
> So spoke Mr. von Rubenstein,
> "My dog, he's not house-trained."

> **Graben Grabengräber Gruben?**
> **Graben Grubengräber Gräben?**
> **Nein!**
> **Grabengräber graben Gräben.**
> **Grubengräber graben Gruben.**
> Do gravediggers dig ditches?
> Do ditchdiggers dig graves?
> No!
> Gravediggers dig graves.
> Ditchdiggers dig ditches.

Ob er über Oberammergau, oder aber über Unterammergau, oder ob er überhaupt
noch kommt, ist ungewiß!
Whether he's coming via Oberammergau, or perhaps via Unterammergau, or not at all is uncertain.

Wenn Grillen Grillen grillen, grillen Grillen Grillen.
When crickets crickets grill, then crickets grill crickets.

> from: http://german.about.com/od/pronunciation/a/tonguetwisters.htm

Finally, the *r* sound can sound a little posh. After a preceding *u, ü, o, ö*, or *i* sound, and followed by a consonant or in word-final position, it almost sounds like a separate syllable like an '-ah'.

nur	only	vor	before
die Uhr	hour	das Tor	gate
für	for	die Körbe	baskets
die Tür	door	die Hörner	horns

2. DAS CH

Ch is a consonant sequence that appears frequently in English. There is more than one way to pronounce this sequence – like the *ch* in "bench" (phonetic symbol /tʃ/) or the *ch* in "Christmas" (/k/).

The *ch* sequence also appears frequently in German, and there are also two ways to pronounce it, both of which are fairly tricky for English-speaking students, since there are no equivalent sounds in English!

On the internet version, click on the audio symbol to hear the pronunciation of these words:

/ç/	/χ/
zeichnen (to draw) möchte (I would like) zum Griechen gehen (to go to the Greek restaurant) gefährlich (dangerous) ich (I) München (Munich)	machen (to do, make) das Schach (chess) die Nacht (night) lachen (to laugh) im Internet suchen (to search in the Internet) kochen (to cook)
the 'ch' is preceded by front-vowels or diphthongs (e, i, ö, ü, ai, ei, ie, äu, eu) or a consonant	the 'ch' is preceeded by back-vowels (a, o, u)
sounds like a hissing cat or air going out of a balloon	sounds like you have a frog in your throat or when you are gargling with mouthwash in the back of your throat

In case you are interested: the main difference between the two sequences is the place of articulation (i.e., the place in your vocal tract where they are formed). The /ç/ is articulated by putting the middle of your tongue below the hard palate (i.e., the front of the roof of your mouth), /χ/ ocurrs with the tongue further back against the area of the soft palate (i.e., as far back as possible on the roof of your mouth).

Don't worry if these sounds are challenging for you at first – you'll get the hang of them soon! And here are, of course, some tongue-twisters for you to practice with:

> **Machen Drachen manchmal nachts echt freche Sachen,**
> **oder lachen Drachen manchmal acht freche Lacher?**
> Do dragons sometimes do really cheeky things at night
> or do dragons sometimes laugh eight cheeky laughs?
>
> **Echte Dichter dichten leichter bei Licht.**
> **Auch freche Fechter fechten mitternachts nicht.**
> Real poets write poetry more easily by light.
> And rascally swordsmen do not fence at midnight.
>
> **Neue Teichfische für den heimischen Fischteich.**
> New pond fish for the fish pond at home.
>
> from: http://www.germanteaching.com/

WebQuests

Go to „WebQuests" on the *Deutsch im Blick* website and get to know more about German television and about the German`s national passion: Fußball. In Kapitel 4, specifically, you will complete the following WebQuests:

1. Finding TV programs that are interesting to you
2. Getting to know soccer teams, *Bundesliga* and the *Nationalteam*
3. Types of Gesellschaftsspiele

Meinungsumfragen

In this chapter, the Interactive Polls focus on how you like to spend your free time, and your attitude towards sports.

Participate in them by going to this chapter's *Deutsch im Blick* website and selecting „Meinungsumfragen".

Verschiedene Freizeitaktivitäten	Different freetime activities
Computerspiele spielen	to play computer games
fernsehen	to watch television
Football spielen	to play football
die Freizeit (no plural)	free time
mit Freunden ausgehen	to go out with friends
Freunde besuchen oder treffen	to visit or meet friends
Gitarre spielen	to play guitar
jagen	to hunt
joggen	to jog
Karten spielen	to play cards
ins Kino gehen	to go to the movies
Kleidung kaufen	to buy clothing
klettern gehen	to go climbing
ins Konzert/ins Theater gehen	to go to the concert/ the theater
malen	to paint
Musik hören	to listen to music
reisen	to travel
schwimmen	to swim
spazieren gehen	to go walking
Sport treiben	to do sports
tanzen	to dance
in den Bergen wandern	to go hiking in the mountains
zeichnen	to draw

Wortschatz

Wein
Messer
Tisch

(QR 4.1 p.203)

Wohin man gehen kann	Where one can go
sich amüsieren	to amuse oneself
der Biergarten (-gärten)	beer garden
in den Biergarten gehen	to go to the beer garden
ins Café gehen (Cafés)	to go to the café café
in die Disco gehen (Discos)	to go to the club
in die Kneipe gehen (Kneipen)	to go to a bar
ins Museum gehen (Museen)	to go to a museum
in die Oper gehen	to go to the opera
in den Park gehen (Parks/Pärke)	to go to the park
einen netten Abend haben	to have a nice evening
das Restaurant (Restaurants)	restaurant
das Theater (Theater)	theater, stage
das Theaterstück (-stücke)	theater play

Kleidung kaufen/tragen	Buying/wearing clothing
Schuhe mit Absätzen	high heels
der Anzug (Anzüge)	suit
der Badeanzug (Badeanzüge)	bathing suit
der BH (BHs)	bra
die Bluse (Blusen)	blouse
die Boxershorts (plural only)	boxer shorts (men's underwear)
die Flip-Flops (used in plural)	flipflops
der Gürtel (Gürtel)	belt
das Hemd (Hemden)	shirt
die Hose (Hosen)	pants
der Hut (Hüte)	hat
die Jeans (plural only)	jeans
das Kleid (Kleider)	dress
die Krawatte (Krawatten)	necktie
der Mantel (Mäntel)	coat
der Pullover/der Pulli (Pullover/Pullis)	sweater
der Rock (Röcke)	skirt
die Sandalen (used in plural)	sandals
der Schal (Schals)	scarf
der Schuh (Schuhe)	shoe
die Shorts (plural only)	shorts
die Socke (Socken)	sock
die Sportjacke (Sportjacken)	sport coat
der Stiefel (Stiefel)	boot
das T-Shirt (T-Shirts)	tshirt
die Unterhose (Unterhosen)	underwear (men)
die Unterwäsche (Unterwäschen)	underwear (women)
tragen	wear
ein Kleid tragen	to wear a dress

das Spiel (Spiele)	Game (games)
das Brettspiel/das Gesellschaftsspiel	board game/group game
Mensch ärgere dich nicht	Sorry!
Schach	chess
das Computerspiel	computer game/video game
das Kartenspiel	card game

Kreative Beschäftigungen	Creative activities
basteln	to do crafts
häkeln	to embroider
nähen	to sew
stricken	to knit
töpfern	to work with clay

Musik und Instrumente	Music and instruments
Bass spielen	to play bass
Cello spielen	to play cello
Flöte spielen	to play flute
Geige spielen	to play violin
Gitarre spielen	to play guitar
das Instrument (Instrumente)	musical instrument
Klarinette spielen	to play clarinet
Klavier spielen	to play piano
die Musik	music
Musik machen	to play music
Schlagzeug spielen	to play drums
singen	to sing

Verschiedene Sportarten	Different kinds of sports
angeln	to fish
die Angel (Angeln)	fishing rod
Basketball spielen	to play basketball
der Basketball (-bälle)	basketball
Billard spielen	to play pool
Fußball spielen	to play soccer
der Fußball (-bälle)	soccer ball
Golf spielen/golfen	to play golf
der Golfball (-bälle)	golf ball
der Golfschläger (-schläger)	golf clubs
kegeln	German bowling
Leichtathletik machen	to do track and field
reiten	to ride horseback
das Pferd (Pferde)	horse
segeln gehen	to go sailing
die Sportart (-arten)	kind of sport
Sport treiben	to do sports
der Sportler (Sportler)	athlete
sportlich	athletic
Tennis spielen	to play tennis
turnen	gymnastics
Volleyball spielen	play volleyball

Wo man essen gehen kann	Where one can go eat
der Chinese	Chinese restaurant
zum Chinesen gehen (zum … gehen)	to go to a Chinese restaurant
essen gehen	to go out to eat
das Gasthaus (-häuser)	traditional restaurant
der Grieche	Greek restaurant
der Italiener	Italian restaurant
der Japaner	Japanese restaurant
der Mexikaner	Mexican restaurant
die Pizzeria (Pizzerias)	pizza restaurant

Ins Kino gehen / Going to the movies

die Eintrittskarte (-karten)	ticket
der Film (Filme)	film, movie
der Abenteuerfilm	adventure
der Dokumentarfilm	documentary
das Drama (Dramen)	drama
der Horrorfilm	horror
der Kinderfilm	children's
die Komödie (Komödien)	comedy
der Krimi (Krimis)	crime, detective
der Liebesfilm	romance
der Spielfilm	movie (general, long, nondrama films)
der Science-Fiction-Film	science fiction
der Zeichentrickfilm	cartoon
Lass uns am Wochenende einen Film sehen!	Let's go watch a movie on the weekend!
Popcorn essen	to eat popcorn
Möchtest du Salz oder Zucker auf deinem Popcorn?	Do you want salt or sugar on your popcorn?
der Schauspieler (-spieler)	actor
die Schauspielerin (-spielerinnen)	actress
der Sitzplatz (-plätze)	seat
einen Sitzplatz (aus)wählen	choose a seat
Wo möchten Sie sitzen?	Where would you like to sit?
in der Mitte/in der Loge/hinten sitzen	to sit in the middle/the balcony/the back
die Vorschau/der Trailer	preview
die Werbung (Werbungen)	commercial, advertisement

Hobbys beschreiben / Describing Hobbies

das Hobby (Hobbys)	hobby
Ich habe keine Hobbys!	I have no hobbies.
Ich habe keine Zeit für Hobbys!	I have no time for hobbies.
entspannend	relaxing
Ich finde mein Hobby entspannend.	(I find that) My hobby is relaxing.
gefährlich	dangerous
Ist das nicht gefährlich?	Isn't that dangerous?
gesund	healthy
interessant	interesting
kreativ	creative
langsam	slow
langweilig	boring
lustig	amusing
schwierig	difficult
Das ist zu schwierig für mich!	This is too difficult for me!
spannend	exciting, thrilling
teuer	expensive
ungewöhnlich	unusual
Das ist aber ein ungewöhnliches Hobby!	that's an unusual hobby!
verrückt – Du bist ja verrückt!	crazy – You're nuts!

QR Codes

4.1	4.2	4.3	4.4	4.5	4.6

Wortschatz · 04_01_int_bg_ freizeit · 04_02_int_ek_ freizeit · 04_03_int_hb_ freizeit · 04_04_int_ju_ freizeit · 04_05_int_ph_ freizeit

4.7	4.8	4.9	4.10	4.11	4.12

04_06_int_ag_ freizeit · 04_07_int_hm_ freizeit · 04_08_int_ec_ freizeit · 04_09_int_sco_ freizeit · 04_10_int_scl_ freizeit · 04_11_int_bg_ kleidung

4.13	4.14	4.15	4.16	4.17	4.18

04_12_int_ek_ kleidung · 04_13_int_hb_ kleidung · 04_14_int_ec_ keidung · 04_15_int_sco_ kleidung · 04_16_int_bg_ musik · 04_17_int_ek_ musik

4.19	4.20	4.21	4.22	4.23	4.24

04_18_int_hb_ musik · 04_19_int_ju_ musik · 04_20_int_ph_ musik · 04_21_int_ec_ musik · 04_22_int_hm_ musik · 04_23_int_scl_ musik

4.25	4.26	4.27	4.28	4.29	4.30

04_24_int_sco_ musik · 04_25_int_ag_ musik · 04_26_int_bg_ filmbuch · 04_27_int_ju_ filmbuch · 04_28_int_hb_ filmbuch · 04_29_int_ju_ sport

4.31	4.32	4.33	4.34	4.35

04_30_int_ek_ sport · 04_31_sik_ petersuesstip · 04_32_sik_ haraldimkino · 04_33_sik_ wburgausgehen · 04_34_intro_ freizeit

Herrschaft der
Schwarzburger Grafen
1208 – 1389

5 FAMILIE, FESTE UND FEIERTAGE

This chapter offers you an exciting tour of families, family life and celebrations in the German-speaking countries: *Geburtstage, eine Hochzeit, Weihnachten, Silvester, Pfingsten, die Sommerferien ...* All the holidays that you can imagine. And all the family as well, who's in yours?

Real or imagined, you can learn to talk about *Eltern, Schwestern, Brüder* and other such sundry relations. As before, you will explore these themes with the help of our native and non-native speaker friends, as well as in the *Sprache im Kontext* videos.

**Online
Book links**

You can find video clips at:
http://coerll.utexas.edu/dib/toc.php?k=5

You can find the vocabulary at:
http://coerll.utexas.edu/dib/voc.php?k=5

Sections
Die Familie • The family
Wie ist meine Familie? • What is my family like?
Feiertage & Feste • Holidays & Celebrations
Feiern & Beziehungen • Celebrating & Relationships

You can find the grammar topics covered in this chapter at:
During the chapter exercises, you are regularly referred to *Grimm Grammar* at the **Deutsch im Blick** website. These are the grammar points the chapter covers, and you need to complete all online exercises in order to get the most benefit from the exercises in this workbook. The points on the left are necessary for completing the exercises in this course packet. The points on the right are recommended if you need some refreshers on parts of speech or what the present tense actually is ☺.

- Possessive determiners
  nominative   http://coerll.utexas.edu/gg/gr/det_04.html
  accusative   http://coerll.utexas.edu/gg/gr/det_05.html

- Cases: month and years   http://coerll.utexas.edu/gg/gr/cas_06.html

- Conversational past   http://coerll.utexas.edu/gg/gr/vcp_01.html
  regular verbs   http://coerll.utexas.edu/gg/gr/vcp_02.html
  irregular verbs with *haben*   http://coerll.utexas.edu/gg/gr/vcp_03.html
  irregular verbs with *sein*   http://coerll.utexas.edu/gg/gr/vcp_04.html
  mixed verbs   http://coerll.utexas.edu/gg/gr/vcp_05.html
  -ieren verbs   http://coerll.utexas.edu/gg/gr/vcp_06.html

- Simple past   http://coerll.utexas.edu/gg/gr/vsp_04.html
  haben   http://coerll.utexas.edu/gg/gr/vsp_05.html
  sein

A. LISTEN   Listen carefully to the pronunciation of each word or phrase in the vocabulary list.

B. REPEAT   Repeat each word or phrase ***out loud*** as many times as necessary until you remember it well and can recognize it as well as produce it. Make a list of the words in this chapter which you find difficult to pronounce. Your teacher may ask you to compare your list with other students in your class. Make sure to learn nouns with their correct gender!

> **Beispiel:**
> die Sprache
> fünf

C. WRITE   Write key words from the vocabulary list so that you can spell them correctly (remember that it makes a big difference whether you cross the Atlantic by ship or by sheep). You may want to listen to the vocabulary list again and write the words as they are spoken for extra practice.

D. TRANSLATION   Learn the English translation of each word or phrase. Cover the German column and practice giving the German equivalent for each English word or phrase. Next cover the English column and give the translation of each.

E. ASSOCIATIONS   Think of word associations for each category of vocabulary. (What words, both English and German, do you associate with each word or phrase on the list? Write down ten (10) associations with the vocabulary from the chapter.

> **Beispiel:**
> der Student/die Universität
> das Flugticket/das Flugzeug

F. COGNATES   Which words are ***cognates?*** (Cognates are words which look or sound like English words.) Watch out for ***false friends***! Write down several cognates and all the false friends from the chapter, create fun sentences that illustrate similarities and differences between the English and German meanings of these words.

> **Beispiel:**
> Nacht/night
> grün/green
> False Friends: *hell* = light, bright vs. *Hölle* = hell

G. WORD FAMILIES   Which words come from word families in German that you recognize (noun, adjective, verb, adverb)? Write down as many as you find in the chapter.

> **Beispiel:**
> das Studium (noun; studies)
> der Student (noun; person)
> studieren (verb)

H. EXERCISES   Write out three (3) „Was passt nicht?" ('Odd one out') exercises. List four words, three of which are related and one that does not fit the same category. Categories can be linked to meaning, grammar, gender, parts of speech (noun, verb, adjective), etc. USE YOUR IMAGINATION! Give the reason for why the odd word does not fit. Your classmates will have to solve the puzzles you provide!

> **Beispiel:**
> grün – blau – gelb – neun
> Here *neun* does not fit, because it is a
> number and all the others are colors.

Wortschatz
Vorbereitung

Always learn nouns with the article!!!

These ideas are sugges tions only. Different learner have different preference and needs for learning an reviewing vocabulary. Tr several of these sugges tions until you find ones tha work for you. Keep in minc though, that knowing man words – and knowing then well, both to recognize an to produce – makes you more effective user of th new language.

Basiswortschatz
Core Vocabulary

The following presents a list of core vocabulary. Consider this list as the absolute minimum to focus on. As you work through the chapter you will need more vocabulary to help you talk about your own experience. To that end, a more complete vocabulary list can be found at the end of the chapter. This reference list will aid your attainment of Chapter 5's objectives.

(QR 5.1 p.247)

Die Familie (Familien) — The family

der Bruder (Brüder)	brother
das Einzelkind (-kinder)	only child
die Eltern (only plural)	parents
das Enkelkind (Enkelkinder)	grandchild
das Familienmitglied (-mitglieder)	family member
die Frau (Frauen)	wife (also: woman)
die Geschwister (plural only)	siblings
die Großmutter (Großmütter), die Oma (Omas)	grandmother
der Großvater (Großväter), der Opa (Opas)	grandfather
das Kind (Kinder)	child
Mama und Papa	Mom and Dad
der Mann (Männer)	husband (also: man)
die Mutter (Mütter)	mother
mütterlicherseits	on my mother's side
der Onkel (Onkel)	uncle
die Schwester (Schwestern)	sister
der Sohn (Söhne)	son
die Tante (Tanten)	aunt
die Tochter (Töchter)	daughter
der Vater (Väter)	father
väterlicherseits	on my father's side
der/die Verwandte (Verwandten)	male/female relative

Wie ist meine Familie? — What is my family like?

blöd	dumb
doof	dumb
dumm	stupid
frech	bold/fresh
intelligent	intelligent
langweilig	boring
lustig	funny
schwerhörig	hard of hearing
schüchtern	shy
sympathisch	likeable
verrückt	crazy

Feiertage & Feste — Holidays & Celebrations

die Ferien (only plural)	holidays/vacation
der Geburtstag (Geburtstage)	birthday
(das) Neujahr	New Year's Day
(der/das) Silvester	New Year's Eve
(der) Tag der deutschen Einheit (3. Oktober)	Unification Day (Oct. 3rd)
(das) Weihnachten	Christmas

Feiern & Beziehungen — Celebrating & Relationships

anrufen	call
besuchen	visit
das Datum	date (as in day)
einladen	to invite
die Einladung (Einladungen)	invitation
feiern	to celebrate
der Freund (Freunde)	male friend, boyfriend
die Freundin (Freundinnen)	female friend, girlfriend
das Geburtstagskind (-kinder)	birthday boy/girl
gern haben	to like
das Geschenk (die Geschenke)	gift, present
gratulieren	to congratulate
die Grußkarte (-karten)	greeting card
schreiben	write
stattfinden	to take place
die Tradition (Traditionen)	tradition

Aktivität 1. Die Familie
What feelings, activities and ideas do you associate with *die Familie*? Jot down as many words as you know in German, then feel free to add to the list in English.

MEINE FAMILIE

meine Eltern   Geburtstag

feiern

Aktivität 2. Wen gibt es in deiner Familie?
Listen to Berna and Jan's video clips titled „Wer ist in deiner Familie?" and circle the correct information based on what Berna and Jan say; each sentence may have more than one correct answer!

Berna hat eine   **kleine • große • normale**   Familie.

Sie hat
eine Mutter • einen Vater • zwei Schwestern • zwei Geschwister.

Ali und Nur sind
Bernas Eltern • Bernas Kinder • Bernas Schwester und Bruder

(QR 5.3 p.247)

Bernas Geschwister   **leben immer noch zu Hause.
studieren an der Uni in Kiel.
studieren in der Türkei.
sind jünger als Berna.**

Jan hat eine   **kleine • große • normale Familie.**

Er hat   **eine Mutter • einen Vater • einen Bruder • drei Brüder.**

Niels ist   **3 Jahre jünger als Jan • 30 Jahre alt • 3 Jahre alt.**

Jans   **Großeltern • Großväter • Großmütter** sind gestorben.

Jan hat auch noch   **eine Tante • einen Cousin • eine Katze.**

(QR 5.4 p.247)

Aktivität 3. Die amerikanischen Studenten: Wer ist in deiner Familie?

Watch the video clips with the American students and write down the information you hear about their families: names of their parents, ages and names of their siblings and any other interesting details they say about their *Familienmitglieder* (*family members*).

	Adan (QR 5.5 p.247)	Hassan (QR 5.6 p.247)	Erin (QR 5.7 p.247)	Sara (QR 5.8 p.247)	Sophia (QR 5.9 p.247)
Eltern (Ihr Name, Alter zum Beispiel)					
Geschwister (Name, Alter zum Beispiel)					
Andere interessante Details					

Aktivität 4. Eva und Peter: Meine Familie

Watch Eva and Peter's video clips („Wer ist in deiner Familie?") and complete the description of their families using the words provided in the box above the texts (each word may be used more than once, as reality requires). Afterwards, answer the two sets of questions regarding families: the first set about Eva and Peter's notions of family, then about yours!

**Bruder • Brüder • Eltern • Familie • Frau • Kinder
Mutter • Neffen • Nichten • Omas • Opas • Schwester
Söhne • Tante • Vater**

A. Evas Familie

Eva hat _____ und _____

und _____. Ihre _____

leben weiter weg, und ihre _____ sind leider

schon gestorben. Ihr Vater hat _____, die zwei

_____. Mütterlicherseits (*on her mother's side*) hat sie

auch einige _____ und _____,

die Kinder von ihrer _____.

(QR 5.10 p.247)

B. Peters Familie

Peter meint, er hat eine ziemlich große _____.

Seine _____ leben immer noch in der Schweiz

und er hat auch zwei _____ mit Familie. Ein

_____ ist vier Jahre älter als Peter, der andere

_____ ist Pilot und ist 10 Jahre jünger als Peter. Er

hat auch eine Familie in Amerika: eine _____ und

vier _____. Ein _____

wohnt in Colorado, die anderen drei immer noch in Austin.

(QR 5.11 p.247)

C. Genauer zuhören

Watch Eva and Peter's video clips again, and listen carefully to the expressions they use to describe their families.

1. Auf die Frage „Ist deine Familie groß?" antwortet Eva mit „Jein". Was bedeutet „Jein"?
2. Aus welchen Familienmitgliedern besteht ihre Familie „im engeren Sinne"? Was heißt „im engeren Sinne"? Wie nennt man diese „Familie" in Ihrer Sprache? Gibt es dafür einen Ausdruck?
3. Sie meint, dass ihre Familie ein bisschen weiter weg wohnt. Was heißt „weit weg" aus Evas Perspektive?
4. Peters Antwort auf die Frage „Haben Sie eine große Familie?" ist:„Es geht." Was bedeutet diese Antwort?
5. Wie oft fährt er in die Schweiz, um seine Familie zu besuchen? Meinen Sie, dass die Familie für Peter sehr wichtig ist?

D. Wie ist es bei Ihnen?

Reflecting back on the answers given by the native speakers and the American students to the questions thus far, answer the following questions based on your family. Is your family similar to or different from the families of the previous respondents?

1. Was ist eine große, kleine, „normale" Familie in Ihrem Land?
2. Wer ist „Familie" und wer sind „Verwandte" in Ihrer Kultur?
3. Wie weit weg wohnt Ihre Familie von anderen Familienmitgliedern?
4. Wie oft besuchen Sie Ihre Familie und Verwandten?

Aktivität 5. Jetzt sind Sie dran!

With your classmates (or other learners), find people who match the following descriptions and write their names in the spaces provided. Of course, you will have to rephrase the statements to questions.

A. Fragen stellen

How do you ask in order to get an answer for the statements in the boxes below? Generate the questions you need to ask!

1. *Hast du eine große Familie?*
2.
3.
4.
5.
6.
7.
8.
9.
10.
11.
12.

B. Finden Sie jemanden, der ...

eine große Familie hat.	mehr als drei Geschwister hat.	einen älteren Bruder hat.	eine jüngere Schwester hat.
keine Tanten hat.	ein Einzelkind ist.	einen Zwillingsbruder/eine Zwillingsschwester hat.	glaubt, dass Haustiere Familienmitglieder sind.
verheiratet ist.	einen Onkel hat.	mit seinen Eltern gut auskommt.	eine Urgroßoma hat.

Aktivität 6. Zurück nach Hause

Watch Berna and Jan's video clips („Zurück nach Hause") and find out how often they travel home to see their families, and how they stay in touch from afar. Answer the questions below in as much detail as possible.

in Kontakt bleiben · anderthalb (1.5)
der Besuch · verbracht · herumgefahren
das Heimweh · zu Weihnachten · besuche
den Touristen/Amerikaner spielen

(QR 5.12 p.247)

(QR 5.13 p.247)

Wie oft reist Berna zurück nach Deutschland?

Bleibt sie die ganze Zeit bei ihrer Familie?

Wie oft reist Jan zurück nach Hause?

Verbringt er die ganze Zeit bei seiner Familie?

Was haben er und seine Eltern gemacht, als sie ihn das letzte Mal besucht haben?

Wie bleibt Jan in Kontakt mit seiner Familie?

Aktivität 7. Welche Mitglieder hat Ihre Familie?

Interview three classmates about their families and take notes about their siblings, parents, contact with their grandparents, etc. Are their answers similar to yours?

Name			
Wie viele Geschwister hat er/sie?			
Wo wohnen seine/ihre Eltern?			
Wie oft besucht er/sie seine/ihre Großeltern jedes Jahr?			
Hat er/sie regelmäßigen (*regular*) Kontakt zu seinen/ihren Cousins/Cousinen?			
Hat er/sie eine Nichte oder einen Neffen?			
Welche Sprachen spricht er/sie in der Familie?			

Grimm Grammar

At home please read the following grammar point on the *Grimm Grammar* website.

<u>possessive determiners: nominative</u>

If the following noun is

A, Masculine or Neuter
mein – my
dein – your
sein – his
ihr – her
sein – its
unser – our
euer – you guys'
ihr – their

B. Feminine or Plural
meine – my
deine – your
seine – his
ihre – her
seine – its
unsere – our
eure – you guys'
ihre – their

Aktivität 8. Referat: Meine Familie

Review the video clips you have seen so far in Kapitel 5 and take notes on the questions that were asked. Select five questions that help you describe your family and answer them. If you feel that your family is too private to discuss – or if you want extra practice – feel free to „make up" or „adopt" a family: borrow somebody else's family life, such as *The Simpsons* (a huge hit in Germany!) or Brangelina or *The Smurfs*, or the British Royal Family. Bring pictures to class, and tell your peers about your family.

Beispiel:

Hast du eine große Familie?

Meine Fragen:		Meine Familie:
_____	?	_____
_____	?	_____
_____	?	_____
_____	?	_____
_____	?	

Aktivität 9. Der Stammbaum: Die Gebrüder Grimm

Fill in the family tree of the Brothers Grimm below. What was the relationship between the family members? The point of reference is the older brother, *Jakob Grimm*. Since his relatives (at least the ones listed below) are all dead, you need to use *war* (was) or *waren* (were) to talk about them.

AUTHENTISCH

Erste Generation

Johannes Herman Zimmer   *war sein Großvater*

Zweite Generation

Philipp Wilhelm Grimm & Dorothea [Zimmer] Grimm
(1752 - 10. Januar 1796) _____

Dritte Generation

Jakob Ludwig Karl Grimm
(4. Januar 1785 – 20. September 1863)

Wilhelm Karl Grimm
(24. Februar 1786 – 16. Dezember 1859) _____
    + Henriette Grimm, geb. Wild _____

Friedrich Hermann Georg Grimm (1783 – 1784)
Karl Friedrich Grimm (1787 – 1852)
Ferdinand Philipp Grimm (1788 - 1844) } _____
Ludwig Emil Grimm (1790 – 1863)
Friedrich Grimm (1791-1792)

Charlotte Amalie Hassenpflug, geb. Grimm (1793-1833) _____
    + Ludwig Hassenpflug _____

geb. = geborene (born)

Aktivität 10. Die Gebrüder Grimm und Sie

Describe the relationships between Jakob Grimm and his family members, then describe the same relatives in your family.

Beispiel:

Johannes Zimmer war sein Großvater.
↘ Mein Großvater heißt Bruno Zwietasch.

Seine Familie	Meine Familie/Meine Verwandten
Philipp Grimm war *sein Vater.*	*Mein Vater heißt ...*
Dorothea Grimm war_____.	
Wilhelm Grimm war_____.	
Henriette war_____.	
Friedrich, Karl und Ludwig waren _____.	
Charlotte war_____.	

Grimm Jakób.

Grimm Wilhelm.

Grimm Grammar

At home please read the following grammar point on the *Grimm Grammar* website.

possessive determiners: accusative

Example: die Großmutter/der Jäger

In this example we're trying to show how *die Großmutter* is related to *der Jäger*.

We select the pronoun based on the gender of the person whose relation is being described (i.e., *der Jäger* → his (sein)).

Then we need an ending based on the gender of the actual relation (i.e., *die Großmutter* → female (e)).

Thus we have *sein + e = seine*.

→ *Die Großmutter ist seine Freundin.*

Aktivität 11. Grimmige Familien

In *Grimm Grammar*, you have met many a family, some not as "traditional" as others. Can you describe the relationships between the following (groups of) individuals?

A. Wer ist wer?

Describe the relationships among the various Grimm characters and replace the underlined words with the appropriate personal pronouns in the nominative case. Specifically, describe how the person on the left of the slash is related to the person on the right of it.

Beispiel:

Rotkäppchen — die Großmutter — *Rotkäppchen ist ihr Enkelkind.*
Aschenputtels Stiefmutter — Aschenputtels Vater — *Die Stiefmutter ist seine Frau.*

1. die böse Königin — Schneewittchen
2. Rotkäppchen — die Mutter
3. Hänsel — Gretel
4. Schneewittchen — der Königssohn
5. sechs Zwerge — Happy
6. Aschenputtel — die Stiefschwestern
7. der Froschkönig — die Prinzessin
8. die Großmutter — der Jäger (?)

ROTKÄPPCHEN   Omas Haus

B. Wer tut was?

Complete the sentences with the correct substitution for the underlined people (and animal).

1. Aschenputtels Vater versteht Aschenputtels Stiefmutter nicht. *ihre Stiefschwestern*
2. Rotkäppchen besucht die Großmutter. *ihn*
3. Die böse Königin hasst Schneewittchen. *ihre Großmutter*
4. Rotkäppchen liebt die Mutter. *seine Schwester*
5. Hänsel beschützt (protects) Gretel. *ihre Mutter*
6. Schneewittchen heiratet den Prinzen. *ihre Stiefmutter*
7. Die sechs Zwerge suchen Happy. *ihren Bruder*
8. Aschenputtel vermeidet (avoids) die Stiefschwestern. *ihren Geliebten*
9. Die Prinzessin küsst den Froschkönig. *sie*

Achtung! Obwohl Aschenputtel und Schneewittchen eigentlich grammatikalisch Neutrum ("das") sind, benutzt man die Possessivpronomen oft in Referenz zum biologischen Geschlecht der Person, also hier weiblich.

Aktivität 12. Und Sie?
What do you do with your family? Love, visit, avoid, protect, kiss? Do tell all ...

A. Mein Stammbaum
On a separate sheet of paper, draw and label a family tree (*Stammbaum*) of your real (or imaginary) family.

B. Meine Familie und anderes Getier ...
("My family and other animals" à la Gerald Durrell). Select 4-5 members of your family (immediate, extended and imaginary members qualify) and describe them with interesting details. Ask yourself: would **you** want to read about the detail? If yes, it's interesting. If not, it's boring, choose something else ☺. Feel free to borrow a relative from the first, a verb from the second and at least one other detail from the third column, but you are very much encouraged to expand beyond these options. Note that *ich* is the subject, and all nouns in box 1 are the direct objects (accusative) of a sentence. In other words, you will start the sentence with the direct object, follow that with the conjugated verb, then add additional information to the sentence to spice things up. Channel Master Yoda: "My parents miss I very much ..."

Beispiel:

Meine Tante sehe ich jedes Wochenende; sie heißt Anika, so wie meine Großmutter. Meinen Onkel David verstehe ich überhaupt nicht. Er kriegt jedes Jahr einen Strafzettel, weil er mit seinem BMW zu schnell fährt.

meine Mutter		
meinen Vater		
meine Großmutter		jedes Wochenende
meine Cousins	besuche	nie
meine Cousinen	verstehe	jeden Tag
meine Geschwister	liebe	überhaupt nicht
meinen Großvater	küsse	nicht
meinen Bruder	hasse	so oft wie möglich
meine Brüder	kenne	an
meine Schwester	suche	per Skype an
meine Schwestern	rufe	sehr
meine Tante	habe	wie die Pest (*like the plague*)
meinen Onkel	sehe	von ganzem Herzen (*with all my* ♥)
meine Nichte	vermisse	wie verrückt (*like crazy*)
meinen Neffen	meide	um jeden Preis (*at all cost*)
meine Haustiere		nur selten, weil er/sie leider schon
meinen Mann		gestorben ist
meine Frau		

ich

1. _____

_____

2. _____

_____

3. _____

_____

4. _____

_____

5. _____

_____

Grimm Gramma

At home please read the following grammar point on the *Grimm Gramma* website.

possessive determiners: accusative

A. If the noun following the determiner is masculine then the following forms are used:
meinen
deinen
seinen
ihren
seinen
unseren
euren
ihren/Ihren

Zum Beispiel:
Ich rufe meinen Vater an.

B. If the following noun is neuter, then the following forms are used:
mein
dein
sein
ihr
sein
unser
euer
ihr/Ihr

Zum Beispiel:
Ich liebe mein Kind.

C. If the following noun is feminine or plural, the following forms are used:
meine
deine
seine
ihre
seine
unsere
eure
ihre/Ihre

Zum Beispiel:
Ich treffe meine Freundin im Café.

Grimm Grammar

At home please read the following grammar point on the *Grimm Grammar* website.

Cases: Monate und Jahreszeiten (months & seasons)

im Winter: im Dezember, Januar, Februar

im Frühling: im März, April, Mai

im Sommer: im Juni, Juli, August

im Herbst: im September, Oktober, November

Feiertage und Feste

Ob mit der Familie, mit Verwandten oder mit Freunden, Feiertage machen viel Spass ... Welche Feiertage feiern Sie? Welche feiert man in den deutschsprachigen Ländern? Das finden Sie im nächsten Teil des Kapitels heraus.

Alles Gute

zur Hochzeit!

FRÖHLICHE WEIHNACHTEN

Alles Gute

zum Geburtstag!

Aktivität 13. Die Deutschen feiern

Watch Berna's, Eva's and Jan's videos „Mein Lieblingsfeiertag", and find out what their favorite holiday is, and how they celebrated it the last time. Before you watch the clips, read the vocabulary in the bubble. While you watch the videos, identify who says which expression. Who thinks Christmas is a good opportunity for bringing a family together? And who is a 70s music fan?

> Fasching • Weihnachten • aufwache • Efeu (*ivory*) • eine gute Gelegenheit
> meinen Geburtstag • kochen • zusammen • gefeiert • nichts Besonderes
> in die Stadt gehen • einladen • ein Paper präsentieren • Eis essen
> verkleidet (*dressed as*) • Geschenke • ganz viel Musik aus den 70er & 80er Jahren

(QR 5.14 p.247)

(QR 5.15 p.247)

(QR 5.16 p.247)

Lieblingsfeiertag			
Wie feiert er/sie (oder seine/ihre Familie)?			
Weitere Details			

Aktivität 14. Die amerikanischen Studenten feiern

Watch the video clips „Mein Lieblingsfeiertag" of the American students, and match up who says what about their favorite holidays. Write the students' name – Adan, Andrew, Erin and Sara – next to the statements that describes their favorite holiday. More than one student's name might match each statement!

(QR 5.17 p.247)

(QR 5.19 p.247)

(QR 5.20 p.247)

(QR 5.18 p.247)

_____ Wir sind nicht sehr religiös, aber wir kommen sehr gern zusammen.

_____ Wir können viel essen und [uns] Football anschauen.

_____ Wir essen zusammen und tauschen Geschenke [aus].

_____ Meine Lieblingsfeiertage sind Halloween und Weihnachten.

_____ Mein Lieblingsfeiertag ist Weihnachten.

_____ Mein Lieblingsfeiertag ist Erntedankfest.

_____ Man trägt viele andere Kleider und Kostüme und isst viel Pumpkinkuchen.

_____ Ich werde immer böse und mufflig (*grumpy*), wenn ich nicht genug Geschenke bekomme.

_____ Für meine Eltern kaufen wir keine Geschenke, weil sie zu teuer sind.

_____ Die Familie meiner Mutter und meine Familie feiern zusammen.

_____ Mein Geburtstag ist mein Lieblingsfeiertag.

_____ Die Familie isst zusammen, und wir kochen immer zusammen.

In Amerika trägt man an Halloween Kostüme, aber wann tragen viele Deutsche - in bestimmten Regionen - gerne Masken und Kostüme? Und warum überhaupt (*at all*)?

Aktivität 15. Wann feiert man ...?

You want to plan ahead and therefore need to match up the following German holidays and celebrations with the correct date in 2020. Then complete the sentence about each of them. You can double check most of the dates at http://www.feiertage.net/uebersicht.php or google them to find out.

A. Im Jahre 2020 feiern wir ...

Feiertage		2020 feiert man ...
Heilige Drei Könige	31.12.2020	
Valentinstag	01.11.2020	
Rosenmontag (Karneval)	03.10.2020	
1. April	29.11.2020	*den ersten April am ersten April!*
Pessach	~~01.04.2020~~	
Ostern	24.02.2020	
Tag der Arbeit	08.04.2020	
Muttertag	12.04.2020	
Tag der Deutschen Einheit	01.05.2020	
Allerheiligen	14.02.2020	
1. Advent	10.05.2020	
Nikolaustag	24.12.2020	
Heiliger Abend/Weihnachten	06.12.2020	
Silvester	06.01.2020	

B. Feiertage im Frühling ...

Which holidays are celebrated in which season in your home country or by your family? Sort the German and American holidays into the correct season/month. Discuss the different holidays you all might celebrate. Are there variations among you and your classmates or do you all celebrate the same holidays, at the same time and in the same way? What might the results suggest about cultural practices?

	in den deutschsprachigen Ländern	in Ihrem Land
Man feiert folgende Feiertage im *Frühling*: im März im April im Mai		
Man feiert folgende Feiertage im *Sommer*: im Juni im Juli im August		
Man feiert folgende Feiertage im *Herbst*: im September im Oktober im November		
Man feiert folgende Feiertage im *Winter*: im Dezember im Januar im Februar		

Zum Nachdenken:

What do the holidays listed in Aktivität 14A tell you about the German-speaking countries? Specifically, about the connection between church and state? Did you know that there is – to this day – a church tax in Germany? All Catholic, Protestant and Jewish residents of Germany pay about 9% of their income along with their income tax to support a church. They have to renounce their religious affiliation and sever relations with the church they were raised in if they wish to go through the lengthy legal procedure of getting out of paying the church tax. For further information, see:

http://www.steuer-forum-kirche.de/church-tax.pdf

Aktivität 16. Ein kleines Interview
Ask a classmate about special holidays he/she celebrates. Take notes, and be prepared to present your peer to the rest of the class.

A. Das Interview

• Wann hast du Geburtstag?

• Wie feierst du deinen Geburtstag (mit Freunden/Familie, großes/kleines Fest, wichtig/unwichtig für dich)?

• Was sind wichtige Feiertage für deine Familie? Wann feiert ihr diese Feiertage?

• Hast du einen Lieblingsfeiertag? Wenn ja, warum hast du diesen Feiertag am liebsten?

• Wie feiert man ihn in deiner Familie/in deinem Freundeskreis?

• Welche Feiertage von der Liste in 14 A feierst du NICHT?

• Gibt es einige Feiertage auf der Liste, die ihr (du und deine Familie/Freunde) an einem anderen Tag feiert?

• In welcher Jahreszeit gibt es in deiner Kultur die meisten Feiertage? Gibt es vielleicht einen Grund dafür (*is there perhaps a reason for that*)?

B. Ein kurzer Bericht
Write a short report about what holidays your partner celebrates, how, what his/her favorite holiday is and why. What holidays does his/her family not celebrate? Do you celebrate the same holidays?

Aktivität 17. Was feiern wir?

There are several greeting cards below. Read each of them, and decide what occasion it was sent for (birthday, wedding, New Years Eve invitation, Christmas, etc.), who sent it and who the addressee is. Take notes on important, useful and fun expressions that are used, especially on what to wish and how to say it!

A.

> Köln, den 13. 10. 2006
> Lieber Marc, liebe Jessica,
> wir wünschen Euch alles
> Gute zur Hochzeit, ein
> schönes Fest und natürlich
> eine rosige Zukunft!!!
> Wir trinken hier in der Ferne
> ein Glas Sekt auf Euch!
> Liebe Grüße ...

Gelegenheit: _____   Ort (Stadt): _____

an: _____   Datum: _____

von: _____

nützliche Ausdrücke: _____

Why are both „Lieber" and „Liebe" included? What are the people drinking from afar (*in der Ferne*)?

Das ist eine deutsch-amerikanische Hochzeitsgesellschaft.

B.

Card text:

ETTLINGEN MAI 2008

LIEBE CARLA,

WIR WÜNSCHEN DIR ZU DEINEM 30. GEBURTSTAG GLÜCK, GESUNDHEIT UND DASS ALL DEINE WÜNSCHE IN ERFÜLLUNG GEHEN.

BLEIB WIE DU BIST!

ICH BIN FROH, DASS ICH DICH KENNE, UND ICH DENKE OFT AN DICH.

HAB EINEN SCHÖNEN TAG MIT DEINEN LIEBEN.

ES GRÜßEN DICH GANZ LIEB UND SCHICKEN DIR 1000 KÜSSE

Gesundheit – good hea[lth]
Wünsche – wishes
bleib – stay
dich kenne – know you
schicken dir – sending y[ou]

Gelegenheit: _____   Ort (Stadt): _____

an: _____   Datum: _____

von: _____

nützliche Ausdrücke: _____

What is „... [wir] schicken dir 1000 Küsse?" And what do you think the abbreviation u. stands for in the closing line?

What do you think is the significance of the Marienkäfer (the ladybug) on this card? Check your answer against a few different sources on the Internet. Is there a similar symbol in your own culture?

C.

Oldenburg, im Juli 99

Liebe Sarah,

wir gratulieren Dir ganz ♥-lich zum Geburtstag und wünschen Dir von Herzen alles Liebe und Gute.

Wir wünschen Dir noch einen schönen Urlaub und hoffen, daß Dir Dein Aufenthalt in Deutschland immer in guter Erinnerung bleiben wird.

Beeta & Wolli

von Herzen
    – with all our heart;
einen schönen Urlaub
    – a good vacation;
dein Aufenthalt in Deutschland
    – your stay in Germany;
in guter Erinnerung
    – will be a happy memory

Gelegenheit: _____   Ort (Stadt): _____

an: _____   Datum: _____

von: _____   What does „♥-lich" mean? _____

nützliche Ausdrücke: _____

D.

HERZLICHEN GLÜCKWUNSCH ZUM GEBURTSTAG!

Lieber Kilian!
Viele liebe Grüße von Oma und Opa aus Deutschland.
Natürlich auch von Sandrin.
Wir wünschen dir viel Spaß beim Lesen!

Tausend Küsse aus Deutschland!
Wir haben euch lieb!

'Hedgehog' by Peter Lavery © Masterfile 2003
Design Copyright The Art Group Limited. Made in England. A658
© Inter IKEA Systems B.V. 2004   IKEA

Gelegenheit: _____   Ort (Stadt): _____

an: _____   Datum: _____

von: _____

nützliche Ausdrücke: _____

E.

Justinchen

tine.zulla@web.de

Anke

ankejz@web.de

AUTHENTISCH

Ohne Dich ist Weihnachten nur halb so schön.

Sheepcards gibt's bei www.sheepworld.de

Meine liebste Jussi-Maus,

wieder ein Weihnachten ohne dich... und Schnee gibt's auch nur auf der Karte... Ich vermisse Dich und wünsche Dir und Micha wunderschöne Weihnachten! Rutscht gut ins neue Jahr.

Liebste Grüße aus dem wilden Westen in das idyllische Rheinland, Anke

Mehr Empfänger   Extras   E-Card absenden

Gelegenheit: _____   Ort (Stadt): _____

an: _____   Datum: _____

von: _____

nützliche Ausdrücke: _____

F.

Nachricht

Hallo Ihr Alle,
Was?   Sommerfest, Life, Freunde
Wo?   bei Connie & Lucas; Sanderring 8.
Wann?   Samstagabend von 18 Uhr bis...
Wie?   Grillen, Tanzen, Gesellschaftsspiele

Wir hoffen, dass ihr kommt!

Bis Samstag,

Connie & Lucas

Einladung zum Grillabend

Gelegenheit: _____   Ort (Stadt): _____

an: _____   Datum: _____

von: _____

nützliche Ausdrücke: _____

Review the greeting cards on the last few pages and summarize your findings:

Gelegenheit	Geburtstags- karten	Hochzeits- glückwünsche	Einladung auf eine Party	Weihnachts- karte
Anrede		Lieber (m)/Liebe (f)		
Wünsche				Fröhliche Weihnachten!
Abschied				
Andere Details	Datum, Ort		wann, wo	

Aktivität 18. Grußkarte schreiben: Jetzt sind Sie dran!

Go to http://www.sheepworld.de, http://www.gruesse.de or http://www.bewegte-grusskarten.de and write a greeting card to your instructor, another student or to a friend (in German, of course ☺). Make sure you include the important information you outlined in the previous exercise (date, greeting, body of text, including the event-appropriate wishes and a closing line, etc.).

Aktivität 19. Ihre Lieblingsfeiertage

What are your "Top 3 Holidays"? Why are they your favorties and why are they particularly important to you? Why do you like them so much? When and how do you celebrate them?

A.

B.

C.

Aktivität 20. Feiertag: ein Gedicht zum Feiern

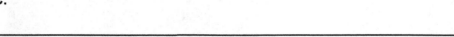

A. Feiertag

Which words (nouns, verbs, adjectives, adverbs) do you associate with the term *Feiertag*?
Write down as many words that begin with the different letters found in *Feiertag* as you can think of. Work together with other students for improved creativity. Have a poetry reading at the end. You get extra points if you can make anything rhyme!

F

E

I   *ich bin glücklich, Imagination, idyllisch, individuell*

E

R

T

A

G

B. Was ist Ihr Lieblingsfeiertag?

Write a second poem, this time dedicated to your favorite holiday. Describe it with two adjectives, three verbs, a phrase or expression, and close your poem with a synonym or another word that you closely associate with this holiday. This is called a cinquain poem.

MEIN LIEBLINGSFEIERTAG

Mein Lieblingsfeiertag ist	
Zwei Adjektive, die diesen Feiertag beschreiben	
Drei Verben, im Zusammenhang mit dem Feiertag	
Ein Ausdruck, Redewendung Satz/Satzteil – a short phrase or sentence that describes the holiday	
Ein Wort: ein Synonym für den Feiertag, eine Definition	

Man soll die Feste feiern, wie sie fallen.

Aktivität 21. Harald: Wie und wo kann man gut feiern?

Watch Harald's *Sprache im Kontext* video „Feiern in Austin" and answer the following questions. What does he say about Oktoberfest? Which cities in the world does he think are the best places to party?

(QR 5.21 p.247)

A. Was erzählt Harald über das Oktoberfest?

- Geht Harald gern aufs Oktoberfest? Warum/warum nicht?

- Wann findet das Oktoberfest statt?

- Wer geht aufs Oktoberfest und wer geht nicht?

B. In welchen Städten kann man, laut Harald, gut feiern?

Die Freunde auf dem Foto trinken aus einem *Maßkrug*. „Das Maß", so nennt man in Süddeutschland nämlich ein 1-Liter Glas oder einen Bierkrug aus dem ausschließlich Bier getrunken wird.

Aktivität 22. Peter und Mario: Feiertage in Bayern

Watch the two *Sprache im Kontext* videos with Peter and Mario and listen for the following information: How and why does Peter think his family's Christmas celebration is different from how other Germans celebrate it? What does Mario say about holidays in Southern and Northern Germany?

(QR 5.22 p.247)
(QR 5.23 p.247)

A. Peter feiert Weihnachten

1. Woher stammt Peters Familie ursprünglich? Seit wann lebt er in Deutschland?

2. An welchem Tag feiert Peters Familie Weihnachten? Und wann schmückt seine Familie den Tannenbaum?

3. Was isst Peters Familie an Heiligabend? Kreisen Sie alle Speisen ein, die Peters Familie isst:

Weißwurst	*Brezeln*
Fisch (besonders Karpfen)	*Gans (in Norddeutschland)*
süßer Senf	*Maultaschen (a pasta filled with spinach and/or meat)*
Sauerkrautsalat mit Pilzen	*Rote-Beete-Suppe*

4. Was passiert an Heiligabend? Stellen Sie die folgenden Aktivitäten in die richtige Reihenfolge:

_____ Man isst Abendessen.

_____ Man packt die Geschenke aus (die Bescherung).

_____ Man macht alles sauber (spült das Geschirr ab).

_____ Die Familie singt Weihnachtslieder.

5. Was essen die Bayern (laut Peter) typischerweise zu Weihnachten? Und was isst man in Norddeutschland?

Zum Nachdenken:

Are holidays determined in your country state by state (or county by county) or at the national level? What does Mario say is the relationship between being Catholic (as a state) and the number of holidays celebrated? Which other two holidays does Mario mention? Why is it important to rest on Christmas night, according to Mario (very tongue-in-cheek, of course!)?

B. Mario: deutsche Feiertage: Which word goes where?
Complete the text with the words in the box to make it meaningful again.
(QR 5.23
p.247)

Feiertage	Weihnachts(feier)tag	Hamburg
darf	Wochen	am 24. 12.
groß	die Bescherung	Freunde
fit zu sein	1990/1989	gemütlich
am 3. Oktober	um 16-17 Uhr	acht

In Deutschland sind _____ Ländersache. Das heißt, dass jedes Bundesland

seine eigenen Feiertage bestimmen _____. Hier zum Beispiel, in Bayern, gibt

es die meisten Feiertage. _____ an der Zahl.

Im nördlichen _____, da es nicht so streng katholisch ist wie hier, gibt es

weniger. Ich glaube, es sind um die fünf Feiertage.

Ostern, zum Beispiel, wird hier ziemlich _____ gefeiert, gerade im südlichen

Teil von Bayern, und wir haben da auch noch zwei _____ Ferien. Die

Studenten leider nicht mehr, aber dafür haben wir kurz davor die Semesterferien. Zudem gibt es

noch Feiertage, der Tag der Deutschen Einheit _____, dieser ist bestimmt

worden, als Ost- – also die ehemalige DDR Ostdeutschland – und die BRD, die Bundesrepublik

Deutschland _____ beziehungsweise _____

zusammengeführt (*connected*) wurden.

Weihnachten feiern wir _____. Am 25. 12. und 26. 12. ist ausschließlich

der erste und zweite _____. Dann besuchen wir unsere Verwandten,

Bekannten und gute _____. Aber wir gehen gewöhnlich am 24. 12. in die

Kirche, ungefähr um _____ Uhr, dann essen wir mit Verwandten

zu Abend, und dann gibt es _____. Das heißt, jeder verteilt an den

anderen Verwandten die Geschenke, und danach sitzt man noch beisammen, trinkt und isst

_____. Und geht dann ins Bett, um am nächsten Tag wieder bei der Oma

oder bei anderen Verwandten weiteressen zu können.

Grimm Grammar

At home please go to the Deutsch im Blick website and read the following grammar point in *Grimm Grammar*
conversational past: regular verbs

conversational past: irregular verbs with *haben*

conversational past: irregular verbs with *sein*

verbs in the conversational past use either sein (e.g. fahren, reisen, sein) or haben (e.g., sehen, kaufen, essen).

Ich bin nach Frankfurt gefahren.
Ich habe dort viele Freunde besucht.

regular verbs take a ge- prefix and the suffix -t: ge-mach-t

irregular verbs have to be learned, as they vary in form: gegessen (essen), gelaufen (laufen), getroffen (treffen).

separable prefix verbs take the -ge- between the prefix and the stem: aus gegangen

simple past of *haben*

ich hatte
du hattest
er/sie/es hatte

wir hatten
ihr hattet
sie/Sie hatten

simple past of *sein*

ich war
du warst
er/sie/es war

wir waren
ihr wart
sie/Sie waren

Aktivität 23. Nikolaustag

Shortly before Christmas, most German children have another reason to celebrate. December 6 is *Nikolaustag*, in honor of Saint Nicholas, the fourth-century bishop. Read a brief description of how Jasmin used to celebrate this day when she was little. Does your family celebrate this holiday? If yes, do you celebrate it the same way as Jasmin?

A. Vor dem Lesen

As a first step in the reading process, scan the text and underline all the nouns and all the verbs. These are so-called content words that help you focus on the meaning of the text. Based on the words you underlined, what do you think are some key points Jasmin raises?

B. Fragen zum Text

a. Who were expecting the arrival of Nikolaus? When did he usually arrive?

b. What was done in preparation for his arrival?

c. Are Santa Clause, *der Weihnachtsmann* and *das Christkind* the same? If yes, how so? If not, how are they different (across the different cultures, across the different holidays, etc.)? You will have to research this a bit on the Internet! Hint #1: part of the answer depends on a distinction between Northern and Southern Germany. Hint #2: Jasmin's family is from the North, but her dad is from the South, and they mixed traditions a bit.

d. What were the two possible outcomes of *Nikolaus'* visit?

If children were _____ the previous year, they ...

If children were _____ the previous year, they...

Am 6. Dezember kam bei uns immer der Nikolaus. Am Abend vor dem 6. Dezember haben mein Bruder und ich immer unsere Stiefel geputzt und sie vor die Haustür gestellt. Der Nikolaus ist nämlich immer in der Nacht gekommen und hat die sauberen Stiefel mit Süßigkeiten und kleinen Geschenken gefüllt, wenn die Kinder im letzten Jahr sehr „brav" gewesen sind. Er sieht ein bisschen aus wie der Weihnachtsmann, ist aber eine ganz andere Person. Bei uns kam aber statt des Weihnachtsmanns zu Weihnachten sowieso das Christkind, daher konnte man den Nikolaus nie mit dem Weihnachtsmann verwechseln. Aber wenn man im letzten Jahr „unartig" gewesen ist oder die Stiefel nicht tadellos sauber waren, dann gab es vom Nikolaus keine Geschenke, sondern nur eine Rute. Deshalb hatten mein Bruder und ich am 5. Dezember trotz aller Vorfreude auch immer etwas Angst, dass der Nikolaus uns nur eine Rute bringen würde. Zum Glück ist das jedoch nie vorgekommen!

Nützliche Wörter:

die Stiefel – boots	*statt* – instead
daher – therefore	*verwechseln* – mix up
tadellos – impeccable (here: *clean*)	
eine Rute – a smallish branch of a birch tree, used for whipping someone	
trotz aller Vorfreude – in spite of our anticipation	

Aktivität 24. Stille Nacht

Did you know that one of the most popular "American" Christmas carols was originally written in the early 19th century by an Austrian priest – Joseph Mohr, from Salzburg – and set to music by Franz Xaver Gruber, an Austrian elementary school teacher? This song celebrates the *Christkind's* birthday on December 24. In the German-speaking countries, it is the *Christkind* who brings presents, which people open on *Heiligabend* (the evening of the 24th). His assistants are angels. There is no specific *Aktivität* to go with this song; just sing along and enjoy! You can hear the music on wikipedia at:

http://en.wikipedia.org/wiki/Stille_Nacht

STILLE NACHT
Text: Joseph Mohr, 1816/1818

Stille Nacht, heilige Nacht,
Alles schläft; einsam wacht
Nur das traute, hochheilige Paar.
Holder Knabe im lockigen Haar,
Schlaf in himmlischer Ruh!
Schlaf in himmlischer Ruh!

Stille Nacht, heilige Nacht,
Hirten erst kundgemacht
Durch der Engel Halleluja,
Tönt es laut von fern und nah:
Christ, der Retter ist da!
Christ, der Retter ist da!

Stille Nacht, heilige Nacht,
Gottes Sohn, o wie lacht
Lieb' aus deinem göttlichen Mund,
Da uns schlägt die rettende Stund'.
Christ, in deiner Geburt!
Christ, in deiner Geburt!

Musik: Franz Xaver Gruber, 1818

Aktivität 25. Lieder & Musik

Tommy Engel – Du bes Kölle. Another very popular celebration in the German-speaking countries is *Karneval*. Köln is especially famous for its celebration of this festival and its *Kölsche Lieder*. Go to the *Deutsch im Blick website* and download the activities under „Lieder & Musk". What do you learn about Köln, *Karneval* and *Kölsch*?

Aktivität 26. Deutsche und Amerikaner: Wie haben sie Geburtstag gefeiert?

One of the most exciting days for many people is their birthday. Different people celebrate in different ways, obviously, and apparently the differences are not across cultures, but across individuals. Watch the interview videos and take notes on how these students celebrated their birthdays the last time: With whom? What did they do at the party? What did they eat, drink, listen to?

A. Die Amerikaner haben so gefeiert ...

Hassan hat _____ Geburtstag.

Das letzte Mal hat er so gefeiert:

(QR 5.24 p.247)

Erin hat _____ Geburtstag.

Das letzte Mal hat sie so gefeiert:

(QR 5.25 p.247)

Sara hat _____ Geburtstag.

Das letzte Mal hat sie so gefeiert:

(QR 5.26 p.247)

B. Und die Deutschen haben so gefeiert ...

(QR 5.27 p.247)

Jan hat _____ Geburtstag.

Das letzte Mal hat er so „gefeiert":

Evas Mutter hatte gerade (*just had*) Geburtstag.

Sie haben ihren Geburtstag so gefeiert:

(QR 5.28 p.247)

Eva hat _____ Geburtstag.

Sie wird (*will*) so feiern:

Das letzte Mal – letztes Jahr – hat sie so gefeiert:

Aktivität 27. Auf der Party

What exactly did Berna, Eva and Jan do on their birthdays? Watch Eva and Jan's clips „Mein Geburtstag" and Berna's clip „Mein Lieblingsfeiertag" and write down all the verbs they used to tell their stories.

(QR 5.27 p.247) (QR 5.14 p.247)

A. Damals

> haben gefeiert
>
> war
>
> sind gekommen

B. Später

Now listen to the part in Eva's video in which she talks about how she was going to celebrate her birthday. Write down all the verbs Eva uses to tell her story.

C. Der Unterschied

What did you notice about the formation of the verbs to talk about the past, on one hand, and to talk about the future, on the other?

> To talk about the past, you ...
>
> To talk about the present, you ...
>
> To talk about the future, you ...

Grimm Grammar

At home please read the following grammar point on the *Grimm Grammar* website.

conversational past: mixed verbs

a small group of verbs take the *ge-* prefix in the conversational past, but also have vowel changes (like strong verbs):

bringen → gebracht
denken → gedacht
kennen → gekannt
nennen → genannt
wissen → gewusst

conversational past: -ieren verbs

In the conversational past verbs with *-ieren* take only the suffix *-t*, but not the *ge-* prefix: *studiert, informiert.*

Aktivität 28. Sprache im Kontext: Mario: Mein Geburtstag
Watch Mario's clip in which he describes how he and his friends celebrated his birthday.
(QR 5.29 p.247)

A. Und alle waren da!
When is his birthday? Who all came and what did they bring?

1. Wann hat Mario Geburtstag?

2. Wie alt ist er gerade geworden?

3. Am Wochenende nach Marios Geburtstag hat man groß gefeiert. Wer hat die Party gegeben (diese Person ist „der Gastgeber")?

4. Und was hat der Gastgeber für die Party mitgebracht?

5. Wer ist zur Party gekommen (diese Leute sind „die Gäste")?

   a. Und was haben diese Leute zur Party mitgebracht?

   b. Wie hat Mario seine Party gefunden?

   c. Was hat er mit seinen Gästen gemacht (angeschaut/gespielt)?

B. Und wie ist es bei Ihnen?
Now think about birthday parties for you and your friends and answer the following questions.

1. Wer gibt die Geburtstagsparty – das Geburtstagskind oder seine Freunde?

2. Was bereitet der Gastgeber/die Gastgeberin für die Party vor?

3. Was machen die Gäste für die Party?

4. Stellen Sie sich mal vor (imagine) … Sie sprechen nun mit Mario über Geburtstagspartys und er fragt:„Wie ist es bei dir?" Welche Gemeinsamkeiten (similarities) mit seiner Beschreibung können Sie fnden? Welche Unterschiede gibt es zwischend er Art (the way in which), wie er und Sie Geburtstag feiern?

5. Und dann fragt Mario:„Wie ihr feiert, ist das typisch in Amerika?" Scheiben Sie eine Antwort auf und besprechen Sie Ihre Antwort mit anderen Kommilitonen. Gibt es überhaupt einen „typisch" amerikanischen Geburtstag?

Aktivität 29. Wer hat die coolste Oma?

Use the statements to figure out whose grandmother gives them what present for their birthday and what hair color their grandmother has. You can work alone or with a partner – try to be the fastest in the class to figure out puzzle. Read the statements and mark the boxes with a "+" if the answer is „Ja" and "-" if the answer is „Nein". Write your findings in the table provided below.

	Omas					Haarfarbe					Geburtstagsgeschenk				
	Oma Hanna	Oma Roswitha	Oma Helga	Oma Angela	Oma Gertrud	lila	grau	schwarz	silber	weiß	€ 10	Auto	Pullover	Schokolade	Teddybär
Tina															
Peter															
Anna															
Susi															
Sebastian															
€ 10															
Auto															
Pullover															
Schokolade															
Wii															
lila															
grau															
schwarz															
silber															
weiß															

- Oma Helga hat silberne Haare.
- Die Oma mit den schwarzen Haaren schenkt ihrem Enkelkind Schokolade. Ihr Enkelkind ist ein Mädchen.
- Oma Hanna schenkt ihrem Enkelkind einen Teddybär zum Geburtstag. Sebastian ist nicht ihr Enkelsohn.

- Susis Oma Roswitha hat seit ihrem letzten Friseurtermin lila Haare. Sie schenkt Susi kein Geld zum Geburtstag.
- Peters Oma hat keine grauen Haare.
- Tina bekommt einen Pullover zu ihrem Geburtstag geschenkt.
- Oma Angela hat einen Enkelsohn und keine Enkeltochter.

	Oma	Omas Haarfarbe	Geburtstagsgeschenk
Tina			
Peter			
Anna			
Susi			
Sebastian			

Aktivität 30. Feiern an der Schule

Young German people love parties! They have massive birthday celebrations, and find any opportunity they can to have a party. Including with schoolmates and their classes. Here are two short blog entries from „Susis Bayernchronik", in which she relates two parties she recently attended. Read the entries and answer the questions below.

	Blogeintrag #1	**Blogeintrag #2**
Titel & Datum *(do you recognize parts of the title words?)*		
Schlüsselwörter *(key words)* – *Wörter, die ich kenne*		
Auf diesen Wörtern basiert das Thema des Blogs:		

15.05.2008   **Katrins und Susis Volljährigkeitsfeier**

Katrin und ich sind gerade 18 geworden! Denn man bis jetzt immer nur mit den Eltern gefeiert hat, wollten wir wirklich was anderes machen! Was *dürfen* wir erst *jetzt* machen? Wählen, Führerschein machen, Alkohol trinken (ohne Eltern). Denn es ist ja unmöglich in der Mitte Mai wählen zu gehen, mussten Autofahren und Alkohol reichen – nicht zur gleichen Zeit! Also, Katrin und ich haben einen kleinen Ausflug gemacht, und von Fürstenfeldbruck nach München gefahren. Wir haben dort einen Stadtbummel gemacht, haben neue Klamotten gekauft und dann später sind wir mit den Kumpels – fast 50 Leuten – bei unseren Cousins Udo und Lucas gefeiert! Wir haben die Nacht durchgetanzt und auch ziemlich viel getrunken, man könnte sagen zu viel. Wir sind erst gegen sechs Uhr schlafen gegangen! Solch einen Kater hab ich noch nie gehabt. Wir haben dann den ganzen Samstag bei Udo und Lucas verbracht, bis 3 Uhr am Nachmittag geschlafen. Später haben wir mit ihnen Filme angeschaut und Pizza gegessen. Sonntagmorgen haben wir amerikanische Pfannkuchen gemacht – mit kleinen Würstchen und Bratkartoffeln – und danach sind wir nach Hause gekommen, und haben mit unseren Eltern und Großeltern wieder gefeiert, Geschenke geöffnet und sind spazieren gegangen! Das Wochenende war echt Klasse!

nützliche Wörter: *wirklich* – really; *wählen* – vote; *der Führerschein* – drivers license; *reichen* – be enough; *der Ausflug* – excursion, daytrip; *der Stadtbummel* – walk around the city; *die Klamotten* – clothes (slang); *die Kumpel* – friends (slang); *der Kater* – hangover

Fragen zum Text

a. What did Katrin and Susi celebrate?

b. What were the three things they were allowed to do as 18-year-olds?

c. Where do they live, and where did they go for their birthday?

d. How did they spend their birthday each day from Friday to Sunday?

10.08.2008 **Die Abiturfeier**

Heute war wieder ein wichtiger Tag in unserem Leben: Wir hatten die Abiturfeier am Gymnasium. Endlich sind wir frei! Die Zeremonie war in der Aula, selbst der Bürgermeister ist gekommen und hat eine Rede gehalten (ziemlich lang und langweilig). Dann haben wir noch die Abiturrede vom Gymnsiumdirektor gehört. Wie jedes Jahr hat der Schulchor wieder gesungen und das Schulorchester gespielt. *Gaudeamus Igitur* und solche *„Klassiker"*. Nachher hat die 13. Klasse die Abiturstreiche begonnen: Das Thema war „Deutschland sucht den Superlehrer" (Nach der Show „Deutschland sucht den Superstar" nach „American Idol"). Zuerst haben die Physiklehrer Experimente geführt – natürlich hat nichts funktioniert! Das hat allen Studenten sehr gut gefallen, besonders den Unterstufenschülern! Danach hat es den Top-Modelwettbewerb gegeben: Gewinner war Frau Lehmann, im 9. Monat schwanger! Die Musiklehrer haben gesungen, Klavier oder Gitarre gespielt. Die 13. Klasse hatte mehrere Proben für sie: Rap, Country, Beatles und sogar Hip-Hop! Am Abend haben wir weiter gefeiert, getanzt, und über die nächsten Monate gequatscht. Alles hat sehr gut geklappt! Katrin und ich haben jede Menge wunderschöne Erinnerungen gesammelt – Fotos habe ich zum Facebook uploadet! Bis dann sind weitere Links zu anderen Abifeiern hier zu finden:

Weitere Links:
Regensburg Abiturfeier:
http://www.youtube.com/watch?v=J7XnsSf3fus

---

nützliche Wörter:
die Aula – auditorium in school;
eine Rede – speech;
der Streich – trick (in this context it usually involves poking fun at teachers);
die Unterstufenschüler – lower classmen, e.g. freshmen;
der Wettbewerb – competition;
der Gewinner – winner;
schwanger – pregnant;
die Probe – challenge (like medieval knights);
die Erinnerung – memory

Fragen zum Text

a. What did Katrin and Susi celebrate here?

b. Who all gave speeches, and who performed what?

c. What 3 events did the teachers have to compete in?

d. How did Katrin und Susi spend the evening?

Aktivität 31. Jetzt sind Sie dran ... Ihre letzte Party

Think about the last party that you went to, then answer the following questions yourself, then use them to interview at least two of your fellow students.

> *Welche Aktivitäten machen Ihnen Spaß?*
>
> *Was war die letzte Party, auf der Sie gewesen sind?*
>
> *Wer hat mit Ihnen gefeiert? · Was haben Sie gefeiert?*
>
> *Was haben Sie alles gemacht? · Wo war die Party?*

	ich	Partner #1	Partner #2
Was war die letzte Party, auf der Sie gewesen sind?			
Wer hat mit Ihnen gefeiert?			
Was haben Sie gefeiert?			
Was haben Sie alles gemacht?			
Wo war die Party?			

Aktivität 32. Eine unvergessliche Party ...

Write a blog entry (ca 250 words) about a truly memorable party you have attended or organized. Use the information you took notes on in the previous exercise and incorporate some of the vocabulary, expressions you learned from your fellow students as well! If this party was memorable for you, make sure it is memorable for your reader as well! Spice up your description with interesting details and varied rhetorical structure as well (e.g., don't always use the subject – verb – direct object pattern in the sentences, do ask a question of the reader, do use some exclamations, etc.).

Eine unvergessliche Party

bitte Photo uploaden

Meine Freunde und ich

einladen
die ganze Nacht
tanzen
hat uns viel Spaß gemacht!
zusammen feiern
wir haben uns verkleidet
tolle Erinnerungen
bei uns zu Hause
gemütlich

bitte Photo uploaden

Um Mitternacht beim Tanzen

Aussprache

Please go to the Deutsch im Blick website, Kapitel 5

Aussprache
Diphthongs and Triphthongs

This chapter takes a closer look at sound- and letter-combinations in German involving vowels. Diphthongs, as the name suggests, consist of two vowels, while triphthongs consist of three vowels.

1. Diphthongs

A diphthong is a vocalic double sound. This means that one vowel "merges" with the other. The following are the three diphthongs in German: *au, ei/ai,* and *eu/äu*. On the chapter website, under „Aussprache", you can click on the icon to hear the pronunciation of these words.

Diphthong	Phonetic Symbol	Examples		
au	[aʊ]	das Haus (house)	die Maus (mouse)	laufen (to run)
ai/ei	[aɪ]	das Einzelkind (single child)	Freitag (Friday)	im Mai (in May)
eu/äu	[ɔy]	das Neujahr (New Year's Eve)	deutsch	du läufst (you run)

There is one more diphthong that occurs pretty much in one interjection only: [ʊɪ] as in *Pfui!* (yuck!)

Note the difference between the *ie* and the *ei* sequence! The former is pronounced like the 'e' in the English "even", whereas the latter is pronounced like an "i":

ie
lieben (to love)
die Geliebte (beloved)
die Schwiegermutter (mother-in-law)
das Genie (genius)
das Bier

ei
bleiben (to stay)
der Freitag (Friday)
schweigen (to stay quiet)
langweilig (boring)
heiraten (to marry)

Point of interest: You may encounter some dialects in Germany, which have a few additional diphthongs than the German you have been learning in *Deutsch im Blick.* For example, High-Bavarian has two additional diphthongs: *ua* and *oa*.

Diphthong	Example from High-Bavarian
ua	Bua – "Bub" (boy)
oa	zwoa – "zwei" (two)

2. Triphthongs

A triphthong is a sound that consists of three vowel sounds and forms exactly one syllable – as you can imagine, the number of triphthongs in standard German is very limited. When you work on this section on the internet, click on the icon below to hear the pronunciation of the example words.

Triphthong	Phonetic Symbol	Examples		
iau/jau	[jaʊ]	Miau (meow)	jauchzen (to cheer)	jaulen (yip)
aue	[aʊɛ]	klauen (steal)	trauen (to trust)	schauen (to see)
aua	[aʊa]	Aua (ouch)		

In Standard German, triphthongs hardly exist because they got simplified over time into diphthongs and simple vowels. However, as with diphthong, triphthongs do appear more often in certain dialects like Styrian (Austrian dialect) or Bernese Swiss German.

Point of interest:

There is another subgroup of vowel clusters that are formed by a diphthong plus a dark *schwa* (remember *Kapitel* 4?). They inevitably include an "e" and an "r" :

[aiɐ]	die Eier (eggs), die Feier (festivity)
[ɔiɐ]	euer (yours), das Feuer (fire)
[aʊɐ]	Bauer (farmer), sauer (sour, angry), dauern (to last)

Finally, here are some fun tongue-twisters for you to practice with!

Bierbrauer Bauer braut braunes Bier.
Beer brewer Bauer brews brown beer.

Der Schweizer Schweißer schwitzt und schweißt.
Der Schweizer Schwitzer schweißt und schwitzt.
Schwitzend schweißt der Schweizer Schweißer.
"The Swiss welder sweats and welds. The Swiss sweater welds and sweats.
Sweating, welds the Swiss welder."

Wenn Fliegen hinter Fliegen fliegen, dann fliegen Fliegen Fliegen nach.
"When flies fly behind flies, then flies fly after flies."

Wenn meine Braut Blaukraut klaut,
dann ist sie eine Blaukrautklaubraut.
"If my bride steals red cabbage,
then she's a red cabbage-stealing bride."

Hinter Herbert Hausmanns Hecke hocken heute hundert Hasen.
"Behind Herbert Hausmann's hedge, there are a 100 rabbits hiding out."

Weil lustige Leute laufend lachen, lachen lustige Leute auch beim Laufen.
"Because funny people laugh running, funny people also laugh while they run."

Mit keiner Kleie und keinem Keim kann kein kleines Korn keimen.
"Without any bran and seed, not a single little seed can germinate (grow)."

From http://german.about.com/od/pronunciation/a/tonguetwisters.htm
http://germanteaching.com/german/tongue-twisters

WebQuests

Go to the *Deutsch im Blick* website to access this chapter's "WebQuests".

1. *Flickr as a segue to understanding about family and celebrations.*
2. *What pertains to family-life according to a Swiss website*

Meinungsumfragen

Go to the *Deutsch im Blick* website to access the „Meinungsumfragen" on the subject of *Familie, Feste und Feiertage.*

In this chapter they deal with friends, family and celebrations (of course!).

Die Familie (Familien)	The family
der Bruder (Brüder)	brother
der Cousin (Cousins)	cousin (male)
das Einzelkind (-kinder)	only child
die Eltern (only plural)	parents
das Enkelkind (-kinder)	grandchild
das Familienmitglied (-mitglieder)	family member
die Frau (Frauen)	wife (also: woman)
die Geschwister (plural only)	siblings
die Großmutter (-mütter), die Oma (Omas)	grandmother
der Großvater (-väter), der Opa (Opas)	grandfather
das Kind (Kinder)	child
Das ist kinderleicht!	that's easy/that's a breeze!
kindisch	childish
kindlich	childlike
die Cousine (Cousinen)	female cousin
Mama und Papa (Mamas und Papas)	Mom and Dad
der Mann (Männer)	husband (also: man)
die Mutter (Mütter)	mother
mütterlicherseits	on my mother's side
der Neffe (Neffen)	nephew
die Nichte (Nichten)	niece
der Onkel (Onkel)	uncle
der Pate/die Patin (Paten/Patinnen)	godfather/godmother
der Schwager (Schwager)	brother-in-law
die Schwägerin (Schwägerinnen)	sister-in-law
die Schwester (Schwestern)	sister
die Schwiegermutter (-mütter)	mother in-law
der Schwiegersohn (-söhne)	son in-law
der Sohn (Söhne)	son
die Stiefmutter (-mütter)	step mother
der Stiefvater (-väter)	step father
die Tante (Tanten)	aunt
die Tochter (Töchter)	daughter
die Urgroßmutter (-mütter)	great grandmother
der Urgroßvater (-väter)	great grandfather
der Vater (Väter)	father
väterlicherseits	on my father's side
der/die Verlobte (Verlobten)	fiance/fiancee
der/die Verwandte (Verwandten)	male/female relative
der Zwillingsbruder (-brüder)	twin (male)
die Zwillingsschwester (-schwestern)	twin (female)
der Zwilling (die Zwillinge)	twin

Wortschatz
Vorbereitung

(QR 5.1 p.247)

Wie ist meine Familie?	What is my family like?
alt	old
ärgerlich	aggravating
blöd	dumb
böse	angry
cool	cool
Er ist ein Depp.	He is a fool.
doof	dumb
dumm	stupid
frech	bold/fresh
fürsorglich	caring
gesprächig	talkative
intelligent	intelligent
jung	young
klug	smart/sharp
komisch	strange
kühl	cold/standoffish
langweilig	boring
liebevoll	loving
lustig	funny
mufflig	grumpy
nervig	annoying/a pain
(un)reif	(im)mature
schweigsam	quiet
ruhig	calm
schwerhörig	hard of hearing
schüchtern	shy
sympathisch	likeable
unerträglich	unbearable/intolerable
unmöglich	impossible
verdrießlich	irksome
verrückt	crazy
witzig	funny

Feiertage & Feste	Holidays & Celebrations
Allerheiligen	All Saints' Day
Aschermittwoch	Ash Wednesday, day after Fat Tuesday
der Fasching	carnival (in southern Germany)
der (religiöse) Feiertag	(religious) holiday
die Ferien (only plural)	holidays/vacation
Winterferien	Winter vacation/holiday
Sommerferien	Summer vacation/holiday
Semesterferien	vacation period between semesters
der Geburtstag (-tage)	birthday
Geburtstag feiern	to celebrate one's birthday
eine Geburtstagsparty (-partys)	birthday party
(der) Karfreitag	Good Friday
(der) Karneval	carnival (in Northern / Western Germany)
das Kostüm (Kostüme)	disguise
ein Kostüm anziehen	to wear a costume
sich verkleiden	to dress up in a costume
der Nationalfeiertag	national holiday
(das) Neujahr	New Year's Day
Prost Neujahr!	Happy New Year!
(die) Ostern	Easter
Frohe Ostern!	Happy Easter!
(das) Pesach/Passah	Passover
Pfingsten	Pentecost
(der/das) Silvester	New Year's Eve
(der) Tag der Arbeit (1. Mai)	Labor Day
(der) Tag der deutschen Einheit (3. Oktober)	Unification Day (Oct. 3rd)
(das) Weihnachten	Christmas

Frohe/Fröhliche Weihnachten!	Merry Christmas!
der Weihnachtsbaum (Weihnachtsbäume)	Christmas tree
den Weihnachtsbaum schmücken	to decorate the Christmas tree
das Weihnachtslied (Weihnachtslieder)	Christmas carol
der Weihnachtsmarkt (Weihnachtsmärkte)	Christmas market
der Christkindlmarkt (Christkindlmärkte)	typical name for christmas markets in southern Germany

Feiern & Beziehungen	**Celebrating & Relationships**
anrufen	call
besuchen	visit
die Blume (die Blumen)	flower
das Datum	date (as in day)
einladen	to invite
die Einladung (Einladungen)	the invitation
die Feier (Feiern)	celebration
feiern	to celebrate
das Fest (Feste)	festival
der Freund (Freunde)	male friend, boyfriend
der Freundeskreis (-kreise)	circle of friends
die Freundin (Freundinnen)	female friend, girlfriend
die Geburt (Geburten)	birth
das Geburtstagskind (-kinder)	birthday boy/girl
gern haben	to like
das Geschenk (die Geschenke)	gift, present
das Gesellschaftsspiel (-spiele)	board games
gratulieren	congratulate
die Grußkarte (-karten)	greeting card
hassen	to hate
heiraten	to marry
die Hochzeit (Hochzeiten)	wedding
die Kerze (Kerzen)	candle
(das) Konfetti (no plural)	confetti
der Kontakt (Kontakte)	contact
küssen	to kiss
lieben	to love
mögen	to like
der Namenstag (-tage)	patron saint's day
die Party (Partys)	party
eine Party geben/schmeißen	to throw a party
der Polterabend (-abende)	prewedding bash
der Plastikbecher (Plastikbecher)	plastic cups, glasses
sich scheiden lassen	to get a divorce
schmücken	to decorate
schreiben	write
der Sekt (no plural)	champagne
der Stammbaum (-bäume)	family tree
stattfinden	to take place
die Serviette (Servietten)	napkins
stammen aus	to come from
die Geburtstagstorte (-torten)	the birthday cake
die Tradition (Traditionen)	tradition
vermeiden	to avoid
vermissen	to miss
verstehen	to understand
die Zeremonie (Zeremonien)	ceremony

QR Codes

5.1	5.2	5.3	5.4	5.5	5.6
Wortschatz	05_29_intro_ feiertage	05_01_int_bg_ familie	05_02_int_ju_ familie	05_03_int_ag_ familie	05_04_int_hm_ familie
5.7	5.8	5.9	5.10	5.11	5.12
05_05_int_ec_ familie	05_06_int_sco_ familie	05_07_int_scl_ familie	05_08_int_ek_ familie	05_09_int_ph_ familie	05_10_int_bg_ hause
5.13	5.14	5.15	5.16	5.17	5.18
05_11_int_ju_ hause	05_12_int_bg_ feiertag	05_13_int_ek_ feiertag	05_14_int_ju_ feiertag	05_15_int_ag_ feiertag	05_16_int_sco_ feiertag
5.19	5.20	5.21	5.22	5.23	5.24
05_17_int_hm_ feiertage	05_18_int_ec_ feiertage	05_19_sik_ haraldoktoberfest	05_20_sik_ peterweihnachten	05_21_sik_ mariofeiertage	05_22_int_hm_ geburtstag
5.25	5.26	5.27	5.28	5.29	5.30
05_23_int_ec_ geburtstag	05_24_int_sco_ geburtstag	05_25_int_ju_ geburtstag	05_26_int_ek_ geburtstag	05_27_sik_ mariogeburtstag	05_28_sik_ gaudiparty

Wortschatz

- *Reisen*
- *Eine Reise buchen*
- *Unterbringungsmöglichkeite*
- *Transportmittel*
- *Reiseziele*
- *Auf einer Reise*
- *Strandurlaub*
- *Sehenswürdigkeiten und Aktivitäten*
- *Wie war dein Urlaub?*
- *Ausgewählte trennbare Verben*
- *Ausgewählte untrennbare Verben*
- *Über das Wetter sprechen*

Aussprache
- *Kapitel 6:* Auslautverhärtung and a helpful guide to recognizing German/English Cognates

Grammatik
Focus
- *Cases: Der Dativ*
- *Irregular Verbs: gefallen*
- *Irregular Verbs: geben*
- *Conversational Past of separable prefix verbs*
- *Conversational Past of inseparable prefix verbs*

Recommended
- *Verbs: Das Perfekt – Einführung*

Videos
Sprache im Kontext
- *Kerstens Flitterwochen*
- *Christines letzte Reise*
- *Mario in Skandinavien*
- *Josh reist nach Amsterda*
- *Ein Wochenende in Schottland*

6 DURCH DEUTSCHLAND UND DIE WELT REISEN

Von der Reiseplanung bis hin zum Reisebericht geht in diesem Kapitel alles ums Reisen und um das Reisewetter! Verhexte (magical) Schlösser in Heidelberg, Kneipen in Amsterdam, verlassene (abandoned) Schönheiten, bizarre Mitbringsel, Reiseberichte, leckere Schokoladentorten, Inselstädte und mehr erwarten Sie!

Nach dem Einführungsvideo geht es an die Materialien.

1. *Arbeiten Sie mit den Interviews der deutschen Muttersprachler und den Interviews der Amerikaner.*
2. *Erweitern Sie Ihren Wortschatz.*
3. *Lernen Sie mit den Videos „Sprache im Kontext" Vokabeln und Ausdrücke im kulturellen Kontext kennen.*
4. *Wenden Sie grammatische Strukturen aus Grimm Grammar besser an.*
5. *Trainieren Sie Ihre Aussprache.*
6. *Vervollständigen Sie WebQuests.*
7. *Verstehen Sie deutsche Gewohnheiten (customs, practices) durch interaktive Umfragen.*

In diesem Kapitel werden Sie viele bekannte europäische Städte und ihre Sehenswürdigkeiten kennen lernen. Sie werden auch Ihre Kenntnisse in der Reiseplanung erweitern und über Ihren Urlaub sprechen können. Sie werden auch das Wetter kommentieren lernen und Wetterberichte besser verstehen.

Vorbemerkung: Alles ist auf einmal auf Deutsch!

Congratulations! After the completion of the first five chapters your German is now good enough to switch the texts for the exercises into German! The following table should help you any time you come across a word or phrase in an exercise that you don't understand. The verbs are listed in alphabetical order. Most verbs are in the imperative; a form you will learn about in Chapter 7, but don't worry you'll still be able to understand the verbs.

auswählen to pick/to choose	Wählen Sie einen Text aus. Pick a text.
achten to pay attention	Achten Sie auf die Aussprache. Pay attention to the pronunciation.
anhören to listen to	Hören Sie sich die Interviews an. Listen to the interviews.
anschauen to look at	Schauen Sie sich das Bild an. Look at the picture.
ansehen to look at	Sehen Sie sich den Text an. Look at the text.
aufschreiben to write down	Schreiben Sie Ihre Meinung auf. Write down your opinion.
beantworten answer	Beantworten Sie folgende Fragen. Answer the following questions.
beenden to finish	Beenden Sie den Satz. Finish the sentence.
berichten to tell	Berichten Sie im Kurs von dem Erlebnis. Tell the class about the experience.
besuchen to visit	Besuchen Sie die Webseite www.berlin.de. Visit the website www.berlin.de.
betrachten to look at	Beatrachten Sie die Bilder. Look at the pictures.
bilden to create	Bilden Sie sechs Sätze. Create six sentences.
einsetzen to fill in	Setzen Sie die Verben in die Lücken ein. Fill the verbs in the blanks.
einüben to rehearse	Üben Sie den Dialog ein. Rehearse the dialog.
verfassen to create	Verfassen Sie ein eigenes Gedicht. Create your own poem.
gehen to go	Gehen Sie zur Webseite www.berlin.de. Go to the website www.berlin.de.

konzentrieren to focus	Konzentrieren Sie sich auf den Text. Focus on the text.
lesen to read	Lesen sie nachfolgenden Text. Read the following text.
nutzen to use	Nutzen Sie das Perferkt. Use the Conversational Past.
sagen to say	Sagen Sie, ob dies richtig ist. Say whether or not this is right.
schreiben to write	Schreiben Sie drei Sätze. Write three sentences.
suchen to look for	Suchen Sie einen günstigen Flug. Look for a cheap flight.
überlegen to think	Überlegen Sie, wohin Sie möchten. Think about where you want to go.
vergleichen to compare	Vergleichen Sie die Preise. Compare the prices.
vervollständigen to complete	Vervollständigen Sie die Lücken. Complete the blanks (with the verbs).
vorspielen to play/enact	Spielen Sie den Dialog vor. Enact the dialog.
vorstellen to imagine	Stellen Sie sich vor, Sie wären Sissi. Imagine you were Sissi.
wählen to pick	Wählen Sie drei der folgenden Begriffe. Pick three of the following terms.
wiederholen to repeat/ eview	Wiederholen Sie den Grammatikteil. Review the grammar-part.
zuordnen to match	Ordnen Sie den Bildern die Begriffe zu. Match the terms with the images.

This chapter helps you with unknown vocabulary in various way:

1. Boxes named „Vokabelhilfe" (*vocabulary-help*) translate or explain the underlined vocabulary.
2. An underlined German word is followed directly by its translation into English.
3. Don't worry, you will always come across a new word or phrase, but you do not need to understand each and every single word!
4. Context will help you to still make sense out of the text.
5. Apply the reading strategies you know (recognizing cognates, looking at key words before you start reading the text for detailed information, etc.).
6. Use a dictionary if you really still want to know what a word means (try: http://www.leo.org, http://www.wordreference.com or http://www.woerterbuch.info)!

Viel Spaß bei Ihren neuen Sprachabenteuern!

Online Book links

Sie können die Videoclips unter folgendem Link finden:
http://coerll.utexas.edu/dib/toc.php?k=6

Sie können die Vokabeln unter folgendem Link finden:
http://coerll.utexas.edu/dib/voc.php?k=6

Sektionen

Reisen • Traveling
Eine Reise buchen • To Book a Travel
Unterbringungsmöglichkeiten • Accomodations
Transportmittel • Means of Transportation
Reiseziele • Travel Destinations
Auf einer Reise • On a trip
Strandurlaub • Beach Vacations
Sehenswürdigkeiten und Aktivitäten • Sights to see and activities to do
Wie war dein Urlaub? • How was your vacation?
Ausgewählte trennbare Verben • Selected Seperable Prefix Verbs
Ausgewählte untrennbare Verben • Selected Inseparable Prefix Verbs
Über das Wetter sprechen • Talking about the weather

Sie können auch die Grammatikthemen aus diesem Kapitel online finden:

Während der Übungen im Kapitel werden Sie regelmäßig auf Grimm Grammar verwiesen (*referred to*). Hier sind die Grammatikthemen, die das Kapitel abdeckt (*covers*); machen Sie alle Online-Übungen, um optimal von den Übungen in diesem Arbeitsbuch (*workbook*) zu profitieren (*to profit from*).

- Cases Der Dativ   http://coerll.utexas.edu/gg/gr/cas_07.htm

- Irregular verbs   http://coerll.utexas.edu/gg/gr/vi_04.html
  gefallen   http://coerll.utexas.edu/gg/gr/vi_03.html
  geben

- Conversational Past   http://coerll.utexas.edu/gg/gr/vcp_07.htm
  of separable prefix verbs   http://coerll.utexas.edu/gg/gr/vcp_08.htm
  of inseparable prefix verbs

- Recommended: http://coerll.utexas.edu/gg/gr/vcp_01.htm
  Verbs: Das Perfekt – Einführung

A. LISTEN

Listen carefully to the pronunciation of each word or phrase in the vocabulary list.

B. REPEAT

Repeat each word or phrase *out loud* as many times as necessary until you remember it well and can recognize it as well as produce it. Make a list of the words in this chapter which you find difficult to pronounce. Your teacher may ask you to compare your list with other students in your class. Make sure to learn nouns with their correct gender!

> **Beispiel:**
> die Sprache
> fünf

C. WRITE

Write key words from the vocabulary list so that you can spell them correctly (remember that it makes a big difference whether you cross the Atlantic by ship or by sheep). You may want to listen to the vocabulary list again and write the words as they are spoken for extra practice.

D. TRANSLATION

Learn the English translation of each word or phrase. Cover the German column and practice giving the German equivalent for each English word or phrase. Next cover the English column and give the translation of each.

E. ASSOCIATIONS

Think of word associations for each category of vocabulary. (What words, both English and German, do you associate with each word or phrase on the list? Write down ten (10) associations with the vocabulary from the chapter.

> **Beispiel:**
> der Student/die Universität
> das Flugticket/das Flugzeug

F. COGNATES

Which words are *cognates?* (Cognates are words which look or sound like English words.) Watch out for *false friends*! Write down several cognates and all the false friends from the chapter, create fun sentences that illustrate similarities and differences between the English and German meanings of these words.

> **Beispiel:**
> Nacht/night
> grün/green
> False Friends: *hell* = light, bright vs. *Hölle* = hell

G. WORD FAMILIES

Which words come from word families in German that you recognize (noun, adjective, verb, adverb)? Write down as many as you find in the chapter.

> **Beispiel:**
> das Studium (noun; studies)
> der Student (noun; person)
> studieren (verb)

H. EXERCISES

Write out three (3) „Was passt nicht?" ("Odd one out") exercises. List four words, three of which are related and one that does not fit the same category. Categories can be linked to meaning, grammar, gender, parts of speech (noun, verb, adjective), etc. USE YOUR IMAGINATION! Give the reason for why the odd word does not fit. Your classmates will have to solve the puzzles you provide!

> **Beispiel:**
> grün – blau – gelb – neun
> Here *neun* does not fit, because it is a number and all the others are colors.

Wortschatz
Vorbereitung

Always learn nouns with the article!!!

These ideas are sugges tions only. Different learner have different preference and needs for learning an reviewing vocabulary. T several of these sugges tions until you find ones th work for you. Keep in min though, that knowing mar words – and knowing the well, both to recognize ar to produce – makes you more effective user of th new language.

Basiswortschatz
Core Vocabulary

The following presents a list of core vocabulary. Consider this list as the absolute minimum to focus on. As you work through the chapter you will need more vocabulary to help you talk about your own experience. To that end, a more complete vocabulary list can be found at the end of the chapter. This reference list will aid your attainment of *Kapitel 6*'s objectives.

(QR 6.1 p.300)

Die Reise	The trip
die Reise (Reisen)	trip, journey
reisen	to travel
nach	to (a location)
der Urlaub (Urlaube)	vacation

Verkehrsmittel	Transportation
das Auto (Autos)	car
der Bus (Busse)	bus
die Bahn (Bahnen)	railroad
der Bahnhof (Bahnhöfe)	train station
das Flugzeug (Flugzeuge)	airplane
der Zug (Züge)	train
der Flughafen (Flughäfen)	airport

Wie war's dort?	How was it there?
günstig	low priced/inexpensive
teuer	expensive
kurz	short
langweilig	boring
schrecklich	terrible/horrible
angenehm	pleasant
anstrengend	exhausting

Zum Einpacken/Mitbringen	To pack/bring along
das Gepäck (no plural)	luggage (suitcases)
die Kamera (Kameras)	camera
das Meer (Meere)	sea
die Muschel (Muscheln)	shell
der See (Seen)	lake
die Sehenswürdigkeit (Sehenswürdigkeiten)	landmark/object of interest
die Sonnenbrille (Sonnenbrillen)	sunglasses
die Sonnencreme (Sonnencremes)	sunscreen
der Strand (Strände)	beach

Was tun?	What to do?
ansehen	to look at/to watch
ausgeben	to spend money
bestellen	to order
entscheiden	to decide
entspannen (sich)	to relax
gefallen	to like
genießen	to enjoy
verabreden (sich)	to agree on/set (a date/an appointment)
verbringen	to spend time
verlassen	to leave (a place/person)
verlaufen (sich)	to get lost
vermissen	to miss
verpassen	to miss (the train, flight)

Über das Wetter	About the weather
das Gewitter (Gewitter)	thunderstorm
der Regen (no plural)	rain
regnen (regnete/geregnet)	to rain
der Schnee (no plural)	snow
die Sonne (sonnig)	sun (sunny)
das Wetter (no plural)	weather
der Wind (windig)	wind (windy)
die Wolke (wolkig/bewölkt)	cloud (cloudy/overcast)
heiß/warm	hot/warm
kühl/kalt	cool/ cold

Aktivität 1. Wer reist gern? Und wohin sind die amerikanischen Studenten schon gereist?

Schauen Sie sich die Videoclips „Reisen" an und schreiben Sie auf, wohin die amerikanischen Studenten schon gereist sind und wohin sie noch reisen möchten.

A. Wir reisen gern!

	Adan (QR 6.2 p.300)	Hassan (QR 6.3 p.300)	Erin (QR 6.4 p.300)	Sara (QR 6.5 p.300)	Sophia (QR 6.5 p.300)
ist schon nach _____ gereist					
möchte noch nach/in _____ reisen					

B. Nützliche Wörter & Ausdrücke

Schauen Sie sich diese Clips noch einmal an und schreiben Sie einige nützliche Wörter und Ausdrücke auf: Wie kann man über REISEN sprechen?

möchte noch besuchen

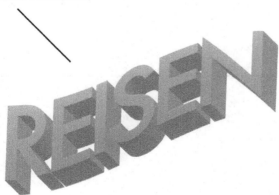

C. Und die Deutschen? Reisen sie auch gern?

Schauen Sie sich jetzt Bernas und Jans Clips an (auch „Reisen"). Was sagen sie über ihre letzten Reisen?

(QR 6.7 p.300)

Berna reist sehr gerne. Ihre letzte Reise führte sie nach Hawaii.

Ihre Reise war _____, _____ &

_____, aber nicht _____.

Berna war auf einer Konferenz, also musste sie auch ein bisschen arbeiten. Sie hatte aber genug Zeit, viele Sehenswürdigkeiten zu sehen. Welche? Was stimmt, was stimmt nicht?

Sie ist auf einen alten Vulkan gewandert (das war anstrengend!).	*richtig*	*falsch*
Sie ist schwimmen gegangen.	*richtig*	*falsch*
Sie hat Bodysurfing probiert.	*richtig*	*falsch*
Sie hat sich Surfer angeschaut.	*richtig*	*falsch*
Sie hat sich die Monumente in Pearl Harbor angeschaut.	*richtig*	*falsch*
Sie hat leider die ganze Zeit im Hotel verbracht.	*richtig*	*falsch*

(QR 6.8 p.300)

Jan reist sehr gerne, denn er

- sieht gerne andere Länder und Kulturen.
- lernt gern andere Sprachen.
- sieht sich gerne in anderen Städten um.

Vor allem reist er gern in Deutschland / Europa / den USA

Seine letzte Reise war nach _____. Dort hat er die folgenden Sehenswürdigkeiten gesehen:

1.

2.

Aktivität 2. Eine Reise planen

Lesen Sie den folgenden Text und beantworten Sie die Fragen vor und nach dem Lesen.

Grimm Gramma

A. Fragen vor dem Lesen

- Was für ein Text ist das? Prosa? Ein Dialog? Ein Gedicht? Wer sind die Hauptfiguren?

- Welche Wörter erkennen Sie schon? Streichen Sie die Wörter, die Sie schon kennen, grün an.

- Was ist Ihr erster Eindruck? Wohin möchte der Reisende fahren?

Wie Sie sehen, ist der Dativ ein wichtiger Kasus in der deutschen Sprache! Bearbeiten Sie zu Hause folgenden Grammatikteil in der *Grimm Grammar*

Dative Case
(Für mehr Hintergrund wissen lesen Sie bitte auch cases overview)

The Dative Case Is used in three main ways

1. with the indirect object of a clause or sentence (e.g., I bought *my mother* a DVD)

2. after dative prepositions (aus, ausser, bei, mit, nach seit, von, zu and with two way prepositions in some instances)

3. as the objects of dative verbs (e.g., danken, ge fallen, etc.).

Im Reisebüro

Kersten und seine Frau möchten in den Urlaub fahren. Leider haben sie nicht viel Geld und wissen nicht genau, wohin sie reisen möchten. Sie gehen deshalb in ein Reisebüro in Hannover, um sich beraten zu lassen.

Kersten betritt das Geschäft. Der Herr am Schreibtisch sagt zu ihm: „Hallo, ich bin Herr Meyer, wie kann ich Ihnen helfen?"

Kersten:	Hallo, ich heiße Kersten Müller, ich möchte eine Reise buchen!
Herr Meyer:	Prima! Bitte setzen Sie sich.
Kersten:	Danke.
Herr Meyer:	Wohin möchten Sie denn?
Kersten:	Ich weiß nicht so genau ...
Herr Meyer:	Das sollten Sie aber schon wissen! Möchten Sie an den Strand oder lieber in die Berge oder lieber in eine Großstadt?
Kersten:	Ich möchte in eine schöne Stadt! Ich bin Student, deshalb kann ich nur € 500,- ausgeben.
Herr Meyer:	Mal sehen ... Wann möchten Sie denn verreisen?
Kersten:	Im August!
Herr Meyer:	Wie wäre denn Rom? Da haben wir im Augenblick ein Sonderangebot.
Kersten:	Nein, da war ich schon und es ist dort auch sehr heiß!
Herr Meyer:	Hmm, nach Rom möchten Sie also nicht. Na gut ... Ich zeige Ihnen einmal einen Prospekt von Österreich. Wie hört sich denn Wien an? Dort ist es nicht so heiß wie in Rom!
Kersten:	Ja, das hört sich gut an! Ich liebe Lipizzaner und ich würde gerne die Show in der Spanischen Hofreitschule sehen! Was kostet das denn?
Herr Meyer:	Das kommt darauf an. Wie viele Sterne soll das Hotel denn haben?
Kersten:	Och, zwei Sterne reichen.
Herr Meyer:	Und reisen Sie allein?
Kersten:	Nein, mit meiner Frau. Und wir möchten ungefähr eine Woche bleiben.
Herr Meyer:	(recherchiert im Computer) Aha, hier haben wir was. Günstiger geht es gar nicht: Flug mit Lufthansa von Hannover nach Wien. 2** Hotel in Wien, 10 Minuten vom Zentrum entfernt, vom 13.08.2013 bis zum 20.08.2013, ohne Verpflegung. Kostet zusammen € 640,- !
Kersten:	Das ist mir zu teuer! Da gucke ich lieber zu Hause im Internet!
Herr Mayer:	Wie Sie wollen ...

Wenn man reist, reist man

nach Österreich, England Bayern, Texas, London Helsinki, Mallorca (Dat aber ohne Artikel)

in die Schweiz, die USA die Karibik (Akk.)

ins Ausland (Akk.)

auf die Seychellen, die Kanaren, eine Insel (Akk.)

---

1. Die Lipizzaner sind Pferde, die in Spaninen und Österreich sehr beliebt sind. Die meisten Lipizzaner sind weiß.
2. Die Spanische Hofreitschule ist eine bekannte Reitschule in Wien. Sie lehrt schwierige Dressurlektionen (dressage steps).

B. Fragen zum Text

- Wohin möchte Kersten reisen?
- Wie viel Geld möchte er ausgeben?
- Mit wem möchte er verreisen?
- Wie lange soll die Reise dauern?
- Welche zwei Städte erwähnt Herr Meyer als mögliche Reiseziele?
- Was für ein Angebot findet Herr Meyer für Kersten?
- Nimmt Kersten das Angebot an?

C. Jetzt sind Sie dran!

Lesen Sie den Dialog „Im Reisebüro" mit einem Partner noch einmal durch, dann spielen Sie ihn dem Kurs vor. Sie können den Dialog natürlich verändern! Kersten kann zum Beispiel andere Wünsche äußern und Herr Meyer kann anders reagieren. Machen Sie sich Notizen!

Wohin?

Wie lange?

Wie viel Geld?

Mit wem?   *eine Reise nach ...*

Wann?

Welches Hotel?

D. Im Reisebüro

In dem Dialog sagt Herr Meyer zu Kersten: „Ich zeige Ihnen einmal einen Prospekt von Österreich." Benennen Sie die Satzteile. Was fällt Ihnen auf? Welche Satzteile erkennen Sie?

Ich	zeige	Ihnen	einmal	einen Prospekt	von	Österreich
			Adverb			

Markieren Sie die <u>Dativ-Ausdrücke</u> im Text (z. B. *im Reisebüro*).

Der Herr am Schreibtisch sagt <u>zu ihm</u> ...   *dative pronoun after a dative preposition*

_____

_____

_____

_____

_____

_____

Aktivität 3. Helfen Sie Kersten bei der Reiseplanung!

Kersten findet das Angebot vom Reisebüro viel zu teuer! Er sucht deshalb nach günstigen Möglichkeiten, eine Woche Urlaub in Wien zu machen. Zuerst sucht er einen Flug. *Germanwings* und *Airberlin* sind Billigflieger (*low-cost carrier*), die er gut kennt.

A. Mit dem Flugzeug nach Wien

Gehen Sie zu den Startseiten von www.germanwings.de, www.airberlin.de, www.lufthansa.de oder www.sta-travel.de und suchen Sie einen günstigen Flug von Hannover nach Wien (5-8 Tage Aufenthalt). Vergleichen Sie die Preise! Welchen Flug würden Sie nehmen?

Bei *Germanwings* kostet der Flug von Hannover (Startflughafen) nach Wien (Zielflughafen) vom

_____ bis zum _____ €_____.

B. Ein Hotel wählen

Suchen Sie nun ein passendes Hotel zum Flug. Sie können bei www.hotel.de oder www.hrs.de schauen. Achten Sie bei der Auswahl des Hotels nicht nur auf den Preis, sondern auch auf die Lage! Sie möchten unbedingt in der Stadtmitte/im Stadtzentrum übernachten!

Ich wähle das Hotel _____. Ich wähle dieses Hotel,

weil _____. Es kostet _____ €.

> **Nota Bene:** Stellen Sie die Sprache auf Deutsch, wenn Sie auf deutschen Webseiten surfen. Viele Webseiten haben eine automatische Ortserkennung und setzen die Sprache auf die des Zugriffslandes (in den USA also Englisch, selbst wenn die Webseite eine deutsche Webseite ist).

Aktivität 4. Lieber mit „Ruf Reisen"!

Kersten hat eine bessere Idee! „Ruf Reisen" organisiert billigen Urlaub für Schüler, Studenten oder Gruppen meistens mit Anreise, Hotel, und Sightseeing inklusive. Oft reist man mit dem Bus in einer bunt gemischten Gruppe. Die meisten Leute, die mit „Ruf Reisen"reisen, sind in ständiger (*constant*) Partylaune.

Bevor Sie die Webseite besuchen, machen Sie einen Wortigel (*mindmap*; lit.: *word hedgehog*) mit nützlichen Vokabeln und Phrasen.

A. Vor dem Schreiben

nach...

Meine RUF-Reise　　　　*inklusive*

B. Eine Reise planen

Besuchen Sie die Webseite www.rufreisen.de und suchen Sie eine Reise aus, die Ihnen gefällt. Stellen Sie Ihre Reise dann Ihren Kommilitonen vor. Wohin würden Sie fahren? Mit wem würden Sie verreisen? Was würde das kosten? Was ist alles inklusive?

Wohin würden (*would*) Sie fahren?

Warum?

Was würde (*would*) die Reise kosten?

Was genau decken die Kosten ab (*what exactly do the costs cover*)?

C. Schreiben

Stellen Sie sich vor, dass Sie diese Reise schon hinter sich haben. Sie hatten ein absolut unvergessliches Erlebnis (*unforgettable adventure*). Schreiben Sie kurz auf, wohin und mit wem Sie gefahren sind, was unterwegs passiert ist. Erzählen Sie uns von Ihrem fantastischen Abenteuer! Was ist passiert?

Meine unvergessliche „Ruf Reisen"-Reise:

Aktivität 5. Günstige Tickets kaufen

Schauen Sie sich jetzt die Videoclips „Günstig reisen" an, Eva und Sara erzählen, wo sie ihre Tickets für ihre letzten Reisen gekauft haben. Passen Sie auf, es kann mehr als eine zutreffende Antwort geben!

A. Eva meint, man sollte keinen Eurailpass kaufen, weil es viel billiger ist,

❏ mit dem Bus zu fahren.
❏ mit Billigfliegern (wie zum Beispiel *Ryanair*) zu fliegen.
❏ im Internet einzelne (*individual*) Zugtickets zu kaufen.

(QR 6.9 p.300)

B. Wo kann man billige Tickets kaufen?

C. Welche Firmen erwähnt (*mentions*) Eva?

D. Sara hat ihren Eurailpass _____ gekauft.

❏ im Internet
❏ an einem Automaten
❏ in München

(QR 6.10 p.300)

E. Laut Sara

Was erzählt Sara über Eurailpässe? Wo kann man sie kaufen? Wie viel kostet ein Eurailpass? Wie lange ist er gültig (*valid*)?

Der Urlaub

Aktivität 6. Mindmap

Erstellen Sie mit Ihren Kommilitonen einen Wortigel zum Begriff „Urlaub". Sammeln Sie mindestens 20 Begriffe, die Ihnen zu diesem Thema einfallen.

Grimm Grammar

Es geht weiter mit dem Dativ. Bearbeiten Sie zu Hause folgenden Grammatikteil in der:

Grimm Grammar:

<u>Dative</u> (cont)

der ⇒ dem
die ⇒ der
das ⇒ dem
die ⇒ den

mein ⇒ meinem
meine ⇒ meiner
mein ⇒ meinem
meine ⇒ meinen

Z.B.:

Sie reist **mit dem** Bus. (mask.)

Sie reist **mit einer Freundin**. (fem.)

Aktivität 7. Verkehrsmittel

Die Deutschen reisen gerne „mit dem Flugzeug" oder „mit der Bahn" in den Urlaub. Die Präposition „mit" zieht Dativ nach sich, und deshalb heißt es nicht „mit **das** Flugzeug" oder „mit **die** Bahn", sondern "mit **dem** Flugzeug" und „mit **der** Bahn". Es gibt aber noch viel mehr Transportmöglichkeiten! Welche Verkehrsmittel wählen die folgenden Personen, um in den Urlaub zu fahren? Setzen Sie die richtigen Formen von *reisen* und die Nomen im Dativ ein.

Das Auto:

Paula _____ mit _____ nach Spanien.

Der Bus:

Thomas _____ mit _____ nach Italien.

Das Flugzeug:

Maria _____ mit _____ nach Deutschland.

Die Bahn:

Tom und Jerry _____ mit _____ nach Schweden.

Das Schiff:

Robert _____ mit _____ in die Karibik.

Das Fahrrad:

_____ du mit _____ in die Schweiz?

Aktivität 8. Memory: „Ich packe meinen Koffer und fliege mit dem Flugzeug nach Ägypten …"

Dieses Konzentrationsspiel fordert ein gutes Gedächtnis (*memory*)! Bilden Sie mit Ihren Kommilitonen einen Kreis. Die erste Person sagt, wohin sie reist und womit sie reist. Die zweite Person wiederholt das und gibt dann selber an, wohin und womit sie reist, und so weiter. Wer sich nicht erinnern (*remember*) kann, muss sich hinsetzen. Wer sich am besten erinnern kann, gewinnt das Spiel!

Beispiel:

Student 1: Ich packe meinen Koffer und reise mit dem Schiff nach Australien.

Student 2: (Name von St. 1) packt seinen/ihren Koffer und reist mit dem Schiff nach Australien. Ich packe meinen Koffer und gehe zu Fuß nach Chile.

Student 3: (Name von St. 1) packt seinen/ihren Koffer und reist mit dem Schiff nach Australien.
(Name von St. 2) packt seinen/ihren Koffer und geht zu Fuß nach Chile.
Ich packe meinen Koffer und fahre mit dem Fahrrad in die Berge...

Reise- und Transportmöglichkeiten	Präposition	Einige Länder, Kontinente und Meere
mit dem Zug fahren/ reisen		Ägypten
mit dem Flugzeug fliegen/reisen		Frankreich
		Italien
		Mexiko
		Polen
		Australien
mit dem Schiff reisen/fahren		England
		Ungarn
		Österreich
		Griechenland
	nach	Finnland
	(+ dative)	Deutschland
		Holland
mit dem Auto/ Mietwagen fahren		Amerika
		Russland
		Kanada
		Schweden
per Autostopp/ Anhalter fahren		Spanien
		Europa
		Afrika
		Asien
		(Nord-/Mittel-/Süd-)
mit dem Fahrrad fahren		Amerika
mit dem Motorrad fahren	in (in this case + accusative)	die Schweiz die USA die Türkei die Niederlande die Berge die Karibik
zu Fuß gehen		
auf einem Pferd reiten	an (in this case + accusative)	die See den See die Nordsee die Ostsee das Meer den Strand
auf einem Kamel reiten		

Nota bene: Man fährt **mit** ... (Verkehrsmittel, Dativ) **nach** ... (Ort, Dativ). Aber es gibt Ausnahmen: „**in** die Schweiz" zum Beispiel (Akkusativ) oder „**an** die See/den See" (Akkusativ). Man muss diese Ausdrücke einfach zusammen lernen! Ach ja, und man fliegt „**auf** eine Insel" (z.B. auf die Seychellen; wieder Akkusativ) …

Grimm Grammar

Wie Sie sehen, ist der Dativ ein wichtiger Kasus in der deutschen Sprache! Bearbeiten Sie zu Hause folgenden Grammatikteil in der *Grimm Grammar*

Wiederholen Sie den <u>Dative Case</u> (lernen Sie die Bedeutung der Dative Verben).

Verbs: <u>geben</u>

Pronouns: <u>Personalpronomen im Dativ</u>

ich ⇒ mir
du ⇒ dir
er ⇒ ihm
sie ⇒ ihr
es ⇒ ihm

wir ⇒ uns
ihr ⇒ euch
sie ⇒ ihnen

Sie ⇒ Ihnen

Aktivität 9. Lieder & Musik
Die Ärzte – „Westerland". Die Ärzte sind eine bekannte Punkrockband aus Berlin. Sie spielen auf vielen Festivals (z.B. *Rock am Ring* oder *Rock im Park*). Gehen Sie zu Kapitel 6 auf der *Deutsch im Blick* Website und laden Sie die Pdf zum Lied runter, um die Aktivitäten zu machen.

Aktivität 10. Geschenke und Mitbringsel: Für deine Reise gebe ich dir …

Ihre Freunde verreisen. Sie geben ihnen Geschenke. Vervollständigen Sie die Sätze mit dem entsprechenden Personalpronomen und Geschenk.

Beispiel:

Christine geht für ein Jahr in die USA.

Ich gebe ___ihr___ ___eine Digitalkamera___

a. Meike reist nach Ägypten. Ich gebe _____ _____.

b. Thomas und Anne fahren für zwei Wochen an den Strand. Ich gebe _____

_____.

c. Tom fährt nach Polen. Ich gebe _____ _____.

d. Maria reist bald nach Mexiko. Ich gebe _____ _____.

e. Peter fährt ans Meer. Ich gebe _____ _____.

f. Anja und Tim fahren in die Türkei. Ich gebe _____ _____.

> Strandtücher • Sonnenbrille • Landkarte • Gummiboot
> Digitalkamera • Sonnencreme • Reiseführer • Sonnenhut

Aktivität 11. Mitbringsel
Wer hat wem was mitgebracht? Diese Austauschstudenten haben ihren Familienmitgliedern und Freunde viele Geschenke aus Amerika zurückgebracht. Bilden Sie einen Satz zu jeder Bilderreihe. Das Beispiel zeigt Ihnen, wie es geht!

Beispiel:

Christina	*ihr Freund*	*eine Baseballmütze*	
⇒ *Christina hat*	*ihrem Freund*	*eine Baseballmütze*	*mitgebracht.*

1. Julia	ihre Freundin	eine Halskette	
2. Til und seine Frau	ihre Eltern	ein Fotoalbum	
3. Peter	sein Bruder	ein Pullover	
4. Christine und Rika	die Cousine	Muscheln	

Und Sie? Bringen Sie jemandem etwas von einer Reise mit? Schreiben Sie 4-5 Sätze darüber, *wem* Sie *was* von ihrer letzten Reise mitgebracht haben.

Jussy hat nichts aus der Türkei für ihre Freundin Anke mitgebracht, aber sie hat eine Postkarte an ihre Freundin nach Texas geschrieben. Schreibst du auch gerne Postkarten?

Aktivität 12. Reiseberichte

A. Peters Reisebericht

Schauen Sie sich Peters Videoclip „Reiseberichte" an und wählen Sie die richtigen Antworten aus der angegeben Auswahl. Passen Sie auf, es gibt öfters mehr als eine zutreffende Antwort!

Peters schönste Reisen waren die Reisen nach

(QR 6.11 p.300)

| Mexiko | Polen | Kanada | Brasilien |

Als sein Gepäck <u>verloren gegangen ist</u> (*got lost*),
❑ hat Peter sich sehr geärgert.
❑ ist es am nächsten Tag wieder aufgetaucht und alles war in Ordnung.
❑ musste er neue Koffer kaufen.

Was meinen Sie, nachdem Sie dieses Video gesehen haben, reist Peter gern?
❑ Ja, er reist sehr gern.
❑ Nein, nur wenn er reisen muss.
❑ Bis jetzt schon, aber nicht mehr!

B. Evas Reisebericht

Hören Sie sich nun den Clip mit Eva an und bringen Sie die <u>durcheinander gewürfelten</u> (*jumbled*) Teile ihres Reiseberichts in die richtige Reihenfolge. In der richtigen Reihenfolge ergibt sich ein Lösungswort. Hinweis: Es ist eine kanadische Delikatesse!

(QR 6.12 p.300)

> Vokabelhilfe:
> der Bär – the bear
> der Campingplatz – the campground
> die Rundreise – a trip that takes one to several places
> die Nachtruhe – the nighttime peace

U) Es gab nämlich viele Bären. Einmal nachts haben wir die Bären sogar auf dem Campingplatz gesehen.

O) In Kanada haben wir eine Rundreise durch Alberta und British Columbia unternommen.

H) Meine letzte Reise ging nach Kanada und in die USA.

R) Danach habe ich in den USA Verwandte, Bekannte und Freunde besucht.

N) Insgesamt war ich 7 ½ Wochen unterwegs.

A) Ich heiße Eva und reise sehr gerne.

P) Da war natürlich die Nachtruhe dahin!

R) Die Reise war sehr schön. Wir haben gezeltet. Ich habe teilweise ganz schön Angst gehabt!

<u>Lösungswort:</u>

1	2	3	4	5	6	7	8	9	10
					S	I			

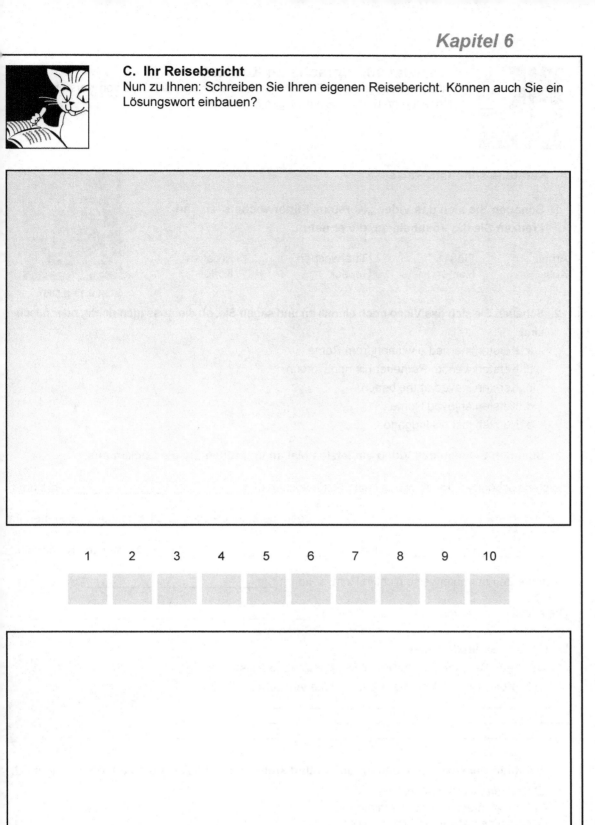

C. Ihr Reisebericht
Nun zu Ihnen: Schreiben Sie Ihren eigenen Reisebericht. Können auch Sie ein Lösungswort einbauen?

1	2	3	4	5	6	7	8	9	10

Foto/Zeichnung von Ihrer Reise mit Beschriftung (*labels*)

Aktivität 13. Sprache im Kontext

Wie waren ihre letzten Reisen? Schauen Sie sich die Clips von Kersten und Christine an und vervollständigen Sie die Übung.

A. Kerstens schönste Reise

1. Schauen Sie sich das Video „Kerstens Flitterwochen" an und kreuzen Sie die Vokabeln an, die er nennt.

Arbeit	Flug	Flitterwochen	Kroatien
Küste	Römer	Gepäck	Koffer

(QR 6.13 p.300)

2. Schauen Sie sich das Video noch einmal an und sagen Sie, ob die Aussagen richtig oder falsch sind.

    a. Kersten married a woman from Rome.

    b. Kersten went to Rome for his honeymoon.

    c. Kersten stayed at the beach.

    d. Kersten enjoyed Rome.

    e. Kersten lost his luggage.

3. Schauen Sie sich das Video ein letztes Mal an und füllen Sie die Lücken aus.

Kerstens schönster Urlaub waren seine Flitterwochen in _____. Ihm hat

_____ besonders gut gefallen. Die Reise war im Sommer, im

_____ und _____. Die meisten Römer sind

zu dieser Zeit normalerweise nicht in Rom, sondern _____. Hat er sein

Gepäck schon mal verloren (*Vorsicht: Witz!*)? _____.

B. Christines letzte Reise

1. Schauen Sie sich das Video "Christines letzte Reise" an und schreiben Sie die Vokabeln auf, die Sie verstehen.

_____	_____	_____
_____	_____	_____
_____	_____	_____

(QR 6.14 p.300)

2. Schauen Sie sich das Video erneut an und kreuzen Sie die Aussagen an, die richtig sind.

    ❑ Christine ist Studentin.

    ❑ Sie hat in einem Zelt geschlafen.

    ❑ Christine hat keinen Freund mehr.

    ❑ Sie war auf einem Basar und hat Gewürze gekauft.

3. Schauen Sie sich das Video ein letztes Mal an und beantworten Sie die Fragen.

a. Wo war Christine im Urlaub? _____.

b. Mit wem war Christine im Urlaub und wie lange? _____

_____

c. Was hat Christine dort gemacht?_____

Aktivität 14. Mein Reiseziel

Sprechen Sie mit anderen Studenten in ihrer Gruppe. Fragen Sie die Studenten, wohin sie reisen möchten und warum (z.B. wegen Sehenswürdigkeiten oder wegen Aktivitäten). Notieren Sie die Antworten in der Tabelle.

Beispiel:

S1: *Wohin möchtest du reisen?*
S2: *Ich möchte nach Florenz reisen.*
S1: *Warum möchtest du nach Florenz reisen?*
S2: *Ich möchte die David-Statue von Michelangelo sehen.*

Name	Reiseziel	Sehenswürdigkeit/Aktivität

Aktivität 15. Heidelberg

A. Kurzinfo Heidelberg

Heidelberg ist eine Stadt in Baden-Württemberg mit rund 140.000 Einwohnern. Die vom Zweiten Weltkrieg relativ <u>unversehrte</u> Stadt ist nach dem Zweiten Weltkrieg zum <u>Hauptquartier</u> der amerikanischen Streitkräfte geworden. <u>Angeblich</u> <u>verbreiteten</u> Amerikaner im Zweiten Weltkrieg folgenden Slogan: „Heidelberg wollen wir verschonen, denn dort wollen wir einmal wohnen!"

Das Heidelberger Schloss gehört zu den <u>beliebtesten</u> Touristenattraktionen in Deutschland. Es ranken sich viele <u>Mythen</u> und <u>Legenden</u> um das Schloss. Einer Legende nach bekommt derjenige das Schloss geschenkt, der es schafft, den eisernen Ring am <u>Schlosseingang</u> zu <u>durchbeißen</u>. Eine Hexe soll dies einmal <u>versucht</u> haben. Sie hat es jedoch nicht geschafft, den Ring zu durchbeißen. Noch heute können Touristen die angeblichen <u>Zahnabdrücke</u> der Hexe am Schlossring begutachten.

Können Sie Heidelberg auf einer Landkarte finden? Was steht noch im Internet über Heidelberg?

<u>Vokabelhilfe:</u>	
unversehrt – undamaged	der Mythos – myth
das Hauptquartier – the headquarters	einer Legende nach – according to legend
angeblich – supposedly	der Eingang – entrance
verbreiten – to spread	durchbeißen – to bite through
beliebt – popular	versuchen – to try
	der Zahnabdruck – dental impression

Grimm Grammar

Einige Verben verlangen ein direktes Objekt (im Akkusativ), andere ein indirektes Objekt (diese stehen im Dativ). Bearbeiten und wiederholen Sie folgende Grammatikteile in der *Grimm Grammar*:

Verbs: gefallen

Reisen gefällt mir.
Reisen gefällt dir.
Reisen gefällt ihm.
Reisen gefällt ihr.
Reisen gefällt ihm.

Reisen gefällt uns.
Reisen gefällt euch.
Reisen gefällt ihnen.
Reisen gefällt Ihnen.

Wiederholung:
Dative Verbs

Wiederholung:
Personal Pronouns in the Dative

ich ⇒ mir
du ⇒ dir
er ⇒ ihm
sie ⇒ ihr
es ⇒ ihm

wir ⇒ uns
ihr ⇒ euch
sie ⇒ ihnen

Sie ⇒ Ihnen

B. Adan & Sophia: Reiseberichte (in Heidelberg)

Sophia und Adan berichten über Heidelberg. Was gefällt ihnen? Was gefällt ihnen nicht? Kreuzen Sie an, welche der Aussagen richtig oder falsch sind.

Sophia:

Heidelberg gefällt Sophia sehr gut.	richtig	falsch
Vor allem die Geschichte Heidelbergs gefällt ihr sehr gut.	richtig	falsch

(QR 6.16 p.300)

Adan:

Heidelberg gefällt Adan nicht.	richtig	falsch
Die vielen Touristen gefallen ihm gar nicht.	richtig	falsch

(QR 6.17 p.300)

Aktivität 16. Was gefällt Ihnen …? Und was nicht?

Gehen Sie ins Internet und finden Sie Informationen über die Sehenswürdigkeiten von München, Berlin und Hamburg. Wählen Sie eine der drei Städte und berichten Sie dem Rest des Kurses mündlich (*orally*), was Ihnen an dieser Stadt gefällt oder nicht gefällt. Sie können sich natürlich Notizen machen.

Beispiel:

Mir gefällt Köln – vor allem der Dom. Es ist eine riesige gothische Kirche. Echt imposant! Mir gefällt auch der Rhein und die Fuß- und Fahrradwege entlang des Ufers. Es gibt acht Brücken. Auf der Hohenzollernbrücke haben tausende Verliebte so genannte Liebesschlösser angebracht. Wirklich romantisch! Die Schlüssel liegen auf dem Grund des Rheins. Die Innenstadt ist nicht weit vom Rheinufer und die Universität in Köln ist auch sehr gut. An Köln gefällt mir nicht so gut, dass immer so viel gebaut wird. Das ist nicht nur laut und nervig, sondern behindert auch den Straßenverkehr … Die Leute sind aber klasse. Sie sprechen witzig und singen gerne Karnevalslieder (übrigens nicht nur während der Karnevalszeit) …

Informationen zu München gibt es im Internet zum Beispiel auf http://www.muenchen.de.
Informationen zu Berlin gibt es im Internet zum Beispiel auf http://www.berlin.de.
Informationen zu Hamburg gibt es im Internet zum Beispiel auf http://www.hamburg.de.

München	• Die Schlossanlage Schleißheim • Das Oktoberfest • Der Christkindlmarkt am Marienplatz • Der Viktualienmarkt • Die Bayerische Staatsbibliothek

Das Stadtwappen der bayrischenLandeshauptstadt

Berlin
- Die Staatsoper
- Das Brandenburger Tor
- Die Love Parade
- Der Reichstag
- Die Berliner Mauer
- Das DDR-Museum

Die Stadfahne der Bundeshauptstadt

Hamburg
- Der Tierpark
- Der Hamburger Fischmarkt
- Die City Beach Clubs
- Die Reeperbahn
- Die Landungsbrücken
- Der Hamburger Michel

Die Stadtfahne von Hamburg

Aktivität 17. Und Ihre Stadt?

Wählen Sie eine Stadt Ihrer Wahl (zum Beispiel Amsterdam, Lima oder Dallas). Was gefällt Ihnen an dieser Stadt? Was gefällt Ihnen nicht? Berichten Sie ihren Kommilitonen und bringen Sie Fotos mit! Lesen Sie sich zur Erinnerung noch einmal das Beispiel aus Aktivität 16 durch – aber nicht kopieren!

Aktivität 18. Die Loreley

A. Die Legende der Loreley
Schauen Sie sich erst die Bilder an. Worum geht es Ihrer Meinung nach in der Sage der Loreley? Dann lesen Sie die kurze Zusammenfassung über die Legende der Loreley (auch: Lorelei).

<u>Vokabelhilfe</u>:		
der Felsen	–	the cliff
anregen	–	to inspire
Nibelungen	–	a Franconian tribe whose epic battles are related in the „Die Nibelungensage." There are gods and heroes, and a treasure in the Rhine. „Der Hort der Nibelungen" is allegedly where the treasure is still hidden!
Clemens Bretano	–	(1778-1842) was a German poet and writer
die Erfindung	–	the invention
Heinrich Heine	–	(1797-1856) was a famous and influential poet
die Sage	–	the legend/ the saga
der Rhein	–	the Rhine (a river in Germany)
wurde vermutet	–	was imagined/ suspected
aufgreifen	–	to refer to/ to pick something up
aufschreiben	–	to write down

Die Loreley ist ein <u>Felsen</u> am <u>Rhein</u>, 132 Meter hoch. Schon im Mittelalter <u>regte</u> der Felsen die Fantasie <u>an</u>, zum Beispiel <u>wurde</u> der Hort der <u>Nibelungen</u> in dem Felsen <u>vermutet</u>.

Im Jahre 1800 inspirierte der Felsen den Schriftsteller <u>Clemens Brentano</u> zur <u>Erfindung</u> einer Fantasiefigur: die Loreley. Später <u>griff</u> der <u>Dichter</u> Heinrich Heine in seinem berühmten Gedicht „Die Loreley" (1824) die Geschichte der Loreley wieder <u>auf</u>.

Die <u>Sage</u> der Loreley ist eine Kunstsage, das heißt, dass ein Autor sie erfunden und <u>aufgeschrieben</u> hat. Nur äußerst selten wird eine Kunstsage zur Volkssage. Eine Volkssage ist eine Sage, die mündlich vom Volk weitergegeben wird, ohne dass ein Autor bekannt ist. Die Sage der Loreley ist eine der wenigen Kunstsagen, die zu Volkssagen wurden. Sie ist sehr populär und wird manchmal im selben Atemzug mit Christian Andersens „kleiner Meerjungfrau" erwähnt.

B. Eine andere Version der Legende ...

Einer Version der Sage nach <u>raubt</u> Loreley <u>aufgrund ihrer Schönheit</u> allen Männern den <u>Verstand</u>. Loreley ist darüber aber nicht glücklich. Ihre einzige Liebe hat sie <u>verlassen,</u> sie möchte keinen anderen Mann. <u>Deshalb</u> entschließt sie sich, ins <u>Kloster</u> zu gehen. Auf dem Weg zum Kloster steigt sie auf einen Felsen, um noch einmal auf den Rhein <u>hinunterzusehen</u>. Loreley <u>stürzt</u> vom Felsen, und <u>der Sage nach</u> sitzt der <u>Geist</u> der Loreley <u>weiterhin</u> auf dem Felsen und ...

Schreiben Sie die Legende zu Ende:

Loreley stürzt vom Felsen, und der Sage nach sitzt der Geist der Loreley weiterhin auf dem Felsen. Eines Tages ...

<u>Vokabelhilfe:</u>

den Verstand rauben	–	to steal one's mind
aufgrund ihrer Schönheit	–	because of/as a result of her beauty
verlassen	–	to leave
deshalb	–	therefore/ that is why
sich entschließen	–	to decide
das Kloster	–	the convent
hinuntersehen	–	(in order to) look down
stürzen	–	to fall
der Sage nach	–	according to the saga
der Geist	–	the ghost
weiterhin	–	still today

C. Heinrich Heines Loreley

Lesen Sie das folgende Gedicht von Heinrich Heine und versuchen Sie herauszufinden, was die Loreley auf dem Felsen macht. Beenden Sie oder verändern Sie dann den oben in Aktivität B begonnenen Satz in der Aufgabenstellung (*instruction*).

Die Loreley – Heinrich Heine (1824)

Ich weiß nicht, was soll es bedeuten,
Dass ich so traurig bin;
Ein Märchen _____ alten Zeiten,
Das kommt _____ nicht aus dem Sinn.

Die Luft ist kühl und es dunkelt,
Und ruhig fließt der Rhein;
Der Gipfel des Berges funkelt
Im Abendsonnenschein.

Die schönste Jungfrau sitzet
Dort oben wunderbar,
Ihr goldnes Geschmeide blitzet,
Sie kämmt ihr goldenes Haar.

Sie kämmt es _____ goldenem Kamme,
Und singt ein Lied dabei;
Das hat eine wundersame,
Gewaltige Melodei.

Den Schiffer im kleinen Schiffe
Ergreift es _____ wildem Weh;
Er schaut nicht die Felsenriffe,
Er schaut nur hinauf in die Höh´.

Ich glaube, die Wellen verschlingen
Am Ende Schiffer und Kahn,
Und das hat mit _____ Singen
Die Loreley getan.

AUTHENTISCH

ihrem · aus · mit
mit · mir

das Geschmeide – jewelry
gewaltig – violent, powerful
ergreifen – catch, hear
das Felsenriff – reef
verschlingen – devour, engulf
der Kahn – boat

Das Gedicht von Heinrich Heine in seiner Vertonung von Friedrich Silcher (1936) finden Sie unter http://www.youtube.com/watch?v=e0_PtHwbCiY. Welche Wirkung (welchen Effekt) hat das Gedicht auf Sie? Welche Bedeutung hat es für Sie?

D. Der Loreley Rap

Modernere Versionen finden Sie mit den passenden Suchbegriffen bei http://www.youtube.com oder http://www.vimeo.com. Ein Anfängerdeutschkurs am Mount Holyoke College hat das Gedicht von Heinrich Heine zu einem Rap gemacht, um ihren Professor zu überraschen. Hier ist der Link: http://youtu.be/hoJ1Jt3Y4Pk. Gefällt Ihnen die Variante? Was ist gut/schlecht? Können Sie es besser? Machen Sie für ihren Lehrer oder Professor ein eigenes Loreley-Musikvideo!

Aktivität 19. Poesie

Kreativität ist gefragt. Wählen Sie mindestens zwei der folgenden Übungen aus.

A. Ein Akrostrichon

Schreiben Sie Ihr eigenes Gedicht: ein Akrostrichon zur „Loreley".

L _____

O _____

R _____

E _____

L _____

E _____

I _____

Muster

Laut singt die Lorelei
Oben auf dem Felsen
Rhein, du gefährlicher Fluss
Ein Mann muss heute sterben
Liebevoll, hoch schaut er
Ertrinkt
In seinen Augen stille
    Trauer versinkt

B. Das Lied vs. Ihre Version

Vergleichen Sie Ihre Version (A18.B) mit der Sage von der Loreley im Lied. Inwieweit (to what extent) stimmt Ihre Version mit der Sage überein? Gar nicht? Ein wenig? Sehr? Was sind Unterschiede?

C. Die Loreley vs. die Moderne

Denken Sie an ein modernes Liebeslied. Vergleichen Sie das Volkslied von der Loreley mit diesem Pop-Song. Welche Änlichkeiten (similarities) und Unterschiede können Sie feststellen?

D. Loreleys Perspektive

Stellen Sie sich vor, Sie sind die Loreley. Was würden Sie in einem kurzen Statement gerne loswerden/aufklären? Schreiben Sie in der 1. Person („Ich").

E. Andere Sagenfiguren

Wählen Sie eine Sagenfigur aus einer Legende (z.B. aus einem Buch, Gedicht, Lied) und berichten Sie Ihren Kommilitonen über sie. Warum haben Sie diese Figur gewählt?

Wilhelm Tell

SAGEN

LEGENDEN

Walpurgisnacht

Aktivität 20. Auf Reisen: Was man alles unternehmen kann

A. Ein Besuch in Wien

Welche Bilder gehören zu welchen Sehenswürdigkeiten oder Aktivitäten? Ordnen Sie die Bilder den Beschreibungen zu. Mehr Informationen zu Wien finden Sie unter http://www.wien.info.

1. Der Wiener Prater (vom Riesenrad aus)

8. Die Wiener Kaffeehäuser

7. Das Schloss Belvedere

2. Der Wienerwald

3. Die Spanische Hofreitschule

1. ____ In diesem Viertel gibt es besonders viele Museen. Viele Leute schauen sich die Ausstellungen in den Museen an.

2. ____ In diesem Schloss finden sich viele Werke von Gustav Klimt, zum Beispiel „Der Kuss". Viele Museumsbesucher denken lange über dieses Bild nach.

3. ____ Dies ist die ehemalige Sommerresidenz von Kaiserin Sissi (Elisabeth). Sie kam sehr gerne hierher.

4. ____ Hier sehen sich viele Leute Freiheitsdressuren (eine Art Reiten) an.

5. ____ Diese Betriebe servieren hervorragenden Kaffee und Kuchen. Es kommt vor, dass Besucher fünf Stück Sachertorte hintereinander essen!

6. ____ Hier gehen viele Leute spazieren.

7. ____ Der Spaß hört hier niemals auf! Hier steigt man in ein großes Riesenrad.

8. ____ Auf diesem Prachtboulevard kann man viel bewundern. Viele Leute kaufen hier schon seit Jahrzehnten gerne ein.

4. Das Museumsquartier

5. Die Ringstraße

6. Das Schloss Schönbrunn

B. Trennbare Verben

In dem Text oben finden Sie viele <u>trennbare Verben</u> (*separable prefix verbs*). Schreiben Sie so viele von diesen Verben auf wie möglich und bilden Sie ihre Infinitive.

1. *Viele Leute schauen sich die Ausstellungen in den Museen an.* Infinitiv: *anschauen*	2.
3.	4.
5.	6.

C. Sehenswürdigkeiten in Ihrer Stadt

Welche Sehenswürdigkeiten gibt es in Ihrer Stadt/Ihrem Land? Was gibt es dort zu tun? Bringen Sie Fotos von 5-6 Sehenswürdigkeiten mit und beschreiben Sie, was man dort alles machen kann. Benutzen Sie möglichst viele von den folgenden Wörtern:

> sich etwas anschauen • über etwas nachdenken • hinfahren
> ankommen • vorkommen • sich etwas ansehen • einkaufen
> spazieren gehen • aufhören • anfangen • kennen lernen
> ausgehen • ausgeben • mitspielen • abbrennen • ausstellen
> darstellen (to present) • sich ausruhen (relax) • mitmachen

_____

_____

_____

_____

_____

_____

_____

Aktivität 21. Einige Studenten verbringen drei Tage in Wien

Grimm Grammar

Bearbeiten Sie zu Hause den folgenden Grammatikteil in der *Grimm Grammar*:
<u>Separable Prefix Verbs</u>

anschauen

ich schaue an
du schaust an
er schaut an

wir schauen an
ihr schaut an
sie schauen an

aber:
... weil wir uns die Museen anschauen.
... weil ich mir die Museen anschauen möchte.

A. Unterwegs

Josh und Doug sind im Augenblick in Wien. Was machen sie dort? Wählen Sie ein passendes Verb aus dem Kasten und vervollständigen Sie den Text im Präsens (nicht alle Verben werden gebraucht).

> ankommen • aufstehen • ausstehen • losgehen • anziehen • mitkommen
> mitbringen • aussteigen • einladen • zustimmen • einsteigen
> aufwachen • anschauen • schwarzfahren • ausschlafen

1. Am Freitagabend _____ Josh und Doug in Wien _____.

2. Am Samstag _____ Josh früh _____. Er kann kaum warten, Wien zu sehen!

3. Doug duscht auch und _____ sich bequeme Kleider _____. Nach einem Frühstück machen sie sich auf dem Weg.

4. An der U-Bahn-Station geht Josh zum Ticketautomaten. Doug will keine Tickets kaufen. „Heute _____ wir _____! " „Nein!" sagt Josh, „wenn uns der Kontrolleur erwischt, kostet uns das 60,- Euro pro Person!" Er kauft zwei Tageskarten.

5. Als die U-Bahn-Linie 1 (U1) kommt, _____ beide in den Zug _____.

6. 15 Minuten später an der Haltestelle „Station Praterstern", _____ sie wieder _____. Sie fahren mit der Loopingbahn und dem Riesenrad und essen viel Zuckerwatte.

7. Später fragt Josh: „Ich gehe heute Abend zur Vorstellung der Spanischen Hofreitschule, _____ du _____?"

8. Doug antwortet: „Nein, ich kann Pferde nicht _____! Ich bin allergisch!" Also geht Josh alleine zur Show, die um 20.00 Uhr beginnt.

Grimm Grammar

Bearbeiten Sie zu Hause den folgenden Grammatikteil in der *Grimm Grammar*:

Review:
Conversational Past

Separable Prefix Verbs in the Conversational Past

haben/sein + Partizip (mit 'ge-')

Ich **habe** *einen Ruck-sack* **mitgebracht**.

Mein Freund **ist mitgekommen.**

B. Wieder zu Hause!

Josh und Doug sind von ihrer Reise nach Wien wieder zurück. Josh schreibt einen Blogeintrag über ihre Reise. Fassen Sie den Text aus Teil A zusammen (**summarize**) und benutzen Sie dazu die trennbaren Verben (*separable prefix verbs*) in der richtigen Form. Nutzen Sie das Perfekt (*conversational past*). Aber zuerst: Was sind die Partizipien der folgenden Verben?

ankommen

ist angekommen

ansehen

hat angesehen

anziehen

hat (sich) angezogen

aufstehen

ist aufgestanden

haben	_____
ignorieren	_____
kaufen	_____
losbrechen	_____
machen	_____
schlafen	_____
sehen	_____
tanzen	_____
warten	_____
ausprobieren	_____
aussteigen	_____
einsteigen	_____
essen	_____
fahren	_____
gehen	_____

Meine Reise nach Wien (von Josh)

Aktivität 22. Welcher Reisetyp bist du
Arbeiten Sie mit einem Partner zusammen.

A. Was denken Sie, welche „Reise- oder Urlaubstypen" gibt es? Wie stellen Sie sich die verschiedenen Typen vor?

Beispiel:

Kreuzfahrturlauber: Schiff, langweilig, alte Leute/Renter, Karibik usw. ...

- ❑ Natururlauber:
- ❑ Winterurlauber:
- ❑ Fitnessurlauber:
- ❑ Familienurlauber:
- ❑ All-Inclusive-Urlauber
- ❑ Aktivurlauber:
- ❑ Kultururlauber:
- ❑ ...

B. Urlaubstyptest. Welcher Urlaubstyp sind Sie?
Im Internet kann man viele Tests finden, um seinen Urlaubstypen zu bestimmen. Zum Beispiel auf der Website des Magazins *GEO*. Googeln Sie nach einem Test im Internet (auf deutsch ntaürlich) und machen Sie den Test online. Notieren Sie ihr Ergebnis und interessante Vokabeln. Alternativ können Sie auch die folgenden Beschreibungen durchlesen und selbst bestimmen (*determine yourself*), welcher Urlaubstyp Sie sind.

Ihr Urlaubstyp

Der Natururlauber
Sie sind am liebsten in der Natur. In jeder freien Minute kann man Sie in der Natur finden. Ob Sie nur in Ihrem Garten arbeiten, einen gemütlichen Abendspaziergang machen oder wandern gehen – die Natur ist ihr liebster Ort. Für längere Reisen nehmen Sie dann auch gerne Ihr Zelt oder sogar Ihren Camper mit. Es spricht einiges dafür, das eigene „Haus" mit in den Urlaub zu nehmen: Man trifft Gleichgesinnte, lebt quasi in der Natur und schläft dabei im „eigenen Bett". Man wird von den ersten Sonnenstrahlen geweckt und kann sich sofort in die Natur begeben.

Der Schneemann
Ob Schlitten-, Schlittschuh- oder Skifahren ist Ihnen ganz egal – Hauptsache es hat Minustemperaturen und Sie können im Anorak, dicken Pullover, langen Strumpfhosen und Winterstiefeln im Freien herum tollen und sich auch sportlich betätigen. Die verschneite Winterlandschaft hilft ihnen sich zu entspannen und neue Energie zu tanken. Dabei lassen Sie sich aber auch gerne abends verwöhnen. Sie genießen gerne ein gutes Abendessen im Hotel bei Kaminfeuer oder entspannen sich nach einem erfolgreichen Skitag in der Sauna.

Der Fitnessfan

Was für viele der Traumurlaub schlechthin ist, ist für andere allerdings ein Alptraum. Der Urlaubertyp Sportskanone findet sein Glück erst, wenn sein Adrenalinspiegel ganz oben ist. Fahrrad fahren, joggen, Tennis spielen, surfen - ganz egal... Hauptsache extrem. Was der normale Mensch Sport nennt ist für Sie Entspannung. Wenn Sie jeden Tag im Urlaub an einem Triathlon teilnehmen könnten, wäre das der perfekte Urlaub für Sie. Dazu kommt natürlich auch gesunde Ernährung - von Hotelbuffets halten Sie gar nichts. Ihr Hotel muss Ihnen eine ausgewogene Ernährung bieten können - am besten noch nach Ihre speziellen Wünsche zubereitet.

Der Familienurlauber

Bei einem Urlaub auf dem Bauernhof mit Ihren Lieben, umgeben von idyllischer Landluft, geht Ihnen das Herz auf. Sie brauchen keinen Großstadttrubel, schicke Hotels oder pausenlos Aktion - vom krähen das Hahnes geweckt zu werden, einen Kaffee zu trinken und danach mit der Familie die Tiere beobachten ist für Sie das höchste. Gelegentlich wandern Sie auch gerne in den nahegelegenen Wäldern oder machen ein Picknick am See.

Der All-Inklusive Urlauber

Strandbar - Hotelbar - Poolbar - Hauptsache ein Bar, an der es etwas zum Trinken und hoffentlich auch zum Essen gibt ohne extra dafür bezahlen zu müssen, das ist fast alles was Ihr Herz begehrt. Oft zeigen Sie sich auch in der Horizontalen am Strand und lassen sich die heisse Sonne auf den Bauch scheinen und schlürfen dabei einen Cocktail. Nach einem anstrengenden Tag des Faulenzens am Strand findet man Sie dann in einem der Hotelrestaurants wo sie sich über ein üppiges Buffet hermachen. Wichtig ist auch, dass die Unterhaltung nicht fehlt und Sie wann immer Sie es wollen durch einen Animateur abgelenkt werden.

Der Aktivurlauber

Für Sie bietet selbst das extremste Peeling keine Herausforderung und den ganzen Tag am Strand zu liegen, finden Sie öde. Sie fühlen sich dort am Wohlsten wo ihnen immer etwas geboten wird und Sie fremde und neue Dinge erfahren können. Alles, was Natur ist und Spannung bietet, spricht Sie an. Extremsport, durch den Amazonas waten, Thailand für drei Monate mit dem Rucksack erkunden bedeutet für Sie: Traumurlaub. Jedoch fühlen Sie sich auch auf dem Wasser sehr wohl: Einen Boom erlebt das Segeln unter den Aktivurlaubern. Hier können Sie vollen Einsatz zeigen und kaum von Bord wartet schon die Unterwasserwelt darauf, entdeckt zu werden.

Der Kulturhungrige

Sie sind ähnlich aktiv wie der Aktivurlauber, jedoch bestehen Sie ihre Abendteuer an Denkmälern, historischen Stätten, Museum und ähnlichem. Sie sind nicht auf Extremsport aus, sondern auf Extrembildung und Kultur. Sie legen viel Wert darauf, während der Reise etwas Neues zu entdecken und fremde Kulturen kennen zu lernen und besser zu verstehen. Kaum in Griechenland angekommen, lassen Sie alle Strände links liegen, um dafür die Spielstätten der Mythologie hautnah zu erleben und die Akropolis Stein für Stein zu inspizieren.

Machen Sie wirklich solche Reisen? Stimmen Sie mit dem Ergebnis überein?

Aktivität 23. Und jetzt sind Sie dran!

Was war Ihre Lieblingsreise? Wohin sind Sie gefahren? Was haben Sie dort gemacht? Was hat Ihnen an dieser Reise besonders gut gefallen? Haben Sie sich schon eimal überlegt einen Reiseblog zu starten, um ihre Erlebnisse zu teilen? Sie können so natürlich auch eigene Fotos oder Videos uploaden und teilen. Versuchen Sie die Benutzereinstellung (*setting*) auf Deutsch zu stellen oder benutzen Sie dieses Template zur Übung:

Meine Lieblingsreise

Bitte **Foto** uploaden:
Meine neuen Freunde

Gästebuch: *Klicke hier*

Meine coolen Reiseausdrücke!
in _____ ankommen
mit Verspätung
sehr spät aufstehen!
jeden Tag mit Freunden ausgehen
exotische Klamotten anziehen
exotische Speisen ausprobieren
tanzen, wandern, neue Leute treffen
Tausende von Fotos machen!
Meine Lieblingsstadt

an den Strand gehen
in den Bergen wandern
einfach nichts tun
zu viele Souveniers kaufen
die Mitbringsel
eine andere Kultur kennen lernen
nach Hause zurückfahren
auspacken
schon die nächste Reise planen

Aktivität 24. Sprache im Kontext

Josh, Doug und Susan sind sehr oft in Europa verreist. Was erzählen sie über ihre verschiedenen Reisen? Schauen Sie sich die Videos an und beantworten Sie die nachfolgenden Fragen.

A. Josh reist nach Amsterdam

1. Beim ersten Hören kreuzen Sie die Ausdrücke (*expressions*) an, die Josh benutzt, um seine Reise zu beschreiben.

❑ Touristen
❑ die Fahrt dauert ungefähr acht Stunden
❑ die Eurokreditkarte
❑ eine Strandstadt
❑ der Aktivurlaub
❑ sich entspannen
❑ im Hotel übernachten

(QR 6.18 p.300)

2. Schauen Sie den Clip erneut an. Beantworten Sie die Fragen in Stichworten.

Wie ist Josh nach Amsterdam gefahren?

Was ist „extrem kalt"?

Was hat Josh in Amsterdam gesehen und gemacht?

3. Schauen Sie den Clip ein drittes Mal und fassen Sie ihn mündlich zusammen.

B. Josh, Doug und Susan in Schottland (und Rom!)
1. Schauen Sie den Clip einmal an und notieren Sie die Wörter, die Sie verstehen.

_____   _____   _____

_____   _____   _____

2. Lesen Sie die folgenden Fragen durch, dann schauen Sie den Clip erneut an und machen Notizen. Nachdem Sie den Clip ein drittes Mal angesehen haben, beantworten Sie die Fragen in einem vollständigen Satz.

Wie sind diese Freunde nach Schottland gefahren?
Wie lange waren sie in Glasgow?
Wo haben sie übernachtet und wie viel hat es pro Nacht gekostet?
Wo haben sie die Tickets für ihre Reise gekauft und wie viel haben sie gekostet?
Was hat Susan an Rom nicht so sehr gefallen?

> Forschen Sie ein bisschen nach! Was können Sie über die Münchner Sehenswürdigkeiten herausfinden?

C. München und Würzburg

1. Welche Sehenswürdigkeiten haben diese Freunde besichtigt?

In München: den Zoo   den Olympiaturm   den Englischen Garten

das Glockenspiel   die Alte Pinakothek   das Hofbräuhaus

In Würzburg: _____   _____   _____

Aktivität 25. Josh und Susan fahren nach Amsterdam

Ergänzen Sie den folgenden Text mit dem zutreffenden untrennbaren (inseparable prefix) Verb aus dem Kasten im Präsens *(present tense)* in der entsprechenden Form.

~~entscheiden~~ • verspäten • erlauben • entspannen • verlassen
beschließen • erblicken • verabreden • erkälten • verbringen • erinnern
genießen • vergnügen • bestellen • verkaufen • verreisen

---

1. Josh und Susan __entscheiden__, nach Amsterdam zu fahren. Susan fragt ihre Mutter, ob sie fahren darf. Susans Mutter und auch Joshs Eltern _____ den beiden zu fahren.
2. Am nächsten Morgen treffen sich die beiden am Bahnhof. Susan _____ nicht gerne viel Zeit im Zug, ihr wird schnell langweilig. Aber heute hat sie gute Laune, weil sie mit dem ICE fahren wird. Der ICE (mit einer Maximalgeschwindigkeit von 330 km/h) braucht von Frankfurt nach Amsterdam nur etwa vier Stunden.
3. Im Zug frühstückt das Paar. Susan _____ einen Milchkaffee und einen Berliner, Josh eine Apfelschorle und ein Stück Donauwelle.
4. In Amsterdam suchen die beiden den Bus, der sie zu ihrem Hotel bringt. Josh fragt Susan: „_____ du dich an die Nummer der Buslinie?" „Ja!", sagt Susan, „Nummer 5".
5. Josh und Susan _____ das Bahnhofsgebäude. Draußen findet Susan den richtigen Bus.
6. Bald darauf _____ Susan und Josh das Nachtleben in Amsterdam. Die Kneipen und Discos sind fantastisch! Die beiden essen Currywurst mit Pommes an einer Pommesbude. Das ist lecker!
7. Am nächsten Tag unternehmen Josh und Susan noch viele andere Dinge in Amsterdam. Sie _____ sich prächtig!
8. Josh sagt zu Sophie: „Schade, dass wir nur die zwei Tage hier _____!"

Grimm Grammar

Lesen und bearbeiten Sie bitte folgenden Grammatikteil in der *Grimm Grammar*:

<u>Inseparable Prefix Verbs in the Present Tense</u>

<u>Inseparable Prefix Verbs in the Conversational Past</u>

haben/sein + Partizip (ohne '*ge-*')

Die Studenten haben zwei Tage in Amsterdam verbracht.

Sie sind am Sonntag verreist.

Aktivität 26. Susan trifft eine Freundin auf der Straße

Susan ist aus Amsterdam zurück. In Würzburg läuft sie zufällig ihrer Freundin Heidi über den Weg. Vervollständige den Dialog im <u>Perfekt</u> (*conversational past*) und benutze die Verben (*inseparable prefix verbs*) aus dem Kasten.

---

beschließen • erlauben • erzählen • verbringen • vergnügen • erkälten • gefallen

---

Heidi: Hi, Susan! Warum bist du Samstag denn nicht auf der Party von Philipp gewesen?

Susan: Oh, ich war in Amsterdam!

Heidi: Ja, das _____ mir Philipp schon _____ (*erzählen*)! Erzähl du mal!

Susan: _____

_____

Heidi: _____

_____

Susan: _____

_____

Heidi: _____

_____

Susan: _____

_____

Heidi: _____

Susan: _____

Aktivität 27. Wohin geht die nächste Reise?

Schauen Sie sich die Clips "Die nächste Reise" von Berna und Jan an. Wohin möchten sie noch reisen? Warum?

(QR 6.22 p.300)

(QR 6.21 p.300)

Aktivität 28. Das Wetter: Auch im Urlaub scheint nicht immer die Sonne!

A. Wetterinformationen aus dem deutschen Fernsehen … wir lachen mit und über die Wetterfee Maxi Biewer

Die Wettervorhersage wird im Anschluss zu einer Nachrichtensendung gezeigt. Manchmal (oder meistens) ist das Wetter leider nicht so unterhaltsam wie die Vorhersage selbst … Die folgenden Aufgaben geben Ihnen einen Einblick.

Gehen Sie zu Maxi Biewers Webseite unter folgendem Link und spielen Sie das Video ab: http://www.maxibiewer.de/index.php?id=22.

❑ Wer oder was ist eine Wetterfee? Wie sagt man dazu in den USA?

❑ Warum lacht Maxi Biewer?

❑ Was haben Sie (nicht) über das Wetter erfahren?

Gehen Sie auf http://wetter.tagesschau.de und schauen Sie einen aktuellen deutschen Wetterbericht an.

❑ Über welches Gebiet/welche Gebiete geht es im Wetterbericht?

❑ Wie ist das Wetter dort?

❑ Ist dieser Bericht wie Wetterberichte in Ihrem Land? Wenn ja, wieso? Wenn nein, wieso nicht?

Spaß-Tipp: Suchen Sie doch mal nach *MC Maxi Beaver Rap by Raab* mit den Suchworten „Maxi Biewer Rap Raab" auf youtube. Was ist in dem Video los?

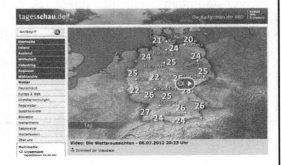

B. Wetterinformationen aus dem Internet

Betrachten Sie nachfolgenden Abbildungen. Worum geht es? Welche Städte sind im Fokus? Gehen Sie auf eine dieser Websites: http://www.wetter.de, http://www.donnerwetter.de oder http://www.dwd.de. Was für Vokabeln erscheinen Ihnen nützlich (*useful*)? Dann sehen Sie sich die Vorhersage einer Stadt ihrer Wahl (*of your choice*) mit den tagesaktuellen Daten an. Machen Sie sich Notizen und geben Sie auch an, wo ihre Stadt liegt (*is located*).

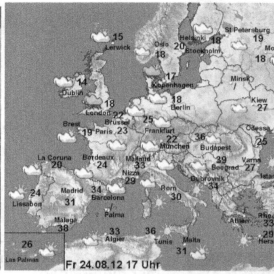

Nützliche Wörter:

C. Celsius oder Fahrenheit?

In Europa wird die Temperatur in Celsius angegeben. Es ist daher nützlich, wenn man weiß, wie man Celsius in Fahrenheit umrechnet. Hier eine Übersicht:

Fahrenheit	-4	14	32	50	68	86	104
Celsius	-20	-10	0	10	20	30	40

Umrechnungsformel:
Umrechnung von Celsius in Fahrenheit: $°F = °C × 1,8 + 32$
Umrechnung von Fahrenheit in Celsius: $°C = (°F − 32) : 1,8$

Vervollständigen Sie nachfolgende Tabelle (einen Temperaturenumrechner (Celsius – Fahrenheit und umgekehrt) finden Sie zum Beispiel auf: http://www.umrechnung.org):

Fahrenheit	46			65	
Celsius		-3	39		23

Aktivität 29. Begriffe rund um das Wetter

Ordnen Sie den Bildern die richtigen Begriffe zu:

1. _b_ die Sonne (die Sonne scheint, es ist sonnig, es ist warm, es ist heiß)
2. ____ der Regen (der Niederschlag, es regnet, es ist regnerisch)
3. ____ der Hagel (es hagelt)
4. ____ der Wind (es ist windig, es ist böig, Wind zieht auf, es gibt einen Sturm, es gibt einen Orkan)
5. ____ das Gewitter (der Blitz, der Donner, es blitzt und donnert, es gibt ein Gewitter)
6. ____ der Nebel (es ist neblig)
7. ____ die Wolke (es ist bewölkt)
8. ____ der Schnee (es schneit, es ist kalt)

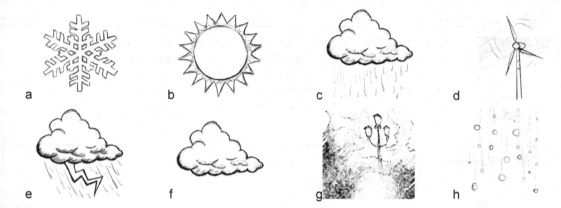

a   b   c   d

e   f   g   h

Aktivität 30. Die Jahreszeiten

Nachfolgend sehen Sie vier Bilder. Welches Bild stellt den Frühling dar? Welches den Sommer, welches den Herbst und welches den Winter?

A. Welche Begriffe (Ideen, Konzepte) assoziieren Sie mit den Jahreszeiten?

Tipp: Das nachfolgende Gedicht hilft Ihnen vielleicht bei der Begriffssammlung!

B. Ein Gedicht über die Jahreszeiten: Welcher der vier Titel passt zu dem Gedicht?

Winterlich • Der Herbst • Sommerliches Gebet • Er ist's

_____

Frühling lässt sein blaues Band
Wieder flattern durch die Lüfte;
Süße, wohlbekannte Düfte
Streifen ahnungsvoll das Land.
Veilchen träumen schon,
Wollen balde kommen.
– Horch, von fern ein leiser Harfenton!
  Frühling, ja du bist's!
Dich hab ich vernommen!

(Eduard Mörike)

Aktivität 31. Wetterberichte auf youtube.com
Schauen Sie sich einige Wetterberichte – mindestens drei – auf http://www.youtube.com an. Gute Suchwörter sind „Wetterbericht" und „Deutschland, Österreich, Schweiz" (oder deine Lieblingsstadt). Schreiben Sie Begriffe und Redewendungen auf, die Sie verstehen. Machen Sie sich Notizen: Wie ist das Wetter heute in den deutschsprachigen Ländern oder Städten?

Nützliche Redewendungen:

Die Stadt/Region				
Höchsttemperatur				
Tiefsttemperatur				
Sonne? (ja, sonnig/ nein, bewölkt)				
Niederschlag? (z.B. Regen, Schnee usw.)				
Sonstiges (z.B. Wind oder Nebel)				

Aktivität 32. Nun zu Ihnen!

Schreiben Sie einen Wetterbericht für Ihr Gebiet. Benutzen Sie möglichst viele Ausdrücke und Redewendungen von der vorigen Übung! Sie können Ihren Wetterbericht live im Kurs vorspielen oder ein Video machen und abspielen.

Guten Abend, meine Damen und Herren!

Aktivität 33. Ein Reisebericht-Spiel im Kurs

Jeder Student nimmt ein leeres Blatt und beginnt oben auf dem Blatt einen Reisebericht („Satz 1"). Er/sie gibt das Blatt seinem/ihrem Nachbarn. Der Nachbar7die Nachbarin liest „Satz 1" und schreibt „Satz 2". „Satz 1" und „Satz 2" müssen zusammen Sinn ergeben. Man knickt das Papier nun so um (*fold over*), dass nur noch „Satz 2" zu sehen ist und gibt es an den nächsten Nachbarn/die nächste Nachbarin, der/die „Satz 3" schreibt. Der Nachbar/die Nachbarin darf NUR den letzten Satz lesen und schreibt einen neuen Satz unter den Satz des Nachbarn/der Nachbarin. Dann wird das Blatt wieder umgeknickt und weitergegeben. Das wird wiederholt, bis das Blatt voll ist. Der jeweilige Autor darf immer nur den vorangegangenen Satz lesen, nicht alle Sätze auf dem Blatt. Am Ende werden die „Reiseberichte" laut vorgelesen. Viel Spaß mit den unglaublichen Geschichten!

Wohin sind Sie gefahren?
Wer ist mitgekommen?
Was haben Sie gesehen?
Was haben Sie gekauft? Gegessen?
Was ist auf der Reise passiert?
Was haben Sie nicht gemacht?
Was haben Sie nicht besuchen können?
Und wie war das Wetter?
...

1. DIE AUSLAUTVERHÄRTUNG

Now that you're familiar with the sounds and letters of the German alphabet, let's see how they can change in different environments. One perfect example is the phonological process known as **Auslautverhärtung** (the hardening of the final consonant in word).

Through this process, the voiced consonants, for example **b**, **d**, and **g**, are transformed into their voiceless counterparts **p**, **t**, and **k** at the end of syllables or words. The term **voiced** describes sounds that make your vocal cords vibrate when you pronounce them, while the term **voiceless** describes sounds that do not make them vibrate. Put your hand on your throat while you say **b** and **p** and you should be able to feel the difference!

The consonants **b** and **p** are really the same sound (same place and manner of articulation); the only difference is that **b** is voiced and **p** is voiceless. For that matter, so are the consonant pairs **k** and **g** as well as **d** and **t**.

Stops

bilabial (pronounced with both of your lips)		alveolar (pronounced with your tongue pressed against that ticklish ridge behind your upper teeth)		velar (pronounced with the back of your tongue pressed against the soft upper part of the roof of your mouth)	
voiceless	*voiced*	*voiceless*	*voiced*	*voiceless*	*voiced*
p	b	t	d	k	g

In German, the voiced consonants **b**, **d**, and **g** are pronounced "normally" as **b**, **d**, and **g** if they begin a word or are in between other sounds (i.e., not at the end of the word), as the following examples show:

At the beginning or in the middle of words

der Bericht	das Angebot	(letter b sounds like German b)
der Dom	im Süden	(letter d sounds like German d)
das Gepäck	die Züge	(letter g sounds like German g)

Now compare these to what these consonants sound like at the end of word:

b	→	**p**	(**b** gets devoiced)
die Urlaube		der Urlaub	
geben		gab	
die Liebe		lieb	

d	→	**t**	(**d** gets devoiced)
die Strände		der Strand	
sandig		der Sand	
einladen		einlud	

g	→	**k**	(**g** gets devoiced)
billiger		billig	
fliegen		der Flug	
die Berge		der Berg	

The same phenomenon occurs with the fricatives **s** and **v**. **z** and **s** are voiced and unvoiced counterparts, as are **v** and **f**.

s as [z]	→	s as [s]	(**s** is pronounced unvoiced at the end)
lesen		las	
die Preise		der Preis	
die Häuser		das Haus	

v	→	f	(**v** is pronounced unvoiced at the end)
brave		brav	

The Second German Consonant Shift: Your friendly guide to German-English cognates

In the early 19th century, scholars were busy deciphering the differences between various Indo-European languages (the language family to which both English and German belong) and noticed a variety of patterned changes from Sanskrit, Latin and Greek to the Germanic branch of this language family. In addition to Friedrich Schlegel and Rasmus Rask, Jakob Grimm of Grimm Grammar fame was quite fascinated and developed a set of statements that described most of the patterns of interest. His descriptions are summarized under **Grimm's Law**, and describe the **First Germanic Sound Shift** (accounting for changes that occurred during the centuries around 1000 BC). These changes included, for example, shifting from the p in pater (father; Latin) to f/v in (father/vater; Germanic languages).

Later in the life of Germanic languages, a second sound shift (over the course of several centuries, starting probably around the 3rd century and before the 9th century) occurred, which accounts for many of the differences that can be seen today between Standard German and English words. Knowing these changes will help you recognize cognates and decipher the meaning of German texts much more efficiently!

So, what does the **High German Sound Shift** (the Second Germanic Consonant Shift) tell us? In a nutshell, it tells us that

a. some fricatives in German (ch, f, s) are voiceless stops (k, p, t) in English
b. some German affricates (a stop plus a fricative: e.g., pf) are voiceless stops (e.g., p) in English
c. some voiceless stops (k, p, t) in German are voiced stops in English

The following chart highlights the differences between German and English consonants, which are a result of the High German Sound Shift.

sound pairs	German	English
ff – p	das Schiff, scharf	ship, sharp
pf – p	der Pfad, das Pfund	path, pound
v – f	vier, die Vorväter	four, forefathers
ss – t	groß, die Straße	great, street
sch [ʃ] – sh/s	scheinen, der Schnee	to shine, snow
z/tz [tz] – t	das Zelt, die Zeit, die Hitze	tent, time, heat
z/tz – c [s]	der Platz, die Gewürze	place, spices
ch [ç/χ] – k	machen, suchen	to make, to seek
ch [ç/χ] – gh	acht, lachen	eight, to laugh
k – ch [tʃ]	die Kirche, das Kind	church, child
k – c [k]	die Küste, die Karte	coast, card
b – v	geben, sieben	to give, seven
t – d	gut, der Tag	good, day
d – δ/θ	der Süden, der Bruder	South, brother
t – δ/θ	das Wetter, der Vater	weather, father
g – y	gestern, gelb, segeln	yesterday, yellow, sail
mm – mb	das Lamm, der Kamm	lamb, comb

Aussprache

Please go to the Deutsch im Blick website, Kapitel 6

Knowing these changes can help you recognize German-English cognates. Below are some sentences in German. Can you decipher what the English equivalents of the **bold italicized** words are?

1. Schneewittchen nimmt ein warmes **Bad**, macht das **Licht** aus und legt sich in das weiche **Bett**.
2. An einem schönen **Tag** nehmen die **Mutter** und der **Vater** Hänsel und Gretel tief in den Wald.
3. Als der Räuber durch die **Tür** ins Haus will, springt die **Katze** ihm ins Gesicht und haut ihre Klauen in sein **Fleisch**.
4. Die Königin befiehlt dem Wirt, **Wasser** aus dem **Keller** zu holen, weil das für den König viel **besser** ist als Wein.
5. Sein Wunsch wird ihm gewährt und bei jedem **Wort**, das er **spricht**, fällt ihm ein goldener **Taler** aus dem Munde.

Answer: 1. bath, light, bed • 2. day, mother, father • 3. door, cat, flesh • 4. water, cellar, better • 5. word, speaks, dollar

You can listen to the *Auslautverhärtung* in this poem by Christian Morgenstern, a German poet who wrote many nonsensical poems (1871–1914):

Himmel und Erde
Von Christian Morgenstern

Der Nachtwindhund weint wie ein Kind,
dieweil sein Fell von Regen rinnt.

Jetzt jagt er wild das Neumondweib,
das hinflieht mit gebognem Leib.

Tief unten geht, ein dunkler Punkt,
querüberfeld ein Forstadjunkt.

Like a child cries the night-greyhound
while on its fur the rain runs down.

Now he wildly chases the wife of the New Moon
who is fleeing, her body all astoop.

Just a dark spot, goes far below,
the forest helper across the meadow

http://www.interdeutsch.de/Uebungen/auslaut.html

WebQuests
In diesem Kapitel finden Sie sechs mögliche WebQuests auf der *Deutsch im Blick*-Webseite:

1. *Im ersten WebQuest werden Ihre Reiseplanungskünste benötigt.*
2. *Im zweiten WebQuest erkunden Sie das Nachtleben in Würzburg.*
3. *Im dritten WebQuest lernen Sie mehr über das Wetter in Deutschland.*
4. *Im vierten WebQuest können Sie in ein deutsches Bundesland reisen, das Ihnen besonders gut gefällt.*
5. *Im fünften WebQuest reisen Sie in die Schweiz.*
6. *Im sechsten WebQuest reisen Sie nach Österreich.*

Meinungsumfragen
Die Themen in diesem Kapitel sind *Reisen* und *Ihre Wetterpräferenzen*. Gehen Sie zur *Deutsch im Blick*-Webseite und klicken Sie auf „Meinungsumfragen".

Reisen	**Traveling**
fahren	to drive/to travel
das Fernweh/die Reiselust	desire to travel (e.g., having the travel bug)
das Heimweh	homesickness
Ich habe Heimweh.	I am homesick.
die Reise (Reisen)	trip, journey
die Weltreise	trip around the world/ world tour
die Rundreise	trip to many places/cities
um die Welt reisen	to travel around the world
auf eine Reise gehen	to go on a journey
reisen	to travel
der Reisebericht (Reiseberichte)	travelogue/account of a journey
der Tourist (Touristen)	tourist
der Urlaub (Urlaube)	vacation
im Urlaub sein	to be on vacation
verreisen	to travel/ to make a journey

Eine Reise buchen	**To Book a Travel**
ausgeben	to spend
der Billigflieger (-flieger)	no frills airline/low budget airline
der Flug (Flüge)	flight
Dieser Flug ist ausgebucht.	This flight is fully booked.
der Flughafen (-häfen)	airport
günstig	low priced/inexpensive
das Land (Länder)	land (rural area), also the countryside
der Ort (Orte)	city/place
planen (plante/geplant)	to plan
der Preis (Preise)	price
Das ist ein guter Preis.	That is a good price.
das Reisebüro (-büros)	travel agency
das Sonderangebot (-angebote)	special offer
die Stadt (Städte)	city
eine europäische Stadt	a European city
die Großstadt	metropolis
die Innenstadt	city center/downtown
teuer	expensive

Unterbringungsmöglichkeiten	**Accomodations**
campen	to camp
der Campingplatz (-plätze)	camping ground
das Hotel (Hotels)	hotel
die Jugendherberge (-herbergen)	youth hostel
das Zelt (Zelte)	tent
zelten	to camp

Transportmittel	**Means of Transportation**
das Auto (Autos)	car
mit dem Auto fahren	to drive by car/ to go by car
per Autostopp/per Anhalter fahren	to hitchhike
die Bahn (Bahnen)	railroad
der Bus (Busse)	bus
mit dem Bus fahren/reisen	to drive/ travel by bus
das Fahrrad (-räder)	bike
mit dem Fahrrad fahren	to bike
das Flugzeug (-zeuge)	airplane
mit dem Flugzeug fliegen	to travel by air
der Fuß (Füße)	foot
zu Fuß gehen	to go by/on foot

der Mietwagen (-wagen)	rental car
einen Mietwagen mieten	to rent a car
auf einem Pferd/Kamel reiten	to ride on a horse/camel
das Schiff (Schiffe)	ship
die Seekrankheit (-krankheiten)	sea sickness
seekrank sein	to be sea sick
das Taxi (Taxis/Taxen)	cab
ein Taxi nehmen/bestellen	to take/ order a cab
mit dem Taxi fahren	to drive/ go by cab
der Zug (Züge)	train

Reiseziele — Travel Destinations

(eine Liste von Ländern finden Sie in Kapitel 1)	(there is a list of countries in Chapter 1)
der Atlantische Ozean	the Atlantic Ocean
der Basar (Basare)	bazaar
auf den Basar gehen	to go shopping at the bazaar
der Berg (Berge)	mountain
in den Bergen wandern	to hike in the mountains
in die Berge fahren	to travel in(to) the mountains
der Felsen (Felsen)	rock/cliff
Die Loreley ist ein Felsen am Rhein.	The Loreley is a rock at the Rhine .
die Karibik	the Caribbean
das Meer (Meere)	sea
ans Meer fahren	to travel to the sea
das Mittelmeer	the Mediterranean
der Pazifische Ozean	the Pacific Ocean
der See (Seen)	lake
auf dem See segeln	to sail on the lake
im See schwimmen	to swim in the lake
die See (Seen)	sea
die Nordsee	the North Sea
die Ostsee	the Baltic Sea
der Strand (Strände)	beach
an den Strand gehen	to go to the beach

Auf einer Reise — On a trip

der Bahnhof (-höfe)	train station
die Fahrkarte (-karten)	ticket (for traveling)
der Fahrkartenautomat (-automaten)	the vending machine (for tickets)
das Gepäck (no pural)	luggage (suitcases)
Mein Gepäck ist nicht angekommen.	My luggage did not arrive.
die Haltestelle (-stellen)	stop
die Karte (Karten)	map
die Landkarte	map
der Koffer (Koffer)	suitcase
der Reiseführer (-führer)	travel guide
der Reisepass (Pässe)	passport
Ihren Reisepass, bitte!	Your (formal) passport, please!
die Reisetasche (-taschen)	travel bag
die Schnellbahn (-bahnen) – abbr.: S-Bahn	high-speed railway
der Sitzplatz (-plätze)	seat (on a train, on an airplane)
die Sitzplatzreservierung	seat reservation
Ich möchte einen Sitzplatz reservieren.	I'd like to reserve a seat.
die Station (Stationen)	station
die Straßenbahn (-bahnen)	tram
der (Ticket-) Schalter (Schalter)	ticket window
die U-Bahn (U-Bahnen)	underground railway
unterwegs sein	to be away/to be out (on business)
verlaufen (sich)	to get lost
Ich habe mich verlaufen.	I got lost.
vermissen	to miss
Ich vermisse dich.	I miss you.
verpassen	to miss (the train, flight)

Ich habe meinen nächsten Flug verpasst!	I missed my connecting flight!
verspäten	to be late
Der Zug ist verspätet.	The train is running late.
der Zoll (Zölle)	customs

(QR 6.1 p.300)

Strandurlaub / Beach Vacations

Strandurlaub	**Beach Vacations**
das Boot (Boote)	boat
der Fisch (Fische)	fish
das Foto (Fotos)	photo
viele Fotos machen	to take lots of pictures
das Fotoalbum (-alben)	photo album
die Kamera (Kameras)	camera
die Insel (Inseln)	the island/the isle
die Küste (Küsten)	coast
die Muschel (Muscheln)	the shell
der Sand (no plural)	the sand
das Segelboot (-boote)	the sailboat
der Sonnenbrand (-bände)	sunburn
die Sonnenbrille (-brillen)	sunglasses
die Sonnencreme (-cremes)	sunscreen
das Ufer (Ufer)	shore
Heute gibt es viele Wellen.	There are many waves today.
das Wasser	water
Das Wasser ist kalt.	The water is cold.

Sehenswürdigkeiten und Aktivitäten / Sights to see and activities to do

Sehenswürdigkeiten und Aktivitäten	**Sights to see and activities to do**
die Ausstellung (Ausstellungen)	exhibition
besichtigen	to visit (a site, famous place, etc.)
Wir haben den Kölner Dom besichtigt.	We visited the Kölner Dom.
das Fest (Feste)	feast/celebration
auf das Oktoberfest gehen	to go to the Oktoberfest
das Festival (Festivals)	festival
Die Band spielt auf dem Festival.	The band plays at the festival.
der Fluss (Flüsse)	river
im Fluss schwimmen gehen	to swim in the river
die Kirche (Kirchen)	church
die Sehenswürdigkeit (Sehenswürdigkeiten)	landmark/the object of interest
das Sightseeing	sightseeing
das Mitbringsel/Souvenir (Mitbringsel/Souvenirs)	souvenir/ the small present
der Souvenirladen (-läden)	souvenir shop
das Schloss (Schlösser)	castle, *also:* lock
Ski fahren	to ski
der Wald (Wälder)	forest
der Zoo (Zoos) also: der Tierpark (Tierparks)	zoo
in den Zoo gehen	to go to the zoo

Wie war dein Urlaub? / How was your vacation?

Wie war dein Urlaub?	**How was your vacation?**
angenehm	pleasant
anstrengend	exhausting
gefallen	to like
Österreich hat mir sehr gut gefallen!	I really liked Austria!
großartig	great
hektisch	hectic
kurz	short
lang	long
langweilig	boring
schrecklich	terrible/ horrible

Ausgewählte trennbare Verben	Selected Seperable Prefix Verbs
ankommen	to arrive
Der Zug ist pünktlich angekommen.	The train arrived on time.
anschauen (sich)	to watch/ to look at
Er schaut sich die Show an.	He is watching the show.
ansehen (sich)	to look at/ to watch
Ich sehe mir den Film an.	I am watching the movie.
ausschlafen	to sleep in
Hans schläft gerne aus.	Hans likes to sleep in.
aussteigen	to get out
Sie steigt aus dem Taxi aus.	She gets out of the cab.
einladen	to invite
Er lädt sie zur Show ein.	He invites her to the show.
einsteigen	to get in
Er steigt in die Bahn ein.	He gets in the train.
mitbringen	to bring along
Er bringt Würstchen zur Party mit.	He brings hot dogs to the party.
mitkommen	to come with/ to come along
Sie kommt zum Konzert mit.	She comes along to the concert.

Ausgewählte untrennbare Verben	Selected Inseparable Prefix Verbs
entspannen (sich)	to relax
Ich entspanne mich vor dem Fernseher	I relax in front of the TV.
genießen	to enjoy
Matthias genießt seinen Urlaub.	Matthias enjoys his vacation.
verabreden (sich)	to agree on /set (a date/ an appointment)
Ich verabrede mich mit ihr.	I make an appointment with her.
verbringen	to spend
Ich verbringe zu viel Zeit mit Hausaufgaben.	I spend too much time on homework.
vergnügen (sich)	to enjoy
Sie hat sich im Zoo nicht vergnügt.	She didn't have a good time at the zoo.

Über das Wetter sprechen	Talking about the weather
aufregend	exciting
deprimierend	depressing
Das Wetter ist deprimierend.	The weather is depressing.
das Eis	ice
Vorsicht! Glatteis!	Attention! Black ice!
jemanden aufs Glatteis führen (fig.)	to lead somebody down the garden path
erfrischend	refreshing
das Gewitter (Gewitter)	thunderstorm
der Blitz (Blitze)	lightning
der Donner (Donner)	thunder
das Unwetter (Unwetter)	bad weather (e.g. a thunderstorm)
der Hagel	hail
es hagelt	it's hailing
heiß	hot
Mir ist heiß/kalt.	I'm hot/cold.
Es ist heiß draußen!	It's hot outside!
der Himmel (Himmel)	sky
Der Himmel ist bedeckt.	The sky is overcast.
ein sternenklarer Himmel	a starlit sky
die Hitze	heat
kühl	cool/chilly
der Nebel	fog
Es ist neblig.	It's foggy/misty.
der Niederschlag (Niederschläge)	precipitation
der Norden	the north
nördlich	northern
der Osten	the east
östlich	eastern
der Regen	rain

regnen — to rain
   Es regnet. — it's raining
   Es gießt wie aus Eimern. (fig.) — It's raining cats and dogs. (fig.)
scheinen — to shine
   Die Sonne scheint den ganzen Tag. — The sun shines all day long.
der Schnee — snow
schneien — to snow
   Es schneit. — It snows/it's snowing.
die Sonne — sun
   Es ist sonnig. — It's sunny.
der Sonnenschein — sunshine
der Sturm (Stürme) — storm
   der Tornado (Tornados) — tornado
   der Hurrikan (Hurrikans/Hurrikane) — hurricane (tropical)
der Süden — the south
   südlich — southern
   im Süden — in the South
die Temperatur — temperature
   Die Höchsttemperatur beträgt 25 °C — The high temperature is 25 °C.
   Die Tiefsttemperatur beträgt -5 °C. — The lowest temperature is -5 °C.
warm — warm
der Westen — the west
   westlich — western
   Der Wind kommt aus dem Westen. — The wind is coming from the West.
das Wetter — weather
der Wetterbericht (Wetterberichte) — weather report
die Wettervorhersage (Wettervorhersagen) — weather forecast
der Wind (Winde) — wind
   Es ist windig. — It's windy.
die Wolke (Wolken) — cloud
   Es ist bewölkt. — It's cloudy/overcast.

QR Codes

6.1 Wortschatz	6.2 06_01_int_ag_ reisen	6.3 06_02_int_hm_ reisen	6.4 06_03_int_ec_ reisen	6.5 06_04_int_sco_ reisen	6.6 06_05_int_scl_ reisen
6.7 06_06_int_bg_ reisen	6.8 06_07_int_ju_ reisen	6.9 06_09_int_ek_ guenstig	6.10 06_10_int_sco_ guenstig	6.11 06_11_int_ph_ bericht	6.12 06_12_int_ek_ reisen
6.13 06_13_sik_ kerstenflitter wochen	6.14 06_14_sik_ christine	6.15 06_15_sik_mario	6.16 06_16_int_scl_ bericht	6.17 06_17_int_ag_ bericht	6.18 06_18_sik_josh-amsterdam
6.19 06_19_sik_ joshetal-scotland	6.20 06_20_int_hb_ naechste	6.21 06_21_int_ju_ naechste	6.22 06_22_int_bg_ naechste	6.23 06_23_intro_ reisen	

Wortschatz
- *Gesund leben*
- *Sport treiben*
- *Sportanlagen*
- *Der menschliche Körper*
- *Körperpflege*
- *Verletzungen*
- *Beschwerden*
- *Ein Kuraufenthalt*
- *Ärzte*
- *Beim Arzt*
- *Die Versicherung*
- *Die Medizin*

Aussprache
- *Kapitel 7: Regional Dialects in Germany*

Grammatik
Focus
- *Miscellaneous: Wortbildung*
- *Verben: Die reflexiven Verben*
- *Verbs: Der Infinitivsatz*
- *Verbs: Der Imperativ*

Recommended
- *Nouns: Overview*
- *Pronouns: Personalpronomen*
- *Conjunctions: Word Order*
- *Modal Verbs: Present Tense*

Videos
Sprache im Kontext
- *Vanessa: Sportausweis*
- *Sara: Sportzentren in Würzburg*
- *Das deutsche Versicherungssystem*
- *Die Körperteile*

7 GESUNDHEIT UND FITNESS

Gesundheit und Fitness sind heutzutage besonders wichtige Themen. Aber was bedeuten „Gesundheit" und „Fitness" überhaupt? Was heißt es, „gesund" und „fit" zu leben? In diesem Kapitel werden Sie diese Fragen untersuchen. Sie werden auch viel über die verschiedenen Aspekte der Gesundheit lernen, zum Beispiel gesund zu essen, Sport zu treiben, den Körper zu pflegen und zum Arzt zu gehen. Das Einführungsvideo wird Ihnen einen kleinen Einblick in dieses Kapitel geben!

Sie werden nach diesem Kapitel
1. *Ihre Aussprache verbessert haben.*
2. *Ihren Wortschatz erweitert haben.*
3. *über Gesundheit und Fitness auf Deutsch sprechen können.*
4. *neue Grammatikthemen beherrschen.*
5. *unterschiedliche Kulturen verstehen.*

Was Sie in diesem Kapitel machen müssen:
1. *mit den Interviews der Muttersprachler und Amerikaner arbeiten.*
2. *mit den „Sprache im Kontext"-Videos arbeiten.*
3. *verschiedene Spiele spielen.*
4. *mit Texten arbeiten.*
5. *Ihre Aussprache üben.*

Online Book links

Sie können die Videoclips unter folgendem Link finden:
http://coerll.utexas.edu/dib/toc.php?k=7

Sie können die Vokabeln unter folgendem Link finden:
http://coerll.utexas.edu/dib/voc.php?k=7

Sections

Gesund leben • healthy living
Sport treiben • Doing sports / exercising
Sportanlagen • Sports facilities
Der menschliche Körper • The human body
Körperpflege • Personal hygiene
Unfälle • Injuries
Beschwerden • Ailments
Ein Kuraufenthalt • A stay at a health resort
Ärzte • Doctors
Beim Arzt • At the doctor
Die Versicherung • Insurance
Die Medizin • Medicine

Sie können auch die Grammatikthemen aus diesem Kapitel online finden:

Während der Übungen im Kapitel werden Sie regelmäßig auf Grimm Grammar verwiesen (*referred to*). Hier sind die Grammatikthemen, die das Kapitel abdeckt (*covers*); machen Sie alle Online-Übungen, um optimal von den Übungen in diesem Arbeitsbuch (*workbook*) zu profitieren (*to profit from*).

- Miscellaneous
  Wortbildung   http://coerll.utexas.edu/gg/gr/mis_02.html

- Verben
  Die reflexiven Verben   http://coerll.utexas.edu/gg/gr/vrf_01.html
  Der Infinitivsatz   http://coerll.utexas.edu/gg/gr/vinf_01.html
  Der Imperativ   http://coerll.utexas.edu/gg/gr/vimp_01.html

- Recommended:
  Nouns: Overview   http://coerll.utexas.edu/gg/gr/no_01.html
  Pronouns: Personalpronomen http://coerll.utexas.edu/gg/gr/pro_01.html
  Conjunctions: Word Order http://coerll.utexas.edu/gg/gr/con_06.html
  Modal verbs: Present Tense http://coerll.utexas.edu/gg/gr/vm_01.html

A. LISTEN

Listen carefully to the pronunciation of each word or phrase in the vocabulary list.

B. REPEAT

Repeat each word or phrase *out loud* as many times as necessary until you remember it well and can recognize it as well as produce it. Make a list of the words in this chapter which you find difficult to pronounce. Your teacher may ask you to compare your list with other students in your class. Make sure to learn nouns with their correct gender!

> **Beispiel:**
> die Sprache
> fünf

C. WRITE

Write key words from the vocabulary list so that you can spell them correctly (remember that it makes a big difference whether you cross the Atlantic by ship or by sheep). You may want to listen to the vocabulary list again and write the words as they are spoken for extra practice.

D. TRANSLATION

Learn the English translation of each word or phrase. Cover the German column and practice giving the German equivalent for each English word or phrase. Next cover the English column and give the translation of each.

E. ASSOCIATIONS

Think of word associations for each category of vocabulary. (What words, both English and German, do you associate with each word or phrase on the list? Write down ten (10) associations with the vocabulary from the chapter.

> **Beispiel:**
> der Student/die Universität
> das Flugticket/das Flugzeug

F. COGNATES

Which words are *cognates?* (Cognates are words which look or sound like English words.) Watch out for *false friends*! Write down several cognates and all the false friends from the chapter, create fun sentences that illustrate similarities and differences between the English and German meanings of these words.

> **Beispiel:**
> Nacht/night
> grün/green
> → False Friends: *hell* = light, bright vs. *Hölle* = hell

G. WORD FAMILIES

Which words come from word families in German that you recognize (noun, adjective, verb, adverb)? Write down as many as you find in the chapter.

> **Beispiel:**
> das Studium (noun; studies)
> der Student (noun; person)
> studieren (verb)

H. EXERCISES

Write out three (3) „Was passt nicht?" ('Odd one out') exercises. List four words, three of which are related and one that does not fit the same category. Categories can be linked to meaning, grammar, gender, parts of speech (noun, verb, adjective), etc. USE YOUR IMAGINATION! Give the reason for why the odd word does not fit. Your classmates will have to solve the puzzles you provide!

> **Beispiel:**
> grün – blau – gelb – neun
> Here *neun* does not fit, because it is a
> number and all the others are colors.

Wortschatz
Vorbereitung

Always learn nouns with the article!!!

These ideas are suggestions only. Different learners have different preferences and needs for learning and reviewing vocabulary. T[...] several of these sugges[...] tions until you find ones tha[...] work for you. Keep in min[...] though, that knowing man[...] words – and knowing the[...] well, both to recognize an[...] to produce – makes you [...] more effective user of th[...] new language.

Basiswortschatz
Core Vocabulary

The following presents a list of core vocabulary. Consider this list as the absolute minimum to focus on. As you work through the chapter you will need more vocabulary to help you talk about your own experience. To that end, a more complete vocabulary list can be found at the end of the chapter. This reference list will aid your attainment of Chapter 7's objectives.

(QR 7.1 p.345)

Gesund sein/Sich fit halten — To be healthy/Staying in shape

die Gesundheit (no plural)	health, well-being
trainieren	to train/work out
Sport treiben	to do sports
das Fitnessstudio (-studios)	gym
der Fußballplatz (-plätze)	soccer field (the real football!)
das Schwimmbad (-bäder)	swimming pool

Die Körperteile — Parts of the Body

der Arm (Arme)	arm
das Auge (Augen)	eye
der Bauch (Bäuche)	stomach
die Brust (Brüste)	breast/chest
der Fuß (Füße)	foot
das Gesicht (Gesichter)	face
das Haar (Haare)	hair
die Hand (Hände)	hand
das Herz (Herzen)	heart
der Kopf (Köpfe)	head
die Nase (Nasen)	nose
der Zahn (Zähne)	tooth

Körperpflege — Personal hygiene

sich die Augenbrauen zupfen	to pluck one's eyebrows
sich das Gesicht waschen	to wash one's face
sich die Haare waschen	to wash one's hair
sich die Hände waschen	to wash one's hands
sich die Zähne putzen	to brush one's teeth
sich rasieren	to shave

Verletzungen und Beschwerden — Injuries and Ailments

sich (z.B. den Arm) brechen	to break one's arm
sich weh tun	to hurt oneself
der Unfall (Unfälle)	accident
die Erkältung (Erkältungen)	common cold
die Grippe (Grippen)	flu
der Schmerz (Schmerzen)	pain, ache
schwach	weak
übel	nauseous
verwirrt	confused
sich ausruhen	to rest
sich erholen	to recuperate

Beim Arzt/im Krankenhaus — At the Doctor's/the Hospital

der Arzt (Ärzte)	physician, doctor
die Ärztin (Ärztinnen)	female physician, female doctor
Angst haben	to be afraid
das Krankenhaus (-häuser)	hospital
nervös	nervous
die Notaufnahme (-aufnahmen)	emergency room
das Rezept (Rezepte)	prescription
eine Spritze bekommen	to get a shot
einen Termin haben	to have an appointment
untersuchen	to examine
versichern	to insure
die Versicherung (Versicherungen)	insurance
die Kopfschmerztablette (-tabletten)	headache medication

Aktivität 1. Leben die Deutschen gesund?

**A. Schauen Sie sich Bernas, Evas und Jans Videos „Gesund leben"
an und füllen Sie die Lücken mit den richtigen Vokabeln aus den
Kästen aus.**

fettige • bewegen Nachbarschaft • Obst gesund • Musik • Sporthalle Gemüse • joggen abschalten • laufe • ungesund spazieren • zu gehen	Bauch-Beine-Po • relativ Luft • Volleyball spielen turne • Kursangebote Aerobic • Sport • ernähr' Fitnesssäle • draußen Basketball spielen • mach'	langweilig • Doktor Aktivitäten • Basketball weiß • Spass • schwimme Fußball • Schwimmen nicht so viel

(QR 7.2 p.345)	(QR 7.3 p.345)	(QR 7.4 p.345)

Bist du ein gesunder Mensch?

Ich versuche _____ zu sein. Ich glaube, manchmal esse ich ein wenig _____, weil ich alles esse, auch Pizza und _____ Sachen. Aber ich versuche schon gesund zu sein, indem ich ab und zu auch mal ein bisschen _____ und _____ esse.

Ja, glaube ich schon. Ich _____ mich sehr gesund, versuch' viel Obst und Gemüse zu essen, _____ viel _____ und bin auch sehr gerne _____ an der frischen _____.

Soweit ich _____, ja! Mein _____ sagt, es ist O.K.

Wo treibst du Sport? Wo kannst du Sport treiben?

Meistens laufe ich in der _____. Manchmal laufe ich auch an der Universität, in der _____.

An der Uni sehr gut und auch _____ günstig. Es gibt große _____, es gibt _____, die man nutzen kann. Es gibt Kurse für _____, Fitnesszirkel, Leichtathletikwettkämpfe, Mannschaften, _____, _____ kann man ...

Ich treibe Sport in unsrem Reccenter. Wir haben einen Reccenter auf dem Campus und dort kann man alle möglichen _____ machen: _____, Laufen, _____ spielen, _____ spielen.

Treibst du Sport lieber alleine oder mit anderen Menschen?

Ich mach' das lieber allein. Ich habe dann meinen Walkman auf, höre _____ und kann dann mal richtig _____ für eine Stunde.

Mit anderen Menschen ist es nicht so _____ _____. Das macht mehr _____.

B. Leben die Amerikaner gesund?

Schauen Sie sich Hassans und Erins Clips „Gesund leben" an und machen Sie sich Notizen. Wie antworten Hassan und Erin auf die folgenden Fragen?

Hassan

Erin

(QR 7.5 p.345)

(QR 7.3 p.345)

Lebst du gesund?

Isst du gesund? Was isst du? Was isst du nicht?

Treibst du Sport? Was machst du?

C. Jetzt sind Sie dran! Brainstorming

Sind Sie ein gesunder Mensch? Was bedeutet es für Sie, gesund zu leben? Lesen Sie die Vorschäge auf der linken Seite durch und schreiben Sie einige Möglichkeiten gesund zu leben auf der rechten Seite auf. Sie dürfen natürlich auch andere Dinge aufschreiben!

- viel Obst und Gemüse essen
- weniger Süßigkeiten essen
- Vitamine nehmen
- viel Sport treiben
- oft spazieren gehen
- zum Arzt gehen
- täglich duschen
- regelmäßig die Hände waschen
- sich oft entspannen
- Stress minimieren (vermeiden)
- genug schlafen
- weniger Alkohol trinken
- keine Zigaretten rauchen

gesund leben

Aktivität 2. Gesund essen

Was essen Eva und Berna zum Frühstück? Zu Mittag? Und zu Abend? Wo können sie gesundes Essen kaufen?

(QR 7.8 p.345)

Was isst Eva zum Frühstück, zu Mittag und zu Abend? Isst sie gesund (was meinen Sie)?

Wo kann man in Würzburg gesundes Essen kaufen?

> Im _____ – die haben oft ein sehr _____
>
> Angebot. In Würzburg würde ich jetzt den _____ empfehlen.
>
> Es ist ein _____ – und _____,
>
> der dreimal die Woche stattfindet und _____ von
>
> Bauern aus der Region anbietet.

(QR 7.7 p.345)

Was isst Berna jeden Tag? Isst sie gesund (was meinen Sie)?

Wo kann man in Austin gesundes Essen kaufen?

> Also ich glaube, es gibt einen _____ – das
>
> ist eine Art Wochenmarkt, wo man frisches Obst und Gemüse kaufen kann.
>
> Es gibt aber auch natürlich viele teuere_____
>
> wie zum Beispiel _____, und ich glaube,
>
> auch bei _____ kann man Gesundes kaufen.

Zusätzliche Fragen:

1. Stimmen Sie mit Berna überein? Kann man an diesen Orten (*places*) in Austin gesundes Essen kaufen?

2. Wo kaufen Sie gesundes Essen? Kaufen Sie überhaupt gesundes Essen?

3. Kostet das gesunde Essen, das Sie kaufen, mehr als andere Lebensmittel? Warum oder warum nicht?

4. Wissen Sie, woher das Essen kommt? Woher?

Aktivität 3. Gesund versus ungesund

Als Antwort auf die Frage *Bist du ein gesunder Mensch?* erwähnen die Muttersprachler und Amerikaner dieselben Dinge: 1) gesund essen und 2) Sport treiben. Was verstehen <u>Sie</u> unter *gesund essen*?

A. Essen und Getränke einordnen: gesund, o.k. oder ungesund?

Mit einem Partner oder einer Partnerin entscheiden Sie, ob die folgenden Lebensmittel und Getränke gesund, o.k. oder ungesund sind. Dann schreiben Sie die Lebensmittel und Getränke in die passenden Kategorien.

> Bier • Brot • Cola Light • Fischstäbchen • Fruchteis • Guacamole • Hamburger • Kaffee • Müsli Pizza • Poptarts • Ramen (asiatische Nudeln) • Saft • Salate • Sandwiches • Schnitzel • Schokolade • Spaghetti • Tacos • Eier • Tofu • Wein • Wurst

gesund	o.k. (un/gesund, aber ...)	ungesund

B. Was macht das Essen gesund?

Wählen Sie zehn der genannten Lebensmittel und Getränke aus und erklären Sie mündlich, warum Sie dieses Lebensmittel/Getränk so bezeichnet haben. Was macht es gesund? Benutzen Sie in Ihrer Erklärung folgende Ausdrücke und achten Sie auf Singular, Plural (Konjugation) und Genus (Pronomen):

Beispiel:

Saft finden wir o.k., weil er vitaminreich ist, aber viel Zucker enthält.

_____		... viele Ballaststoffe/wenig Ballaststoffe enthält/enthalten.
_____		... wenig Cholesterin/viel Cholesterin enthält/enthalten.
_____		... kein Koffein/viel Koffein enthält/enthalten.
_____	*finden wir...*	... wenig Fett/viel Fett enthält/enthalten.
_____	*gesund / o.k. /*	... keine Konservierungsstoffe/viele Konservierungsstoffe enthält/enthalten.
_____	*ungesund, weil es/er/sie ...*	... kalorienarm/kalorienreich enthält/enthalten.
_____	*(, aber ...)*	... wenig Salz/viel Salz enthält/enthalten.
_____		... alkoholfrei/alkoholisch ist/sind.
_____		... vitaminreich/vitaminarm ist/sind.
_____		... wenig Zucker/viel Zucker enthält/enthalten.

Aktivität 4. Ein kleines Interview: Gesund essen

A. Interview

Beantworten Sie zuerst die folgenden Fragen auf der linken Seite. Dann stellen Sie Ihrem Partner/Ihrer Partnerin dieselben Fragen und schreiben Sie seine/ihre Antworten auf. Benutzen Sie vollständige Sätze!

1. Welche gesunden Lebensmittel essen Sie?   *... isst Ihr Partner/Ihre Partnerin?*

2. Welche ungesunden Lebensmittel vermeiden Sie?   *... vermeidet Ihr Partner/Ihre Partnerin?*

3. Welche gesunden Getränke trinken Sie?   *... trinkt Ihr Partner/Ihre Partnerin?*

4. Welche ungesunden Getränke vermeiden Sie?   *... vermeidet Ihr Partner/Ihre Partnerin?*

B. Fragen zum Thema Essen

Diskutieren Sie in Gruppen mit drei anderen Studenten/Studentinnen die folgenden Fragen zum Thema *gesund essen*. Notieren Sie Ihre Meinungen sowie die Meinungen Ihrer Gruppenmitglieder.

1. Was bedeutet „gesund essen"?

2. Ist es wirklich so wichtig, aus persönlichen oder sozialen Gründen, dass man gesund isst? Anders gesagt: Kann jemand gesund sein, ohne dass er/sie gesund isst?

3. Können Studenten gesund essen?

Aktivität 5. Sport treiben

In Aufgabe 1 haben die Muttersprachler und Amerikaner auch *Sport treiben* erwähnt, als Sie über Gesundheit gesprochen haben. Ist Sport treiben auch für Sie ein wichtiger Teil der Gesundheit? Welchen Sport treiben Sie?

> **Sprachtipp:** *Sport treiben* hat zwei Bedeutungen: "to play sports" und "to exercise". Man treibt Sport, wenn man eine Sportart wie zum Beispiel Fußball spielt, aber auch, wenn man einfach wandern geht.

A. Warum treiben Sie Sport?

Lesen Sie die folgenden Aussagen (*statements*). Dann entscheiden Sie sich, ob dies ein Grund ist, warum Sie Sport treiben. Kreuzen Sie alle zutreffenden (*applicable*) Aussagen an.

Ich treibe Sport, weil ...

- ❑ ... es dem Herz-Kreislauf-Sytsem (*cardiovascular system*) hilft.
- ❑ ... ich gern unter Leuten bin.
- ❑ ... ich Wettkampf (*competition*) mag.
- ❑ ... es mir hilft, mein Gewicht zu halten (*maintains my weight*).
- ❑ ... es Spaß macht.
- ❑ ... es mich entspannt.
- ❑ ... Ärzte sagen, dass man sich mindestens dreimal pro Woche 30 Minuten bewegen sollte.
- ❑ ... es mir gut tut (*it makes me feel well*).
- ❑ ... ich gern draußen in der frischen Luft bin.

B. Welchen Sport treiben Sie?

Schauen Sie die folgende Liste an. Kreisen Sie alle Aktivitäten ein, die Sie selber machen.

Aerobic	Karate	Schwimmen
Baseball	Klettern	Sit-ups
Basketball	Laufen	Spazieren gehen
Football	Paintball	Tanzen
Fußball	Pilates	Tennis
Gewicht heben	Racquetball	Volleyball
Golf	Radfahren	Yoga
Joggen	Reiten	Wandern

Sonst noch was ...?

Nein danke, ich treibe keinen Sport!
Ich bin gar nicht sportlich, aber ich sammle Briefmarken.

C. Ein kleines Interview

Arbeiten Sie mit einem Partner/einer Partnerin zusammen und schreiben Sie 5-8 Fragen zum Thema Gesundheit und Sport auf. Stellen Sie sich gegenseitig die Fragen und dann schreiben Sie einen kurzen Bericht über Ihren Partner/Ihre Partnerin.

Mögliche Fragen:

Antworten von meinem Partner/ meiner Partnerin:

Mein(e) Partner(in) ist ein/kein sehr gesunder Mensch, denn ...

Aktivität 6. Sprache im Kontext: Der Sportausweis an der Uni-Würzburg

Sehen Sie im Video „Vanessa: Sportausweis", wie Vanessa den Sportausweis (*sports pass*) beschreibt, den man an der Uni Würzburg bekommen kann. Was sagt sie darüber?

A. Schauen Sie sich den Clip einmal an und kreuzen Sie die Vokabeln an, die Sie hören:

- ❑ Sportausweis
- ❑ schlafen
- ❑ Sport treiben
- ❑ Fitnessstudio
- ❑ Sportanlagen
- ❑ Anlagen

(QR 7.9 p.345)

B. Schauen Sie den Clip ein zweites Mal an und beantworten Sie die Fragen:

1. Warum musste Vanessa einen Sportausweis kaufen?
   a. Jeder Student muss einen kaufen.
   b. Sie treibt sehr gern Sport.
   c. Ihre Freundinnen haben sie darum gebeten.

2. Wieviel kostet ein Sportausweis?
   a. 25 Euro
   b. 50 Euro
   c. 15 Euro

3. Was macht man, wenn man das Fitnesszentrum benutzen möchte?
   a. Man muss noch einen Sportausweis kaufen. Das kostet 25 Euro.
   b. Man bringt den Sportausweis einfach mit.
   c. Man darf das Fitnesszentrum nicht benutzen. Es ist nur für den Lehrkörper (*faculty*).

4. Wie findet Vanessa das Fitnesszentrum?
   a. Sie findet die Kosten günstig und die Anlage schön.
   b. Sie findet die Kosten etwas teuer und die Anlage nicht sehr gut.
   c. Sie findet die Kosten etwas teuer, aber die Anlage schön.

C. Schauen Sie den Clip erneut an und denken Sie dabei daran, wie es bei Ihnen aussieht. Müssen Studenten einen Sportausweis kaufen oder ist der Preis schon in den Studiengebühren (*tuition fees*) enthalten? Wenn ja, wie viel kostet der Sportausweis? Finden Sie den Preis günstig?

Aktivität 7. Sprache im Kontext: Sportzentren an der Uni Würzburg

Vanessa erwähnt, dass es ein Sportzentrum an der Uni gibt. Es gibt tatsächlich zwei – die Sportanlage am Hubland und das Sportzentrum Mergentheimer Straße. Im nächsten Clip, „Sara: Sportzentren", beschreibt Sara die beiden Sportzentren in Würzburg.

(QR 7.10 p.345)

A. Sehen Sie sich Saras Video an und schreiben Sie Vokabeln auf, die Sie wichtig finden:

Verben	Nomen	Andere *(Other)*

B. Sehen Sie sich das Video erneut an – wie beschreibt sie diese Zentren? Ordnen Sie jede Beschreibung (auf der rechten Seite) dem richtigen Sportzentrum (auf der linken Seite) zu.

... hat viele Fußballplätze.

Das Sportzentrum Mergentheimer Straße ...

... hat ein Bootshaus zum Rudern, das nicht sehr gut ist.

... ist ein älteres Zentrum.

... ist wo die Uni-Sportfakultät ist.

... ist auf der anderen Seite des Mains.

... hat auch Klassenzimmer [Seminarräume].

... hat ein Track [einen Sportplatz].

... ist ein neues Zentrum – es wurde im Jahr 2000 gebaut.

Die Sportanlage am Hubland ...

... hat kleine und sehr alte Kraft- und Cardioräume.

... ist nicht weit weg.

Grimm Grammar

Wie Sie sehen, bestehen viele deutsche Worte aus mehreren Wörtern! Bearbeiten Sie zu Hause das folgende Grammatikthema in der *Grimm Grammar* Miscellaneous: Wortbildung

C. Was haben die Sportzentren noch?

Sara hat eine gute Beschreibung von beiden Sportzentren gegeben, aber was gibt's noch? Lesen Sie unten die Auflistungen und versuchen Sie, die deutschen Wörter den entsprechenden englischen Wörtern zuzuordnen.

Die Sportanlage am Hubland:

1 Hauptfeld	gym
1 Rasenfeld	beach volleyball courts
1 Kunstrasenfeld	multi-purpose room
5 Tennisplätze	grass field
3 Beachvolleyballfelder	artificial turf field
1 Dreifachhalle (DrfH Hub)	main field
1 Mehrzweckhalle (MzH Hub)	three-fold room
1 Fitnessstudio (FS)	tennis courts

Das Sportzentrum Mergentheimer Straße:

Spielhalle (SpH)	gymnastics room
Turnhalle (TuH)	sauna
Mehrzweckhalle (MzH)	arcade
Schwimmhalle (SwH)	cardio room
Gymnastikhalle (GymH)	gymnasium
Hörsaal (HS)	multi-purpose room
Kraftraum	lecture hall/auditorium
Cardioraum	indoor swimming pool
Sauna	weight room

Nota Bene: Sie haben sicher bemerkt, dass fast jedes der obigen Wörter eigentlich aus mehreren Wörtern besteht. Zum Beispiel besteht das Wort *Spielhalle* aus zwei Wörtern – Spiel und Halle. Das Wort Beachvolleyballfelder besteht sogar aus drei Wörtern – Beach, Volleyball und Felder. Solche Wörter kommen in der deutschen Sprache sehr oft vor. Sie heißen Komposita (*compound words*) und sind eine Art Wortbildung (*word formation*).

Aktivität 8. Die Sportanlagen auf Ihrem Campus

Stellen Sie sich vor, Sie sind Uni-Repräsentant auf Ihrem Campus. Beschreiben Sie, welche Sportanlagen es auf dem Campus gibt. Wie viele Felder, Plätze, Räume, Stadien und Zentren gibt es und wie sind sie (z.B. neu oder alt; groß oder klein). Wie kommt man hinein? Dürfen nur Studenten diese Sportanlagen benutzten? Was kostet es, sie zu nutzen? Benutzen Sie Ihre neuen Kenntnisse (*new knowledge*) über die Wortbildung dazu neue, bedeutungsvolle Wörter zu bilden. Viel Spass!

Aktivität 9. Der menschliche Körper
A. Zum Thema Gesundheit und Fitness gehört natürlich auch der menschliche Körper (*the human body*).
Glücklicherweise gibt es hier viele deutsche Wörter, die dem Englischen ähnlich sind! Können Sie raten, was hier zusammenpasst? Ordnen Sie den deutschen Wörtern die richtigen Buchstaben zu.

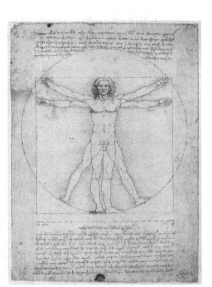

der Arm	_____	a. finger
das Auge	_____	b. foot
die Brust	_____	c. shoulder
der Ellbogen	_____	d. lip
der Finger	_____	e. hand
der Fuß	_____	f. nose
die Haare	_____	g. breast/chest
die Hand	_____	h. knee
das Knie	_____	i. arm
die Lippe	_____	j. ear
die Nase	_____	k. hair
das Ohr	_____	l. eye
die Schulter	_____	m. elbow

B. Und es gibt noch mehr!
Nennen Sie zuerst die fehlenden Körperteile (#1, #2, #5, #8, #9, #12, #17) auf Deutsch (diese Körperteile kennen Sie schon!). Dann lesen Sie die Wörter für die übrigen Körperteile und versuchen Sie, die entsprechenden englischen Wörter zu raten.

Körperteile	Auf Deutsch		Auf Englisch
	1. _____	=	_____
	2. _____	=	_____
	3. der Kopf	=	_____
	4. der Hals	=	_____
	5. _____	=	_____
	6. der Daumen	=	_____
	7. das Handgelenk	=	_____
	8. _____	=	_____
	9. _____	=	_____
	10. der Bauch	=	_____
	11. der Oberschenkel	=	_____
	12. _____	=	_____
	13. das Schienbein	=	_____
	14. der Zeh	=	_____
	15. die Wade	=	_____
	16. der Knöchel	=	_____
	17. _____	=	_____
	18. der Hintern/der Po	=	_____
	19. der Rücken	=	_____
	20. der Oberarm	=	_____
	21. der Unterarm	=	_____

Aktivität 10. Sprache im Kontext

Sehen Sie im Video „Die Körperteile", wie der Student Stephan erklärt welche Körperteile er hat und wozu man sie benutzen kann.

A. Sehen Sie sich das Video an

Schreiben Sie wietere und alternative Begriffe auf, die Stephan für die Körperteile benutzt.

Weitere Begriffe

_____

_____

_____

_____

(QR 7.22 p.345)

Alternative Begriffe

_____

_____

_____

B. Schauen Sie das Video erneut an

Welche Ausdrücke benutzt Stephan? Und zu welchem Körperteil gehören die Ausdrücke? Machen Sie sich Notizen und fügen Sie diese dann in die Tabelle ein.

die Füße	gehen	Mit den Füßen geht man.

C. Was fällt Ihnen ein? Was kann man mit den Körperteilen noch machen? Ergänzen Sie die Tabelle mit Ihren Ideen.

Aktivität 11. Körperpflege

Was für die Gesundheit auch sehr wichtig ist, ist Körperpflege. Auch wenn man gesund isst und Sport treibt, muss man seinen Körper pflegen, um völlig gesund zu sein. Wie pflegt man den Körper?

Man benutzt Deo.
Man benutzt Q-Tips/Ohrenstäbchen.
Man bürstet sich/kämmt sich die Haare.
Man duscht sich.
Man putzt sich die Zähne.
Man rasiert sich.
Man wäscht sich das Gesicht.
Man wäscht sich die Haare.
Man wäscht sich die Hände.
Man zupft sich die Augenbrauen.

Denken Sie nun an Ihre eigene Körperpflege und beantworten Sie die folgenden Fragen.

←---→

zweimal/dreimal (oder mehr) am Tag	jeden Tag	zweimal/dreimal (oder mehr) die Woche	jede Woche	zweimal/dreimal (oder mehr) pro Monat

Wie oft ...

1. ... zupfen Sie sich die Augenbrauen?

2. ... duschen Sie sich?

3. ... waschen Sie sich das Gesicht?

4. ... bürsten/kämmen Sie sich die Haare?

5. ... waschen Sie sich die Haare?

6. ... waschen Sie sich die Hände?

7. ... rasieren Sie sich?

8. ... putzen Sie sich die Zähne?

Aktivität 12. Eine kurze Beschreibung

Benutzen Sie Ihre Antworten, um Ihre Körperpflege zu beschreiben. Wie pflegen Sie Ihren Körper? Was machen Sie, um gesund zu bleiben?

Beispiel:

Meine Körperpflege ist sehr gut. Ich putze mir dreimal am Tag die Zähne.
Meine Zähne sind natürlich sehr sauber. Ich wasche mir immer die Hände.

Grimm Gramma

Wie Sie vielleicht bemerkt haben, sind viele Wörter, die wir brauchen, um das Thema *Gesundheit* zu besprechen, reflexive Verben. Um mehr über sie zu erfahren, bearbeiten Sie das folgende Grammatikthema in der *Grimm Grammar*:

Verbs:
Die reflexiven Verben

Aktivität 13. Schlaf und Gesundheit

Es wird oft übersehen (*overlooked*), dass Schlaf eine große Rolle für der Gesundheit spielen kann. Studien zeigen, dass zu wenig, aber auch zu viel Schlaf ungesund ist.

A. Wie viele Stunden schlafen sie pro Nacht?

Schauen Sie sich die Videos „Schlaf, Kindlein Schlaf" von den Muttersprachlern (Berna, Eva, Jan) und den Amerikanern (Hassan, Erin, Sara) an. Wie viele Stunden schlafen sie jede Nacht? Kreisen Sie die richtige Zahl ein. Ist das genug und gesund? Und was glauben die Studentinnen/Studenten: Leben die Deutschen oder die Amerikaner gesünder?

(QR 7.11 p.345)

2   3   4   5   6   7   8   9   10

Berna findet das **genug/nicht genug.**

Sie meint, dass das **gesund/nicht gesund** ist.

Wer ist gesünder: **Amerikaner/Deutsche,** weil …

(QR 7.12 p.345)

2   3   4   5   6   7   8   9   10

Eva findet das **genug/nicht genug.**

Sie meint, dass das **gesund/nicht gesund** ist.

Wer ist gesünder: **Amerikaner/Deutsche,** weil …

(QR 7.13 p.345)

2   3   4   5   6   7   8   9   10

Jan findet das **genug/nicht genug.**

Er meint, dass das **gesund/nicht gesund** ist.

Wer ist gesünder: **Amerikaner/Deutsche,** weil …

(QR 7.14 p.345)

2   3   4   5   6   7   8   9   10

Hassan findet das **genug/nicht genug.**

Er meint, dass das **gesund/nicht gesund** ist.

Wer ist gesünder: **Amerikaner/Deutsche,** weil …

(QR 7.15 p.345)

2   3   4   5   6   7   8   9   10

Sara findet das genug/nicht genug.

Sie meint, dass das **gesund/nicht gesund** ist.

Wer ist gesünder: **Amerikaner/Deutsche,** weil …

(QR 7.16 p.345)

2   3   4   5   6   7   8   9   10

Sara findet das **genug/nicht genug.**

Sie meint, dass das **gesund/nicht gesund** ist.

Wer ist gesünder: **Amerikaner/Deutsche,** weil …

B. Schlafen
Diskutieren Sie mit einem Partner/einer Partnerin die folgenden Fragen:

1. Wie viele Stunden schlafen Sie jede Nacht? Ist das genug für Sie? Ist das gesund?

2. Stimmen Sie zu, dass Schlaf ein wichtiger Teil der Gesundheit ist? Finden Sie, dass Schlaf Stress abbaut (*relieves stress*)? Wenn ja, warum, wenn nicht, warum nicht?

3. Warum könnte (*could*) es ungesund sein, zu viel Schlaf zu bekommen?

4. Mit wem stimmen Sie überein: Leben die Deutschen oder die Amerikaner gesünder?

Aktivität 14. Jetzt sind Sie dran! Verletzungen!
Natürlich versuchen Sie, so gut wie möglich auf sich aufzupassen (*to take care of yourself*). Sie essen gesund, Sie treiben Sport, Sie kümmern sich um Ihren Körper, und Sie bekommen möglichst viel Schlaf – nicht wahr? ☺. Aber manchmal geht das nicht und etwas geht schief (*goes awry*) – Sie verletzen sich irgendwie, vielleicht gerade beim Sport!

A. Was ist Ihnen schon passiert?

Kreisen Sie jeweils die richtige Antwort ein. Ist Ihnen so etwas schon einmal passiert?

Ich habe schon einmal ein blaues Auge gehabt.	Ja	Nein
Ich habe einen Autounfall gehabt.	Ja	Nein
Ich habe einen blauen Fleck gehabt.	Ja	Nein
Ich habe eine Gehirnerschütterung gehabt.	Ja	Nein
Ich habe einen Sportunfall gehabt.	Ja	Nein

Lesen Sie die folgenden Angaben und kreisen Sie alle Antworten ein, die auf Sie zutreffen.

Ich habe mir **den Arm/den Finger/den Fuß/das Handgelenk/den Knöchel/die Nase/den Zeh gebrochen.**
(**oder**) Ich habe mir noch kein Körperteil gebrochen.

Ich habe mir **den Ellbogen/den Finger/das Handgelenk/das Knie/den Knöchel/die Schulter/den Zeh verstaucht.**
(**oder**) Ich habe mir noch kein Körperteil verstaucht.

B. Was ist Ihrem Partner/Ihrer Partnerin passiert?
Hat er/sie einmal schon ein blaues Auge gehabt? Wie ist das passiert? Vergleichen Sie Ihre eigenen Antworten mit den Antworten Ihres Partners/Ihrer Partnerin. Wer hat die schlimmste VErletzung gehabt? Wer scheint mehr Unfälle zu haben? Wer hat mehr Pech?

Lesen Sie folgende Angaben und kreisen Sie die Antworten ein, die <u>auf Ihren Partner/Ihre Partnerin</u> zutreffen.

Er/Sie hat sich **den Arm/den Finger/den Fuß/das Handgelenk/den Knöchel/die Nase/den Zeh** gebrochen.
(**oder**) Er/sie hat sich noch kein Körperteil gebrochen.

Er/Sie hat sich **den Ellbogen/den Finger/das Handgelenk/das Knie/den Knöchel/die Schulter/den Zeh** verstaucht.
(**oder**) Er/sie hat sich noch kein Körperteil verstaucht.

Aktivität 15. Forumeinträge: Verletzungen

Die Webseite http://www.netdoktor.de bietet Foren (*forums*) – oder auf Neudeutsch *Communities* – an, in denen man Fragen stellen oder auch beantworten kann. Wenn Sie auf der Webseite den Button "Community" anklicken, können Sie die Diskussionsthemen einsehen. Hier sind einige Auszüge, falls Sie keinen Internetzugang haben.

A. Vor dem Lesen

1. Was glauben Sie, wer diese Foren benutzt?

2. Überfliegen (*scan, skim*) Sie den Text und ordnen Sie die folgenden Wörter der richtigen Bedeutung zu:

die Schwellung	joint
das Gelenk	to dislocate
auskugeln	hurts
schmerzt	worries me
die Bewegung	affected
die Ruhigstellung	movement
macht mir Sorge	swelling
in Mitleidenschaft gezogen	x-ray
das Röntgenbild	immobilization

3. Lesen Sie nun den Eintrag und die Antwort.
Eintrag:

Community:
Muskeln, Knochen & Gelenke

‹ Zurück zu allen Diskussionen

Empfehlen   Twittern 0   +1 0

roror

Finger ausgekugelt, was jetzt?

Hallo,
ich habe mir gestern beim Handballspielen den Ringfinger ausgekugeln. Es war das mittlere Gelenk und hat fürchterlich weh getan, bis ein Mannschaftskollege kräftig dran gezogen hat und er wieder drin war.
Heut schmerzt er mir bei der Bewegung (VIEL weniger als wo er ausgekugelt war) und ist aber eigtl frei beweglich. Nur die starke Schwellung macht mir bisschen Sorge.
Hier meine Frage: Muss ich zum Arzt gehen? Kann da was kaputt sein?
Grüße

Muskeln, Knochen & Gelenke   Finger   Gelenke   Ausgekugelt

14.02.2011 11:14 Uhr Lesenswert 1

Merken   Antwort schreiben

Antwort:

Hi.
An deiner Stelle würde ich schon zum Arzt gehen. Ein Röntgenbild kann dir Sicherheit verschaffen ob irgendwelche knöchernen Strukturen in Mitleidenschaft gezogen wurde. Danach würde sich dann auch die Therapie orientieren.
Außerdem kann dir der Arzt eine Schiene zur Ruhigstellung verschreiben und dir zeigen wie man den Finger richtig mit einem Tape-Verband versorgt, für den Zeitpunkt wo du wieder mit Handball anfängst!
Grüße Free

freeway86

14.02.2011 11:18 Uhr   Hilfreich? 0   #1

 Empfehlen   Twittern 0   +1 0

Missbrauch melden

B. Nach dem Lesen
Beantworten Sie die folgenden Fragen über die Einträge, die Sie gerade gelesen haben.

1. Der Benutzer/die Benutzerin beschreibt einen kleinen Unfall. Wie ist dieser Unfall passiert?

_____

_____

2. Kann er/sie den Finger noch bewegen? Tut es weh?

_____

_____

3. Der/die zweite Benutzer/Benutzerin, die antwortet, berät (*advises*) den Verletzten/die Verletzte. Was sollte er/sie tun? Warum rät er/sie ihm/ihr das?

_____

_____

_____

4. Was ist dein Ratschlag? Glaubst du auch, dass der Verletzte/die Verletze zum Arzt gehen sollte? Wenn ja, warum, wenn nein, warum nicht?

_____

_____

_____

C. Jetzt sind Sie dran!

1. Forumeintrag: Wählen Sie eine Verletzung aus, die Sie gehabt haben, und schreiben Sie einen kurzen Forumeintrag (wie *Eintrag* und *Antwort* oben). Beschreiben Sie, was Ihnen passiert ist und wie es zu Ihren Beschwerden (*ailments*) ge-kommen ist. Was tut weh? Was möchten Sie jemanden fragen?

2. Forumantwort: Tauschen Sie Ihren Eintrag mit einem Partner/einer Partnerin und antworten Sie auf seinen/ihren Eintrag. Geben Sie ihm/ihr eine gute Auskunft (*information*) und einen Rat (*advice*).

Dieses deutsche Verkehrszeichen weist darauf hin, dass ein Krankenhaus in der Nähe zu finden ist.

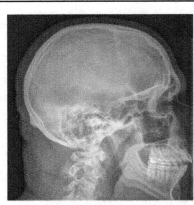

Dieses Röntgenbild zeigt einen menschlichen Schädel von der Seite.

Aktivität 16. Krank sein

Verletzungen sind nicht die einzigen Probleme, mit denen Sie zu tun haben. Sie müssen auch gegen verschiedene Krankheiten ankämpfen. Lesen Sie die Liste von Symptomen, die Sie haben können, wenn Sie krank sind (oder werden) und suchen Sie das richtige Leiden aus der Vokabelliste aus.

1. Ihnen ist sehr warm. Ihre Temperatur ist 102 Grad Fahrenheit (fast 39 Grad Celsius). Sie müssen ein Eisbad nehmen, um Ihre Temperatur zu senken. Was ist mit Ihnen los?

→ Ich _____.

das Bewusstsein verlieren
erkältet sein
Fieber haben
flau im Magen
die Grippe haben

2. Sie waren gerade in einem Restaurant und haben etwas Neues auf der Speisekarte probiert. Das Essen hat gut geschmeckt, aber sie fühlen sich auf einmal nicht mehr so wohl. Was ist mit Ihnen los?

→ Mir ist _____.

3. Sie sind beim Arzt. Der Arzt nimmt Ihnen Blut ab. Plötzlich fühlen Sie sich unwohl. Ihnen wird sehr warm und Sie können sich nicht mehr so gut konzentrieren. Was ist mit Ihnen los?

→ Ich _____.

4. Sie waren stundenlang am Computer, denn Sie müssen morgen einen Aufsatz einreichen. Jetzt sind Sie sehr müde und auch ein bißchen schwindelig (*dizzy*). Sie nehmen ein paar Aspirin. Was ist mit Ihnen los?

→ Ich _____.

5. Sie haben Husten und Schnupfen. Ihnen ist manchmal sehr warm und manchmal sehr kalt. Sie brauchen viele Taschentücher und Hustenbonbons. Was ist mit Ihnen los?

→ Ich _____.

Welche Beschwerden hat das Kind?
Was macht die große Schwester?
Waren Sie als Kind oft oder selten krank?

Aktivität 17. Sprache im Kontext: Krank sein

A. Joel: Ich gehe zum Arzt
Schauen Sie sich Joels Kontextvideo an und füllen Sie die Lücken mit den richtigen Wörtern (rechts) aus. Was macht Joel, wenn er krank ist? (Achtung: Es bleiben Vokabeln übrig!)

(QR 7.17 p.345)

Je nachdem, wie _____ ich bin.

Normalerweise, wenn's wirklich _____ ist,

gehe ich zum _____, klar, aber ansonsten

_____ man es _____.

krank	schrecklich
schlimm	sehr
hält	aus
Arzt	

B. Und Sie?
Sie wissen jetzt, was Joel macht, wenn er krank ist. Was machen Sie, wenn Sie krank sind? Beantworten Sie die Fragen und benutzen in Ihren Sätzen die folgenden Ausreden.

zum Arzt gehen	ein Heizkissen benutzen
sich ausruhen	sich hinlegen
ein paar Aspirin-Tabletten nehmen	eine Nudelsuppe essen
ein warmes/kaltes Bad nehmen	einen Tee trinken
im Bett bleiben	viel Wasser trinken

1. Was machen Sie, wenn Ihnen übel ist?

_____

2. Was machen Sie, wenn Sie sich schwach fühlen?

_____

3. Was machen Sie, wenn Sie Rückenschmerzen haben?

_____

4. Was machen Sie, wenn Sie die Grippe haben?

_____

5. Was machen Sie, wenn Ihr Kopf weh tut?

_____

6. Was machen Sie, wenn Sie Fieber haben?

_____

Aktivität 18. Klassenspiel: Wer verdient das goldene Pflaster?

Die Spielregeln:

1. Einer beginnt und berichtet von seiner schlimmsten Krankheit oder Verletzung.
2. Der nächste berichtet von seiner schlimmsten Krankheit oder Verletzung, die natürlich viel schlimmer war.
3. Es geht reihum immer so weiter.

Das Ziel: Am Ende entscheidet die ganze Gruppe, wer die schlimmste Krankheit/Verletzung hatte.

Hier ist ein Beispiel:

Person 1: Als ich 6 war, habe ich mir das Bein gebrochen. Das war so schlimm, dass ich vier Wochen lang einen Gips tragen musste und nicht laufen konnte.

Person 2: Ach, das ist ja gar nichts! Ich lag drei Wochen im Krankenhaus wegen einer Hirnhautentzündung mit hohem Fieber und den schrecklichsten Schmerzen!

Person 3: Papperlapapp! Wenn ihr hört, was mir mit 15 passiert ist ...

Einige nützliche Begriffe:

Herrje!/Herrjemine!	Criminy!
Ach, hör doch auf!	Get away with you!
Das ist doch gar nichts!	That's nothing!
Mir ging es viel schlechter!	I was feeling even worse!
Mir ging es am schlechtesten!	I was feeling worst!
Nein, mir ging es am allerschlechtesten (allerallerallerschlechtesten), weil ...	No, it was me who felt the very worst (the very very vey, very ...), because ...
Alles halb so schlimm!	Half as bad!
Ich war am schlimmsten dran!	I was off worst of all!
Mumpitz! Hört hierher!	Don't talk rot! Listen to me!
Das sind doch Kinkerlitzchen!	That's geegaw!
Papperlapapp!	Fiddlesticks!

Aktivität 19. Ärzte

Normalerweise geht man zum Arzt, wenn man sich nicht wohlfühlt. Welche Ärzte gibt es?

A. Wer ist wer?

Ordnen Sie die folgenden Vokabeln einander zu.

der Augenarzt/die Augenärztin	_____	a. gynecologist
der Chiropraktiker/die Chiropraktikerin	_____	b. ear-nose-throat doctor
der Frauenarzt/die Frauenärztin	_____	c. dentist
der Fußspezialist/die Fußspezialistin	_____	d. dermatologist
der Hausarzt/die Hausärztin	_____	e. veterinarian
der Hautarzt/die Hautärztin	_____	f. ophthalmologist
der Hals-Nasen-Ohren-Arzt/die -Ärztin	_____	g. chiropractor
der Kinderarzt/die Kinderärztin	_____	h. podiatrist
der Heilpraktiker/die Heilpraktikerin	_____	i. psychiatrist
der Orthopäde/die Orthopädin	_____	j. general practitioner
der Psychiater/die Psychiaterin	_____	k. doctor of naturopathy
der Tierarzt/die Tierärztin	_____	l. orthopedist
der Zahnarzt/die Zahnärztin	_____	m. pediatrician

B. AUA! Schmerzen!

Es gibt viele Arten von Schmerzen. Versuchen Sie in Ihrem Kurs, eine Liste von möglichen Schmerzen zusammenzustellen.

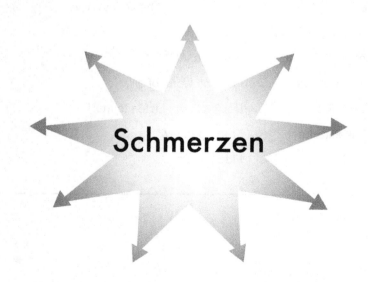

C. Definitionen
Versuchen Sie nun, fünf Ärzte von der Ärzteliste in Aktivität 19A zu definieren und benutzen Sie Ihre Antworten aus Aktivität 19B!

Beispiel:

Wenn man Zahnschmerzen hat, geht man zum Zahnarzt.

1.

2.

3.

4.

5.

Zum Nachdenken:
Zum Arzt zu gehen ist nicht immer die einzige Lösung, besonders für Leute in den deutschsprachigen Ländern. Dort ist es üblich, in ein Bad (*spa*) oder einen Kurort (*health resort*) zu fahren, wenn man sich von einer Krankheit oder Verletzung erholen möchte. Auch wenn man nur etwas gestresst ist, fährt man oft dorthin. Aber viele Leute lassen sich die Kur von einem Arzt verschreiben, soweit die Versicherung das bezahlt.
 Bäder waren in der Vergangenheit besonders wichtig – wenn Sie eine Karte von Deutschland ansehen, sehen Sie sofort, dass viele Dörfer und Städte den Namen „Bad ..." tragen. In diesen Bädern gab (und gibt es) Heilwasser, das man trinken kann. Man kann in diesem Wasser auch baden (z.B. Baden Baden).

Aktivität 20. Harald beim Arzt
Harald hat immer etwas Witziges zu sagen. Was sagt er über Zahnärzte und Psychiater? Schauen Sie sich Haralds Video „Beim Arzt" an und beantworten Sie dann die Fragen.

A. Beim Zahnarzt
Wie oft geht Harald zum Zahnarzt? Warum?

_____

_____

_____

(QR 7.19 p.345)

B. Beim Psychiater
Geht Harald zum Psychiater?

_____

Was hält Harald von Psychiatern? Wer ist seiner Meinung nach der beste Psychiater?

_____

_____

Grimm Grammar

In der nächsten Aufgabe benutzen wir viele Modalverben. Bitte gehen Sie zu

Grimm Grammar

und wiederholen Sie das folgende Grammatikthema:

Verbs:
<u>modal verbs present tense</u>

dürfen → ich darf
können → ich kann
mögen → ich mag/
　　　　 ich möchte
müssen → ich muss
sollen → ich soll
wollen → ich will

Aktivität 21. Zum Arzt gehen

A. Ein Termin

Egal welche Schmerzen hat, wenn es weh tut, muss man zum Arzt gehen. Hier ist eine Liste von Sätzen, die beschreiben, was beim Arzt passiert. Setzen Sie die Sätze in die richtige Reihenfolge.

_____ Der Patient/Die Patientin wartet im Wartezimmer. Er/Sie kann eine Zeitschrift lesen.

_____ Der Arzt/Die Ärztin muss Fragen stellen und soll den Patienten/die Patientin untersuchen.

_____ Der Patient/Die Patientin muss zurück zum Arzthelfer/zur Arzthelferin.

_____ Der Patient/Die Patientin kommt in die Arztpraxis. Er/Sie muss dann die Versichertenkarte vorzeigen.

___1___ Der Patient/Die Patientin muss zuerst die Arztpraxis anrufen, um einen Termin zu bekommen.

_____ Dann ruft der Arzthelfer/die Arzthelferin den Patienten/die Patientin auf. Er/Sie wird ins Behandlungszimmer geführt.

_____ Der Arzthelfer/Die Arzthelferin druckt das Rezept für die Medizin aus.

_____ Der Arzt/Die Ärztin möchte wissen, warum er/sie gekommen ist.

_____ Der Patient/Die Patientin darf dann zur Apotheke, um die Medizin zu holen.

_____ Der Arzt/Die Ärztin verschreibt die Medizin.

_____ Der Arzt/Die Ärztin kommt ins Zimmer.

B. Wichtige Vokabeln

Ein Wortigel. In Aktivität 19 haben Sie viele neue Vokabeln rund um die Arztpraxis gelernt. Versuchen Sie nun eine Vokabelliste zu erstellen. Welche Wörter muss man kennen, wenn man zum Arzt geht. Ergänzen Sie auch die Artikel (maskuline und feminine Formen) der Nomen

Aktivität 22. Ein Tag beim Arzt

Sie haben die Sätze in Aktivität 21 in die richtige Reihenfolge gebracht. Sie können die Geschichte aber auch verkürzen (*shorten*). Versuchen Sie die folgenden Sätze zusammenzusetzen. (Tipp: Einige Sätze können nicht verkürzt werden!)

Beispiel:

Der Patient muss zuerst den Arzt anrufen. Der Patient bekommt einen Termin.

Der Patient muss zuerst den Arzt anrufen, um einen Termin zu bekommen.

1. Der Patient soll 15 Minuten vor dem Termin in der Arztpraxis sein. Der Patient muss dann die Versichertenkarte vorzeigen.

2. Der Arzthelfer muss den Patienten ins Wartezimmer bitten. Der Patient wartet im Wartezimmer.

3. Der Arzt/Die Ärztin kommt ins Zimmer. Der Arzt/Die Ärztin muss Fragen stellen und soll den Patienten/die Patientin untersuchen.

4. Der Patient/Die Patientin muss zurück zum Arzthelfer/zur Arzthelferin. Der Arzthelfer/Die Arzthelferin druckt das Rezept für die Medizin aus.

5. Der Patient/Die Patientin darf dann zur Apotheke. Dann kann der Patient/die Patientin die Medizin holen.

Aktivität 23. Sprache im Kontext: Wenn ich krank bin

Nach dem Arzttermin. Schauen Sie sich Joels Video noch einmal an und beantworten Sie die folgenden Fragen.

Wo kauft Joel seine Medizin?

_____

Wie bekommt Joel seine Medikamente?

(QR 7.17 p.345)

_____

_____

Grimm Gramma

Bitte gehen Sie zu *Grimm Grammar* und schauen Sie sich folgende Grammatikteile an:

Verbs: Der Infinitivsatz

• zu + Infinitiv (to)

• ohne ... zu + Infinitiv (without)
• um ... zu + Infintiv (in order to)

An der Uni ist es einfach, fit zu sein.
Man kann nicht gesund sein, ohne Sport zu treiben.
Ich treibe Sport, um gesund zu sein.

Grimm Grammar

In der nächsten Aufgabe üben wir Befehle. Bitte gehen Sie zu *Grimm Grammar* und schauen Sie sich folgende Grammatikteile an:

<u>Verbs: Der Imperativ</u>

du → Rauche nicht!
ihr → Raucht nicht!

wir → Rauchen wir nicht!
Sie → Rauchen Sie nicht!

Aktivität 24. Versicherung

Eine Versicherung ist ein Muss, wenn man nicht viel mehr Geld für Ärzte und Medikamente ausgeben will. In Deutschland haben alle Hochschulstudenten Anspruch auf *(to be eligible)* eine gesetzliche Krankenversicherung *(compulsory insurance)* – solange sie jünger als 30 Jahre alt sind und weniger als 14 Fachsemester studiert haben. Lesen Sie die Versichertenkarte und beantworten Sie die Fragen über Ihre eigene Versicherung.

Der Name der Versicherung ist AOK, eine Abkürzung von Allgemeine Ortskrankenkasse. Die AOK ist der größte gesetzliche Versicherungsträger Deutschlands.

Der vollständige Name des Versicherten ist Andrew Michael Meyer.

Diese Versichertenkarte ist nur bis Juli 2014 gültig.

Der Versicherte ruft diese Telefonnummer an, wenn er Fragen oder Probleme hat.

	Informationen über Andrews Versicherung	Informationen über Ihre Versicherung
1. Wie heißt die Versicherung?		
2. Welche Informationen sind auf der Karte zu finden?		

Aktivität 25. Sprache im Kontext: Das deutsche Versicherungssystem

Schauen Sie sich den Clip von Andrea an, um mehr über das deutsche Versicherungssystem zu erfahren.

(QR 7.21 p.345)

A. Welche Wörter aus dem Clip kennen Sie (grün unterstreichen) und welche sind neu für Sie (rot unterstreichen)?

Sozialversicherungsfachangestellte   Krankenkasse   Arbeit   freiwillig

Gesetz   das private Versicherungsunternehmen   privat

B. Schauen Sie den Clip erneut an und kreuzen Sie die richtigen Aussagen an

❏ Man kann sich in Deutschland freiwillig krankenversichern.

❏ Es gibt ein Sozialgesetzbuch, das die Krankenversicherung regelt.

❏ Wer in Deutschland Arbeit hat, ist direkt krankenversichert.

❏ Wer viel Geld verdient, muss sich privat versichern.

C. Sehen Sie sich den Clip ein letztes Mal an und sagen Sie in eigenen Worte, was Sie von Andrea gelernt haben (mündlich)

Seit dem 1.1. 2009 gibt es ein neues Gesetz. Was sagt dieses Gesetz?

_____.

D. Wie sieht es bei Ihnen aus? Wie sind Sie versichert?

1. Sind Sie über die Uni versichert? Wenn nicht, wie sind Sie versichert? Wie heißt Ihr Versicherungsunternehmen?

2. Wie viel kostet Ihre Versicherung? Finden Sie den Preis günstig oder teuer? Warum? Wer bezahlt die Versicherung?

3. Wie lange sind Sie noch bei dieser Versicherung versichert? Können Sie auch nach Ihrem Studium bei diesem Unternehmen bleiben oder gibt es eine Alterseinschränkung?

Aktivität 26. Ratschläge zur Gesundheit
A. Beim Arzt.

Sie waren gerade beim Arzt und es sieht nicht gut aus. Der Arzt hat Ihnen Ratschläge gegeben, um gesund und fit zu bleiben. Arbeiten Sie mit einem Partner und sagen Sie Ihrem Partner, was Ihr Arzt Ihnen gesagt hat. Sie müssen die formelle Form „Sie" benutzen, denn Sie sind der Arzt!

Beispiel:

Ich soll regelmäßig zum Arzt kommen. → *Kommen Sie regelmäßig zum Arzt!*

1. Ich soll gut auf meine Gesundheit achten.

2. Ich muss gesünder essen.

3. Ich soll jede Nacht acht Stunden schlafen.

4. Ich muss jeden Tag mindestens acht Gläser Wasser trinken.

5. Ich darf nicht mehr rauchen.

6. Ich soll keinen Alkohol trinken.

7. Ich soll viel spazieren gehen.

8. Ich soll mein Gewicht halten.

B. Jetzt sind Sie dran!

Ein Freund von Ihnen lebt sehr ungesund. Er raucht viel zu viel, trinkt viel Cola, Bier und Alkohol. Außerdem macht er kaum Sport. Sie möchten ihm helfen und geben ihm Rat – in direkter Form!

Beispiel:

Mach mehr Sport!

-
-
-
-
-
-
-

Aktivität 27. Beim Arzt: ein Drehbuch

Sie sind Drehbuchautor/Drehbuchautorin! Schreiben Sie mit einem Partner zusammen eine Szene aus einem Drehbuch mit der Überschrift „Beim Arzt"! Bevor Sie anfangen, denken Sie an die folgenden Fragen:

- Was ist das gesundheitliche Problem? Was ist mit dem Patienten/der Patientin los?
- Was für ein Arzt soll es sein? (Es muss nicht der „richtige Arzt" sein für das Problem ☺)
- Was passiert? Gibt der Arzt Ihnen irgendwelche Ratschläge?
- Wird das Problem gelöst oder nicht?

Wenn Sie mit dem Drehbuch fertig sind, stellen Sie es Ihrem Kurs vor! Nehmen Sie zusätzliches (*additional*) Papier; wenn sie künstlerisch begabt sind, können Sie auch Screenshots zu der Szene zeichnen.

Aktivität 28. Der BMI

Wer gesund lebt, achtet auch auf ein gesundes Gewicht. Der Body-Mass-Index (BMI) hilft Ihnen herauszufinden, ob ihr Gewicht gesund ist. Idealerweise sollte der **BMI** für 17- bis 24-Jährige zwischen 19 und 25 liegen. Am wichtigsten ist aber, dass man sich in seinem Körper wohl fühlt (*to feel comfortable in one's body*).

Ein BMI unter (*below*) 19 bedeutet **Untergewicht** und ein BMI über (*above*) 25 bedeutet **Übergewicht**.

In Deutschland rechnen wir in Kilogramm (kg), Metern (m) und Zentimetern (cm). Hier die passenden Werte:

Körpergewicht: 1 kg = 2.2046 pounds

Körpergröße: 1 m = 3.28 feet; 1 cm = 0.3937 inches

Berechnen Sie Ihren BMI (Körpergewicht dividiert durch die Körpergröße hoch zwei). Wenn Sie nicht schon wissen, was Ihr B-M-I ist, helfen Ihnen folgende Informationen:

Mein Körpergewicht: Mein Gewicht (in pounds) x $\frac{\text{1 Kilogramm}}{\text{2.2046 pounds}}$ = _____ Kilogramms

Meine Körpergröße: Meine Körpergröße (in feet) x $\frac{\text{1 Meter}}{\text{3.28 feet}}$ = _____ Meters

Mein BMI: $\frac{\text{Gewicht (in kg)}}{\text{Körpergröße (in cm) x Körperröße (in cm)}}$ = _____ BMI

Aktivität 29. Ein guter Vorsatz für das neue Jahr

Viele Amerikaner (und auch viele Deutsche!) haben gute Vorsätze für das neue Jahr (*new year's resolution*). Die beliebtesten Vorsätze handeln von Gesundheit und Fitness. Schreiben Sie Ihre Top 3 Vorsätze zum Thema Gesundheit. Würden Sie diese Vorsätze beibehalten? Wie lange? Bevor Sie anfangen, denken Sie an die verschiedenen Themen des Kapitels!

gesund essen	schlafen
Sport treiben	Verletzungen/Krankheiten
Körperpflege	zum Arzt gehen

1. _____

2. _____

3. _____

Aktivität 30. Im Fitnessstudio

Sie haben sich entschlossen, Ihre Vorsätze zum Neujahr endlich zu realisieren, und Sie stehen im Fitnessstudio und sprechen gerade mit einem Trainer über Ihre Gesundheit und Fitnesspläne. Als letzte Übung dieses Kapitels spielen Sie den Dialog vor: *Was sind Ihre Vorsätze? Wie oft können Sie trainieren? Was möchten Sie am liebsten tun, um gesund und fit zu sein? Was müssen Sie essen? Was dürfen Sie <u>nicht</u> essen? Welchen Sport werden Sie treiben? Warum wollen Sie fitter und gesünder werden? Wie werden Sie dieses Jahr endlich Erfolg haben (erfolgreich sein)?*

Schreiben Sie einen Dialog und vergessen Sie nicht, dass man mit Humor alle Probleme lösen kann (oder sich zumindest beim Versuch amüsieren kann!).

Aktivität 31. Lieder & Musik

Fußballsongs: „Wo die Weser einen großen Bogen macht" und „Stern des Südens" – In diesem Kapitel finden Sie unter „Lieder & Musik" auf der *Deutsch im Blick* Website eine pdf zur Bearbeitung von zwei Liedern, die mit Fußball zu tun haben.

Aussprache
Regional Dialects in Germany

In the next three chapters we will take a closer look at dialects in Germany, Switzerland and Austria. Even though it is not possible to discuss all different dialects in each country, the samples provided here give a good overview of the distinct dialects spoken in these three countries. After we have looked at the general dialect categories we will take a look at some of the dialects in Germany.

1. Overview: Regional Dialects in the German-speaking Countries

Up until now we've used Standard German as the basis for our discussion of the German language. This is because as foreign language learners, you need to know the particular variety that will enable you to communicate MOST efficiently and effectively! However, when you actually travel to the German-speaking countries, you'll soon realize that there are a LOT of regional varieties – or **dialects** – of German. Dialects are characterized not only by pronunciation, but also by grammar and vocabulary.

The dialects of the German-speaking countries are traditionally grouped into three categories:
1. *Niederdeutsch*; 2. *Mitteldeutsch*; and 3. *Oberdeutsch*.

Niederdeutsch (Low German dialects)	→	northern Germany
Mitteldeutsch (Central German dialects)	→	central Germany
Oberdeutsch (Upper German dialects)	→	southern Germany, Alsace, Austria, Liechtenstein, Switzerland

No, that's not a typo – the Low German dialects are actually found in northern Germany while the Upper German dialects are found in southern Germany, Austria, and Switzerland! This may seem confusing, but just remember that the terms Low German and Upper German refer to the *topography* (i.e., elevation) of the regions where they are spoken.

The Low German dialects are spoken in the low coastal regions bordering the North Sea and in the flat plains regions of northern Germany (above the red line; the one furthest north). The Upper German dialects are spoken in the mountainous regions of the Bavarian Alps in southern Germany as well as in the Austrian and Swiss Alps (below the orange and purple lines; the two lines south on the map). The Central German dialects are spoken in the regions in between (between the red and purple lines, the middle area). There you will find more regional variations as well.

The **Benrath Line** (the line to the north) separates the Low German dialects from the Central German dialects, and the **Germersheim Line/Speyerer** Line (the two lines below; oftentimes comprised to one) separate the Central German dialects from the Upper German dialects.

source: http://www.aboutaustria.org/german_language_2.htm

Aussprache

Please go to the Deutsch im Blick website, Kapitel 7

2. The High German Sound Shift

The High German Sound Shift was already outlined in the last chapter (Kapitel 6) so we will not go into too much detail describing it here. You should know, however, that the differences it describes are not only between German and English, but also between the Southern and North-German dialects.

The High German sound shift affected the Upper German dialects and, to a lesser extent, the Central German dialects. (Think of the area where the Central German dialects are spoken as a kind of in-between zone – most, but not all, of the sound shift took place here.) Since these particular dialects eventually formed the foundation for a standardized German language (i.e., High German), the shift is known as the High German sound shift.

What about the Low German dialects? Yep, you guessed it – the shift did not affect them. Nor did it affect other Germanic languages like Dutch and English. Take a look at the chart below. You'll notice that the sounds of certain Low German words are the same as Dutch and English words!

Pre-shift	Post-shift	Low German (Northern Germany)	Dutch	English	Upper/Central German (affected by shift)
$d \rightarrow t$		Dag, Dach	dag	day	Tag
$k \rightarrow ch$		maken, moaken, maaken	maken	to make	machen
$p \rightarrow f/ff$		Schipp, Schepp	schip	ship	Schiff
$p \rightarrow pf$		Peper, Päpa	peper	pepper	Pfeffer
$t \rightarrow ss/ß$		eten, äten	eten	to eat	essen
$t \rightarrow z$		teihn, tian	tien	ten	zehn
$v, w, f \rightarrow b$		Leev	lief	love	Liebe

You may find another dialectal sound shift not indicated in the above chart. When you travel from Northern Germany to Southern Switzerland you notice that in Switzerland the initial *K* is very often pronounced as ch. So, instead of saying *Knie* (knee) the Swiss say *Chnü* or instead of *Kind* (child) they say *Chind*.

3. Plattdeutsch, Berlinerisch, Kölsch, Bayrisch

In the following sections we will look at four dialects in Germany. These are definitely not the only ones but perhaps they are the most famous ones. For each dialect we provide a short overview of the pronunciation and a list of words compared to the Standard German equivalent. There are manz websites in Germany that deal with dialect differences and smartphone applications are on the rise. In fact, many dialects are supported by city state or federal funds. Kölsch for example has a dictionary, grammar handbook and various literature. Many Germans spend time on contributing to the dialect format of Wikipedia. Have a look.

Wikipedia in *Kölsch*:
http://ksh.wikipedia.org/wiki/Wikipedia:Houpsigk
Wikipedia in *Bayrisch*:
http://bar.wikipedia.org/wiki/Hauptseitn
Wikipedia in *Plattdeutsch*:
http://nds.wikipedia.org/wiki/Wikipedia:H%C3%B6%C3%B6ftsiet

PLATTDEUTSCH

Plattdeutsch (also: Niedersächsisch) is a group of dialects spoken in the state of Lower Saxony, the word *platt* meaning flat in the sense of either elevation or manner of speaking. These dialects did not take part in the High German sound shift that altered the consonants **p, t, k**, etc., so they are deemed Low German.

Dialect features	*Beispiele* *(Standard German → Platt)*
pf is pronounced *f* at the beginning of words	Pfeffer → Feffer
s is not pronounced *sch* at the beginning of words	schmieren → smeeren schlafen → slapen Schwein → Swien Stein → Steen
g is pronounced *j* at the beginning of syllables and words	geht → jeht
long vowels are shortened in words with only one syllable	Hut → Hutt
r is pronounced as a uvular roll (i.e., in the back of the throat like you're gargling mouthwash)	
at the end of words, the letter *g* (which has a *k* sound due to *Auslautverhärtung*) is pronounced *ch*	zwanzig → zwanzich
t is left off the end of words	nicht → nich

Grammatical changes:
a. accusative and dative case are interchangeable
  für mich → für mir

b. plural nouns occasionally formed with *s*
  der Onkel → die Onkels
  der Doktor → die Doktors

c. *sein* instead of *haben* is used in past perfect of *anfangen* and *beginnen*
  ich habe begonnen → ich bin begonnen
  ich habe angefangen → ich bin angefangen

Vocabulary differences to Standard German:

Morgen! → Moin moin!
Abendessen → Abendbrot
das Butterbrot → die Stulle
sehen → kucken/kieken
der Fleischer → der Schlachter

Frisch Water ut den Soot
is vör alle Wehdag god

Water rein un hell
is de wahre Lebensquell

"Fresh water from the well, is good for every pain.
Water pure and clear is the true source of life."

Could you rewrite it in Standard German?

BERLINERISCH

Berlinerisch is spoken in and around Germany's capital city. The city's location on the Benrath Line has lent the dialect its (mainly) Low German phonological features (i.e., *ich → ick* and *Apfel → Appel*), while its many immigrants have introduced vocabulary into the dialect from French and Turkish, for example.

Dialect features	*Beispiele* *(Standard German → Berlinerisch)*
pf is pronounced *f* at the beginning of words	*Pfeffer → Feffer*
g is pronounced *j* at the beginning of syllables and words	*geht → jeht*
r is pronounced as a uvular roll (i.e., in the back of the throat like you're gargling mouthwash)	
diphthongs *au* and *ei* are pronounced *oo* and *ee*, respectively	*auch → ooch* *keiner → keener*
at the end of words, the letter *g* (which has a *k* sound due to Auslautverhärtung) is pronounced *ch*	*zwanzig → zwanzich*
t is left off the end of words	*nicht → nich*

Grammatical changes:
a. accusative and dative case are interchangeable
   für mich → für mir

b. plural nouns occasionally formed with *s*
   der Onkel → die Onkels
   der Doktor → die Doktors

c. *sein* instead of *haben* is used in past perfect of *anfangen* and *beginnen*
   ich habe begonnen → ich bin begonnen
   ich habe angefangen → ich bin angefangen

Vocabulary differences to Standard German:

Morgen! → Moin moin!
Abendessen → Abendbrot
das Butterbrot → die Stulle
sehen → kucken/kieken
der Fleischer → der Schlachter

„Wat heulst'n kleener Hampelmann?"
– „Ick habe Ihr'n Kleenen 'ne Krone jeschnitzt, nu will er se nich!"
(Titel of Caricature *auf Berlinerisch* reads in Enlish: "What are you crying about, little jumping jack?"
– "I made a crown for your little one, now he doesn't want it!")

The caricature mocks the failure of the "lesser German solution" (Friedrich Wilhelm IV. [1795–1861] rejected the German Imperial Crown, shown to the right in the caricature). On the left we see the president of the German national parliament (*Parlamentspräsident*) Heinrich Wilhelm August Freiherr von Gagern (1799–1880).
First published in: *Düsseldorfer Monatshefte*. 1849.
Lithograph: Ferdinand Schröders (1818–1857).

KÖLSCH

Kölsch is spoken in and around Cologne, in the western German state of North Rhein-Westphalia. Cologne lies just south of the Benrath Line that separates the Low German dialects from the Middle German dialects. Thus, while Kölsch shares some phonological features with Berlinerisch, for example, it is really a Middle German dialect. Kölsch is well known for sounding nasal and sing-songy, two qualities which stem in part from its contact with the French language during Napoleon Bonaparte's 21-year-long occupation of Cologne.

Dialect features	*Beispiele* *(Standard German → Kölsch)*
g is pronounced *j* at the beginning of syllables and words	*geht → jeht*
r is pronounced as a uvular roll (i.e., in the back of the throat like you're gargling)	
diphthongs *ei*, *au*, and *eu* become their long vowel counterparts *i*, *u*, and *ü*, respectively	*Wein → Wing* *Frau → Fruu* *Freund → Fründ*
umlauts *ö* and *ü* are pronounced *e* and *i*	*schön → scheen* *Brüder → Brieder*
short *a* is pronounced short *o*	*schlafen → schlofen*
b is pronounced *v*	*Weib → Wiiv*
ch is pronounced *sch*	*ich → isch* *mich → misch*
at the end of words, the letter *g* is pronounced *ch*	*zwanzig → zwanzich*
final *n* dropped at the end of words	*machen → mache*
final schwa dropped at the end of words	*heute → heut*

Grammatical changes:

a. different past participles for certain verbs
       gedacht → gedenkt
       gewinkt → gewunken

Vocabulary differences to Standard

zu Hause → daheim
nicht → net/nit
nicht wahr? → gell?
der Fleischer → der Metzger
der Rotkohl → das Rotkraut

> Nohjemaate Krützblom jenau
> esu jroß wie bovve op
> denne Domtürm
> 9,50 m huh 4,60 m breit
> E Zeiche doför, dat dä Dom
> 1880 fädich jewoode es

"Replica of a finial of the same size as found on top the these towers of the cathedral, 9,50 m high 5,60 m wide. A sign for the completion of the construction of the cathedral in 1880."

But what would it be in Standard German and how do you pronounce the words (and the numericals)?

BAYRISCH

Bayrisch is a group of dialects spoken in the southernmost German state of Bavaria. (The word Bayerisch refers to the political territory of Bavaria. In the late 1800s, Bavarian King Ludwig I insisted on retaining the Greek y in the spelling of his beloved territory.) The High German sound shift was entirely realized here.

Dialect features	*Beispiele* *(Standard German → Bayrisch)*
schwa deleted from prefixes	*gesehen → gsehen*
r is pronounced as an alveolar roll (trilled)	
ch is pronounced *sch*	*ich → isch*
umlauts *ö* and *ü* are pronounced *e* and *i*	*schön → scheen/Brüder → Brieder*
short *a* is pronounced short *o*	*schlafen → schlofen*
st and *sp* are pronounced *scht* and *schp*, when they appear in the middle of words	*Fest → Fescht* *Wespe → Weschpe*
additional diphthongs used (i.e., *ia, ua, oa, ai, ou, oa, ea*)	*allein→ allioa* *bleich → bloach*
final *n* dropped at the end of words	*machen → mache*
final schwa dropped at the end of words	*heute→ heut*
diminutive endings *-chen* and *-lein* are pronounced *-le* (singular) and *-la* (plural)	*Mädchen → Mädle/Mädla*

Grammatical changes:
a) *some nouns take different genders*
    die Butter → der Butter
    das Radio → der Radio
b) past tense is almost entirely expressed through the present perfect tense (i.e., no imperfect tense)
    hatte → hat gehabt
c) *sein* is used in present perfect tense of verbs to indicate motion of the body (i.e. legen, sitzen, stehen)
    ich habe gelegen → ich bin gelegen
e) different past participles for certain verbs
    gedacht → gedenkt
f) different plural forms
    die Wagen → die Wägen
    die Stücke → die Stücker
    die Stiefel → die Stiefeln

Vocabulary differences to Standard

das Brötchen → die Semmel
zu Hause → daheim
nicht wahr? → gell?
nicht → net/nit
der Fleischer → der Metzger
immer → alleweil
sehr → arg
der Junge → der Bub
die Kartoffel → der Erdapfel
die Straße → die Gasse
sehen → schauen
nicht mehr → nimmer
die Apfelsine → die Orange

O Wanderer, du sollst es wissen,
vui Leut hat's scho am Berg daschmiss'n,
drum geh' langsam, nimm dir Zeit,
denn schnell bist in da Ewigkeit!

"O hiker, you should know, many men already fell off the cliff. So walk slowly, take your time, because fast you'll be in eternity!"

What would you think if you saw this sign hiking the Alps?

Work found at http://commons.wikimedia.org/wiki/File:Spruch_in_Bairisch_-_O_Wanderer_du_sollst_es_wissen.JPG / CC BY-SA 3.0 (http://creativecommons.org/licenses/by-sa/3.0/)

WebQuests

Zu diesem Kapitel gehören sechs mögliche WebQuests, die Sie wie gewohnt auf der *Deutsch im Blick* Webseite finden und bearbeiten können:

1. *Im ersten WebQuest werden Sie mehr über gesundes Essen lernen.*
2. *Im zweiten WebQuest erfahren Sie mehr über Gesundheit und Fitness.*
3. *Im dritten WebQuest schreiben Sie ein Grußkarte: Gute Besserung*

Meinungsumfragen

Gehen Sie zur *Deutsch im Blick* Website und machen Sie die Meinungsumfrage zum Thema *Gesundheit und Fitness* (keine große Überraschung, was?).

Gesund leben	Healthy living
der Alkohol	alcohol
alkoholisch	alcoholic (beverage)
alkoholfrei	alcohol-free (beverage)
der Ballaststoff (Ballaststoffe)	fiber, roughage
das Cholesterin (no plural)	cholesterol
das Fett (Fette)	fat
fit sein	to be fit
die Gesundheit (no plural)	health, well-being
gesund	healthy
gesund sein	to be healthy
das Koffein (no plural)	caffeine
die Kalorie (Kalorien)	calorie
kalorienarm/kalorienreich	low-calorie/high-calorie
das Vitamin (Vitamine)	vitamin
vitaminarm/vitaminreich	vitamine-poor/vitamine-rich

Sport treiben	Doing sports/exercising
Aerobic machen	to do aerobics
Gewichte heben	to lift weights
Pilates machen	to do Pilates
Racquetball spielen	to play Racquetball
tanzen	to dance
trainieren	to train
Yoga machen	to do yoga

Sportanlagen	Sports facilities
das Beachvolleyballfeld (-felder)	beach volleyball court
das Fitnessstudio (-studios)	gym
das Footballstadion (-stadien)	(American) football stadium
der Fußballplatz (-plätze)	soccer field (the real football!)
der Kraftraum (-räume)	weight room
die Sauna (Saunen/Saunas)	sauna
das Schwimmbad (-bäder)	swimming pool
das Sportzentrum (-zentren)	sports center
der Tennisplatz (-plätze)	tennis court
die Turnhalle (-hallen)	gymnasium

Wortschatz

(QR 7.1 p.345)

Der menschliche Körper	The human body
der Arm (Arme)	arm
das Auge (Augen)	eye
die Augenbraue (-brauen)	eyebrow
die Backe (Backen)	cheek
der Bauch (Bäuche)	stomach
die Brust (Brüste)	breast/chest
der Daumen (Daumen)	thumb
der Ellbogen (Ellbogen)	elbow
der Finger (Finger)	finger
der kleine Finger	pinky finger
der Mittelfinger	middle finger
der Ringfinger	ring finger
der Zeigefinger	index finger
der Fuß (Füße)	foot
das Fußgelenk (-gelenke)	ankle
das Gesicht (Gesichter)	face
das Haar (Haare)	hair
der Hals (Hälse)	neck
die Hand (Hände)	hand
das Handgelenk (-gelenke)	wrist
das Herz (Herzen)	heart
der Hintern (Hintern)	buttock
die Hüfte (Hüften)	hip
das Knie (Knie)	knee
der Knöchel (Knöchel)	knuckle
der Kopf (Köpfe)	head
die Leber (Lebern)	liver
die Lippe (Lippen)	lip
die Lunge (Lungen)	lungs
der Muskel (Muskeln)	muscle
die Nase (Nasen)	nose
der Oberschenkel (-schenkel)	thigh
das Ohr (Ohren)	ear
der Rücken (Rücken)	back
die Schulter (Schultern)	shoulder
die Stirn (Stirnen)	forehead
die Wange (Wangen)	cheek
der Zahn (Zähne)	tooth
der Zeh (Zehen)	toe
die Zunge (Zungen)	tongue

Körperpflege	Personal hygiene
sich die Augenbrauen zupfen	to pluck one's eyebrows
das Deo (Deos)	deodorant
sich das Gesicht waschen	to wash one's face
die Gesichtscreme (-cremes)	facial cream
sich die Haare waschen	to wash one's hair
sich die Hände waschen	to wash one's hands
der Rasierer (Rasierer)	electric shaver
die Slipeinlage (-einlagen)	thin pantiliner
der Tampon (Tampons)	tampon

Verletzungen	Injuries
der blaue Fleck (Flecken)	bruise, hematoma
das blaue Auge (Augen)	black eye, shiner
sich (z.B. den Arm) brechen	to break one's arm
die Gehirnerschütterung (-erschütterungen)	concussion
sich (z.B. den Knöchel) verstauchen	to sprain one's ankle
sich weh tun	to hurt oneself
der Unfall (Unfälle)	accident
der Autounfall	car accident

Beschwerden	Ailments
das Bewusstsein verlieren/in Ohnmacht fallen	to pass out
bewusstlos	unconscious
die Erkältung (Erkältungen)	common cold
sich erkälten	to catch a cold
eine Erkältung haben	to have a cold
das Fieber (no pural)	fever
Fieber haben	to have a fever
die Grippe (Grippen)	flu
die Grippe haben	to have the flu
der Husten (no plural)	cough
husten	to cough
der Schmerz (Schmerzen)	pain, ache
Bauchschmerzen haben	to have a stomachache
Halsschmerzen haben	to have a sore throat
Kopfschmerzen haben	to have a headache
Rückenschmerzen haben	to have a backache
Zahnschmerzen haben	to have a toothache
Schnupfen haben	to have a runny nose, sniffles
schwach	weak
sich schwach fühlen	to feel weak
übel	nauseous
Mir ist übel.	I feel nauseous.
sich übergeben	to throw up
unwohl	sick, queasy
sich unwohl fühlen	to feel sick, queasy
verschwitzt	sweaty
verwirrt	confused
wehtun	to hurt, to ache
Mein Bauch tut weh.	My stomach hurts.

Ein Kuraufenthalt	A stay at a health resort
sich ausruhen	to rest
sich entspannen	to relax
sich erholen	to recuperate
die Erholung (no plural)	recuperation
das Heilbad (-bäder)	spa
die Kur (Kuren)	treatment at a health resort
der Kurort (-orte)	health resort

Ärzte	Doctors
der Arzt (Ärzte)	physician, doctor
die Ärztin (Ärztinnen)	female physician, female doctor
der Augenarzt (-ärzte)	ophthamologist
der Chiropraktiker (-praktiker)	chiropractor
der Frauenarzt (-ärzte)	gynecologist
der Fußspezialist (-spezialisten)	podiatrist
der Hausarzt (-ärzte)	general practitioner
der Hautarzt (-ärzte)	dermatologist
der Hals-Nasen-Ohren Arzt	ear-nose-throat doctor
der Kinderarzt (-ärzte)	pediatrician
der Orthopäde (Orthopäden)	orthopedist
der Psychiater (Psychiater)	psychiatrist
der Tierarzt (-ärzte)	veterinarian
der Zahnarzt (-ärzte)	dentist
der Heilpraktiker (-praktiker)	homeopathic doctor

Note: Even though female forms exist (by adding -in), it is common to refer to the type of doctor in the (general) male form.

Beim Arzt	At the doctor
Angst haben	to be afraid
Keine Angst!	Don't be afraid!
der Arzthelfer (-helfer)	physician's assistant
die Arzthelferin (-helferinnen)	female physician's assistant
die Arztpraxis (-praxen)	doctor's office
das Krankenhaus (-häuser)	hospital
die Krankenschwester (-schwestern)	nurse (female only)
der Krankenpfleger (-pfleger)	male nurse
die Krankenpflegerin (-pflegerinnen)	female nurse
der Krankenwagen (-wagen)	ambulance
nervös	nervous
die Notaufnahme (-aufnahmen)	emergency room
die Panik (no plural)	panic
Keine Panik!	Don't panic!
der Patient/die Patientin (Patienten/Patientinnen)	patient
das Rezept (Rezepte)	prescription
ein Röntgenbild machen lassen	to get an X-Ray
Ich lasse mich röntgen.	I'm having an X-ray taken.
eine Spritze bekommen	to get a shot
einen Termin haben	to have an appointment
untersuchen	to examine
verschreiben	to prescribe
das Wartezimmer (-zimmer)	waiting room

Die Versicherung	Insurance
versichern	to insure
der Versicherte/die Versicherte (Versicherten)	insured (male/female)
die Versichertenkarte (-karten)	insurance card
die Versicherung (Versicherungen)	insurance
die Autoversicherung	car insurance
die Krankenversicherung	medical insurance
der Versicherungsträger (-träger)	insurance carrier

Die Medizin	Medicine
das Antibiotikum (Antibiotika)	antibiotic
das Aspirin	aspirin
das entzündungshemmende Medikament	anti-inflammatory medication
der Hustensaft (-säfte)	cough syrup
das Hustenbonbon (-bonbons)	cough drops
der Inhalator (Inhalatoren)	inhaler
die Kopfschmerztablette (-tabletten)	headache medication
das Pflaster (Pflaster)	bandage, band-aid

QR Codes

7.1

Wortschatz

7.2

07_01_int_bg_
gesundleben

7.3

07_02_int_ek_
gesundleben

7.4

07_03_int_ju_
gesundleben

7.5

07_04_int_hm_
gesundleben

7.6
07_05_int_ec_
gesundleben

7.7

07_06_int_bg_
gesundessen

7.8

07_07_int_ek_
gesundessen

7.9

07_08_sik_
vanessa
sportausweis

7.10

07_09_sik_
sarasportzentren

7.11

07_10_int_bg_
schlafen

7.12

07_11_int_ek_
schlafen

7.13

07_12_int_ju_
schlafen

7.14

07_13_int_hm_
schlafen

7.15

07_14_int_ec_
schlafen

7.16

07_15_int_sco_
schlafen

7.17

07_16_sik_
joelkrank

7.18

07_17_int_hb_
gesundleben

7.19

07_18_int_hb_
beimarzt

7.20

07_19_intro_
gesundheit

7.21

07_20_sik_
versicherung
system

7.22

07_21_sik_
koerperteile

8 DAS TRAUMLEBEN: BEZIEHUNGEN, WOHNEN UND DIE KARRIERE

Haben wir nicht alle einmal davon geträumt ein Star, ein/eine Sänger/Sängerin, ein/ eine Schauspieler/Schauspielerin zu sein? Oder möchten wir nicht alle auf einer Insel (island) leben, den ganzen Tag schwimmen und uns sonnen und den perfekten Partner neben uns liegen haben?

Das perfekte Traumleben kann in Erfüllung gehen! In diesem Kapitel werden Sie viel über Beziehungen, das Wohnen und die Karriere von Deutschen, Schweizern und Amerikanern lernen. Was ist ihnen wichtig? Wie leben sie? Und vieles mehr!

Außerdem werden Sie in diesem Kapitel die Chance haben viel über Ihr Traumleben zu erzählen. Lassen Sie uns gemeinsam das Traumleben erleben!

Das Einführungsvideo wird Ihnen einen kleinen Einblick in dieses Kapitel geben! Also los, ran an den Speck!

Sie werden nach diesem Kapitel
1. über Beziehungen, Karriere und Wohnen auf Deutsch sprechen können,
2. neue Wörter und Grammatikthemen beherrschen,
3. unterschiedliche Kulturen und kulturelle Unterschiede besser verstehen.

Online Book links

Sie können die Videoclips unter folgendem Link finden:
http://coerll.utexas.edu/dib/toc.php?k=8

Sie können die Vokabeln unter folgendem Link finden:
http://coerll.utexas.edu/dib/voc.php?k=8

Sections

Leute, die man kennt • People you know
Beschreibungen von Leuten • Descriptions of people
Einander kennenlernen • Getting to know each other
Es wird ernst • It's getting serious
Wo möchten Sie leben? • Where would you like to live?
Arbeit, Arbeit, Arbeit ... • Work, work, work ...
Was ist deutsch? • What is German?

Sie können auch die Grammatikthemen aus diesem Kapitel online finden:

Während der Übungen im Kapitel werden Sie regelmäßig auf *Grimm Grammar* auf der *Deutsch im Blick*-Website verwiesen (*referred to*). Hier sind die Grammatikthemen, die das Kapitel abdeckt (*covers*); machen Sie alle Online-Übungen, um optimal von den Übungen in diesem Arbeitsbuch (*workbook*) zu profitieren (*to profit from*).

- Adjectives – Komparativ und   http://coerll.utexas.edu/gg/gr/adj_05.html
  Superlativ

- Verbs – Konjunktiv II im Präsens   http://coerll.utexas.edu/gg/gr/vsub_02.htm

- Recommended:
  Adjectives: Overview   http://coerll.utexas.edu/gg/gr/adj_01.html
  Subjunctive: Overview   http://coerll.utexas.edu/gg/gr/vsub_01.htr

A. LISTEN Listen carefully to the pronunciation of each word or phrase in the vocabulary list.

B. REPEAT Repeat each word or phrase *out loud* as many times as necessary until you remember it well and can recognize it as well as produce it. Make a list of the words in this chapter which you find difficult to pronounce. Your teacher may ask you to compare your list with other students in your class. Make sure to learn nouns with their correct gender!

> **Beispiel:**
> die Sprache
> fünf

C. WRITE Write key words from the vocabulary list so that you can spell them correctly (remember that it makes a big difference whether you cross the Atlantic by ship or by sheep). You may want to listen to the vocabulary list again and write the words as they are spoken for extra practice.

D. TRANSLATION Learn the English translation of each word or phrase. Cover the German column and practice giving the German equivalent for each English word or phrase. Next cover the English column and give the translation of each.

E. ASSOCIATIONS Think of word associations for each category of vocabulary. (What words, both English and German, do you associate with each word or phrase on the list? Write down ten (10) associations with the vocabulary from the chapter.

> **Beispiel:**
> der Student/die Universität
> das Flugticket/das Flugzeug

F. COGNATES Which words are *cognates?* (Cognates are words which look or sound like English words.) Watch out for *false friends*! Write down several cognates and all the false friends from the chapter, create fun sentences that illustrate similarities and differences between the English and German meanings of these words.

> **Beispiel:**
> Nacht/night
> grün/green
> → False Friends: *hell* = light, bright vs. *Hölle* = hell

G. WORD FAMILIES Which words come from word families in German that you recognize (noun, adjective, verb, adverb)? Write down as many as you find in the chapter.

> **Beispiel:**
> das Studium (noun; studies)
> der Student (noun; person)
> studieren (verb)

H. EXERCISES Write out three (3) „Was passt nicht?" ('Odd one out') exercises. List four words, three of which are related and one that does not fit the same category. Categories can be linked to meaning, grammar, gender, parts of speech (noun, verb, adjective), etc. USE YOUR IMAGINATION! Give the reason for why the odd word does not fit. Your classmates will have to solve the puzzles you provide!

> **Beispiel:**
> grün – blau – gelb – neun
> Here *neun* does not fit, because it is a
> number and all the others are colors.

Wortschatz
Vorbereitung

Always learn nouns with the article!!!

These ideas are suggestions only. Different learner have different preference and needs for learning an reviewing vocabulary. T several of these suggestions until you find ones th work for you. Keep in min though, that knowing mar words – and knowing ther well, both to recognize ar to produce – makes you more effective user of th new language.

Basiswortschatz
Core Vocabulary

The following presents a list of core vocabulary. Consider this list as the absolute minimum to focus on. As you work through the chapter you will need more vocabulary to help you talk about your own experience. To that end, a more complete vocabulary list can be found at the end of the chapter. This reference list will aid your attainment of Chapter 8's objectives.

(QR 8.1 p.386)

Leute, die wir kennen — People We Know

der/die Bekannte (Bekannten)	acquaintance
der Chef (Chefs)	male boss
die Clique (Cliquen)	clique
der Freund (Freunde)	friend, boyfriend
die Freundin (Freundinnen)	female friend, girlfriend
der Kumpel (Kumpels)	buddy, pal
der Nachbar (Nachbarn)	male neighbor
die Partnerin (Partnerinnen)	female partner

Menschen beschreiben — Describing People

dick	big
dünn	thin
eingebildet	conceited
freundlich	friendly
grantig	grumpy
hübsch	handsome
humorvoll	humorous
nett	nice
schlank	slender
süß	cute
sympathisch	likeable
treu	faithful, loyal

In einer Beziehung — In a Relationship

das Geheimnis (Geheimnisse)	secret
die Harmonie (Harmonien)	harmony
kuscheln	to cuddle
sich mögen	to like one another
reden	to speak or talk
sich sehen	to see each other
träumen	to dream
sich treffen	to meet (up)
die Verabredung (Verabredungen)	date
zusammen sein	to date (older than high school)
die Beziehung (Beziehungen)	relationship
die Ehe (Ehen)	marriage
heiraten	to get married
die Hochzeit (Hochzeiten)	wedding ceremony
die Liebe	love
die Scheidung (Scheidungen)	divorce
der Streit (Streite)	fight
sich trennen	to separate, split up
sich verlieben	to fall in love
sich verloben	to get engaged
vertrauen	to trust

Wo und mit wem wohnen? — Living where and with whom?

alleine	alone
mit Mitbewohnern	with roommates
in der Nähe von ...	near...
in der Stadt	in the city
auf dem Land	in the countryside
im Ausland	abroad

Arbeit und Karriere — Work and Career

der Beruf (Berufe)	profession, job
das Gehalt (Gehälter)	salary (paid periodically/monthly)
das Interview (Interviews)	interview (in German not used for jobs)
das Vorstellungsgespräch (-gespräche)	job interview
der Lebenslauf (-läufe)	curriculum vitae/resume
jobben	to do a temp job
verdienen	to earn

I. Beziehungen

Aktivität 1. Beziehungen

Was bedeutet *Beziehung*? Bevor Sie über Beziehungen sprechen, versuchen Sie das Wort *Beziehung* zu definieren. Was assoziieren Sie mit dem Begriff *Beziehung*? Sie können Verben, Nomen, Adjektive etc. benutzen.

Wie Sie wahrscheinlich schon festgestellt haben, gibt es verschiedene Arten von Beziehungen: die persönliche Beziehung, die Liebesbeziehung, die Beziehung zu Familie und Freunden etc. In den nächsten Aufgaben werden Sie mit verschiedenen Beziehungen arbeiten und verschiedene Beziehungen entdecken!

Aktivität 2. Persönliche Beziehungen: Sind Sie gern unter Menschen?

A. Eva und Erin im Gespräch!

Sind Eva und Erin gesellig oder nicht? Finden Sie heraus, mit wem sie sich treffen. Schauen Sie zuerst Evas Video an und beantworten Sie die Fragen!

Sind Eva persönliche Beziehungen wichtig? Woher wissen Sie das?

_____

Wo trifft sie Menschen?

_____

(QR 8.2 p.386)

Was ist mit Erin? Schauen Sie sich ihr Video an und beantworten Sie die folgenden Fragen!

Sind Erin persönliche Beziehungen wichtig? Woher wissen Sie das?

_____

Wo trifft sie Menschen?

_____

(QR 8.3 p.386)

B. Persönliche Beziehungen: Wer sagt was?

Schauen Sie sich auch Bernas, Jans und Saras Video zum Thema persönliche Beziehungen und Freunde an. Was sagen sie dazu? Ordnen Sie die Aussagen der richtigen Person zu:

(QR 8.4 p.386)

A. Ja, es ist wichtig Freunde zu haben, wenn man Probleme hat zum Beispiel oder auch, wenn's einem gut geht.

(QR 8.5 p.386)

B. Manchmal, aber nicht immer. Meine Familie ist sehr eng und ich habe einige sehr enge Freunde, aber meistens, nee, ich gehe sehr gern allein.

(QR 8.6 p.386)

C. Ja, persönliche Beziehungen sind mir sehr wichtig. Ich brauch' viele Freunde. Ich brauche auch Nachbarn und Mitbewohner, damit man sich halt austauschen kann, wenn man Probleme hat oder auch, wenn man glücklich ist.

C. Eine Frage der Kultur?

Nachdem Sie die Videos gesehen und die Fragen beantwortet haben, denken Sie kurz über das Folgende nach: Eva, Berna und Jan kommen aus Deutschland und Erin und Sara kommen aus den USA! Gibt es Unterschiede zwischen den beiden Gruppen und ihren persönlichen Beziehungen und Freunden? Wenn ja, warum glauben Sie, dass es Unterschiede gibt? Wenn nein, warum nicht? Machen Sie sich ein paar Notizen und besprechen Sie dann Ihre Gedanken mit Ihrem Kurs!

Wie Sie festgestellt haben, kann man auf der Grundlage von wenigen Personen nicht verallgemeinern (*to generalize*). Wie man seine Zeit mit Freunden verbringt, kommt ganz auf die Person an und die Kultur, in der man lebt.

D. Jetzt sind Sie dran!

Sind Ihnen persönlich Beziehungen und Freunde wichtig? Schreiben Sie einen kurzen Absatz darüber!

Tipp: Nicht vergessen: Im Deutschen muss das Verb an zweiter Stelle stehen. Weitere Informationen dazu finden Sie in Kapitel 2.

Aktivität 3. Liebesbeziehungen

Schauen Sie sich die *Sprache im Kontext* Videos von Christian und Guido – „Willst du mit mir gehen?" und „Guidos Meinung zum Dating"– an und bearbeiten Sie die folgenden Aufgaben.

A. Beim ersten Hören

Kreuzen Sie die Wörter an, die im Clip vorkommen.

individuell • Familie • Gespräch • weggehen

Beziehungen • unwichtig • langweilen

unternehmen

(QR 8.7 p.386)

B. Schauen Sie sich das Video von Christian noch einmal an.

Wie funktioniert laut Christian das Dating in Deutschland? Füllen Sie die Lücken aus.

Also, das ist ganz _____ anders und ich glaube, es entwickelt

sich _____ über _____, wenn man eben zusammen

_____, zusammen was _____ oder so, dass man dann

anfängt ins _____ zu kommen. Es ist nicht so _____, wenn

man ausgeht zusammen, das ist jetzt nicht so was _____ oder so, sondern man fängt

einfach an _____ mit der Person zusammen zu unternehmen.

C. Guidos Meinung zu Dating

Schauen Sie sich das Video von Guido an. Wie funktioniert laut Guido das Dating in der Schweiz? Kreuzen Sie auch hier beim ersten Hören die Vokabeln an, die vorkommen, und füllen Sie dann die Lücken mit den richtigen Vokabeln aus.

Paar • zusammen • ähnlich • Fall • quatschen

funken • Eltern • Freunde • Clique

(QR 8.8 p.386)

In der Schweiz ist es fast wie in Deutschland oder sehr _____ wie in Deutschland.

Normalerweise _____ man sich in einer _____ und das ist

also die _____ Freunde oder Freundinnen und dann _____ man

zusammen _____. Und dann kann es _____ und wenn's funkt,

dann geht's von dort weiter. Und man _____ sich dann normalerweise auch

mit _____. Dann irgendwann ist man dann ein _____.

Aber so wie hier, wo man sagt, gut, jetzt _____ wir was essen

_____, nur die beiden, ist eigentlich nicht so der _____.

D. Ein Wortigel
Versuchen Sie eine kleine Vokabelliste von Christians und Guidos Videos zu erstellen: Was sind wichtige Wörter und Redensarten für das Thema *Dating und Beziehungen*?

die Liebe

Dating/Beziehungen

E. Und Sie?
Beschreiben Sie das Dating in Ihrem Land oder Ihre persönliche Einstellung zu diesem Thema. Wie funktioniert es? Gibt es eine Art von Dating, zum Beispiel: So funktioniert Dating in den USA? Was ist gut und was nicht so gut? Machen Sie sich einige Notizen und schreiben Sie einen kurzen Bericht. Teilen Sie Ihre Erfahrungen dem Kurs mit.

F. Vergleichen Sie Christians und Guidos Bemerkungen.
Schauen Sie sich Christians Video nochmal an und schauen Sie sich auch Guidos Video zum Thema *Dating* an. Nun vergleichen Sie auch diese zwei Videos und die Informationen, die sie darin bekommen mit Ihren Erfahrungen.

- Wie funktioniert das *Dating* für Christian?

- Was denkt Guido über das *Dating*?

- Was ist anders oder genauso bei Ihnen?

- Welche Art von *Dating* gefällt Ihnen? Warum?

Aktivität 4. Traumpartner: Berna, Erin und Jan
Schauen Sie sich die Interviews an und markieren Sie die richtigen Informationen für jede Person. Was ist ihnen wichtig an einem Partner?

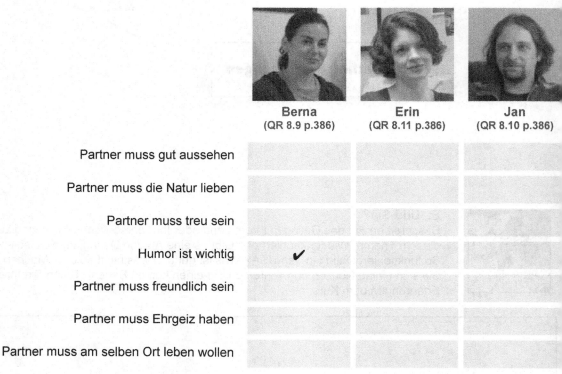

	Berna (QR 8.9 p.386)	Erin (QR 8.11 p.386)	Jan (QR 8.10 p.386)
Partner muss gut aussehen			
Partner muss die Natur lieben			
Partner muss treu sein			
Humor ist wichtig	✔		
Partner muss freundlich sein			
Partner muss Ehrgeiz haben			
Partner muss am selben Ort leben wollen			

Aktivität 5. Wie ist Ihr idealer Partner/Ihre ideale Partnerin?
Nun wissen Sie, was Berna, Erin und Jan wichtig an einem Partner ist. Was ist Ihnen wichtig? Zur Hilfe finden Sie hier einige Adjektive und Ausdrücke.

Adjektive:

nett	*freundlich*	*lustig*	*humorvoll*	*sympathisch*	*gutaussehend*	*schön*
schlank	*süß*	*gut gelaunt*	*dick*	*hübsch*	*pummelig*	*treu* *groß* *klein*

Ausdrücke:

sich verabreden   sich gut verstehen   sich treffen   sich sehen   zusammen gehen

zusammen sein   in den Arm nehmen   den ganzen Abend   für immer   Fernbeziehung

Kurzbeziehung   funken (es funkt)   sich verlieben   sich streiten   sich trennen

heiraten   sich verloben   Schluss machen   sich unterhalten

Andere/Eigene:

A. Wie soll Ihr Partner/Ihre Partnerin sein?

Zuerst machen Sie sich Notizen: Was ist Ihnen an einem Partner wichtig? Sie können die Vokabeln in den beiden Kästen oben benutzen. Fangen Sie so an:

In einer Beziehung muss mein Partner nett sein. Er/Sie ...

B. Befragung

Jetzt fragen Sie einen Kommilitonen/eine Kommilitonin, was ihm/ihr wichtig ist, und erzählen Sie ihm/ihr, was Ihnen an einem Partner wichtig ist. Machen Sie sich gute Notizen! Fangen Sie so an:

Was ist dir wichtig an einem Partner?

C. Eine Reportage

Jetzt berichten Sie Ihrem Kurs, was Sie über Ihren Kommilitonen/ihre Kommilitonin herausgefunden haben. Schreiben Sie Ihren Bericht auf einem separaten Blatt. Fangen Sie so an:

Ich habe mit _____ gesprochen. Ihm/Ihr ist an seinem/ihrem Partner _____ wichtig ...

Aktivität 6. Liebe

Liebe bedeutet für jede Person etwas anderes. Lesen Sie sich das folgende Liebesgedicht „Liebe ist ..." durch. Besprechen Sie die Zeilen mit einem Partner und entscheiden Sie, ob Sie diesen Worten zustimmen oder nicht. Dann bearbeiten Sie *A* und *B* auf den folgenden Seiten.

Grimm Gramma

In den letzten Aufgaben sind Adjektive sehr wichtig gewesen. Bitte gehen Sie zu *Grimm Gramma* und lesen Sie folgende Grammatikteile:

Adjectives overview

A. Ihre Meinung

Arbeiten Sie mit einem Partner/einer Partnerin zusammen und füllen Sie die Tabelle mit detaillierten Antworten aus.

Liebe ist ...	Stimmen Sie zu?	Warum? Warum nicht?
... mit kleinen Gesten zu zeigen, was man fühlt.		
... wenn sie die Hauptrolle in seinem Leben spielt.		
... beim Kuscheln das Handy auszuschalten.		
... wenn sie ihm wichtiger ist als der Sportteil.		
... sie nicht nur am Valentinstag zu verwöhnen.		
... wenn da immer noch ein kleines Geheimnis bleibt.		
... wenn sie keinen Schlaf findet, weil seine Betthälfte leer ist.		

Hier sind einige Ausdrücke zur Unterstützung:

Es stimmt/Es stimmt nicht, denn ...
Es ist (nicht) realistisch, denn ...
Es ist wichtig, dass ...

Das ist dumm/blöd/falsch/richtig ...
Ich glaube, ich sehe das anders ...
Das sehe ich nicht so.

Das sehe ich nicht ein, denn ...
Liebe für mich ist ...
Ich weiß, dass ...

Ausschnitte aus der *Bild* zum Thema „Liebe ist ...".

Kulturtipp: *Bild,* früher und offiziell die *Bild-Zeitung,* ist eine deutsche Tageszeitung, die vom Axel-Springer-Verlag montags bis samstags gedruckt wird. *Bild* wird in 44 Ländern verkauft. Die Tageszeitung ist sehr bekannt und beliebt, aber auch recht umstritten, wegen ihrer reißerischen und teils oberflächlichen Berichterstattung. Sonntags erscheint eine spezielle Auflage in einem speziellen Stil, *Bild am Sonntag.*

B. Kreative Ecke

Schreiben Sie ihr eigenes Liebesgedicht oder gestalten Sie ihren eigenen Zeitungsauschnitt zu „Liebe ist ..."! Zeigen Sie Ihren Ausschnitt dem Kurs und wählen Sie den Besten aus! Sie können zum Beispiel auch buntes Papier und verschieden Farben benutzen – seien Sie kreativ!

Aktivität 7. Liebe auf den ersten Blick!

A. Persönliche Fragen
Beantworten Sie die folgenden Fragen.

1. Waren Sie schon einmal verliebt? Wie alt waren Sie damals?

2. Haben Sie schon Liebe auf den ersten Blick erlebt?

3. Wie fühlt sich Liebe auf den ersten Blick an? Kreuzen Sie die Antworten an, die für Sie zutreffen.

- ♥ zittrig
- ♥ energiegeladen
- ♥ Herzklopfen

- ♥ nervös
- ♥ Ich falle gleich in Ohnmacht.
- ♥ strahlende Augen

- ♥ Flugzeuge im Bauch
- ♥ Ich kann nicht atmen.
- ♥ glücklich

4. Man sieht Liebe auf den ersten Blick in vielen Filmen. Welche Filme kennen Sie, die das zeigen? Glauben Sie, dass das realistisch ist? Wenn ja, warum? Wenn nicht, warum nicht?

B. Im Gespräch
Glauben Sie an die Liebe auf den ersten Blick? Besprechen Sie in kleinen Gruppen, ob es die Liebe auf den ersten Blick gibt. Was denken Sie darüber? Benutzen Sie Vokabeln und Ihre Notizen aus 7A.

> Ich glaube, ..., denn...
> Ich finde ..., denn...
> Meinst du...
> Kann man...

Kulturtipp: Die *Bravo* ist Deutschlands größtes, ältestes und erfolgreichstes Jugendmagazin. Es beschäftigt sich nicht nur mit allen Themen rund um Stars und Sternchen, sondern beantwortet auch Fragen rund um das Thema Liebe und Sexualität. Viele Deutsche sagen, dass sie von der *Bravo* aufgeklärt (t*o learn about the birds and the bees/to be enlighten*) worden sind.

Aktivität 8. Lieder & Musik
Die Fantastischen Vier 4 – Die da! In diesem Kapitel finden Sie dieses Beziehungs-Lied einer bekannten Hip-Hop-Gruppe aus Stuttgart. Gehen Sie zu „Lieder & Musik" auf der *Deutsch im Blick* Website, laden Sie die passende Pdf herunter und bearbeiten Sie die Aufgaben.

Aktivität 9. Ratgeber

A. Vor dem Lesen

1. Was bedeutet „Ratgeber"? Kann ein Ratgeber auch ein Mensch sein?

2. Gibt es auch Ratgeber in Ihrer Heimat? Wo kann man sie finden?

3. Der Titel von diesem Text lautet: „Liebe auf den ersten Klick". Was bedeutet das? Was thematiesier der Text Ihrer Ansicht nach?

B. Beim Lesen

Beantworten Sie die folgenden Fragen:

1. Wie viele Menschen suchen ihren Partner im Internet?

2. Wieso finden nicht alle den perfekten Partner?

3. *Freizeit Spaß* bietet einige Tipps. Welche Tipps bekommt der Leser?

C. Nach dem Lesen

Was ist Ihre Meinung? Glauben Sie an die Liebe auf den ersten Klick? Warum/Warum nicht? Was sind Ihre Erfahrungen? Sind Online-Partnerbörsen hilfreich/gefährlich/abstoßend/faszinierend? Schreiben Sie Ihre Meinung auf, lesen SIe sie dann einem Partner vor und besprechen Sie Ihre Meinungen.

Nur Mut: 26 Prozent der Singles werden im Internet fündig...

nen. Internet-Adressen finden Sie z.B. unter www.kontaktanzeigen-ratgeber.de oder www.singleboersen-vergleich.de. Dort erfahren Sie auch, wo sich die meisten Solisten Ihres Alters tummeln.

▶ Kontaktanzeigen sind sehr beliebt – unverbindliches Kennenlernen und Flirten erlaubt. Bei www.friendscout24.de kann man z.B. live im Séparée Kontakte knüpfen. www.datingcafe.de bietet auch Single-

Am Anfang war der Flirt...

reisen und Blinddates an. bei www.singles.freenet.de finden sich viele einsame Herzen aus den neuen Bundesländern. Die Kosten: Wer sich nicht nur die Anzeigen ansehen will, sondern selbst inserieren möchte, muss mit

zehn bis 25 € pro Monat rechnen. **Tipp:** Die Anzeige ist Ihr Aushängeschild! Vermeiden Sie Negatives (z.B. Mein Ex war ein Reinfall), lieber mit hübschem Foto auffallen!
▶ **Vermittlungen** sind anonym: Sie beschreiben sich, Ihr Profil wird in einer Datenbank gespeichert – der passende Partner professionell ermittelt. Mit 4,2 Mio. Nutzern ist www.parship.de z.B. die größte Agentur. www.elitepartner.de hat sich auf Akademiker spezialisiert (mit Seriositätsprüfung). Hier werden Singles mit Niveau fündig. www.dzf.de zielt auf Alleinstehende über 40 ab.

So viel Service kostet: Mitglieder zahlen monatlich 16 bis 50 €, für Frauen ist's oft gratis. **Tipp:** Das Kleingedruckte lesen! Meist verlängern sich Mitgliedschaften automatisch. Diese bei Anmeldung gleich kündigen.

Datenschutz ist wichtig

▶ **Vorsicht, Nepp!** Wird der Kontakt über SMS- oder Servicenummern angeboten? Finger weg! Hier geht's oft nur um teure SMS-Abzocke. Auf die AGB achten: Anbieter sollten Daten nicht weitergeben.

Eine andere Form der Beziehung ist die Beziehung zu Mitbewohnern. In den nächsten Aufgaben geht es um das Thema *Wohnen*: alleine wohnen, mit Mitbewohnern zusammen wohnen. Sie lernen auch, darüber zu sprechen, wo man leben und wohnen kann und möchte. Viel Spass dabei!

Grimm Gramma

Bitte gehen Sie zu *Grimm Grammar* und bearbeiten Sie folgende Grammatikteile:

Adjectives: comparative and superlative

zum Beispiel:

alt – älter – am ältesten
nett – netter – am nettesten
intelligent – intelligenter – am intelligentesten
kalt – kälter – am kältesten

und

gut – besser – am besten

Aktivität 10. Mit Mitbewohnern oder lieber allein?

A. Wer lebt lieber alleine, wer lebt gerne mit anderen Menschen?
Schauen Sie sich die Videos „Mitbewohner" von Eva, Sara und Jan an und vervollständigen Sie die folgenden Sätze:

Eva
(QR 8.12 p.386)

Sara
(QR 8.13 p.386)

Jan
(QR 8.14 p.386)

Es war nicht sehr _____ für Eva mit sechs anderen Mädels in England zu leben.	Jetzt hat Sara so _____ Platz.	Momentan ist es sehr _____ für ihn, dass er mit anderen Leuten zusammen wohnt.
Zu sechst in einer WG zu wohnen, das ist zu _____.	Diese Wohnung ist echt sehr _____.	Einmal, weil man viele Probleme dadurch etwas _____ macht.
Die verschiedenen Nationalitäten hatten einfach verschiedene kulturelle Hintergründe und da auf einen gemeinsamen Zweig zu kommen, war sehr _____.	Und sie hat die Wohnung sehr _____, aber im nächsten Jahr wird es sehr _____, aber es geht.	Man kann z.B. die Rechnungen _____ bezahlen.

B. Wohnen sie lieber alleine?
Ist es einfacher alleine zu wohnen? Nachdem Sie die Videos gesehen haben, füllen Sie den Text mit den richtigen Adjektivformen aus. Sie können Aufgabe **10A** als Hilfe benutzen. Benutzen Sie die jeweils angegebenen Adjektive, aber vergessen Sie nicht diese in die richtige/passende Form (Komparativ/Superlativ) zu setzen!

schwierig • <s>gern</s> • einfach

Eva lebt _lieber_ alleine. Es ist _____ alleine, als mit Mitbewohnern zu leben. Eva hat in England mit sechs anderen Mitbewohnerinnen zusammen gelebt. Sie kamen aus verschiedenen Ländern. Das machte es _____, als mit Mitbewohnerinnen aus dem gleichen Land zusammen zu leben.

gern • viel • süß • eng

Sara hat jetzt _____ Platz als sonst in ihrer Wohnung. Diese Wohnung ist _____ als die letzte Wohnung. Sie hat diese Wohnung _____ als ihre letzte Wohnung. Im nächsten Jahr hat sie eine Wohnung, die _____ als diese Wohnung ist.

gut • gut • leicht • gern

Jan lebt _____ mit Mitbewohnern. Momentan ist es _____ für ihn. Dadurch sind die Probleme _____. Die Rechnungen lassen sich _____ zu dritt bezahlen als alleine.

C. Jetzt sind Sie dran!

Schreiben Sie einen kleinen Absatz über Ihre Situation: Leben Sie lieber alleine oder mit anderen Menschen zusammen? Wie leben Sie momentan? Wie gefällt Ihnen die Situation? Ist das besser oder schlechter? Was ist Ihnen wichtig, wenn es um das Wohnen geht (*when talking about living*)? Was finden Sie am schwierigsten/am besten, wenn Sie mit anderen Studenten zusammen wohnen? Was sind die Vorteile (*advantages*) und Nachteile (*disadvantages*) von Mitbewohnern? Geben Sie wohlüberlegte (*well-considered*) Antworten!

Aktivität 11. Sprache im Kontext: Wer wohnt am liebsten allein? Guido oder Berna?

A. Guido: Mitbewohner ja oder nein?
Beim ersten Hören notieren Sie die Vokabeln, die Sie kennen.

(QR 8.15 p.386)

B. Beim zweiten Schauen
Schauen Sie sich Guidos Video erneut an und setzen Sie die folgenden Aussagen in die richtige Reihenfolge

_____ Mitbewohner muss ich sagen – nee, vielleicht nicht, weil ich hab' gern meinen eigenen Platz, meine eigenen Räumlichkeiten (*space*).

_____ Ich mach die Sauerei; wenn der Kühlschrank leer ist, weiß ich, wann er leer ist, und dann kann ich auch selber mal einkaufen gehen.

_____ Ja, das kommt drauf an!

_____ Für andere, die können nicht ohne Mitbewohner leben.

_____ Ich wohn' alleine, vielleicht mit einer Freundin zusammen.

C. In einem Satz
Sagen Sie, ob Guido lieber alleine wohnt, und wenn ja, warum.

_____.

Grimm Grammar

Bitte gehen Sie zur
Grimm Grammar-
Website und lesen
Sie die folgenden
Grammtikteile.

Complete Übung 1 and
2 under adjectives:
<u>comparative and super-</u>
<u>lative</u>

<u>Subjunctive: overview</u>

<u>Subjunctive: present</u>
<u>tense</u>

(QR 8.16 p.386)

D. Berna: Mitbewohner
Schauen Sie nun Bernas „Sprache im Kontext"-Clip „Mitbewohner" und
notieren Sie beim ersten Hören die Vokabeln, die Sie kennen.

E. Beim zweiten Hören
Beantworten Sie die folgenden Fragen:

Wie findet Berna das Leben alleine?

Wie lebt Berna momentan? Wie gefällt ihr das?

Warum gefällt Berna ihre jetzige Wohnsituation?

F. In einem Satz
Sagen Sie, ob Berna gerne mit Mitbewohnern zusammen wohnt, und wenn ja, warum.
_____.

Aktivität 12. Sprache im Kontext: Wo würde Jan gern leben?
Schauen Sie sich Jans Video „Jan: Wo würdest du gerne leben?" an und füllen
Sie die Lücken mit den richtigen Wörtern aus.

> würde • würde • leben • leben • leben • leben
> möchte • gefallen • könnte • könnte

Ich _____ dort _____, wo das Wetter schön ist.

Wo ich ein bisschen Kultur habe um mich herum. Also so ganz alleine auf dem

Land _____ es mir nicht so _____. Ich muss

eine große Stadt in der Nähe haben. Und ja, insofern _____ ich zum

Beispiel gerne im Süden der USA _____. Das gefällt mir. Vielleicht

in der Nähe von Atlanta _____ ich gut _____. Ich

_____ auch in Texas gut _____, oder Kalifornien.

**(QR 8.17
p.386)**

Aktivität 13. Umfrage: Wo würden Sie gern leben?

A. Umfrage: Gehen Sie in Ihrem Kurs herum und fragen Sie drei Kommilitonen, wo sie gern leben würden. Füllen Sie die Tabelle aus.

S1: *Wo würdest du gern leben?*
S2: *Ich würde gern in Nordafrika leben.*
S1: *Warum möchtest du dort leben?*
S2: *Nordafrika ist sehr schön. Das Mittelmeer ist schön und ich möchte Arabisch lernen.*
S1: *Könntest du dir vorstellen in Deutschland, Österreich oder in der Schweiz zu leben?*
S2: *Ja, warum nicht! Ich könnte in Österreich oder auch in der Schweiz leben. Aber ich könnte nicht in Deutschland leben.*
S1: *Warum könntest du in Österreich und in der Schweiz leben, aber nicht in Deutschland?*
S2: *In Österreich, in Wien, gibt es viel Kultur, wie die Oper zum Beispiel. Die Schweiz hat auch etwas Besonderes für mich. Sie sprechen viele Sprachen dort. Deutschland ist auch schön, aber es regnet viel. Ich glaube, ich würde lieber in Österreich oder in der Schweiz leben.*

Name:			
Wo würdest du gern leben?			
Warum?			
Könntest du dir vorstellen, in den deutschsprachigen Ländern zu leben?			
Warum/Warum nicht?			

B. Eine Reportage

Wählen Sie einen/eine von Ihren Kommilitonen/Kommilitoninnen und schreiben Sie einen kurzen Bericht über ihn/sie. Wo möchte er/sie leben? Warum? Könnte er/sie sich vorstellen, in den deutschsprachigen Ländern zu leben? Warum/Warum nicht? Stimmen Sie mit seinen/ihren Antworten überein?

Beispiel:

Ich habe mit Jan gesprochen. Jan würde gern im Süden der USA leben. Der Süden der USA gefällt ihm sehr...

Aktivität 14. In einem neuen Land leben!

A. Vor dem Lesen

Schauen Sie sich den folgenden Text an und bearbeiten Sie die folgenden Aufgaben.

1. Was für eine Textform ist das?

2. Unterstreichen Sie alle die Vokabeln, die Sie schon kennen.

3. Finden Sie die folgenden Wörter im Text, lesen Sie die Sätze, in denen sie vorkommen, und versuchen Sie zu raten (*guess*), was diese Vokabeln bedeuten:

____ *ursprünglich*	a. to save money
____ *geflohen (fliehen)*	b. husband
____ *jein*	c. female pilot
____ *vermissen*	d. originally
____ *in Rente gehen*	e. female reporter
____ *sparen*	f. fled (*to flee*)
____ *Ehemann*	g. to miss
____ *Pilotin*	h. to retire
____ *Journalistin*	i. yes and no

B. Beim Lesen: Beantworten Sie die folgenden Fragen

1. Wo lebt Siham?

2. Woher kommt sie? (Tipp: Es ist möglich, dass es nicht nur eine richtige Antwort gibt.)

3. Wo könnte Siham leben? Warum?

4. Wo würde Siham gern leben, wenn sie in Rente geht?

5. Könnte sie dort in Rente gehen? Was bräuchte sie dafür?

6. Was denkt Siham über Nordeuropa?

7. Was ist Sihams Traumberuf? Warum würde sie das gern machen?

Siham, du lebst in Österreich. Gefällt es dir hier?

Ja, mir gefällt Österreich sehr. Ich lebe hier schon seit 15 Jahren. Ich komme ursprünglich aus dem Libanon und bin mit fünf Jahren mit meiner Familie nach Österreich geflohen. Das Leben hier ist gut.

Vermisst du dein Land?

Jein. Ich kann mich an manche Sachen erinnern, aber am meisten vermisse ich meine Familie und Freunde; meine Oma und meinen Opa und so.

Würdest du gern in einem anderen Land leben?

Ich könnte mir gut vorstellen, in Südeuropa zu leben. Ich würde auch gern mal in Lateinamerika wohnen. Ich habe sehr viel über Lateinamerika gelesen und gehört. Ich möchte gern sehr viel reisen und mir die Länder und Kulturen anschauen. Ich könnte auch in Spanien leben. Ich mag das Meer sehr und deswegen würden viele Länder in Frage kommen.

Wo würdest du gern in Rente gehen?

Naja, wenn es möglich wäre, dann würde ich gern irgendwann wieder im Libanon leben. Vielleicht könnte ich in meinen späten Jahren dort leben. Dafür müsste ich viel Geld verdienen und sparen. Außerdem müsste mein Ehemann bereit sein, mit mir dorthin zu ziehen. Mal schauen!

Könntest du dir vorstellen in Nordeuropa zu leben? Oder ist das zu kalt für dich?

Also, Nordeuropa ist sehr schön! Ich bin sogar schon ein paar Mal in Holland, Dänemark und Schweden gewesen. Ich war leider noch nie in Finnland. Finnland würde ich gern besuchen. Dort zu wohnen ... bin mir nicht so sicher. Ich könnte mir vorstellen immer wieder nach Nordeuropa in den Urlaub zu fahren. Aber dort ist es wirklich zu kalt für mich. Ich könnte nicht lange dort wohnen. Der Winter ist dort viel länger als der Sommer.

Und, Siham, was ist dein Traumberuf?

Oh, das ist schwierig. Ich würde gern Pilotin werden. Das ist schon immer mein Traum gewesen. Ich möchte gern andere Länder besuchen und durch den Himmel fliegen. Dort oben ist es so schön! Vielleicht könnte ich auch Managerin werden. Dann könnte ich auf einer Insel oder so ein Hotel besitzen.

Das ist sehr interessant. Also möchtest du am liebsten viele verschiedene Länder sehen und dabei arbeiten?

Ja, ich würde gern mein Interesse an Kulturen und Reisen mit meiner Arbeit verbinden. Das wäre ganz toll! Journalistin, so wie Sie, das könnte ich mir auch gut vorstellen!

Na, dann versuche ich dir eine Praktikumsstelle zu beschaffen. Vielen Dank für deine Zeit. Ich wünsche dir alles Gute für die Zukunft.

Ich danke auch! Das nächste Mal können wir das Interview vielleicht in einem anderen Land führen.

Nach dem Lesen: Besprechen Sie mit einem Partner folgende Fragen

1. Kennen Sie Menschen in Ihrem Heimatland, die nicht dort geboren sind?

2. Was sind ihre Erfahrungen?

3. Was wissen Sie über Immigranten in Ihrem Land?

II. Die Welt der Arbeit

Aktivität 15. Lieder & Musik

Die Prinzen – Millionär. In diesem Kapitel finden Sie auch dieses Lied von einer beliebten deutschen a capella-Gruppe aus Leipzig. Gehen Sie zu „Lieder & Musik" auf der *Deutsch im Blick* Website, laden Sie die passende pdf herunter und bearbeiten Sie die Aufgaben.

Aktivität 16. Im Ausland arbeiten!

A. Vor dem Lesen

1. Was für ein Text ist das?

2. Die Überschrift lautet: „Fürs Praktikum auf Weltreise." Wovon glauben Sie handelt der Text?

3. Wer ist die Zielgruppe für diesen Text?

4. Versuchen Sie zu raten, was diese Vokabeln bedeuten:

_____ *Praktikum*	a. academic student
_____ *Ehrgeiz*	b. contest/competition
_____ *Reiselust*	c. requirements
_____ *Hochschüler*	d. internship
_____ *Teilnehmer*	e. emerging talent
_____ *anspruchsvoll*	f. deadline
_____ *Auslandsaufenthalt*	g. ambition
_____ *Nachwuchstalent*	h. participants
_____ *Wettbewerb*	i. desire to travel
_____ *Bewerbungsschluss*	j. challenging
_____ *Voraussetzung*	k. stay abroad

Fürs Praktikum auf Weltreise

Die Welt sehen und gleichzeitig an der Karriere feilen? Kein Problem! Mit dem Praktikumsprogramm von MLP und Junge Karriere bringen Studierende beruflichen Ehrgeiz und Reiselust unter einen Hut.

Join the best - so lautet das ehrgeizige Motto, unter dem sich Hochschüler aller Fachrichtungen für eine von 14 Praktikumsstellen rund um den Globus bewerben können. Das Programm läuft bereits im fünften Jahr. Ob als Jurist in Chicago, als Chemiker in Singapur oder als Wirtschaftswissenschaftler in Warschau: Die Teilnehmer erwarten anspruchsvolle Aufgaben in führenden Unternehmen. Je nach Vereinbarung dauert der Auslandsaufenthalt zwischen zwei und sechs Monaten. Dazu schnürt MLP ein Rundum-sorglos-Paket. Der Finanzberater zahlt Flug, Unterkunft und Versicherung und stellt den Nachwuchstalenten eine Kreditkarte zur Verfügung.

Allein im vergangenen Jahr beteiligten sich rund 3400 Studierende am Wettbewerb um Praktikumsplätze in internationalen Metropolen. Bewerbungsschluss für einen Auslandsaufenthalt im Jahr 2009 ist der 9.November 2008. Teilnehmen können alle deutschsprachigen Studenten ab dem dritten Semester sowie Absolventen, Referendare und Doktoranden. Sie sollten mindestens ein erfolgreiches Praktikum absolviert haben.

Stipendiaten 2009: Praktika rund um den Globus

Unternehmen	Einsatzort/-land
Allianz Group	Jakarta/Indonesien*
Axel Springer AG	Warschau/Polen*
Baker & McKenzie	Chicago/USA*
BASF SE	Singapur*
Deloitte Consulting GmbH	Tokio/Japan*
Evonik Industries AG	New York/USA*
Heidelberger Druckmaschinen AG	Quigpu bei Schanghai/China*
Hochtief AG	Johns River bei Sydney/Australien*
Hypo Vereinsbank/Unicredit Group	Moskau/Russland*
Pricewaterhouse Coopers AG	Warschau/Polen*
Procter & Gamble Service GmbH	Genf/Schweiz*
SAP AG	Palo Alto/USA*
Siemens Managment Consulting	New York/USA*
T-Systems Enterprise Services GmbH	Puebla/Mexiko*

* Änderungen - auch der Zielorte - sind vorbehalten. Es besteht kein Rechtsanspruch auf Erhalt eines bestimmten Praktikumsplatzes
Quelle: www.jointhebest.info

Voraussetzung ist außerdem ein Abiturdurchschnitt von 2,5 oder besser. Ein Online-Bewerberfragebogen lässt sich im Internet unter www.jointhebest.info abrufen. Wer auf Nummer sicher gehen will, kann sich übrigens von erfahrenen MLP-Beratern unter die Arme greifen lassen. Beim Bewerbungscoaching analysieren Professionals die Unterlagen der Teilnehmer. Angeboten wird auch ein Training für das finale Assessment-Center.

Selbst für Studierende, die es nicht unter die ersten 14 schaffen, lohnt sich die Kandidatur. Wer in die letzte Runde kommt, hat die Chance auf einen von mehr als 100 Praktikumsplätzen in ganz Deutschland. Ein weiterer Bonus für Nachwuchstalente: Sie werden in das Join-the-best-Karrierenetzwerk aufgenommen und regelmäßig über interessante Jobangebote oder Veranstaltungen informiert.

Bewerbung: So kommen Sie gut an

Per Mausklick zum Traumpraktikum: Anmeldungen für das Join-the-best-Stipendium 2009 sind ausschließlich online unter www.jointhebest.info möglich. Noch bis zum 9. November 2008 können Kandidaten hier ihre Unterlagen hinterlegen. Abgefragt werden zum Beispiel Informationen zu Studienfächern, Praktika sowie Sprach- und Computerkenntnissen. Wer die erste Hürde genommen hat, wird am 28. oder 29. November 2008 zu einem Assessment-Center in einer MLPGeschäftsstelle vor Ort eingeladen. Dort erwartet die Bewerber ein Sprach- und Zahlenlogiktest. Darüber hinaus stellen sie ihre Fähigkeiten in Gruppenübungen und einer Selbstpräsentation unter Beweis. Am 15. und 16. Januar 2009 findet in der MLP-Zentrale in Wiesloch das finale Assessment-Center statt. Für die 14 erfolgreichen Kandidaten heißt es anschließend: Ab ins Ausland! www.jointhebest.info

Hochtief AG • Allianz AG • BASF AG • Procter & Gamble GmbH
Deloitte & Touche GmbH Wirtschaftsprüfung • Siemens Management Consulting
PricewaterhouseCoopers AG • SAP • HypoVereinsbank AG
Baker & McKenzie • Evonik Industries AG • Axel Springer AG

B. Beim Lesen: Beantworten Sie die Fragen

1. Wie lange gibt es dieses Programm schon?

2. Wie lange dauert der Auslandsaufenthalt?

3. Was enthält das MLP-Paket?

4. Wann ist der Bewerbungsschluss für das Jahr 2009?

5. Wer kann an diesem Programm teilnehmen?

6. Was sind die Voraussetzungen für die Teilnahme?

7. Was wird in der Online-Anmeldung abgefragt?

C. Nach dem Lesen: Arbeiten Sie in einer Gruppe und beantworten und besprechen Sie folgende Fragen:

1. Gibt es für Sie ähnliche Möglichkeiten? Wenn ja, welche und wie viele Studierende machen das? Wenn nein, warum nicht?

2. Wohin würden Sie gehen? Wo würden Sie Ihr Praktikum machen?

3. Welche Vorteile hat ein Auslandspraktikum gegenüber einem Praktikum zu Hause?

4. Würden Sie ein Praktikum im Ausland machen? Warum? Warum nicht?

5. Glauben Sie, Europäer reisen mehr ins Ausland als Einwohner anderer Länder? Warum?

Aktivität 17. In zehn Jahren ...

A. Sprache im Kontext Video: Guido: In 10 Jahren
Schauen Sie sich Guidos Video an und schreiben Sie gemeinsam auf, wie man folgende Wörter und Ausdrücke auf Deutsch sagt:

(QR 8.26 p.386)

no idea	
to have a career	
eternal student	
as a professor	
private business	
computer company	
it depends on where the job is	
probably not in Germany	
career suicide	
it doesn't matter (to me)	

B. Wie sieht ihr Leben in zehn Jahren aus?
Schauen Sie sich die Videos von Eva, Erin und Jan (Interviews: „Mein Leben in 10 Jahren") an. Was erzählen sie über ihre Träume und ihr Leben in zehn Jahren? Machen Sie sich Notizen und beantworten Sie folgende Fragen.

Eva
(QR 8.18 p.386)

Erin
(QR 8.19 p.386)

Jan
(QR 8.20 p.386)

1. Was für einen Beruf hat Eva in zehn Jahren?

2. Ist sie verheiratet und hat Kinder?

3. Hat sie schon den richtigen Partner für die Zukunft?

4. Was macht Erin in zehn Jahren und wo lebt sie dann?

5. Als was arbeitet Jan in zehn Jahren? Und wo arbeitet er?

C. Jetzt sind Sie dran!
Fragen Sie zwei Kommilitonen/Kommilitoninnen, was sie in zehn Jahren machen, und berichten Sie dann dem ganzen Kurs davon.

Name:		
Wie sieht dein Leben in zehn Jahren aus?		
Was für einen Beruf möchtest du haben? Was möchtest du werden?		
Wo möchtest du gern arbeiten?		

der Anwalt/die Anwältin
der Chemiker/die Chemikerin
der Lehrer/die Lehrerin
der Arzt/die Ärztin
der Diplomat/die Diplomatin
der Ingenieur/die Ingenieurin
der Geschäftsmann/die Geschäftsfrau
der Pilot/die Pilotin
der Journalist/die Journalistin
der Psychiater/die Psychiaterin

D. Eine Reportage: Berichten Sie dem Kurs, was Ihre Kommilitonen/Kommilitoninnen in zehn Jahren machen/arbeiten

Partner #1:

Partner #2:

Er/Sie arbeitet ...

Er/Sie arbeitet ...

Aktivität 18. Was ist Ihnen wichtig an Ihrer Arbeit?

A. Im Gespräch

Besprechen Sie mit einem Partner, was für Sie die fünf wichtigsten Kriterien für die Arbeit sind. In dem Kasten finden Sie einige Vokabeln als Hilfe. Welches Kriterium steht für Sie an erster Stelle? Welche sind im Rang niedriger? Sind Ihre Liste und die Liste Ihres Parters ähnlich?

---

mit anderen Menschen arbeiten • im Freien arbeiten • ein privates/großes Büro haben
Spaß haben • viel Geld verdienen • flexibel sein • viele/wenige Stunden arbeiten
viel Urlaub haben • mit Tieren arbeiten • alleine arbeiten • anderen Menschen helfen
von zu Hause aus arbeiten • (k)einen Chef/(k)eine Chefin haben • kreativ sein
intellektuelle Tätigkeit • viel reisen können

Fangen Sie so an:

An meiner Arbeit ist es mir am wichtigsten, kreativ zu sein.
Das zweitwichtigste Kriterium ist...

1.

2.

3.

4.

5.

B. Interviews: Was ist wichtig an der Arbeit? Eva, Jan und Berna erzählen, was ihnen an ihrer Arbeit wichtig ist. Füllen Sie die Tabelle mit den richtigen Informationen aus.

Eva
(QR 8.22 p.386)

Jan
(QR 8.23 p.386)

Berna
(QR 8.24 p.386)

C. Interview: Sie haben die Möglichkeit Eva, Jan und Berna zu befragen. Welche weiteren Fragen würden Sie ihnen stellen?

Fragen:

1.

2.

3.

4.

5.

D. Ein Sketch: Beim Berufsberater

Arbeiten Sie mit einem Partner/einer Partnerin und stellen Sie sich vor, dass Sie beim Berufsberater sind. Einer von Ihnen ist der Berater, der andere ist der Bewerber (applicant). Der Bewerber versucht einen Job zu finden, der seinen Hauptkriterien (die Sie oben erwähnt haben) und Qualifizierungen wirklich gut entspricht. Benutzen Sie die Vokabeln aus Teil A, die Antworten von Berna, Eva und Jan sowie die Fragen in Teil C, um einen kleinen Sketch (ca. 3-5 Minuten) zu schreiben und im Kurs vorzuführen.

Sie sollten den Dialog NICHT Wort für Wort aufschreiben und auswendig lernen!!! Machen Sie sich lieber Notizen und lernen Sie die Bedeutung der Fragen und mögliche Antworten auf diese Fragen!

Notizen:

Mögliche Themen und nützliche Ausdrücke

E. Der letzte Schritt vor dem Vorstellungsgespräch!

Sie haben sich für ein traumhaftes Praktikum beworben, und Sie haben es geschafft! Sie sind unter den zehn besten Kandidaten; nur die besten drei werden aber zu einem Vorstellungsgespräch eingeladen. Für die nächste Runde müssen Sie zwei Absätze schreiben, um die letzten Fragen Ihres zukünftigen (hoffentlich) Chefs zu beantworten.

Was ist Ihr Traumjob? _____

Absatz #1:

Was ist Ihnen an der Arbeit am wichtigsten? Warum sind Sie der beste Kandidat/die beste Kandidatin?

Absatz #2:

Wie lösen Sie Konflikte bei einem Teamprojekt? Was tun Sie, wenn Sie hoffnungslos viele Aufgaben haben?

Aktivität 19. Spiel: Speeddating

Ferrero Deutschland stellt die beliebte Milch und Schokolade Kombination *Kinderschokolade* und *Kinderriegel* her und hat in den letztan Jahren eine Webekampagne gestartet, in der sich *Frau Milch* und *Herr Schokolade* bei einem Speed-Dating-Event kennenlernen und verlieben. Suchen Sie im Internet nach diesem Werbespot, um in die richtige Stimmung zu kommen. Dann sehen Sie sich den Fragebogen an und spielen ihr eigenes Speed-Dating. Für jede Runde haben Sie 5 Minuten Zeit. Machen Sie sich Notizen zu den Antworten ihrer "Dates", um am Ende ihren Favoriten zu wählen. Wer weiß, vielleicht finden Sie im Deutschkurs den Mann/die Frau ihres Lebens!

Frage	Date 1	Date 2	Date 3	Date 4	Ja!	Nein!
Wie heißt du?						
Was ist dein Traumberuf?						
Wo würdest du gerne leben?						
Möchtest du gerne Kinder haben oder lieber einen Porsche fahren?						
Lebst du alleine oder in einer WG?						
Vollende bitte diesen Satz: Ich habe eine Schwäche für ...						
Wie sollte deine Traumfrau/dein Traummann sein?						
...						

Aktivität 20. Zusammenfassung

A. Gehen Sie zu Aktivität 5 und vergleichen Sie Evas, Jans und Bernas Antworten. Was ist ihnen an ihren Partnern wichtig/wichtiger/am wichtigsten? Mit wem stimmen Sie selbst überein und warum?

Partner

B. Gehen Sie zu Aktivität 10 und vergleichen Sie Evas, Saras und Jans Antworten. Wer lebt gern/lieber/am liebsten alleine oder mit Mitbewohnern? Mit wem stimmen Sie selbst überein und warum?

Wohnen

C. Gehen Sie zurück zu Aktivität 19 und vergleichen Sie Jans, Evas und Bernas Antworten. Was ist ihnen an ihrer Arbeit wichtig/wichtiger/am wichtigsten? Mit wem stimmen Sie selbst überein und warum?

Arbeit

In Köln am Rhein findet man tausende Sicherheitsschlösser (teils graviert oder bemalt) an dem Gitter, das die Bahnstrecke von dem Fußgängerüberweg auf der Hohenzollernbrücke trennt. Seit etwa 2004 werden es immer und immer mehr. Verliebte, beste Freunde und viele andere hängen ein Schloss an den Zaun, geben sich ein Versprechen und schmeißen dann den Schlüssel in den Fluß. Das (Liebes-/ Freundschafts- ...) Versprechen soll so abgesiegelt werden. Wie finden Sie das? Würden Sie auch ein Schloss anhängen? Mit wem? Warum? Warum nicht?

Aktivität 21. Ihr Traumleben

Jetzt sind Sie dran! Wo würden Sie gern leben? Was ist Ihnen an Beziehungen (zur Familie, zu Freunden, zu Mitarbeitern) wichtig? Wo möchten Sie arbeiten und warum? Was ist Ihnen an der Arbeit am wichtigsten/gar nicht wichtig? Anders gesagt, wie sieht Ihr Traumleben aus?

Herzlichen Glückwunsch! Sie haben dieses Kapitel durchgearbeitet! Jetzt können Sie über Beziehungen, das Wohnen und die Karriere mit anderen Studenten ganz fröhlich diskutieren!

Aussprache
Regional Dialects in Switzerland –
SCHWEIZERDEUTSCH (Schwiizerdütsch)

In the previous chapter we explored the different dialects in Germany. This chapter takes a closer, though only partial, look at the different Swiss German dialects. Below is a map of Switzerland indicating the different languages and dialects spoken.

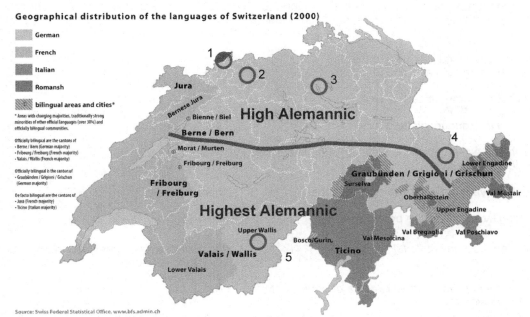

As you can see, Switzerland has four main languages and four main language areas (although most Swiss people are multilingual): Swiss-German is spoken in the middle part of Switzerland, Swiss-French is mostly spoken in the West and South-West, Italian in the *Kanton Tessin* and Retho-Romanisch (a Latin derivative) in the *Kanton Graubünden* (a canton is Switzerland's political unit, like a state in Germany or Austria). In this chapter we concentrate on the Swiss German "part" of Switzerland.

The thick line in the picture above approximates the division between the **High-** and **Highest Alemannic** dialect areas. This does not mean that in each of the speech regions only one dialect is spoken. On the contrary, dialects differ within the two regions as well as between *Kantone*, or even within a *Kanton*, to the point where neighboring townships might have quite distinct dialects. If you are interested in listening to samples from the different regions you can find them at http://www.dialekt.ch/default.htm. Here we will focus on a few varieties of Swiss German.

Let's take a brief look at the dialectal differences. The five circles (numbered to match the following table) in the above picture illustrate the dialect diversity that exists in Switzerland.

English	German	1. Basel-City	2. Basel-Canton	3. Zürich	4. Graubünden	5. Wallis
understand	verstehen		verstoo	verstaa		
bag	Tüte	Sagg	Sak			
not	nicht		nit	nööd		net
cold	kalt	kiel	chalt			
we go	wir gehen		mir gönd		miar göönd	wiär gääh
church	Kirche		Chillä		Kircha	

Schweizerdeutsch is the national variety of German spoken in multilingual Switzerland (which also recognizes French, Italian, and Romansch as national languages). Due to its location (i.e., to the southwest of Germany, Switzerland underwent the High German sound shift just as southern Germany and Austria did. However, as a result of its constant exposure to other languages (especially French), *Schweizerdeutsch* has a unique sound as well as unique vocabulary, which distinguishes it from the other Upper German dialects.

Dialect features	*Beispiele (Standard German → Schweizerdeutsch)*
at the beginning of words, *k* is pronounced +	*kalt → chalt* *Küche → Chuchi*
schwa deleted from prefixes	*gesehen → gsee*
r is pronounced as an alveolar roll (i.e., when the tongue makes contact with the roof of your mouth)	*es regnet regelmäßig in Regensburg*
ch is pronounced 'hard' *[χ]* at the beginning, middle and end of a word	*ich → iich* *die Milch → die Milch*
umlaut *ü* is pronounced as u+ä	*Brüder → Bruäder*
short *a* is pronounced long o	*schlafen → schlofä*
st and *sp* are pronounced *scht* and *schp* in the middle of words	*Fest → Fescht* *Wespe → Wäschpii*
final *schwa* dropped at the end of words	*heute → hütt*
diminuitive endings are pronounced *–li*	*Hauslein --> Hüüsli*
differences in institutional language	der Bundestag → der Nationalrat die Bundesländer → die Kantone die Fahrkarte → das Billet
many French words used in place of equivalent German words	der Schaffner → der Kondukteur vielen Dank! → merci vielmals das Fahrrad → das Velo der Bürgersteig → das Trottoir schnell → geschwind nicht wahr? → gell?/gäll?
some vocabulary different from Standard German	zu Hause → dahei der Junge → d'r Buäb sehen → luägä/luäge die Sahne → d'r Rahm der Fleischer → d'r Metzger Guten Tag → Grüezi

Nota Bene: A German dialect resembling Swiss German is spoken in France on the border of France, Switzerland and Germany. This dialect is called *Elsässisch* (Alsacian).

This is the image of the Swiss Commemorative Coin 2011.

Berner Zibelemärit? What could that be? Can you figure it out? The images on the coin give you a hint.

How much is it worth in US $?

WebQuests

Zu diesem Kapitel gehören zwei WebQuests, die Sie wie gewohnt auf der *Deutsch im Blick* Webseite finden und bearbeiten können:
1. Telefonanschlüsse in Deutschland
2. Zeitschriften und Magazine.

Meinungsumfragen

Gehen Sie zur *Deutsch im Blick* Website und machen Sie die Meinungsumfrage zum Thema *Beziehungen, Karriere und Wohnen* .

Wortschatz

(QR 8.1 p.386)

Leute, die man kennt	People you know
der Arbeitskollege (-kollegen)	male co-worker
die Arbeitskollegin (-kolleginnen)	female co-worker
der/die Bekannte (Bekannten)	acquaintance
ein guter Bekannter	a good male friend
eine gute Bekannte	a good female friend
der Chef (Chefs)	male boss
die Chefin (Chefinnen)	female boss
die Clique (Cliquen)	clique
der Freund (Freunde)	friend, boyfriend
die Freundin (Freundinnen)	female friend, girlfriend
ein Freund/eine Freundin von mir	a friend of mine
der Kollege (Kollegen)	colleague or good friend
die Kollegin (Kolleginnen)	female colleague
der Kumpel (Kumpels) – no female form!	buddy, pal
der Nachbar (Nachbarn)	male neighbor
die Nachbarin (Nachbarinnen)	female neighbor
der Partner (Partner)	male partner
die Partnerin (Partnerinnen)	female partner

Beschreibungen von Leuten	Descriptions of people
arrogant	arrogant
dick	big
dünn	thin
dürr	skinny
eingebildet	conceited
fett	fat
freundlich	friendly
gesellig	social
grantig	grumpy
gutaussehend	goodlooking
gut gelaunt	in a good mood
hübsch	handsome
humorvoll	humorous
lustig	funny
mager	skinny
muffelig	grumpy
nett	nice
pummelig	chubby
schlank	slender
schön	beautiful
süß	cute
sympathisch	likeable
treu	faithful, loyal

Einander kennenlernen	Getting to know each other
abholen	to pick someone up
Ich hol' dich von zu Hause ab.	I'll pick you up at home.
anfangen	to start or begin
Wann fängt der Film denn an?	When does the movie start?
anmachen	to hit on someone
ein Bier trinken gehen	to go have a beer
einen Kaffee trinken gehen	to have a cup of coffee
Sollen wir mal zusammen einen Kaffee trinken?	Want to go and have a cup of coffee?
Eis essen gehen	to go out for ice cream
flirten (flirtete - hat geflirtet)	to flirt
Flugzeuge/Schmetterlinge im Bauch haben	to have butterflies in one's stomach
funken (funkte - hat gefunkt)	to spark
das Geheimnis (Geheimnisse)	secret
die Harmonie (Harmonien)	harmony
das Herzklopfen	heartthrob
Ich fall' gleich in Ohnmacht!	I'm about to faint!
Ich gebe dir einen aus.	Can I buy you a drink?

Ich lade dich ein.	means: Let me pay for this.
kuscheln	to cuddle
das Meeting (Meetings)	official meeting
sich mögen	to like one another
quatschen	to chit chat
reden	to speak or talk
Ich muss mit dir reden.	I have to talk to you. (sounds serious)
Mit dir kann man nicht reden.	There's no talking to you.
Er lässt nicht mit sich reden.	He won't budge.
sich sehen	to see each other
träumen	to dream
Ich hab' von dir geträumt.	I dreamt about you.
sich treffen	to meet (up)
Treffen wir uns mal auf ein Glas Wein?	Should we go have a glass of wine some time?
Treffen wir uns dann da?	Should we meet there then?
das Treffen (Treffen)	meeting
der Treffpunkt (-punkte)	meeting point
sich unterhalten	to talk, have a conversation
sich verabreden	to agree to meet, to arrange a date
die Verabredung (Verabredungen)	date
das Verständnis (usually no plural)	understanding
sich gut verstehen	to get along well
Wer zahlt die nächste Runde?	Who's buying the next round?
zusammen/miteinander gehen	to date (high school level)
Willst du mit mir gehen?	Do you want to date me?
zusammen sein	to date (older than high school)

Es wird ernst.	**It's getting serious.**
die Beziehung (Beziehungen)	relationship
die Fernbeziehung	longdistance relationship
die Ehe (Ehen)	marriage
Darf ich dich küssen?	May I kiss you?
Du siehst toll aus.	You look great.
heiraten	to get married
die Heirat (no plural)	wedding
die Hochzeit (Hochzeiten)	wedding ceremony
Kann ich dich in den Arm nehmen?	Can I give you a hug?
die Liebe	love
Liebe auf den ersten Blick	love at first sight
sich scheiden lassen	to get divorced
die Scheidung (Scheidungen)	divorce
Schluss machen	to break up
Mary hat mit mir Schluss gemacht.	Mary broke up with me.
der Streit (Streite)	fight
sich streiten	to fight or argue
sich trennen	to separate, split up
die Trennung (Trennungen)	separation
das Verhältnis (Verhältnisse)	relationship; ratio
Meine Eltern und ich haben ein gutes Verhältnis.	I have a good relationship with my parents.
Ich glaube, ihr Mann hat ein Verhältnis.	I think her husband is having an affair.
sich verlieben	to fall in love
sich verloben	to get engaged
die Verlobung (Verlobungen)	engagement
vertrauen	to trust
sich zanken	colloquial for to fight
die Zukunft (no plural)	future

Wo möchten Sie leben?	Where would you like to live?
alleine	alone
an einem warmen/kalten Ort	in a warm/cold place
auf einer Insel	on an island
auf dem Land	in the countryside
im Ausland	abroad
im Weltraum	in space
in den Bergen	in the mountains
in der Nähe von ...	near ...
in der Stadt	in the city
in einer Großstadt	in a big city
mit einigen Freunden	with some friends
mit Mitbewohnern	with roommates

Arbeit, Arbeit, Arbeit...	Work, work, work...
die Stellenanzeige (-anzeigen)	job ad
der Anzug (Anzüge)	suit
der Arbeitslose (-losen)	unemployed male person
die Arbeitslose (-losen)	unemployed female person
die Arbeitslosigkeit (no plural)	unemployment
die Arbeitslosenzahl (-zahlen)	number of unemployed people
die Arbeitsstelle (-stellen)	position
die Beförderung (Beförderungen)	promotion
der Beruf (Berufe)	profession, job
Was sind Sie von Beruf?	What is your profession?
sich (für eine Stelle) bewerben	to apply (for a position/job)
eine Stelle bekommen/verlieren	to get/lose a job
das Büro (Büros)	office
die Flexibilität	flexibility
das Gehalt (Gehälter)	salary (paid periodically/monthly)
das Vorstellungsgespräch (-gespräche)	job interview
der Job (Jobs)	(temporary) job
jobben	to do a temp job
das Kostüm (Kostüme)	suit for a woman
die Karriere (Karrieren)	career
die Krawatte/der Schlips (Krawatten/Schlipse)	necktie
die Kreativität (usually no plural)	creativity
der Lebenslauf (-läufe)	curriculum vitae/resume
der Lohn (Löhne)	wages (e.g., hourly)
pensioniert	retired
die Rente (Renten; often used in plural)	retirement pay
die Rente (no pural)	retirement
in Rente gehen	to retire
verdienen (viel/wenig)	to earn (a lot/little)
die Vorbereitung (Vorbereitungen)	preparation

Berufe	Professions
der Anwalt/die Anwältin	lawyer
der Apotheker/die Apothekerin	pharmacist
der Arzt/die Ärztin	doctor
der Baumeister/die Baumeisterin	builder
der Berater/die Beraterin	counselor
der Buchhalter/die Buchhalterin	accountant
der Chemiker/die Chemikerin	chemist
der Diplomat/die Diplomatin	diplomat
der Dolmetscher/die Dolmetscherin	interpreter (synchronous)
der Geschäftsmann/die Geschäftsfrau	businessman, businesswoman
der Ingenieur/die Ingenieurin	engineer
der Journalist/die Journalistin	journalist
der Kellner/die Kellnerin	waiter
der Koch/die Köchin	chef
der Krankenpfleger/die Krankenpflegerin	male nurse/ female nurse
die Krankenschwester	female nurse
der Künstler/die Künstlerin	artist
der Lehrer/die Lehrerin	teacher (school, high school)
der Musiker/die Musikerin	musician
der Nachrichtensprecher/die Nachrichtensprecherin	TV anchor
der Pilot/die Pilotin	pilot
der Professor/die Professorin	professor (college, university)
der Psychologe/die Psychologin	psychologist
der Schauspieler/die Schauspielerin	actor
der Sportler/die Sportlerin	athlete
der Übersetzer/die Übersetzerin	translator
der Unternehmer/die Unternehmerin	enterpreneur

QR Codes

8.1 Wortschatz

8.2 08_01_int_ek_beziehungen

8.3 08_02_int_ec_beziehungen

8.4 08_03_int_sco_beziehungen

8.5 08_04_int_bg_beziehungen

8.6 08_05_int_ju_beziehungen

8.7 08_06_sik_christian-dating

8.8 08_07_sik_guido-dating

8.9 08_08_int_bg_partner

8.10 08_09_int_ju_partner

8.11 08_10_int_ec_partner

8.12 08_11_int_ek_mitbewohner

8.13 08_12_int_sco_mitbewohner

8.14 08_13_int_ju_mitbewohner

8.15 08_14_sik_guido-mitbewohner

8.16 08_15_int_bg_mitbewohner

8.17 08_16_sik_jangerneleben

8.18 08_17_int_ek_lebenin10

8.19 08_18_int_ec_lebenin10

8.20 08_19_int_ju_lebenin10

8.21 08_20_int_bg_lebenin10

8.22 08_21_int_ek_arbeit

8.23 08_22_int_ju_arbeit

8.24 08_23_int_bg_arbeit

8.25 08_24_intro_traumleben

8.26 08_25_sik_guido-in10jhrn

9 WAS IST DEUTSCH?

*Eine Google-Suche im Sommer 2012 nach dem Satz „Was ist deutsch" hat 597,000
Treffer auf deutschen Websites ergeben. Im Vergleich kam der Satz „Was ist
österreichisch" 1,470 mal auf Websites aus Österreich vor, und in der Schweiz gab es
8,490 Sites mit „Was ist schweizerisch". Diese Suche ist zwar sehr rudimentär, aber
sie zeigt trotzdem, dass die Frage der Identität für Deutsche sehr wichtig ist.*

*In diesem Kapitel werden wir versuchen, die folgende Frage zu beantworten: Was
ist deutsch? Wir werden die Frage von Identität sowie Selbst- und Fremdbilder
besprechen, um besser zu verstehen, was es heißt, Deutscher/Deutsche zu sein. Im
deutschsprachigen Kontext sind folgende Themen besonders wichtig:*

1. *Sind Sie politisch engagiert?*
2. *Schule und Ausbildung*
3. *Krieg und Frieden*
4. *Die Umwelt*

Am Ende des Kapitels können Sie:
1. *ausländische Nationalbilder über Deutsche und Deutschland vergleichen.*
2. *verstehen, wie junge Deutsche über Politik sprechen.*
3. *das deutsche Parteienspektrum beurteilen und Ihre eigene Position angeben.*
4. *das deutsche Bildungssystem beschreiben und mit anderen Ländern
   vergleichen.*
5. *über Berufsinteressen sprechen.*
6. *Ausbildungsbedingungen in Deutschland und in Ihrem Heimatland vergleichen.*
7. *die Rolle der Umwelt und des Umweltschutzes in Deutschland verstehen.*

Online Book links

Sie können die Videoclips unter folgendem Link finden:
http://coerll.utexas.edu/dib/toc.php?k=9

Sie können die Vokabeln unter folgendem Link finden:
http://coerll.utexas.edu/dib/voc.php?k=9

Sections

Was ist deutsch? • What is German?
Die Umwelt • The Environment
An der Schule • At School
Nach der Schule • after school (upon graduation)
Die Politik • Politics

Sie können auch die Grammatikthemen aus diesem Kapitel online finden:

Während der Übungen im Kapitel werden Sie regelmäßig auf *Grimm Grammar* auf der *Deutsch im Blick*-Website verwiesen (*referred to*). Hier sind die Grammatikthemen, die das Kapitel abdeckt (*covers*); machen Sie alle Online-Übungen, um optimal von den Übungen in diesem Arbeitsbuch (*workbook*) zu profitieren (*to profit from*).

- Verbs: Der Infinitivsatz — http://coerll.utexas.edu/gg/gr/vinf_01.html
- Conjunctions: Subordinierende Konjunktionen — http://coerll.utexas.edu/gg/gr/con_04.html

- Recommended:

Verbs: Overview — http://coerll.utexas.edu/gg/gr/v_01.html
Verbs: Konjunktiv II im Präsens — http://coerll.utexas.edu/gg/gr/vsub_02.htm
Conjunctions: Overview — http://coerll.utexas.edu/gg/gr/con_01.html
Conjunctions: Word Order — http://coerll.utexas.edu/gg/gr/con_06.html
Conjunctions: Coordinating Conjunctions — http://coerll.utexas.edu/gg/gr/con_03.html

A. **LISTEN**

Listen carefully to the pronunciation of each word or phrase in the vocabulary list.

B. **REPEAT**

Repeat each word or phrase *out loud* as many times as necessary until you remember it well and can recognize it as well as produce it. Make a list of the words in this chapter which you find difficult to pronounce. Your teacher may ask you to compare your list with other students in your class. Make sure to learn nouns with their correct gender!

> **Beispiel:**
> die Sprache
> fünf

These ideas are sugge
tions only. Different learne
have different preference
and needs for learning ar
reviewing vocabulary. T
several of these sugge
tions until you find ones th
work for you. Keep in min
though, that knowing ma
words – and knowing the
well, both to recognize ar
to produce – makes you
more effective user of th
new language.

C. **WRITE**

Write key words from the vocabulary list so that you can spell them correctly (remember that it makes a big difference whether you cross the Atlantic by ship or by sheep). You may want to listen to the vocabulary list again and write the words as they are spoken for extra practice.

D. **TRANSLATION**

Learn the English translation of each word or phrase. Cover the German column and practice giving the German equivalent for each English word or phrase. Next cover the English column and give the translation of each.

E. **ASSOCIATIONS**

Think of word associations for each category of vocabulary. (What words, both English and German, do you associate with each word or phrase on the list? Write down ten (10) associations with the vocabulary from the chapter.

> **Beispiel:**
> der Student/die Universität
> das Flugticket/das Flugzeug

F. **COGNATES**

Which words are *cognates?* (Cognates are words which look or sound like English words.) Watch out for *false friends*! Write down several cognates and all the false friends from the chapter, create fun sentences that illustrate similarities and differences between the English and German meanings of these words.

> **Beispiel:**
> Nacht/night
> grün/green
> → False Friends: *hell* = light, bright vs. *Hölle* = hell

G. **WORD FAMILIES**

Which words come from word families in German that you recognize (noun, adjective, verb, adverb)? Write down as many as you find in the chapter.

> **Beispiel:**
> das Studium (noun; studies)
> der Student (noun; person)
> studieren (verb)

H. **EXERCISES**

Write out three (3) „Was passt nicht?" ('Odd one out') exercises. List four words, three of which are related and one that does not fit the same category. Categories can be linked to meaning, grammar, gender, parts of speech (noun, verb, adjective), etc. USE YOUR IMAGINATION! Give the reason for why the odd word does not fit. Your classmates will have to solve the puzzles you provide!

> **Beispiel:**
> grün – blau – gelb – neun
> Here *neun* does not fit, because it is a
> number and all the others are colors.

Eigenschaften und Werte — Characteristics and Values

sich anpassen	to fit it, assimilate
die Bildung (no plural)	education
die Ehrlichkeit (usually no plural)	honesty
auf etwas/jemanden Einfluss haben	to have influence on something / someone
die Gerechtigkeit (Gerechtigkeiten)	justice
der Glaube (Glauben)	faith, belief
hilfsbereit	helpful
die Höflichkeit (Höflichkeiten)	politeness
der Mut (no plural)	courage
die Sicherheit (Sicherheiten)	security
die Toleranz (usually no plural)	tolerance
die Unabhängigkeit (Unabhängigkeiten)	independence
die Verantwortung (Verantwortungen)	responsibility
das Vertrauen (usually no plural)	trust
die Wahrheit (Wahrheiten)	truth

Politik — Politics

das Bundesland (Bundesländer)	federal state
engagiert	involved, engaged
die (politische) Einstellung (Einstellungen)	(political) attitude, inclinations
die Hauptstadt (Hauptstädte)	capital city
die Nachkriegszeit	postwar period
die Partei (Parteien)	political party
selbstbewusst	self-assured, self-confident
die Wahl (Wahlen)	choice, election
das Wahlprogramm (Wahlprogramme)	party platform
wählen	to vote, choose
der Wähler (Wähler)	male voter
die Wählerin (Wählerinnen)	female voter

Bildung und Ausbildung — Education and Training

sich bewerben	to apply
bei einer Firma, Schule	to a firm, school
um eine Stelle	for a position
abschließen	to graduate
die Bildung (no plural)	education
die Kenntnis (Kenntnisse; nearly always plural)	knowledge
die Pflicht (Pflichten)	obligation
die Schule besuchen	to attend school

Die Umwelt — The Environment

der Abfall (Abfälle)	trash
das Abgas (Abgase, usually in plural)	exhaust fume
achten (auf etwas achten)	to watch out for, observe
das Aussehen	appearance
die Energie (Energien)	energy
fördern	to encourage
die Gefahr (Gefahren)	danger
der Müll (no plural)	garbage
die Mülltrennung (usually no plural)	trash sorting
sparen	to save
der Strom (no plural)	electricity
trennen	to separate
die Umwelt (usually no plural)	environment
die Veranstaltung (Veranstaltungen)	event
der Verkehr (no plural)	traffic

Aktivität 1. Typisch deutsch?

A. Was Sie schon wissen

Lesen Sie die folgende Liste durch und markieren Sie die Charakteristiken, die Sie besonders *deutsch* finden.

Familie	Einfluss auf andere Menschen? Länder?
Gerechtigkeit	gemütliche Cafés
Respekt gegenüber anderen Menschen	finanzielle Sicherheit im Beruf
Freiheit	tolle Gastgeber
Hilfsbereitschaft	unverschämt direkt
Verantwortungsgefühl	unhöfliche Möchtegern-Amerikaner
Höflichkeit	sarkastisch, aber superlustig
Bildung	liebevoll und langweilig
Sicherheit	geschmacklos
Unabhängigkeit	sofort zum Punkt kommen
Friedfertigkeit	Fleiß
Toleranz	Ehrlichkeit
Fleiß	die besten Buchläden auf der Welt!
Vertrauen gegenüber anderen Menschen	Autos, die am Zebrastreifen halten
Leistungsbereitschaft	extrem unhöfliche Leute
Lebensgenuss	Man meldet sich mit Namen am Telefon
Mut	Brot, das schön knusprig (*crispy*) ist
Sparsamkeit	schlecht gelaunte Menschen in Geschäften
Respekt vor Autorität	das entscheidende Verb ans Ende setzen
Tradition	intensive Debatten über **alle Themen**
Gerechtigkeit	
Religiosität (Religion)	
Patriotismus	

B. Sprache im Kontext: „Typisch deutsch"

(QR 9.27 p.430)

1. Sehen Sie sich den kurzen Film „Typisch deutsch" an und überlegen Sie sich die Antworten auf folgende Fragen. Schreiben Sie ein paar Notizen auf.

Wovon handelt der Videoclip?

Was machen die Leute im Videoclip?

2. Schauen Sie sich das Video noch einmal an und markieren Sie alle Wörter, die Sie hören.

❑ schlafen	❑ Demokratie
❑ Pünktlichkeit	❑ Oktoberfest
❑ Fußball	❑ Autos
❑ Sprache	❑ Wildpferde
❑ Land	❑ Disziplin
❑ Bier	❑ Ausbildung

3. Schauen Sie den Clip ein drittes Mal an. Was ist nun deutsch? Markieren Sie die Sätze, die laut dem Video zutreffen.

    a. German is the relatedness to the country.
    b. German is not to eat or laugh.
    c. German is the language that forms your thinking.
    d. German cars are low quality.
    e. Germans are disciplined.
    f. Germans criticize others.

4. Sehen Sie sich den Clip ein letztes Mal an. Beantworten Sie die Fragen in eigenen Worten.

    Warum finden diese Leute es schwer, die Frage „Was ist typisch deutsch?" zu beantworten?

    Welche Eigenschaften finden Sie auch „typisch amerikanisch"?

Aktivität 2. Ihre Meinung: Was ist deutsch?

A. Ideen sammeln

Die Listen in den vorigen Aktivitäten sind Beschreibungen von Deutschen über sich selbst: deutsche Selbstbilder. Können Sie als Ausländer solchen Beschreibungen vertrauen? Können diese Charakteristiken Ihnen dabei helfen, Deutsche besser zu verstehen? Wie? Können diese Beschreibungen problematisch sein? Warum? Sind Selbstbilder realistisch? Schreiben Sie Ihre Gedanken auf undfragen Sie zwei Kommilitonen, was sie meinen.

Meiner Meinung nach ...

sind diese Beschreibungen nützlich, weil ...	*sind solche Beschreibungen problematisch, weil ...*

B. Weitere Adjektive/Begriffe

Schauen Sie sich die Liste (das Selbstbild der Deutschen) noch einmal an. Fehlen noch andere Wörter und Ausdrücke, die SIE benutzen würden, um die Deutschen zu beschreiben? Was Sie vielleicht von Verwandten, aus Filmen, der Literatur oder Kultur über Deutschland oder die Deutschen gelernt haben?

weitere Wörter & Ausdrücke zum *Deutschsein*

Was ich über die Deutschen weiß, habe ich ...

- ❑ **aus literarischen Texten**
- ❑ **aus den Nachrichten**
- ❑ **von meinen Eltern**
- ❑ **von Verwandten**
- ❑ **in der Schule/an der Uni**
- ❑ **aus Filmen**
- ❑ **im Internet**
- ❑ **aus Illustrierten** (*tabloids*)

... gelernt.

Aktivität 3. Sind Sie politisch engagiert?

A. Ein Wortigel

Was ist Politik? Was bedeutet das Wort für Sie? Bevor wir über Politik sprechen, versuchen Sie das Wort *Politik* zu definieren. Welche Wörter beziehungsweise Ausdrücke und Ideen assoziieren Sie mit diesem Begriff?

wählen

Politik

Aktivität 4. Welche Rolle spielt die Politik in unserem Leben?

A. Eva: Politisch engagiert

Schauen Sie sich Evas Videoclip an und vervollständigen Sie die Interviews mit den zutreffenden Wörtern aus dem Kasten.

> Mitte • engagiert • aufgeklärt • mag
> Wie • Grund • wählst • überhaupt • liberal

(QR 9.3 p.430)

Interviewer:	Bist du politisch _____ ?
Eva:	Nein, ähm, _____ nicht.
Interviewer:	Und warum nicht?
Eva:	Ähm, dazu bin ich im Sportverein zu aktiv, hab ich überhaupt keine Zeit mehr dafür, was eigentlich auch nicht der richtige _____ ist, aber …
Interviewer:	_____ du regelmäßig?
Eva:	Ich gehe zum Wählen und bin davor auch immer relativ gut _____ dann [darüber], was ich wähle.

B. Erin, Berna und Jan: Sind sie politisch engagiert?

Diese Studenten sprechen über ihr Verhältnis zur Politik. Schauen Sie sich die folgenden Videoclips an und vervollständigen Sie die Tabelle mit möglichst vielen Informationen über jede Person. Wenn es keine Antwort auf eine Frage gibt, dann schreiben Sie einfach „keine Antwort".

	(QR 9.5 p.430)	(QR 9.6 p.430)	(QR 9.7 p.430)
Politisch engagiert?			
Interesse an Politik?			
Politische Orientierung?			
Wählt regelmäßig?			

Zum Nachdenken

Die Deutschen haben gesagt, dass sie politisch *nicht* engagiert sind, aber auch, dass sie immer wählen gehen und sich vor der Wahl gründlich informieren. Ihrer Meinun nach, wie verstehen diese drei Studenten „politisch engagiert"? Hat dieser Ausdruck auch für <u>Sie</u> dieselbe Bedeutung? Ist *wählen gehen* dasselbe wie *politisch engagiert sein*?

C. Welche Rolle spielt Politik in Ihrem Leben?

Beantworten Sie die folgenden Fragen selbst, und fragen Sie dann zwei Kommilitonen/Kommilitoninnen, was sie meinen.

	ich	*Partner 1*	*Partner 2*
Interessieren Sie sich für politische Nachrichten?			
Wo informieren Sie sich über Politik? Im Internet? In den Zeitungen? Im Fernsehen (*Daily Show* usw.)? In den Illustrierten (*tabloids*)?			
Halten Sie sich für politisch engagiert?			

Aktivität 5. Über Politik sprechen

In Deutschland ist es normal, dass junge Leute zu verschiedenen politischen Fragen Stellung nehmen können. Das können Sie yum Beispiel im Forum http://www.talk-portal.com in „Diskuission & Politik" sehen. Gehen Sie selbst auf die Suche nach Inhalten oder nutzen Sie diesen Thread: http://www.talk-portal.com/thread/threadid=3964

A. Einträge lesen

Lesen Sie drei bis fünf Einträge und beantworten Sie die folgenden Fragen. Danach vergleichen Sie Ihre Antworten mit den Antworten von Ihrem Partner/Ihrer Partnerin.

a. Welche Parteien kommen vor?

b. Welche Einträge sind **Ihren** politischen Einstellungen ähnlich? Was steht in diesen Einträgen?

c. Was überrascht Sie an den Einträgen? Warum?

Meine Ergebnisse	*Die Ergebnisse meines Partners/meiner Partnerin*

B. Nützliche Ausdrücke

Lesen Sie die Einträge, die Sie und Ihr Partner/Ihre Partnerin ausgewählt haben, noch einmal durch und schreiben Sie nützliche Wörter, Ausdrücke und Redewendungen auf, die Sie besonders wichtig finden, um über Politik sinnvoll und verständlich sprechen zu können.

Ich bin ganz deiner Meinung!

C. Jetzt sind Sie dran!

Schreiben Sie nun Ihren eigenen Eintrag in diesem Forum. Schreiben Sie mindestens fünf bis sechs Sätze, und benutzen Sie möglichst viele von den neuen Ausdrücken, die Sie ausgesucht haben. Hier sind noch einige wichtige Redewendungen:

Ich sehe (nicht) ein, dass …	*Ich würde sagen, dass …*	*Ich meine …/Was meinst du?*
Zum Beispiel …	*Ich bin ganz anderer Meinung!*	
Ich stimme mit dir völlig überein!		
Ich muss darüber ein bisschen nachdenken!		

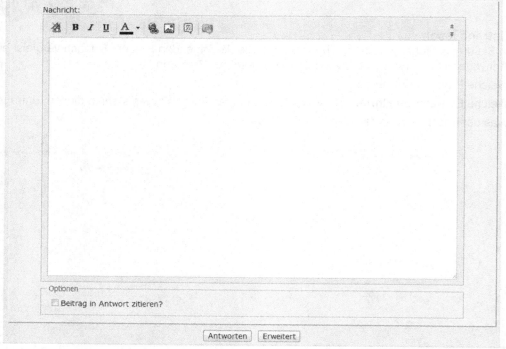

Aktivität 6. Lieder & Musik

Parkas – Lärmen lernen. In diesem Kapitel finden Sie einen Song von Parka, der politische und soziale Kritik ausübt. Laden Sie die passende Pdf unter „Lieder & Musik" von der *Deutsch im Blick* Website in Kapitel 9 herunter und bearbeiten Sie die Aufgaben.

Grimm Gramma

Ähem … UM über Politik besser reden ZU können, brauchen Sie die „um … zu"-Konstruktion: Infinitivsätze. UM diese Konstruktion ZU wiederholen, bearbeiten Sie zu Hause das folgende Grammatikthema in *Grimm Grammar:*
Verbs – der Infinitivsatz

Aktivität 7. Politische Ziele

In der Politik braucht man oft ein Ziel (*a goal*) und dann die Mittel (*means*), um dieses Ziel zu erreichen. Sie finden unten Beispiele für wichtige politische Ziele. Wie kann man diese Ziele erreichen? Vervollständigen Sie die folgenden Sätze, indem Sie erklären, was SIE machen würden.

Um bessere Schulen zu haben, …

Um einen Krieg zu vermeiden (*avoid*), …

Um eine Weltmacht zu werden, …

Um ein unvergesslicher Politiker zu werden, …

Um Studenten stärker für den politischen Prozess zu begeistern (zu interessieren), …

Tipp: Auch hier steht das konjugierte Verb wieder an zweiter Stelle! Allerdings gilt der gesamte Teil von „Um … zu + Infinitiv" als „erste Stelle". Das konjugierte Verb kommt also direkt nach dem Komma. Weitere Informtionen dazu finden Sie in: *Grimm Grammar* Conjunctions: Word Order

Aktivität 8. Politisch informiert

Bevor man sich politisch engagiert, sollte man sich politisch richtig informieren. Wie tun das Berna, Eva, Harald, Jan und Peter? Sehen Sie sich ihre die Videoclips an und beantworten Sie die Fragen in der ersten Spalte. Versuchen Sie auch festzustellen, wer die folgenden Ausdrücke benutzt:

(QR 9.8 p.430)　(QR 9.9 p.430)　(QR 9.10 p.430)　(QR 9.11 p.430)
(QR 9.12 p.430)

„Ich muss gestehen (*confess*), dass ich den ‚Stern' lese …"

„Ich bin ein Nachrichtenjunkie"

„Außenpolitik • Innenpolitik"

„Die Nachrichten sind sehr provinziell"

„Viele deutsche Familien organisieren ihren Tagesablauf um die Tagesschau"

„Nein, ich abonniere nicht"

„Das Erste und das Zweite sind die Standardsender …"

A. Die Deutschen & ein Schweizer

	Berna	Eva	Harald	Jan	Peter
Sie lesen diese Zeitungen, um sich zu informieren:					
Sie sehen sich diese Sendungen im Fernsehen an, um sich zu informieren:					
Sie sehen diese Unterschiede zwischen den europäischen & amerikanischen Nachrichten:					

Sehen Sie sich jetzt die Videoclips „Politisch informiert" von Sara und Erin an und beantworten Sie dieselben Fragen. Danach beantworten Sie die Fragen selbst: Wie informieren Sie sich über Politik und die Welt? Welche Zeitungen lesen Sie? Welche Sendungen sehen Sie sich im Fernsehen an? Danach stellen Sie einem Partner/einer Partnerin die Fragen.

B.
Die amerikanischen Studenten

(QR 9.13 p.430)   (QR 9.15 p.430)   **SIE**   **Ihr Partner/ Ihre Partnerin**

Sie lesen diese Zeitungen, um sich zu informieren:			
Sie sehen sich diese Sendungen im Fernsehen an, um sich zu informieren:			
Sie sehen diese Unterschiede zwischen den europäischen & amerikanischen Nachrichten:			

Die Politik der Bundesrepublik Deutschland

Aktivität 9. Über die Bundesrepublik

Hören Sie sich das Interview „Politische Systeme" von Sara an. Sie erzählt uns über das politische System, die Bundesländer und die politischen Parteien in Deutschland. Beantworten Sie danach die Fragen (in ganzen Sätzen).

Wieviele Bundesländer gibt es in Deutschland?

Was ist die Hauptstadt von Deutschland?

(QR 9.16 p.430)

Welche politischen Parteien gibt es? (Wie heißen sie?)

Internet-Tipp
Tolle Links – leicht zu verstehen und schnell informiert!

Die News: http://www.tivi.de/fernsehen/logo/start/index.html

Die Bundesländer: http://www.tivi.de/fernsehen/logo/index/00095/index.html

Die Bundesregierung: http://www.schekker.de

Aktivität 10. Die deutschen Parteien

Sie haben in Saras Interview die Abkürzungen der deutschen Parteiennamen gehört. Wie aber lauten die vollen Namen? Und was vertreten die Parteien? Lesen Sie folgenden Text über die Parteien und beantworten Sie danach die Fragen.

A. Vor dem Lesen

In den USA gibt es zwei große Parteien: die Demokratische Partei (eher liberal und progressiv) und die Republikanische Partei (eher konservativ). Die inoffizielle Farbe der Demokraten ist blau, die Farbe der Republikaner – auch inoffiziell – ist rot. Die deutschen politischen Parteien haben ebenso ihre eigenen Farben.

Können Sie erraten (*guess*), welche Farben welche Ideologien symbolisieren?

schwarz (auch orange)   *eine Partei, die sich für die Natur (Umwelt) interessiert*

rot (auch b**un**t)   *eine eher liberale Partei, links von der Mitte*

gelb (und **blau**)   *eine konservative Partei*

grün   *eine Partei, die die Nazizeit heraufbeschwört*

braun   *eine liberale Partei, die finanziell etwas konservativer ist*

Überfliegen (*scan*) Sie nun den Text auf den nächsten Seiten und finden Sie diese Farben. Welche Schlüsselwörter (und Konzepte) werden in den sieben kleinen Texten mit diesen Farben assoziiert? Unterstreichen Sie diese Schlüsselwörter, **bevor** Sie den Text genauer lesen!

B. Beim Lesen

Beantworten Sie die folgenden Aufgaben, während Sie den Text genauer bearbeiten.

1. Ordnen Sie die politischen Parteien von links (liberal) nach rechts (konservativ) ein.

liberal ⟷ konservativ

2. Welche bekannten Namen assoziiert man mit den einzelnen Parteien?

3. Welche Themen oder Fragen sind für die einzelnen Parteien wichtig?

Ein buntes Parteienspektrum
Das politische System Deutschlands

Schwarz, Rot und Gelb hieß lange Zeit die politische Farbenlehre in Deutschland. Anfang der 80er Jahre kam Grün hinzu, später auch noch Dunkelrot - um in der Logik der Farben zu bleiben. Und das Spektrum wächst weiter.

[Source: http://www.dw-world.de/]

Autor: Klaus Dahmann, Heike Mohr

Redaktion: Peter Stützle, Hartmut Lüning

Von Konrad Adenauer über Helmut Kohl bis Angela Merkel

Die Christlich-Demokratische Union (CDU) im Verbund mit ihrer rein bayerischen Schwesterpartei, der Christlich-Sozialen Union (CSU), hat über die längste Zeit den Bundeskanzler gestellt. In der Nachkriegszeit hatten sie ihre Anhänger vor allem unter den früheren Wählern der katholisch geprägten Zentrumspartei gefunden. Die volkstümliche Bezeichnung der Unionsparteien als "die Schwarzen" stammt auch vom Zentrum, denn für dieses saßen einst viele schwarz gewandete katholische Priester im Parlament. "Christlich" tragen beide Parteien im Namen und werden im Parteienspektrum als "konservativ" eingeordnet. Traditionell stehen sie für christlich geprägte Ideale. Als Volksparteien suchen sie allerdings auch einen möglichst breiten Konsens in der Bevölkerung. Als Koalitionspartner bevorzugen die Unionsparteien oft die liberale Freie Demokratische Partei (FDP). Zur Not gehen sie aber auch so genannte "Große Koalitionen" mit der Sozialdemokratischen Partei Deutschlands (SPD) ein. Das gab es auf Bundesebene erstmals Ende der 1960er-Jahre und auch von 2005 bis 2009.

Rot und sozialdemokratisch

Dazwischen hatten immer mal wieder SPD-geführte Koalitionsregierungen entweder mit der FDP oder den Grünen im Bund das Sagen. Für die Sozialdemokraten stehen die Bundeskanzler Willy Brandt, Helmut Schmidt und zuletzt Gerhard Schröder. Das Rot ihres Banners verweist auf die Wurzeln in der Arbeiterbewegung in der zweiten Hälfte des 19. Jahrhunderts. Die SPD gab es unter diesem Namen bereits in der Weimarer Republik. Sie wurde aber, wie alle anderen Parteien, von den Nationalsozialisten verboten; viele ihrer Mitglieder starben in Konzentrationslagern.

Nach dem Krieg belasteten ideologische Streitigkeiten die Partei. In ihrem "Godesberger Programm" beschloss die SPD im Jahr 1959, sich inhaltlich und ideologisch von einer sozialistischen Arbeiterpartei zu einer sozialdemokratischen - und damit für mehr Bürger wählbaren - Volkspartei zu wandeln.

Grün – mehr als nur ökologisch

Bis Mitte der 1980er-Jahre gab es für die Sozialdemokraten bei der Suche nach einem Koalitionspartner nur die Wahl zwischen der FDP und - wie in den 1960er-Jahren - der "Großen Koalition" mit den Unionsparteien. Im Laufe der 1980er-Jahre betrat ein neuer Koalitionspartner die politische Bühne: die Grünen. Sie haben ihre Wurzeln in der Anti-Atomkraft- und der Friedensbewegung der 1970er-Jahre, aber auch in der Frauenbewegung sowie Bürgerinitiativen. Nach und nach gab es die ersten vorsichtigen Bündnisse auf Lokal- und Landesebene mit den Grünen, bis man Rot-Grün 1998 unter dem damaligen Bundeskanzler Gerhard Schröder auch im Bund umsetzte.

Im Mai 2011 wurde Winfried Kretschmann schließlich zum ersten grünen Ministerpräsidenten gewählt: Seither regiert in Baden-Württemberg eine grün-rote Koalition, also ein Bündnis aus Grünen und SPD. Mehr als 30 Jahre nach ihrer Gründung, stehen die Grünen damit zum ersten Mal an der Spitze einer Landesregierung. Daneben wird inzwischen sogar Schwarz-Grün - zumindest auf Lokal- und Landesebene - praktiziert. Eigentlich heißen die Grünen offiziell "Bündnis 90/Die Grünen", denn 1993 vereinigten sich die im "Bündnis 90" zusammengefassten Bürgerbewegungen Ostdeutschlands mit den Grünen. Seitdem trägt die Partei einen Doppelnamen..

Gelb steht für liberal

Die Freie Demokratische Partei (FDP), die im Farbenspektrum traditionell gelb erscheint, hat ihre Position als einziges Zünglein an der Waage zwischen den Unionsparteien und den Sozialdemokraten verloren. Die FDP war Juniorpartner fast jeder Bundesregierung, sofern die nicht schwarz-rot oder rot-grün war.

Die Partei sieht sich in der Tradition des Liberalismus in Deutschland und lehnt staatliche Überregulierung ab. Die FDP vertritt oft die Interessen kleiner und mittlerer Unternehmen und wird gerne auch als "Partei der Besserverdienenden" gebrandmarkt.

Seit 2009 stellt die FDP gemeinsam mit der CDU/CSU die deutsche Bundesregierung. Bei der Landtagswahl in Mecklenburg-Vorpommern im September 2011 kam die Partei allerdings nur noch auf 2,8 Prozent der Stimmen; eine ähnlich große Niederlage erlebte die FDP im gleichen Monat auch bei der Berlin-Wahl: Mit einem Verlust von knapp 6 Prozent der Stimmen ist sie nicht mehr im Berliner Abgeordnetenhaus vertreten. Dafür sorgte ein Neuling in der deutschen Parteienlandschaft für eine politische Sensation.

Erst entern, dann ändern: Die Piratenpartei

Denn die 2006 gegründeten Piraten zogen im September 2011 zum ersten Mal in ein deutsches Landesparlament ein: Während die FDP in Berlin auf nur 1,8 Prozent kam, erreichten die unter einem Orange-farbenen Logo segelnden Piraten auf Anhieb 8,9 Prozent.

Fast schon traditionelles Hauptthema der noch jungen Piratenpartei ist das Internet. Die Piraten fordern einen Gratiszugang zum Internet und wollen den Online-Kopierschutz entschärfen: Jeder soll freien Zugang zu allen Informationen haben, die im Internet verfügbar sind. Außerdem setzen sich die Piraten gegen das Speichern persönlicher Daten durch staatliche Behörden ein. Angespornt durch den Berliner Erfolg peilen die Polit-Neulinge in Orange inzwischen bundespolitische Mitwirkung an.

Rot-Rot, für viele SPD-Mitglieder noch ein rotes Tuch

Seit einigen Jahren erstarkt die Linkspartei, deren Farbe ebenfalls rot ist und die zur Unterscheidung von den Sozialdemokraten auch gerne als dunkelrot bezeichnet wird. Die Linkspartei zieht vor allem Wähler der SPD an. Bei den Sozialdemokraten wiederum gibt es heftige parteiinterne Diskussionen, wie die SPD zur Linken stehen soll. Doch mehrheitlich haben die etablierten Parteien ein Problem mit der Linken. Das hat mit ihrer Entstehungsgeschichte zu tun: Ihre Wurzeln im Osten sind in der früheren Sozialistischen Einheitspartei Deutschlands (SED) der DDR zu finden, deren Mitglieder zunächst nach der Wiedervereinigung die Partei des Demokratischen Sozialismus (PDS) gründeten. Diesen wird immer noch eine personelle und ideologische Nähe zum einstigen Regime vorgeworfen. Der westliche Wurzelstrang ist eine junge Abspaltung der SPD: die Wahlalternative Soziale Gerechtigkeit (WASG). PDS und WASG haben sich inzwischen zur Linkspartei vereinigt, die soziale Missstände anprangert und sich als Vertreter des kleinen Mannes versteht. Auch mit einem radikalen Pazifismus versucht die Linke zu punkten.

Rechtsextreme in der deutschen Parteienlandschaft

Für Aufsehen haben stets Erfolge der Rechtsextremen gesorgt. Unter ihnen macht vor allem die Nationaldemokratische Partei Deutschlands (NPD) von sich reden. Sie war schon in den 1960er-Jahren in mehrere Landesparlamente eingezogen und errang auch in den letzten Jahren immer einmal wieder Landtagssitze.

Ein Verbotsverfahren gegen die NPD wurde 2003 vom Bundesverfassungsgericht wegen Verfahrensfehlern gestoppt. Seitdem wird hin und wieder über ein neues Verbotsverfahren diskutiert - besonders in jüngster Zeit, nachdem die Mordserie der rechtsextremistischen Terrorgruppe "Nationalsozialistischer Untergrund" bekannt geworden ist und es deutliche Hinweise auf Verbindungen zwischen den Tätern und NPD-Mitgliedern gibt. Auch andere Gruppierungen am rechten Rand - wie die Republikaner und die Deutsche Volksunion (DVU) - konnten vorübergehend in Landtage einziehen. Allerdings ist es noch keiner rechtsextremen Partei gelungen, bei Bundestagswahlen über die Fünf-Prozent-Hürde zu kommen.

C. Jetzt sind Sie dran!

Welche politischen Parteien gibt es in Ihrem Land? Welche politischen Einstellungen haben Sie? Verwenden Sie die Wörter und Sprache vom Text „Ein buntes Parteienspektrum". Mit welchen deutschen Parteien könnte man Ihre Parteien vergleichen?

die Demokratische Partei – die Demokraten die Grüne Partei – die Grünen	die Republikanische Partei – die Republikaner die Libertäre Partei – die Libertarier

Der Name und die Abkürzung der Partei			
Konzepte, Ideologie, Werte			

Aktivität 11. Politische Systeme: Ist ihr Bundesland liberal oder konservativ?

Sehen Sie sich Bernas und Evas Videos an, in denen sie über ihre Bundesländer sprechen. Welche Informationen geben sie über ihre Bundesländer?

A. Wie ist Ihr Bundesland?

Sehen Sie sich Bernas und Evas Videos an, in denen sie über ihre Bundesländer sprechen. Welche Informationen geben sie über ihre Bundesländer?

(QR 9.17 p.430)

(QR 9.18 p.430)

	Aus welchem Bundesland kommt sie?	
	Was ist die Hauptstadt von diesem Bundesland?	
	Ist dieses Bundesland eher liberal oder konservativ?	
	Ist sie eher liberal oder konservativ?	

B. Geografische Unterschiede in der Politik

Forschen Sie im Internet nach, ob es in Deutschland in der Politik geografische Unterschiede gibt oder nicht: Sind die nördlichen Bundesländer eher liberaler oder konservativer? Und die im Süden? Im Westen? Im Osten?

1. Welche geografischen Unterschiede gibt es in der Politik in Deutschland, Österreich und in der Schweiz?

2. Welche geografischen Unterschiede gibt es in der Politik in Ihrem Land?

3. Wo wohnen Sie?

4. Stimmen Sie politisch mit der Mehrheitsmeinung von Ihrem Bundesstaat überein?

Schule und Ausbildung

Das dritte Thema, das wir untersuchen, um die Frage "Was ist deutsch?" zu beantworten, ist die Ausbildung: Wie ist das Schulsystem in Deutschland?

Was wollten Sie als 10-jähriges Kind werden?

Als erstes, versuchen Sie sich daran zu erinnern, was Sie als 10-jähriges Kind, in der 4. Klasse, vorhatten. Wussten Sie schon damals, was Sie von Beruf werden wollten? Wo Sie weiter lernen/studieren wollten? Haben Sie in diesem Alter darüber überhaupt schon nachgedacht?

Aktivität 12. An der Grundschule

A. Denken Sie nun an die 4. Klasse (Sie waren ungefähr 10 Jahre alt).

Wie sagt man *Grundschule* in Ihrem Land? Wann hat für Sie die nächste Schulform (*level of education*) begonnen? Wie viele Schulformen gibt es in Ihrem Land? Besprechen Sie diese Fragen mit anderen Kommilitonen/Kommilitoninnen und versuchen Sie, die Schullaufbahn in Ihrem Land bis zum 18. bzw. 19. Lebensjahr zu beschreiben. Verwenden Sie dabei keine übersetzten Namen, z. B. "High School" ist "High School" und nicht „Hochschule".

Wie hat Ihre erste Schulform geheißen?

Bis wann haben Sie sie besucht?

Was war die zweite Schulform?

Welche Jahrgänge hat sie umfasst?

Blieben alle Schüler an dieser zweiten Schule zusammen oder wurden sie auf verschiedenen Schulen verteilt (*were they split up*)? (ja • nein)

Wenn ja, wohin? Wie hießen die nächsten Schulformen?

Gab es eine dritte Schulform? Wie hat sie geheißen?

In welchem Alter beendet man in Ihrem Land seine Schulausbildung (Sekundarausbildung)?

Was glauben Sie, wie ist es in Deutschland? Schauen Sie sich die Abbildung dazu an.

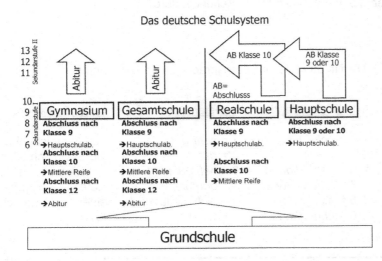

Das deutsche Schulsystem

Aufgrund einer Schulreform (2007) absolvieren Gymnasiasten/Gymnasiastinnen in allen Bundesländern (Ausnahme ist Rheinland-Pfalz) nur noch 12 Jahre (anstatt 13 Jahre). Schülern soll dadurch ermöglicht werden eher mit dem Studium zu beginnen – entsprechend dem amerikanischen System.

Aktivität 13. Schulausbildung

A. Lesen Sie den Text und verbinden Sie die Wörter mit den passenden Definitionen.
[Source: http://www.tatsachen-ueber-deutschland.de/**]**

Tatsachen über Deutschland

Gute Startchancen für alle sind wichtig für Bildung und Leistung. In Deutschland gilt für alle Kinder eine neunjährige Schulpflicht. Der Besuch öffentlicher Schulen ist kostenfrei. In der Regel besuchen die Kinder mit sechs Jahren für vier Jahre die Grundschule. Anschließend gibt es unterschiedliche weiterführende Schulen: Hauptschule, Realschule, Gymnasium. Sie unterscheiden sich in den Leistungsanforderungen und in der Gewichtung von Praxis und Theorie. Daneben gibt es Gesamtschulen, an denen Schulpflichtige aller Leistungsgruppen parallel unterrichtet werden. Ein Wechsel zwischen den verschiedenen Gruppen (Schulformen) ist dort leicht möglich. Die Hauptschule umfasst die 5. bis 9. Klasse als Pflichtunterricht, das 10. Schuljahr ist freiwillig. Die Realschule steht zwischen Hauptschule und Gymnasium, umfasst die Klassen 5 bis 10 und führt zur „Mittleren Reife". Das Gymnasium vermittelt eine vertiefte allgemeine Bildung. Es endet je nach Bundesland nach zwölf oder 13 Schuljahren mit der Allgemeinen Hochschulreife. Die meisten Schulen sind Halbtagsschulen.

Realschule	Erste Schule für alle deutschen Kinder
Gymnasium	Abschluss der Realschule
Hauptschule	Legt Wert auf eine allgemeine Bildung, dauert bis zur 12. bzw. 13. Klasse
Abitur/Allgemeine Hochschulreife	Umfasst die Klassen 5 bis 10
Mittlere Reife	Umfasst die Klassen 5 bis 9 (die 10. ist möglich)
Grundschule	Abschluss des Gymnasiums

1. Wie also heißt die erste Schulform, die alle Schüler/Schülerinnen besuchen müssen?

2. Und wie heißen die drei Schularten der Sekundarstufe?

Die Noten in den deutschsprachigen Schulen sind so:

In Deutschland	In Österreich	In der Schweiz
1 = *sehr gut*	1 = *sehr gut*	In den meisten Kantonen reicht die Skala von 6 bis 1. Aber Achtung! Hier ist 6 die beste Note, 4 ist genügend, und mit einer 1 fällt man durch (*one fails*).
2 = *gut*	2 = *gut*	
3 = *befriedigend*	3 = *befriedigend*	
4 = *ausreichend*	4 = *genügend*	
5 = *mangelhaft*	5 = *nicht genügend*	
6 = *ungenügend*		

B. Die Schularten der Sekundarstufe

Die große Frage ist nun, wie sich die drei Schularten der Sekundarstufe unterscheiden? Lesen Sie die Abschnitte auf der nächsten Seite und vervollständigen Sie die Tabelle.

	Hauptschule	Realschule	Gymnasium
Jahre/Dauer			
Fokus			
Kurse (Beispiele)			
Orientierung praktisch/theoretisch			
sonstige Informationen			

C. Welche Ausbildung?

Welche Berufe kann man mit einem Hauptschulabluss erlernen? Informieren Sie sich hier.

Hauptschule

Die Hauptschulen sind Pflichtschulen für alle Schüler, die nach dem Besuch der Grundschulen nicht auf eine andere weiterführende Schule gehen. Sie enden mit der 9., in einigen Ländern mit der 10. Klassenstufe … Die Hauptschule vermittelt eine allgemeine Bildung als Grundlage für eine praktische Berufsausbildung.

Hauptschüler bekommen Orientierungshilfen für die spätere Berufswahl. Solide Kenntnisse und Fertigkeiten in Deutsch, Mathematik, Englisch und in den musischen Fächern sind unverzichtbar – wie für die anderen Schularten auch. Doch es gibt Unterschiede: In der Hauptschule gehen die Lehrer im Unterricht nicht vorwiegend theoretisch und abstrakt vor, sondern eher konkret-anschaulich, lebensnah, praxisbezogen und exemplarisch. Lernen durch eigenes Tun ermöglicht vielen Kindern und Jugendlichen erst den Schulerfolg.

Realschule

Die Realschule umfasst die Jahrgangsstufen 5 bis 10.

Das Bildungsangebot der Realschule richtet sich an junge Menschen, die an theoretischen Fragen interessiert sind und gleichzeitig praktische Fähigkeiten und Neigungen haben. Die Bayerische Realschule vermittelt eine allgemeine und berufsvorbereitende Bildung.

Die Bayerische Realschule bietet drei Ausbildungsrichtungen, die sog. Wahlpflichtfächergruppen, an. Diese setzen ab der 7. Jahrgangsstufe verschiedene Bildungsschwerpunkte.

Gymnasium

Das Gymnasium umfasst derzeit die Klassen 5 bis 12 (oder 13) … Das Gymnasium vermittelt eine vertiefte Allgemeinbildung, die für ein Hochschulstudium unabdingbar ist. Damit schafft es zugleich auch Voraussetzungen für eine berufliche Ausbildung.

Das Gymnasium bietet ein breites Fächerprogramm, das sich von sprachlich-künstlerischen über mathematisch-naturwissenschaftliche bis zu gesellschaftswissenschaftlichen Fächern erstreckt. Jeder Schüler erlernt mindestens zwei Fremdsprachen.

Weitere Informationen finden Sie hier:
http://de.wikipedia.org/wiki/Gegliedertes_Schulsystem
http://www.studentenpilot.de/studium/studienabschluesse/

Aktivität 14. Sprache im Kontext: Die Ausbildung in der Schweiz

A. Guido: Die Ausbildung in der Schweiz

Sehen Sie sich Guidos „Sprache im Kontext" Videoclip an und notieren Sie unbekannte und bekannte Begriffe.

Bekannte Begriffe	Unbekannte Begriffe

(QR 9.19 p.430)

B. Beim zweiten Schauen

Er spricht über vier verschiedene Schulformen und die weiterführenden Ausbildungsmöglichkeiten nach diesen Schulen. Füllen Sie die Tabelle aus.

Schule	Weiterführende Möglichkeiten

C. Beim dritten Schauen

Schauen Sie sich den Videoclip noch einmal an und beantworten Sie diese Fragen:

1. Gelten Guidos Bemerkungen für die ganze Schweiz? Falls nicht, für welchen Bereich (*area*) gelten sie?_____

2. Wie alt ist man am Anfang der Schulzeit? _____

3. Wie viele Jahre sind Pflichtjahre? _____

4. Wie lange dauert die Primarschule? _____

5. Wie lange dauern die nächsten drei möglichen Schulen nach der Primarschule? _____

D. Deutschland und die Schweiz: Ein Vergleich
Welche sind die (mehr oder weniger) parallelen Schulformen in Deutschland und in der Schweiz?

Deutsche Schulen	Schweizerische Schulen
Grundschule	
Hauptschule	
Realschule	
Gymnasium	
Ausbildung	

Schulen ohne Analogie in der Schweiz oder in Deutschland

Aktivität 15. Meinungsumfrage
Wussten Sie schon, als Sie zehn Jahre alt waren, was Sie von Beruf werden wollten? Wussten Ihre Lehrer und Eltern, wozu Sie fähig waren? Lesen Sie die folgenden Äußerungen und entscheiden Sie, ob Sie mit ihnen einverstanden sind oder nicht. Besprechen Sie Ihre Antworten mit anderen Kommilitonen.

Als ich zehn Jahre alt war, wusste ich genau, was ich von Beruf werden wollte.	**Ja**	**Nein**
Alle Lehrer und Eltern wissen genau, was für ein Beruf zu den Kinder passen wird, wenn sie 20 Jahre alt werden.	**Ja**	**Nein**
Als zehnjähriges Kind wollte ich Lokführer werden, und das will ich immer noch werden.	**Ja**	**Nein**
Ich möchte meine Kinder in Deutschland oder in der Schweiz zur Schule schicken.	**Ja**	**Nein**
In der Grundschule hatte ich sehr gute Noten und hätte auf das Gymnasium gehen können.	**Ja**	**Nein**
Als ich 10 Jahre alt war, interessierte ich mich viel mehr für Lego als für Latein.	**Ja**	**Nein**
Ich will heute immer noch denselben Beruf ergreifen wie mit zehn.	**Ja**	**Nein**

Aktivität 16. Ausbildung nach der Schule

Nach der Schule ist man natürlich noch nicht bereit, sofort in die Arbeitswelt einzutreten (*enter*). Man muss entweder eine Ausbildung machen oder studieren. Viele Jugendliche machen auch eine Berufsausbildung in der "dualen Berufsausbildung". Das System heißt „dual", weil man gleichzeitig (*simultaneously*) bei einer Firma arbeitet und an einer Berufsakademie studiert. Es gibt ungefähr 350 Berufe, die eine Ausbildung erfordern (*require*).

Nota bene: Die *Wörter* studieren und *Studium* sind nur in Verbindung mit Hochschulen zu benutzen (z.B. Uni, Musik- oder Filmhochschulen).

A. Wie wär´s für Sie in Deutschland?
Im nächsten Teil werden Sie verschiedene Berufsmöglichkeiten und deren Ausbildungen entdeckten.

Schritt 1
Was möchten Sie von Beruf sein?

_____ *Mechaniker*	_____ *Bankangestellte*	_____ *Buchhalter*
_____ *Chemikerin*	_____ *Rechtsanwältin*	_____ *Professor*
_____ *Krankenpfleger*	_____ *Künstler*	_____ *Zahnarzt*
_____ *Sekretärin*	_____ *Architektin*	_____ *Schauspieler*
_____ *Gymnasiallehrer*	_____ *Bibliothekar*	_____ *?*
_____ *Bäcker*	_____ *Informatikerin*	

Schritt 2
Gehen Sie auf die *BerufeNet* Website (http://berufenet.arbeitsagentur.de/berufe/index.jsp) und geben Sie Ihren Beruf in die Suchbox ein. Ein Beispiel wäre „Fachkinderkrankenschwester" (pediatric nurse specialist).

Bundesagentur für Arbeit

BERUFENET — **Berufsinformationen einfach finden**

AUTHENTISCH

Was ist BERUFENET?

Neue und neu geordnete Ausbildungsberufe

Hinweise zum Verlinken

Suche

Berufsbezeichnung(en)/Suchbegriff(e)

| Fachkinderkrankenschwester | Suche starten |

⊞ Eingrenzen auf Gruppen

Schritt 3

Klicken Sie auf ein Ergebnisse (unter „Berufsbezeichnung") und lesen Sie die Berufsinformationen über diesen Beruf.

» Suche

Informationen zum Beruf

▪ **Kurzbeschreibung**
▪ Kompetenzen

Zusätzliche Informationen

▪ Stellen- und Bewerberbörsen
▪ Zahlen/Daten/Fakten

» Vormerkliste (0 Einträge)

» BERUFETV /
berufskundliche Filme

» BERUFE-Universum

Fachkinderkrankenschwester/-pfleger

Druckauswahl	In Vormerkliste

Die Tätigkeit im Überblick

Hauptaufgabe von Fachkinderkrankenschwestern und -pflegern ist die eigenständige Pflege und mitverantwortliche Betreuung von Patienten und Patientinnen im Kindes- und Jugendalter in bestimmten medizinisch-pflegerischen Fachgebieten. Sie führen vor allem pflegerische, diagnostische und therapeutische Maßnahmen nach ärztlichen Anweisungen aus. Darüber hinaus leiten sie Pflegepersonal an und bilden den Fachkräftenachwuchs aus.

Die Ausbildung im Überblick

Fachkinderkrankenschwester/-pfleger ist eine landesrechtlich geregelte Weiterbildung im Gesundheitswesen.

Weiterbildungslehrgänge werden von Weiterbildungseinrichtungen für Gesundheitsberufe angeboten. Sie dauern in Vollzeit mindestens 1 Jahr, in Teilzeit/Blockunterricht bis zu 4 Jahre.

Die Weiterbildung wird in folgenden Fachgebieten angeboten:

- Fachkinderkrankenschwester/Fachkinderkrankenpfleger - Hygiene
- Fachkinderkrankenschwester/Fachkinderkrankenpfleger für Intensivpflege/Anästhesie
- Fachkinderkrankenschwester/Fachkinderkrankenpfleger für Nephrologie
- Fachkinderkrankenschwester/Fachkinderkrankenpfleger - Onkologie
- Fachkinderkrankenschwester/Fachkinderkrankenpfleger - Operations-/Endoskopiedienst
- Fachkinderkrankenschwester/Fachkinderkrankenpfleger für Palliativ- und Hospizpflege
- Fachkinderkrankenschwester/Fachkinderkrankenpfleger in der Psychiatrie
- Fachkinderkrankenschwester/Fachkinderkrankenpfleger - Rehabilitation/Langzeitpflege

Schritt 4

Klicken Sie zunächst auf der linken Seite auf Ausbildung und schreiben Sie sich auf, welche Kurse, Praktika und weitere Qulifikationen dieser Beruf verlangt.

Schritt 5

Arbeiten Sie mit anderen Studenten zusammen und vergleichen Sie welche Ausbildung für verschiedene Berufe verlangt wird. Was müssen Sie in Ihrem Land tun, um Ihren Beruf ausüben zu können?

	Mein Beruf	Der Beruf meines Partners/ meiner Partnerin
Ausbildung in Deutschland		
Ausbildung in meinem Land		

Grimm Grammar

Wenn Sie den Konjunktiv wiederholen wollen, dann klicken Sie auf den Link zur *GrimmGrammar:*

Verbs – Konjunktiv II im Präsens

Sie können diese Sätze auch anders sagen, indem Sie subordinierende Konjunktionen verwenden. Bearbeiten Sie zu Hause das folgende Grammatikthema in *Grimm Grammar:*

Conjunctions – Subordinierende Konjunktionen

Aktivität 17. Die Umwelt

Die Umwelt gehört, wie die Schule, zum deutschen Alltag (*everyday life*). Man soll die Umwelt schützen, wo man lebt und arbeitet. Sehen wir uns an, was das für die deutschsprachigen Länder bedeutet!

A. Mülltrennung

In Deutschland trennt man den Müll. Verbinden Sie die Mülltonnen mit der richtigen Müllkategorie. Dann identifizieren Sie alle Gegenstände (*items*) aus dem Müll.

[Images from http://www.bmu-kids.de/Spiele/Muellspiel/daten/spiel.php]

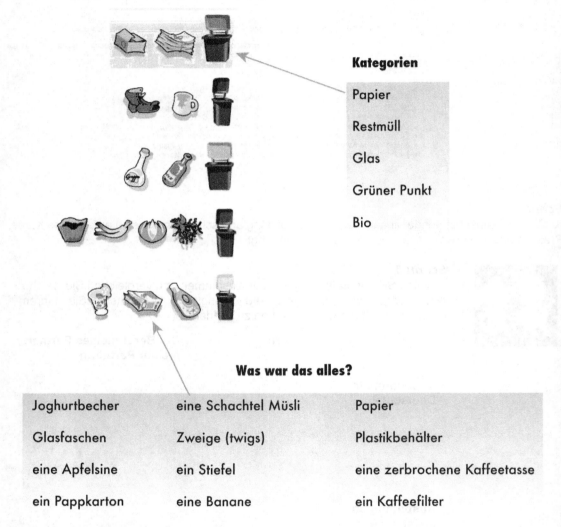

Kategorien

Papier

Restmüll

Glas

Grüner Punkt

Bio

Was war das alles?

Joghurtbecher	eine Schachtel Müsli	Papier
Glasfaschen	Zweige (twigs)	Plastikbehälter
eine Apfelsine	ein Stiefel	eine zerbrochene Kaffeetasse
ein Pappkarton	eine Banane	ein Kaffeefilter

B. Wie ist es bei Ihnen zu Hause?

Machen Sie nun eine Umfrage im Unterricht. Verfassen Sie eine kleine Reportage über die Ergebnisse, zum Beispiel: Zwei Drittel aller Befragten sprechen nur über das Recycling von Altpapier ... Die Hälfte überlässt das Mülltrennen einem anderen im Haushalt ...

- Wer wirft den gesamten (*all*) Abfall in einen Eimer (kein Recycling)?

- Wer trennt den Müll zu Hause?

- In wie viele Müllarten trennen sie den Müll?

- Nimmt die Müllabfuhr (*garbage truck*) den gesamten Abfall mit, oder muss man recycelbare Materialien selber wegbringen?

Zu Hause trennen wir den Müll so …

Und nun üben Sie selbst! Besuchen Sie die folgende Website und spielen Sie mit dem Fröschlein mit!

http://www.bmu-kids.de/kreativ/spiele/muellspiel/muellspiel.htm

Aktivität 18. Wir können mehr für die Umwelt tun als nur den Müll trennen, zum Beispiel, in dem wir weniger Engergie verbrauchen

Wie viel Energie verbrauchen Sie zu Hause? Könnten Sie auch mit weniger Energie (Strom) leben?

A. Nützliche Wörter

Raten Sie mit einem Partner, was die folgenden Wörter und Ausdrücke bedeuten könnten. Schreiben Sie zusammmen kurze Definitionen auf Deutsch.

ein Zimmer beleuchten	*ein Zimmer lüften*	*tropfen*
Energie sparen	*das WC/die WC-Spülung*	*das Gerät*
die Fenster sind auf/geschlossen	*der Wasserhahn*	*bauen*

B. Jetzt sind Sie dran! Machen Sie einen Umweltcheck und reflektieren Sie über ihr Verhalten.

Was sind Ihe Stärken und Schwächen?

Wo oder wie verbrauchen Sie die meiste Energie? Warum? Ist es notwendig?

Wie könnten Sie besser Energie sparen?

Schreiben Sie mindestens vier Ideen auf. Folgen Sie den Beispielen im Kasten.

Ich könnte mehr Energie sparen, wenn ...

ich meine Klimaanlage seltener benutzen würde.
ich ein kleines Haus kaufen würde.

C. Meine Versprechen ...

Ja, ja, träumen kann man, aber was genau werden Sie tun, um die Umwelt zu schützen? Machen Sie ein Versprechen (*promise*).

Beispiel:

Ich werde mit dem Fahrrad fahren, um weniger Benzin zu verbrauchen.
Ich werde meine Klimaanlage weniger benutzen, um Energie UND Geld zu sparen.

Schreiben Sie noch fünf Äußerungen auf, was SIE machen können, um die Umwelt zu schützen. In die erste Spalte sollten Sie Ihre eigenen Versprechen schreiben, dann diskutieren Sie Ihre Ideen mit anderen Kommilitonen/ Kommilitoninnen und schreiben diese Versprechen in die übrigen Spalten.

Ich	Partner 1	Partner 2	Partner 3
1.	1.	1.	1.
2.	2.	2.	2.
3.	3.	3.	3.
4.	4.	4.	4.
5.	5.	5.	5.

D. Deine persönlichen Umwelttipps
Bitten Sie einen Partner um Tipps zum Energiesparen. Fangen Sie so an:

Du, ich verbrauche zu viel _____. Wie kann ich _____?

ODER

Kannst du mir sagen, wie ich weniger _____ verbrauchen kann?

Der Partner könnte antworten:

Naja, ich würde vorschlagen, dass _____

ODER

Hast du versucht, _____ zu _____?

E. Vervollständigen Sie die folgenden Aussagen. Achten Sie auf die Wortstellung!

1. Solange wir den ganzen Abend in allen Zimmern Licht anlassen (auch wenn niemand da ist), …

2. Obwohl es mir ein bisschen kalt in der Wohnung ist, …

3. Wir halten die Klimaanlage bei 75 Grad Fahrenheit, obwohl …

4. Wasser sparen könnte einfach sein, solange …

5. Wir könnten es kühl halten, ohne dass …

Aktivität 19. Deutsche und die Umwelt

Dass man die Umwelt schützen solle, ist selbstverständlich. Wir werden am Beispiel des Radfahrens sehen, dass Umweltschutz, gesundes Leben und Leben mit der Natur ein Teil des Alltags sein können.

A. Vor dem Lesen
Sehen Sie sich den folgenden Artikel an und beantworten Sie diese Fragen.

1. Was sehen Sie auf dem Bild?

2. Was sind die drei Schlüsselwörter im Titel?

3. Worum geht es also in diesem Text?

4. Was meinen Sie: Wie viele Teile hat dieser Text?

5. Eine Einführung, und was sonst noch?

6. Welche Informationen sollten in diesen Teilen stehen?

Aktivität 20. Und was macht Ihre Stadt für die Umwelt?

Entwerfen Sie nun eine „Website" für Ihre Heimatstadt. Beschreiben Sie die existierenden Umweltprogramme und auch, was die Stadt neu einführen möchte, um noch mehr für die Umwelt zu tun. Verwenden Sie nützliche Ausdrücke aus den beiden Texten, die Sie gelesen haben.

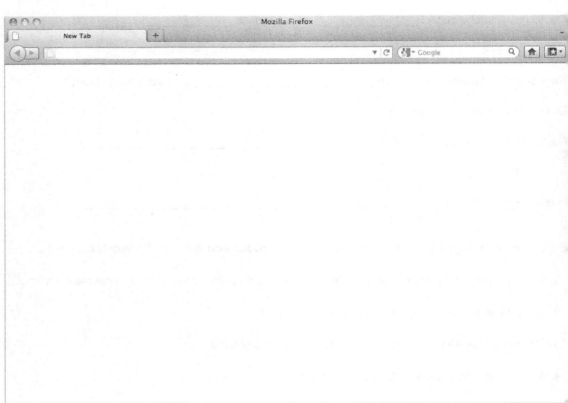

Können Sie diese Schrift entziffern (*decode*)?

Was steht über dem Fenster an dieser Berghütte in Bayern?

An wen ist es gerichtet (*addressed*)?

Was sagt es, wie soll man mit der Natur (nicht) umgehen?

Und zurück zur Frage „Was ist deutsch?"

Aktivität 21. Was ist den Deutschen wichtig?
Das Selbstbild der Deutschen
Es gab vor Kurzem zwei Umfragen, die diese Frage auf verschiedene Weise gestellt haben. Die erste Umfrage (von *Reader´s Digest*) fragte nach den wichtigsten Werten der Deutschen. Was ist ein Wert? Das ist eine Eigenschaft (Charakteristik) oder eie Haltung, die wir für sehr wichtig bzw. essentiell halten. Zum Beispiel *Ehrlichkei* ... Für Deutsche ist es am wichtigsten, dass man ehrlich ist. Was denken Sie?

A. Vor dem Lesen
Sehen Sie sich die Liste von Werten im orangen Kasten an. Welche Werte sind für Sie am wichtigsten? Diskutieren Sie mit einem anderen Studenten/einer anderen Studentin und stellen Sie eine Rangliste (*ranking*) auf. Sie müssen eine gemeinsame Liste zusammenstellen!!!.

1.   6.

2.   7.

3.   8.

4.   9.

5.   10.

Sehen Sie sich nun die Rangliste von *Reader´s Digest* an. Vergleichen Sie diese mit Ihrer Liste. Was ist wichtiger für Sie? Für Deutsche? Schreiben Sie mindestens fünf Vergleiche auf.

So wichtig sind 24 ausgesuchte Werte
Sind Ihnen diese Werte **sehr wichtig?**

Ehrlichkeit	74%
Familie	68%
Gerechtigkeit	64%
Respekt vor anderen	61%
Freiheit	60%
Hilfsbereitschaft	54%
Verantwortungsgefühl	53%
Höflichkeit	51%
Bildung	50%
Sicherheit	43%
Unabhängigkeit	41%
Friedfertigkeit	37%
Toleranz	35%
Fleiß	33%
Vertrauen in andere	26%
Leistungsbereitschaft	21%
Lebensgenuss	26%
Mut	21%
Sparsamkeit	19%
Respekt vor Autorität	18%
Tradition	15%
religiöser Glaube	14%
Patriotismus	8%
Einfluss auf andere	4%

B. Die Deutschen äußern sich im *Spiegel*

Das Thema „Werte" untersuchte auch eine große Umfrage der deutschen Zeitschrift *Spiegel*. Diese zweite Umfrage hat andere Fragen gestellt. Bevor wir die Ergebnisse dieser Umfrage lesen, beantworten Sie selbst manche Fragen, indem sie ankreuzen oder eine kurze Antwort geben.

1. Sehen Sie sich eher als Einwohner Ihres Bundesstaats oder als US-Amerikaner?

2. Wie zufrieden sind Sie mit der Demokratie in den USA und dem ganzen politischen System?

    ___ sehr   ___ einigermaßen   ___ gar nicht

3. Wie wichtig ist für Sie …

Sparsamkeit	___ sehr wichtig	___ ziemlich wichtig	___ egal	___ nicht wichtig
freie Meinungsäußerung	___ sehr wichtig	___ ziemlich wichtig	___ egal	___ nicht wichtig
Disziplin	___ sehr wichtig	___ ziemlich wichtig	___ egal	___ nicht wichtig

4. Glauben Sie an ein Leben nach dem Tod?   ___ ja   ___ nein

5. Kinder zu schlagen …
    ___ … ist grundsätzlich verkehrt (*twisted*)
    ___ … ist allenfalls das letzte Mittel (*last resort*)
    ___ … gehört zur Erziehung

6. Würden Sie in einem Krieg Ihr Leben oder das Ihrer Angehörigen (relatives) aufs Spiel setzen, um Amerika zu verteidigen?
    ___ ja   ___ nein

7. Ich bin …   ___ stolz   ___ ziemlich stolz   ___ gar nicht stolz Amerikaner zu sein.

8. Eine Frau, die Kinder hat, sollte nicht mehr arbeiten gehen.
    ___ stimmt   ___ stimmt nicht

9. Aktivität am Morgen. Kreuzen Sie bitte die Aktivitäten an, die zu Ihrer Morgenroutine gehören.
    ___ Radio hören   ___ frühstücken   ___ Zeitung lesen   ___ fernsehen

10. Wie lange brauchen Sie im Durchschnitt im Bad? _____ Minuten

11. Auf der nächsten Seite finden Sie die deutschen Antworten auf dieselben Fragen. Vergleichen Sie diese Meinungen mit ihren eigenen Antworten.

Was ist gleich?

Was ist anders?

Was hat Sie überrascht?

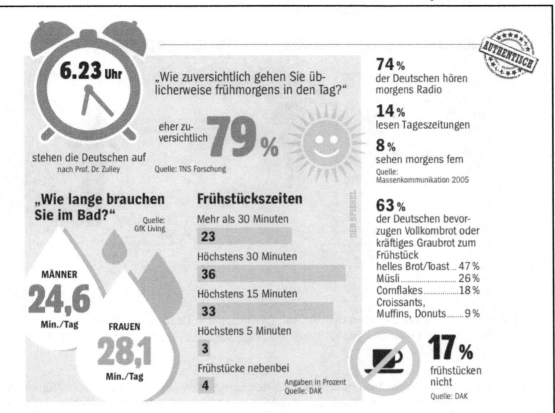

6.23 Uhr

stehen die Deutschen auf
nach Prof. Dr. Zulley

„Wie zuversichtlich gehen Sie üb-
licherweise frühmorgens in den Tag?"

eher zu-
versichtlich **79 %**

Quelle: TNS Forschung

AUTHENTISCH

74 %
der Deutschen hören
morgens Radio

14 %
lesen Tageszeitungen

8 %
sehen morgens fern
Quelle:
Massenkommunikation 2005

**„Wie lange brauchen
Sie im Bad?"**
Quelle:
GfK Living

MÄNNER
24,6
Min./Tag

FRAUEN
28,1
Min./Tag

Frühstückszeiten

Mehr als 30 Minuten
23

Höchstens 30 Minuten
36

Höchstens 15 Minuten
33

Höchstens 5 Minuten
3

Frühstücke nebenbei
4

Angaben in Prozent
Quelle: DAK

63 %
der Deutschen bevor-
zugen Vollkornbrot oder
kräftiges Graubrot zum
Frühstück
helles Brot/Toast... 47 %
Müsli.................... 26 %
Cornflakes..............18 %
Croissants,
Muffins, Donuts....... 9 %

17 %
frühstücken
nicht
Quelle: DAK

Sind die Ergebnisse überraschend (*surprising*) für Sie oder hätten Sie die Deutschen so eingeschätzt (*assess*)?

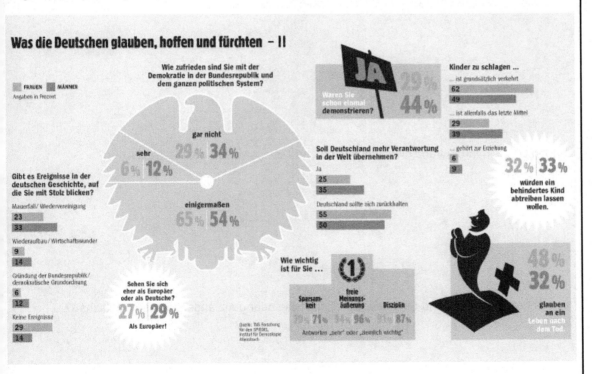

Was die Deutschen glauben, hoffen und fürchten – II

FRAUEN   MÄNNER
Angaben in Prozent

Wie zufrieden sind Sie mit der
Demokratie in der Bundesrepublik und
dem ganzen politischen System?

gar nicht
29 % 34 %

sehr
6 % 12 %

einigermaßen
65 % 54 %

Gibt es Ereignisse in der
deutschen Geschichte, auf
die Sie mit Stolz blicken?

Mauerfall/ Wiedervereinigung
23
33

Wiederaufbau/ Wirtschaftswunder
9
14

Gründung der Bundesrepublik/
demokratische Grundordnung
6
12

Keine Ereignisse
29
14

Sehen Sie sich
eher als Europäer
oder als Deutsche?
27 % 29 %
Als Europäer!

JA
Waren Sie
schon einmal
demonstrieren?
29 %
44 %

Soll Deutschland mehr Verantwortung
in der Welt übernehmen?

Ja
25
35

Deutschland sollte sich zurückhalten
55
50

Wie wichtig
ist für Sie ...

Sparsam-
keit
29 % 71 %

freie
Meinungs-
äußerung
34 % 96 %

Disziplin
87 %

Antworten „sehr" oder „ziemlich wichtig"

Quelle: TNS Forschung
für den SPIEGEL,
Institut für Demoskopie
Allensbach

Kinder zu schlagen ...

... ist grundsätzlich verkehrt
62
49

... ist allenfalls das letzte Mittel
29
39

... gehört zur Erziehung
6
9

32 % 33 %
würden ein
behindertes Kind
abtreiben lassen
wollen.

48 %
32 %
glauben
an ein
Leben nach
dem Tod.

Alle Daten und Grafiken entstammen dem Artikel „Der König von Deutschland," im *Spiegel* am 21. April 2008, Ausgabe 17/2008. URL: http://www.spiegel.de/spiegel/print/d-56670297.html.

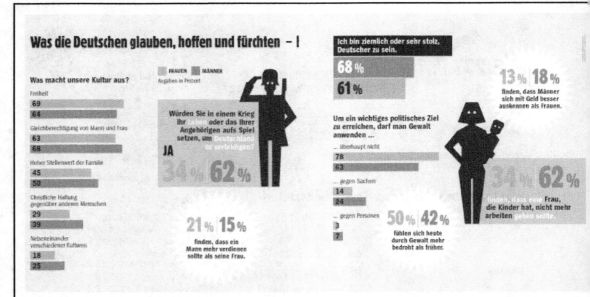

Die Daten und Grafik entstammen dem Artikel „Der König von Deutschland," im *Spiegel* am 21. April 2008, Ausgabe 17/2008. URL: http://www.spiegel.de/spiegel/print/d-56670297.html.

Tipp: Auf der *Spiegel* Website können Sie auch den kompletten Atikel als pdf-Datei herunterladen. Mit weiteren Statistiken und Illustrationen lernen Sie so noch mehr über die Deutschen und ihre Lebensweisen.

Was meinen Sie, wie würden die Prozentanteile in Ihrem Land aussehen?

Haben Leute in Ihrem Land dieselben Werte und Lebensweisen wie die Deutschen?

In welchen Bereichen sind Sie entweder ähnlich wie oder ganz anders als die Deutschen?

Aktivität 22. Deutschland und die USA: Gegenseitiges Lernen

Sehen Sie sich die folgenden Videoclips an. Was könnten die USA von Deutschland lernen? Und was könnte Deutschland von den USA lernen? (Tipp: Nicht alle Studenten haben alle Fragen beantwortet!)

	Was sollte Deutschland von den USA lernen?	Was sollten die USA von Deutschland lernen?	Stimmen Sie mit diesen Meinungen überein? Wenn nicht, was ist Ihre Meinung?
(QR 9.22 p.430)			
(QR 9.23 p.430)			
(QR 9.24 p.430)			
(QR 9.4 p.430)			
(QR 9.25 p.430)			
(QR 9.26 p.430)			

1. Sehen Sie kulturelle Trends in den Antworten? Sind die Meinungen der Amerikaner anders als die Meinungen der Deutschen? Oder sind die Unterschiede eher persönlich?
2. Was zeigen uns die Äußerungen dieser Studenten über ihre Selbstbilder und Fremdbilder? Wie würden Sie auf der Grundlage (*according to*) dieser Äußerungen definieren, was „deutsch" und was „amerikanisch" ist?
3. Haben SIE dasselbe Selbstbild (über Amerika oder über Ihr eigenes Land) und dasselbe Fremdbild (über Deutschland) wie diese Studenten? Warum?

Aktivität 23. Die Deutschen kommen (... und wie lieb wir sie haben)

Das *Schweizer Fernsehen* (SF) zeigt eine Reportage über Deutsche, die in die Schweiz einwandern. Das ganze Video dauert ungefähr 48 Minuten, und Sie können es direkt auf der Webseite des *Schweizer Fernsehens* finden (http://www.srf.ch/player/tv/dok/video/die-deutschen-kommen-und-wie-lieb-wir-sie-haben?id=c7c55599-3594-49c5-bfd5-82ac2fb6de16 ; Titel: *DOK - Die Deutschen kommen*.)

A. Clip 1

Im ersten Clip wird nach der Meinung mancher Schweizer über Deutsche gefragt.
Was würden Sie sagen – ist der Ton der Bemerkungen überwiegend positiv oder negativ? Warum?

Es folgt eine Liste von kritischen Aussagen der Schweizer über die Deutschen. Welche finden Sie besonders negativ?

> unfreundlich, uncharmant
> Es erinnert noch ein wenig an "Kaiserreich".
> Sie haben eine große Klappe (Mund).
> Sie hauen schon gern auf die Pauke (show off, party too loudly).
> Sie sprechen zu schnell und zu viel.
> Sie passen sich nicht an.
> Einzeln sehr angenehm, in Horden schwierig.
> Hochnäsig
> Sie sind nicht ehrlich. Sie ziehen dich über den Tisch (*to trick you*), wenn sie können.

B. Clip 2

Frau Rosen und ihre Familie sind Deutsche, die jetzt in der Schweiz wohnen. Frau Rosens Erfahrungen sind zum großen Teil positiv gewesen, aber sie hat einige Beschwerden (*complaints*). Hören Sie ihr zu und versuchen Sie den Text zu vervollständigen.

---

unsicher • wunderschön • Brüdern • Kanton • wunderschön
Schweizer • Volk • Berge • Zürich • Geld

Was ich nicht mag an der Schweiz ist, dass ein _____ gegen den anderen

ist, dass man einfach _____ wird, was man überhaupt sagt. Wenn ich sage,

„Luzern ist _____", dann sagt man in Niedwalden: „Ja, meine Güte, und wir?

Wir haben die _____ und das ist alles wunderschön." Wenn ich sage: „Jetzt

fahre ich nach _____, weil ich einfach mal wieder nach Zürich muss." Dann

sagt mir jemand: „Ja, also du musst nicht dein _____ nach Zürich bringen.

Das sind keine _____." Das find ich nicht gut an der Schweiz. Eigentlich

müsst ihr doch das so wie ihr das bei euch habt „ein einzig _____ von

_____ sein", oder?

> →Was will Frau Rosen mit diesem letzten Satz sagen?

C. Clip 3

Dieser Clip hat mit dem Arbeiten in der Schweiz zu tun. (12:58 – 13:30)

Um welche Deutschen geht es in diesem Videoclip?

Welche Arbeit machen sie?

Wie nennt man die Deutschen? Warum ist dieser Satz besonders provokativ?

Haben Sie so eine Beschreibung im Zusammenhang mit einer anderen Personengruppe je gehört? Erklären Sie.

Aktivität 24. Die Amis kommen ...
Wie würde eine solche „Reportage" über Amerika aussehen? Schreiben Sie zu jeder Frage einen Absatz. Sie haben hier freie Hand (*free reign*). Sie können sich ein bisschen im Internet oder bei deutschsprachigen Bekannten informieren, wenn Sie wollen. Das müssen Sie aber nicht. Hauptsache, Sie sind kreativ. Verwenden Sie das, was Sie schon gelernt haben, und drücken Sie sich klar und deutlich aus.

Absatz 1:   Wie sieht man Amerika und die Amerikaner in den deutschsprachigen Ländern?

Absatz 2:   Wie sehen SICH die Amis selbst?

Absatz 3:   Wer sollte seine Perspektive/sein Benehmen ändern: die Deutschen/ Schweizer/Österreicher oder die Amerikaner?

Aktivität 25. Lieder & Musik
Die Prinzen – Deutschland. Sie finden noch einen Song in Kapitel 9! Laden Sie die passende pdf-Datei unter „Lieder & Musik" von der *Deutsch im Blick* Website herunter und bearbeiten Sie die Aufgaben.

Aussprache
Regional Dialects in Austria

In this chapter we take a look at the dialects spoken in Austria: **Österreichisches Deutsch**. Austria is a central European country located to the southeast of Germany. Since the High German sound shift took place in Austria as well, Österreichisches Deutsch shares many linguistic features with Upper German dialects (including, and especially with, Bavarian dialects). Yet despite the similarities in pronunciation and grammar, there are some significant differences between these varieties of German.

Work found at http://commons.wikimedia.org/wiki/ File:Austria_states_german.png / CC BY-SA 3.0 (http:// creativecommons.org/licenses/by-sa/3.0/)

German is considered pluricentric, in that it has several standard languages, and speakers of these standards identify closely with the national variety they speak. Austrian German is no different. There is a standard Austrian German, and there are a number of regional dialects:

- ***Central Austro-Bavarian:*** (Northern and Northwestern parts of Austria)

- ***Southern Austro-Bavarian*** (spoken in the rest of Austria except in Voralberg; reflects considerable linguistic influence from neighboring countries for historical reasons: Slovenia, Hungary, Czech Republic, Italy)

- ***Voralbergisch*** (spoken in the state of Voralberg; a High Alemannic dialect, closer to Swiss-German linguistically than to Standard Austrian)

Due to space limitations, and given the introductory nature of these Aussprache segments, we will focus primarily on the Austrian Standard dialect in comparison to Standard German and will provide only a brief introduction into the Viennese dialect of Austrian German. However, visit http://www. oeaw.ac.at/dinamlex to learn more about Austrian dialects.

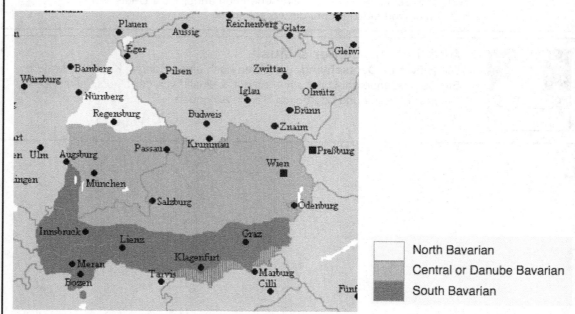

	North Bavarian
	Central or Danube Bavarian
	South Bavarian

Work found at http://en.wikipedia.org/wiki/File:Bairisches_Mundartgebiet.png / CC BY-SA 3.0 (http://creativecommons. org/licenses/by-sa/3.0/)

1. ÖSTERREICHISCHES DEUTSCH

While Austro-Bavarian dialects are generally mutually intelligible (with the exception of some versions of Tyrolean), Austrian varieties differ from German dialects in terms of vocabulary especially, due to historical reasons (close connection between the Habsburg and French royal families, which led to an influx of French words through education, diplomacy, court language, etc.). Below is a table comparing a few words from the Austrian dialect with Standard German.

Aussprache

Please go to the Deutsch im Blick website, Kapitel 9

Dialect features	Beispiele (Standard German → Dialect)
Pronunciation vocalization of *l* and *r* after *e* and *i* voiceless stops are voiced (softened)	*viel → vui/vüü* *die Gruppe → die Grubbm*
Grammar verbs that involve body positions take "sein" instead of "haben" in conversational past loss of genitive case	*habe gesessen → bin gesessen* *habe gestanden → bin gestanden* *des Mannes → vom Mann*
Vocabulary differences in institutional language foreign influences from Italian, Czech, Slovakian, Slovenian, Hungarian ***lots*** of vocabulary different from Standard German!	*der Bundestag → der Nationalrat* *das Abitur → die Matura* *grüne Bohnen → die Fisolen* *der Blumenkohl → der Karfiol* *der Mais → der Kukuruz* *die Pflaume → die Zwetschke* *die Tomaten → die Paradeiser* *Tag! → Servus!* *(no equivalent) → Grüss Gott!* *Januar → Jänner* *Februar → Feber* *die Aprikose → die Marille* *die Schlagsahne → das Schlagobers* *sparsam → glua* *der Wasserhahn → die Pippe* *der Strom → das Natz*

2. WIENERISCH

The Viennese dialect overlaps almost completely with Standard Austrian (and ergo Bavarian) German. The features that Wienerisch shares with these dialects are:

softening the voiceless stops ($p \rightarrow b$)
vocalizing 'l' and 'r' sounds after vowels (*kalt → kööd; viel → vüü*)
unrounding vowels (*Glück → Glick*)

But there are some distinct sounds to be found in Viennese German as well:

making monophthongs out of diphthongs (*heiße → haas*)
lengthening vowels at the end of a sentence (*war → woooa*)

Grammatically speaking, Viennese German is like Standard Austrian. It is most distinct its vocabulary. Viennese contains many lexical items, which have their origin in other parts of the former Habsburg Empire since Vienna served as the melting pot of the constituent populations. Here is some uniquely Viennese vocabulary:

English	Standard German	Viennese	Borrowed from
shirt	Hemd	Hemad	Old High German
slimy mass	Schleim	Baaz	Middle High German
long underpants	lange Unterhosen	Gattihosn	Hungarian
appetite	Appetit	Gusta	Italian
sidewalk	Gehsteig	Trottoa	French

Der Ausschnitt aus der Zeitschrift *Der Floh von* 1875 zeigt Wagner in Wien.

Text: "Do, rö, mü, fa, so, la, si, do. Im Nomen vün da Journalistik, was Se hassen, waanen kennt mer, bring' ich Ihnen, weil Se kä Zeitung lesen, waanen kennt mer, ä classische Antwort, was in kaaner Zeitung, sündern im Goethe steht ünd ünter üns gesagt ä scheen's Compliment ist – waanen kennt mer!"

Any clue what this could be all about? What would the text be in standard German?
Research it.

WebQuests

Dieses Kapitel hat zwei WebQuests, die Sie auf der *Deutsch im Blick*-Website finden und bearbeiten können:
1. Die Bundesrepublik Deutschland – Sie machen eine virtuelle Reise nach Deutschland durch das Deutschlandportal
2. Recycling in Deutschland – viel Spass beim Müllquiz!!!

Meinungsumfragen

In diesem Kapitel konzentriert sich die Umfrage auf die Themen *politische und soziale Fragen, Arbeitslosigkeit, „Fremde", und die Umwelt.*

Sie können an diesen Meinungsumfragen teilnehmen, indem Sie zur Website des 9. Kapitels gehen und „Meinungsumfragen" anklicken.

Was ist deutsch?	What is German?
sich anpassen	to fit it, assimilate
das Benehmen	behavior
die Bildung (no plural)	education
charmant	charming
die Ehrlichkeit (usually no plural)	honesty
der Einfluss (Einflüsse)	influence
auf etwas/jemanden Einfluss haben	to have influence on something / someone
einzeln	one by one
ernst	serious
fertig	ready
fleißig sein	to be diligent, hard-working, industrious
die Gerechtigkeit (usually no plural)	justice
geschmacklos	tasteless
der Glaube (no plural)	faith, belief
hilfsbereit	helpful
hinzufügen	to add
hochnäsig	snobby
die Höflichkeit (Höflichkeiten)	politeness
die Horde (Horden)	horde
die Klappe (Klappen)	mouth (slang)
Halt die Klappe!	Shut up!
die Leistung (Leistungen)	achievement
der Mut (no plural)	courage
die Sicherheit (Sicherheiten)	security
sparsam	thrifty
sauber	clean
die Toleranz (usually no plural)	tolerance
die Unabhängigkeit (Unabhängigkeiten)	independence
unverschämt	unashamed, brazen
verantwortlich	responsible
die Verantwortung (Verantwortungen)	responsibility
das Vertrauen (no plural)	trust
die Wahrheit (Wahrheiten)	truth
der Zebrastreifen (-streifen)	crosswalk

Die Politik	Politics
aufgeklärt	informed
der Anhänger (Anhänger)	follower
das Aufsehen	furor, sensation
der Bund	federation
das Bundesland (Bundesländer)	federal state
engagiert	involved, engaged
eingeschüchtert	intimidated
die (politische) Einstellung (Einstellungen)	(political) attitude, inclinations
der Eintrag (Einträge)	entry
gut erzogen	well-bred
Kinder erziehen	to raise children
alleinerziehende Mutter	single-mother
die Hauptstadt (-städte)	capital city
der Lärm	noise
lärmen	to make noise, raise a fuss
die Nachkriegszeit	postwar period
die Partei (Parteien)	political party
die Regulierung (Regulierungen)	regulation
das Unternehmen (Unternehmen)	business
der Unternehmer (Unternehmer)	male entrepreneur
die Unternehmerin (Unternehmerinnen)	female entrepreneur
regelmäßig	regularly
selbstbewusst	self-assured, self-confident
Stellung nehmen	to take a position
überraschen	to surprise

Wortschatz

(QR 9.1 p.430)

die Wahl (Wahlen)	choice, election
der Wahlkampf (-kämpfe)	election campaign
das Wahlplakat (-plakate)	election poster
das Wahlprogramm (-programme)	party platform
wählen	to vote, choose
der Wähler (Wähler)	male voter
die Wählerin (Wählerinnen)	female voter
wütend	furious

An der Schule — At School

das Abitur (no plural)	*Gymnasium* diploma qualifying for admission to university
abschließen	to graduate
allgemein	general
die Ausbildung (Ausbildungen)	education, training
der/die Auszubildende/Azubi (Auszubildende/Azubis)	apprentice
der Berufsberater (-berater)	employment counselor
die Berufsberaterin (-beraterinnen)	female employment counselor
die Berufsschule (-schulen)	vocational school
sich bewerben (bei einer Firma, Schule)	to apply (for something)
der Gymnasiast (Gymnasiasten)	male student at a secondary school (see below: Gymnasium)
die Gymnasiastin (Gymnasiastinnen)	female secondary school student
das Gymnasium (Gymnasien)	secondary school preparing for university studies
die Hauptschule (-schulen)	secondary school preparing for vocational careers
der Hauptschüler (-schüler)	male student at a Hauptschule
die Hauptschülerin (-schülerinnen)	female student at a Hauptschule
die Jahrgangsstufe (-stufen)	grade level
die Kenntnis (Kenntnisse; nearly always plural)	knowledge
öffentlich	public
die Pflicht (Pflichten)	obligation
die Realschule (-schulen)	secondary school preparing for midlevel, white collar work
der Realschüler (-schüler)	male student at a Realschule
die Realschülerin (-schülerinnen)	female student at a Realschule
die Richtlinie (-linien)	policy, guideline
an der Schule sein	to be at school
die Schule besuchen	to attend school
zur Schule gehen	to go to school
der Schüler (Schüler)	male pupil (elementary and secondary school)
die Schülerin (Schülerinnen)	female pupil (elementary and secondary school)
sitzen bleiben	to fail (a grade level)
sich unterscheiden	to differentiate
verbindlich	binding, mandatory

Nach der Schule — After graduation

der Zivildienst	civil service (mandatory service for men)
Zivildienst machen	to do civil service
Er ist Zivi.	He is doing his national service.
der Wehrdienst	military service
Wehrdienst machen	to do military service
die Kaserne (Kasernen)	barracks

Die Umwelt	The Environment
der Abfall (Abfälle)	trash
das Abgas (Abgase)	exhaust fume
achten (auf etwas achten)	to watch out for, observe
das Aussehen	appearance
beleuchten	to illuminate, to light up
der Eimer (Eimer)	bucket
die Energie (Energien)	energy
(erneuerbare) Energiequellen	(renewable) energy sources
das Fenster (Fenster)	window
die Fenster sind auf/zu	the windows are open/closed
die Fenster auf-/zumachen	to open/close the windows
die Folge (Folgen)	consequence
fördern	to encourage
die Gefahr (Gefahren)	danger
die Glühbirne (Glühbirnen)*	lightbulb
die Heizung (Heizungen)	heating
mangeln an	to lack
hier mangelt es an Umweltbewusstsein	there is a lack of environmental awareness here
der Müll (no plural)	garbage
die Mülltrennung (usually no plural)	trash sorting
das Ozon (no plural)	ozone
das Recycling (no plural)	recycling
sparen	to save
der Strom (no plural)	electricity
die Taste (Tasten)	button (on electronics)
teilnehmen an etwas (an etwas teilnehmen)	to participate (in)
der Treibhaus-Effekt (no plural)	greenhouse effect
trennen	to separate
tropfen	to drip
die Umwelt (usually no plural)	environment
die Umwelt schonen	to protect the environment
das Umweltbewusstsein	environmental awareness
umweltfreundlich	environmentally friendly
der Umweltmuffel (-muffel)	a dullard when it comes to environmental issues
der Unfall (Unfälle)	accident
verbrauchen	to use
verträglich	bearable, sustainable
die Veranstaltung (Veranstaltungen)	event
der Verkehr (no plural)	traffic
der Wasserhahn (hähne)	spigot
den Wasserhahn zudrehen	to turn off the spigot

Glühbirnen are now forbidden in Germany, only *Energiesparbirnen (energy aving bulbs)* are allowed as *Leuchtmittel (lighting)*.

QR Codes

9.1	9.2	9.3	9.4	9.5	9.6
Wortschatz	09_01_intro_ deutsch	09_02_int_ek_ engagiert	09_03_int_hm_ gegenseitig	09_04_int_ec_ engagiert	09_05_int_bg_ engagiert

9.7	9.8	9.9	9.10	9.11	9.12
09_06_int_ju_ engagiert	09_07_int_bg_ informiert	09_08_int_ek_ informiert	09_09_int_hb_ informiert	09_10_int_ju_ informiert	09_11_int_ph_ informiert

9.13	9.14	9.15	9.16	9.17	9.18
09_13_int_ec_ informiert	09_13_int_hm_ engagiert	09_14_int_sco_ informiert	09_15_int_sco_ systeme	09_16_int_bg_ systeme	09_17_int_ek_ systeme

9.19	9.20	9.21	9.22	9.23	9.24
09_18_sik_guido- ausbildung	09_19_sik_ florian-zivildienst	09_20_sik_guido- militaerdienst	09_21_int_bg_ gegenseitig	09_22_int_ek_ gegenseitig	09_23_int_ju_ gegenseitig

9.25	9.26	9.27	9.28
09_25_int_ec_ gegenseitig	09_26_int_sco_ gegenseitig	09_27_sik_ typischdeutschdw	09_28_sik_ dienstfrauen

Wortschatz

- (Deutsche) Geschichte
- Krieg und Frieden
- Über berühmte Personen sprechen
- Rund um Deutschland und die Deutschen
- Opern und andere Sehenswürdigkeiten
- Armut, Verzweiflung und Hoffnung
- Nach dem Weg fragen
- Wegbeschreibungen

Aussprache

- Kapitel 10: German Dialects Spoken in the US

Grammatik

Focus
- Wissen/kennen
- Das Imperfekt: Regelmäßige Verben
- Modalverben im Präsens
- Modalverben in der Vergangenheit
- Das Adverb: Wann? Wie oft? Wie viel? Wie sehr?
- Das Adverb: Wie? Wo? Wohin? Woher?
- Das Adverb: Narration/Erzählung

Recommended
- Das Imperfekt: sein
- Das Imperfekt: Haben
- Wortstellung
- Two-way prepositions

Videos

Deutsche und Schweizer
- Lieblingsepoche
- Showtickets
- Ins Theater gehen
- Was man wissen muss ...

Amerikanische Studenten
- Lieblingsepoche
- In die Oper gehen
- Ins Theater gehen
- Was man wissen muss ...

10 *AUF NACH BERLIN!*

Auf Wiedersehen, Würzburg! Nach einem langen Aufenthalt in dieser schönen süddeutschen Stadt reisen Sie in den Norden, um die Hauptstadt Deutschlands zu besichtigen. In diesem (letzten) Kapitel geht alles um Berlin, ein Symbol der deutschen Geschichte und der deutschen Kultur. Wie schon zuvor werden Ihnen die Themen durch die Interviews der Deutschen und Amerikaner wie auch durch die „Sprache im Kontext"-Videos näher gebracht.

In diesem Kapitel werden Sie die unglaublich facettenreiche Stadt Berlin kennenlernen. Sie werden über die bedeutendsten Ereignisse und berühmtesten Persönlichkeiten aus der Geschichte Berlins in einer neuen Zeitform, dem Imperfekt, lesen und schreiben können und Sie werden sich über die vielen Sehenswürdigkeiten der Stadt mit neuen Adverbien besser als zuvor ausdrücken können.

Online Book links

Sie können die Videoclips unter folgendem Link finden:
http://coerll.utexas.edu/dib/toc.php?k=10

Sie können die Vokabeln unter folgendem Link finden:
http://coerll.utexas.edu/dib/voc.php?k=10

Sections

- (Deutsche) Geschichte • (German) History
- Krieg und Frieden • War and Peace
- Über berühmte Personen sprechen • Talking about Famous People
- Rund um Deutschland und die Deutschen • On Germany and the Germans
- Opern und andere Sehenswürdigkeiten • Operas and other Objects of Interest
- Armut, Verzweiflung und Hoffnung • Poverty, Desperation, and Hope
- Nach dem Weg fragen • Asking for directions
- Wegbeschreibungen • directions

Sie können auch die Grammatikthemen aus diesem Kapitel online finden:

Während der Übungen im Kapitel werden Sie regelmäßig auf *Grimm Grammar* auf der *Deutsch im Blick*-Website verwiesen (*referred to*). Hier sind die Grammatikthemen, die das Kapitel abdeckt (*covers*); machen Sie alle Online-Übungen, um optimal von den Übungen in diesem Arbeitsbuch (*workbook*) zu profitieren (*to profit from*).

• wissen/kennen	http://coerll.utexas.edu/gg/gr/vi_15.html
• Imperfekt (regelmäßige Verben)	http://coerll.utexas.edu/gg/gr/vsp_01.htm
Wiederholung: Imperfekt (haben)	http://coerll.utexas.edu/gg/gr/vsp_04.htm
Wiederholung: Imperfekt (sein)	http://coerll.utexas.edu/gg/gr/vsp_05.htm
Imperfekt (unregelmäßige Verben)	http://coerll.utexas.edu/gg/gr/vsp_02.htm
Imperfekt (gemischte Verben)	http://coerll.utexas.edu/gg/gr/vsp_03.htm
• Adverbien:	
Zeit, Häufigkeit, Menge, Intensität	http://coerll.utexas.edu/gg/gr/adv_01.htm
Art und Weise, Ort, Richtung	http://coerll.utexas.edu/gg/gr/adv_02.htm
in Aufsätzen	http://coerll.utexas.edu/gg/gr/adv_03.htm
• Modalverben:	
Präsens	http://coerll.utexas.edu/gg/gr/vm_01.htm
Imperfekt	http://coerll.utexas.edu/gg/gr/vm_01.htm
• Wechselpräpositionen	http://coerll.utexas.edu/gg/gr/cas_09.htm
Review:	
Akkusativ &	http://coerll.utexas.edu/gg/gr/cas_03.htm
Dativ	http://coerll.utexas.edu/gg/gr/cas_07.htm
• Review: Imperativ	http://coerll.utexas.edu/gg/gr/vimp_01.htm

Wortschatz
Vorbereitung

Always learn nouns with the article!!!

A. **LISTEN**   Listen carefully to the pronunciation of each word or phrase in the vocabulary list.

B. **REPEAT**   Repeat each word or phrase *out loud* as many times as necessary until you remember it well and can recognize it as well as produce it. Make a list of the words in this chapter which you find difficult to pronounce. Your teacher may ask you to compare your list with other students in your class. Make sure to learn nouns with their correct gender!

> **Beispiel:**
> die Sprache
> fünf

C. **WRITE**   Write key words from the vocabulary list so that you can spell them correctly (remember that it makes a big difference whether you cross the Atlantic by ship or by sheep). You may want to listen to the vocabulary list again and write the words as they are spoken for extra practice.

D. **TRANSLATION**   Learn the English translation of each word or phrase. Cover the German column and practice giving the German equivalent for each English word or phrase. Next cover the English column and give the translation of each.

E. **ASSOCIATIONS**   Think of word associations for each category of vocabulary. (What words, both English and German, do you associate with each word or phrase on the list? Write down ten (10) associations with the vocabulary from the chapter.

> **Beispiel:**
> der Student/die Universität
> das Flugticket/das Flugzeug

F. **COGNATES**   Which words are *cognates?* (Cognates are words which look or sound like English words.) Watch out for *false friends*! Write down several cognates and all the false friends from the chapter, create fun sentences that illustrate similarities and differences between the English and German meanings of these words.

> **Beispiel:**
> Nacht/night
> grün/green
> → False Friends: *hell* = light, bright vs. *Hölle* = hell

G. **WORD FAMILIES**   Which words come from word families in German that you recognize (noun, adjective, verb, adverb)? Write down as many as you find in the chapter.

> **Beispiel:**
> das Studium (noun; studies)
> der Student (noun; person)
> studieren (verb)

H. **EXERCISES**   Write out three (3) „Was passt nicht?" ('Odd one out') exercises. List four words, three of which are related and one that does not fit the same category. Categories can be linked to meaning, grammar, gender, parts of speech (noun, verb, adjective), etc. USE YOUR IMAGINATION! Give the reason for why the odd word does not fit. Your classmates will have to solve the puzzles you provide!

> **Beispiel:**
> grün – blau – gelb – neun
> Here *neun* does not fit, because it is a
> number and all the others are colors.

These ideas are sugge tions only. Different learne have different preference and needs for learning ar reviewing vocabulary. T several of these sugge tions until you find ones th work for you. Keep in min though, that knowing mar words – and knowing the well, both to recognize ar to produce – makes you more effective user of t new language.

Basiswortschatz
Core Vocabulary

The following presents a list of core vocabulary. Consider this list as the absolute minimum to focus on. As you work through the chapter you will need more vocabulary to help you talk about your own experience. To that end, a more complete vocabulary list can be found at the end of the chapter. This reference list will aid your attainment of Chapter 10's objectives.

(QR 10.1 p.483)

(Deutsche) Geschichte	(German) History
auswandern (wanderte aus - ausgewandert)	to emigrate
die Bundesrepublik Deutschland (BRD)	the Federal Republic of Germany (BRD)
die Deutsche Demokratische Republik (DDR)	the German Democratic Republic (DDR)
die ehemalige DDR	former East Germany
die Epoche (Epochen)	era/ the epoch
das Ereignis (Ereignisse)	event/ the incident
die Gegenwart	present
hoffen	to hope
der Kanzler (Kanzler)	chancellor
der Kanzlerin (Kanzlerinnen)	female chancellor
die Kirche (Kirchen)	church
kritisieren (kritisierte - kritisiert)	to criticize
die Kultur (Kulturen)	culture
der Mauerfall	the fall of the Berlin Wall
der Staat (Staaten)	state/ country/ federal state
die Wiedervereinigung	the (German) reunification
die Wirtschaft	economy
die Wirtschaftskrise (Wirtschaftskrisen)	economic crisis/the depression
die Zukunft	future
der Krieg (Kriege)	war
furchtbar	terrible/awful
die Gewalt	violence
die Hilfe/Hilfeleistung (Hilfen/Hilfeleistungen)	help
die Hoffnung (Hoffnungen)	hope
der Kampf (Kämpfe)	fight
kämpfen	to fight, battle
verlieren (verlor - verloren)	to lose
der Verlierer (Verlierer)	loser

Rund um Deutschland und die Deutschen	On Germany and the Germans
arrogant sein	to be arrogant
bewundern (bewunderte - bewundert)	to admire
der Bürger (Bürger)	citizen (male)
die Bürgerin (Bürgerinnen)	citizen (female)
die Gesellschaft (Gesellschaften)	society
keinen Humor haben	to have no sense of humor
jammern	to whine/to moan/to complain
pünktlich sein	to be on time
überpünktlich sein	to be overly punctual/to be exceedingly on time
tauschen	to swap/ to trade
die Tradition (Traditionen)	tradition
das Vorurteil (Vorurteile)	prejudice

Opern und andere Sehenswürdigkeiten	Operas and other Objects of Interest
die Aufführung (Aufführungen)	performance/the act/the showing
beeindruckend	impressive
sich befinden (befand sich - sich befunden)	to be located
gegründet	founded/started
die Oper (Opern)	opera
der Reiseführer (Reiseführer)	travel guide
suchen	to search
die Vorstellung (Vorstellungen)	screening/the show/ the performance

Nach dem Weg fragen	Asking for directions
Ich kenne mich hier nicht aus.	I don't know my way around.
Können Sie mir vielleicht helfen?	Could you help me?
Wo ist der Zoo?	Where is the zoo?

Wegbeschreibungen	Giving directions
Biegen Sie rechts/links ab.	Turn right/ left.
Der Zoo ist in der Nähe von …	The zoo is near the …
Nehmen Sie die nächste Kreuzung rechts/links.	Take a right/ left on the next intersection.
einsteigen (stieg ein - eingestiegen)	to board (busses, trams, trains, etc.)
aussteigen (stieg aus - ausgestiegen)	to de-board (busses, trams, trains, etc.)

I. Die Stadt kennen lernen

Berlin ist die Hauptstadt von Deutschland. In Berlin sind Geschichte und Natur, Erholung und Erlebnis und vieles mehr vereint und es bietet für jeden Besucher etwas.

Aktivität 1. Begriffe zu Berlin

Sie wissen gewiss mehr über Berlin, als Sie denken! Sammeln Sie mit der Klasse Begriffe, die Ihnen zu Berlin sofort in den Sinn kommen.

Aktivität 2. Was wissen Sie über Berlin?

Arbeiten Sie mit einem Partner/einer Partnerin zusammen, um die Fragen im folgenden Berlin-Quiz zu beantworten.

1. Wissen Sie, wann die Berliner Mauer gebaut wurde?

Ja, das weiß ich. Die Berliner Mauer wurde
_____ gebaut.

a. 1961
b. 1949
c. 1945
d. 1989

2. Wissen Sie, von wem die berühmt gewordene (*now reknowned*) Bemerkung „Ich bin ein Berliner"* stammt?

Ja, das weiß ich. Es war _____
_____.

a. Michail Gorbatschow
b. Ronald Reagan
c. Angela Merkel
d. John F. Kennedy

*Haben Sie schon gehört, dass diese Bemerkung grammatisch falsch sein soll? Das stimmt nicht! Viele Berliner sagen „Ich bin ein Berliner/eine Berlinerin".

Grimm Grammar

In der letzten Aufgabe sind die Verben „kennen" und „wissen" oft vorgekommen. Bitte gehen Sie zu *Grimm Grammar* und lesen Sie folgende Grammatikteile:

wissen/kennen

3. Kennen Sie, Marlene Dietrich?

Hmmm ... nein, ich kenne sie nicht, aber ich weiß, dass sie eine berühmte deutsche

_____ aus Berlin war. (Sie ist 1992 gestorben.)

a. Politikerin   c. Sängerin und Schauspielerin

b. Autorin   d. Modedesignerin

4. Kennen Sie einen deutschen Film, der in Berlin spielt?

Ja, ich kenne einen: _____ .

a. *Metropolis* (1927)

b. *Lola rennt* (1998)

c. *Nosferatu* (1922)

d. *Das Boot* (1982)

e. *M - eine Stadt sucht einen Mörder* (1931)

f. _____

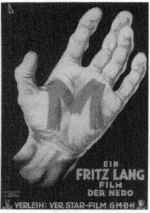

Work found at http://en.wikipedia.org/ wiki/File:M_poster.jpg / CC BY-SA 3.0 (http://creativecommons.org/licenses/ by-sa/3.0/)

5. Wissen Sie, welche vier Länder Berlin am Ende des Zweiten Weltkriegs unter sich aufgeteilt (*partitioned*) haben?

Ja, das weiß ich. Es waren _____, _____,

_____ und _____.

a. Großbritannien, Italien, Österreich und die USA

b. Großbritannien, Österreich, die Sowjetunion und die USA

c. Frankreich, Großbritannien, die Sowjetunion und die USA

d. Frankreich, Großbritannien, Japan und die Sowjetunion

6. Wissen Sie, wie viele Goldmedaillen der Amerikaner Jesse Owens bei den olympischen Sommerspielen 1936 in Berlin gewonnen hat?

Er hat _____ Goldmedaillen gewonnen.

a. 3

b. 6

c. 2

d. 4

7. Wissen Sie, was die Berliner Luftbrücke war?

Das war _____.

a. die Evakuierung (*evacuation*) Ost-Berlins nach dem

    Fall der

    Berliner Mauer

b. eine altmodische Berliner Transportart

c. die Versorgung West-Berlins durch die Westalliierten

    (23. Juni1948 – 12. Mai 1949)

d. eine Achterbahn (*rollercoaster*) in Berlin

8. Kennen Sie einen Sänger oder eine Band, die aus Berlin kommt?

Nein, ich kenne keine, aber ich weiß, welcher Sänger bzw. welche Band aus Berlin kommt. Das ist doch ganz klar: _____ sind Berliner.

a. *Die Toten Hosen* und *Herbert Grönemeyer*

b. *Scooter* und *Fettes Brot*

c. *Seeed*, *Nina Hagen* und *Die Ärzte*

d. *Oomph!*, *Falko* und *Die Prinzen*

Aktivität 3. Lieder & Musik

Berlin in Liedern. In diesem Kapitel lernen Sie viel über Berlin: die Geschichte der Stadt, die Sehenswürdigkeiten, die sich dort befinden, und berühmte Leute, die dort gelebt und gearbeitet haben. Aber die Stadt hat auch ein bestimmtes Gefühl, das viele Künstler und Besucher bezaubert (*enchant*). Laden Sie die passende pdf-Datei unter „Lieder & Musik" von der *Deutsch im Blick*-Website in Kapitel 10 herunter und bearbeiten Sie die Aufgaben. Vielleicht bekommen Sie ein bisschen mit, was dieses Gefühl eigentlich ist.

[Source: http://www.karneval-berlin.de/]

Aktivität 4. Berlin: Eine multikulturelle Stadt

Berlin ist heute eine besonders multikulturelle Stadt. Wie multikulturell genau, wird in den neuesten statistischen Informationen des Berliner Integrationsbeauftragten (*integration commission*) erklärt.

A. Vor dem Lesen: Wortbildung

Die folgenden Wörter sind im Text sehr wichtig. Lesen Sie die Wörter und ihre Bedeutungen auf der linken Seite und raten Sie dann, was die Wörter auf der rechten Seite bedeuten.

der Zuwanderer = immigrant   →   die Zuwanderung = _____

die Staatsangehörigkeit = citizenship   →   der Staatsangehörige = _____

bevölkerungsreich = populous   →   die Bevölkerung = _____

> **Vokabelhilfe**
>
> ausmachen – to account for   der Bezirk – district
> Anteil haben an – to take part in   ungleichmäßig verteilt – unevenly
> verlaufen – to run (along)   aufweisen – to have distributed

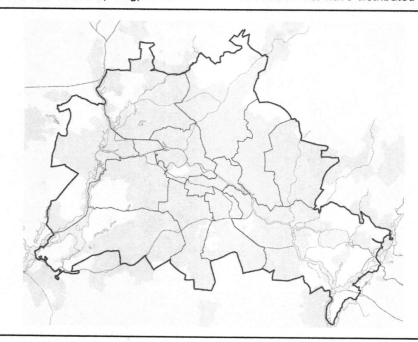

Zuwanderer und Einwohner Berlins nach Staatsangehörigkeit

Berlin ist die bevölkerungsreichste Stadt Deutschlands und nach St. Petersburg die zweitgrößte im gesamten Ostmitteleuropa. Unter den insgesamt ungefähr 3,4 Millionen Einwohnern machen nicht-deutsche Staatsangehörige 13,7 Prozent aus. Mehr als jede achte Person in Berlin besitzt demnach keine deutsche Staatsangehörigkeit. Die nicht-deutsche Bevölkerung Berlins ist ungleichmäßig über die Stadt verteilt. Zwischen den Bezirken variiert die Quote der nicht-deutschen Staatsangehörigen zwischen 3,6 Prozent (Marzahn-Hellersdorf) und 28,7 Prozent (Mitte). Die Teilung verläuft einerseits zwischen dem Osten und dem Westen der Stadt. Das alte Ost-Berlin hatte keinen Anteil an der Zuwanderung von Arbeitsmigranten („Gastarbeiter") vor 1989, daher leben bis heute nur sehr wenige Personen mit z.B. italienischer, griechischer oder türkischer Staatsangehörigkeit im Osten der Stadt. Andererseits verläuft eine Trennlinie zwischen den Innenstadtbezirken und den Außenstadtbezirken. Die Innenstadtbezirke (Mitte, Friedrichshain-Kreuzberg, Neukölln) weisen alle eine Quote für nicht-deutsche Staatsangehörige von deutlich über 20 Prozent auf. Wie in den Vorjahren stammten im Jahr 2008 die meisten Personen nicht-deutscher Staatsangehörigkeit aus der Türkei (111.285 Personen), gefolgt von Staatsbürgern aus Polen mit 43.700 Personen. Die drittstärkste Gruppe bilden Staatsbürger aus dem ehemaligen Serbien und Montenegro mit 22.251 Personen.

Zuwanderer in Berlin nach Staatsangehörigkeit (2008)

Staatsangehörigkeit (Gebiet)	Berlin	Staatsangehörigkeit (Gebiet)	Berlin	Staatsangehörigkeit (Gebiet)	Berlin
Türkei	111.285	Portugal	2.794	Belgien	1.344
Polen	43.700	Japan	2.767	Sri Lanka	1.299
Serbien[2]	22.251	Schweden	2.811	Kuba	1.263
Italien	14.964	Brasilien	2.532	Marokko	1.189
Russische Förderation[1]	14.915	Indien	2.417	Slowenien[1]	1.175
USA	14.186	Ungarn	2.348	Peru	1.174
Frankreich (einschließlich Korsika)	13.133	Syrien, Arabische Republik	2.274	Jordanien	1.067
Vietnam	12.494	Dänemark und Färöer	2.560	Georgien[1]	1.065
Kroatien[1]	10.752	Irak	2.025	Aserbaidschan[1]	1.038
Bosnien und Herzegowina[1]	10.556	Kanada	1.862	Angola	981
Großbritannien und Nordirland	10.196	Ägypten	1.830	ehem. Tschechoslowakei[4]	819
Griechenland	9.582	Irland	1.811	Kolumbien	1.011
Österreich	8.982	Ghana	1.766	Mexiko	967
Ukraine[1]	8.706	Kasachstan[1]	1.661	Philippinen	939
Libanon	7.553	Kamerun	1.652	Algerien	909
Bulgarien	7.375	Tunesien	1.635	Bangladesch	884
Spanien	7.044	Australien	1.565	Chile	790
China	6.023	Mongolei	1.542	Kenia	720
Thailand	5.772	Pakistan	1.511	Slowakei[1]	704
Schweiz	4.583	Finnland	1.510	Taiwan	692
Mazedonien[1,3]	4.575	Weißrussland[1]	1.478	Moldau, Republik[1]	655
Iran	4.355	Norwegen	1.444	Äthiopien	602
Niederlande	3.961	Indonesien	1.430	Afghanistan	597
ehem. Sowejunion[4]	3.796	Tschechische Republik[1]	1.413	Argentinien	586
Rumänien	3.771	Nigeria	1.375	Armenien[1]	543
Korea, Republik	2.894	Litauen[1]	1.360	Mosambik	474
Israel	2.849	Lettland[1]	1.360		

Staatenlos	1.637	[1] soweit unter dieser Staatsangehörigkeit gemeldet
Ungeklärt	11.839	[2] einschließlich ehemaliges Serbien und Montenegro
Ohne Angabe	58	[3] vorläufige Bezeichnung
Gesamt	470.051	[4] Zuordnung auf die Nachfolgestaaten nicht möglich

Quelle: Statistisches Landesamt Berlin (Stand: 31. Dezember 2008). Besuchen Sie auch http://www.berlin.de/lb/intmig/statistik/demografie/einwohner_staatsangehoerigkeit.html für aktuellere Daten oder finden Sie Informationen zu der Einbürgerungskampagne „Der deutsche Pass hat viele Gesichter".

Grimm Grammar

Es gibt in der deutschen Sprache zwei Zeitformen (*tenses*), die man benutzen kann, um über die Vergangenheit zu sprechen: das Perfekt (*conversational past*) und das Imperfekt (*simple past*). Das Perfekt wird vor allem in der gesprochenen Sprache häufig verwendet. Das Imperfekt wird mehr in formelleren Gesprächen und vor allem in der Schriftsprache genutzt, obwohl einige bestimmte Verben auch in der Umgangssprache (*everyday speech*) regelmäßig im Imperfekt vorkommen.

Mehr dazu finden Sie auf der nächsten Seite.

B. Beim Lesen: Fragen zum Text
Beantworten Sie folgende Fragen zum Text.

1. Wie viele Einwohner hat Berlin insgesamt?

2. Wie viele dieser Einwohner haben eine nicht-deutsche Staatsangehörigkeit? (Geben Sie bitte absolute Zahl, nicht die Prozentzahl an. Tipp: Sie brauchen einen Taschenrechner dafür.)

3. Warum leben bis heute nur sehr wenige Personen mit nicht-deutscher Staatsangehörigkeit im Osten der Stadt?

4. In welchen Bezirken der Stadt liegt die Quote für nicht-deutsche Staatsangehörige über 20 Prozent?

5. Aus welchem Land kamen im Jahr 2007 die meisten Personen nicht-deutscher Staatsangehörigkeit?

6. Wie viele Staatsangehörige Ihres Landes leben in Berlin?

C. Nach dem Lesen: Fragen zur Diskussion
Diskutieren Sie im Unterricht folgende Fragen.

1. Warum ist Berlin so multikulturell? (Welche Gründe haben Menschen anderer Länder nach Berlin einzuwandern?)

2. Wie multikulturell ist Ihre Stadt Ihrer Meinung nach?

3. Wissen Sie, aus welchen Ländern die meisten Personen nicht-amerikanischer Staatsangehörigkeit in Ihrer Stadt stammen?

4. Welche Vorteile und möglichen Nachteile gibt es, Ihrer Meinung nach, wenn viele Menschen aus vielen unterschiedlichen Kulturen zusammen leben? Möchten Sie gerne in einer multikulturellen Stadt leben? Wo? Warum/warum nicht?

Der deutsche Pass hat viele Gesichter.

EUROPÄISCHE UNION

BUNDESREPUBLIK DEUTSCHLAND

PASST UNS!

Berlin bürgert ein.

II. Berlin und die neuere deutsche Geschichte

Jahrhundertelang (*for centuries*) hat Berlin eine sehr wichtige Rolle in der Geschichte Deutschlands gespielt. Im nächsten Teil des Kapitels betrachten Sie die neuere Geschichte Deutschlands anhand der neueren Geschichte Berlins.

Aktivität 5. Berlin als Hauptstadt

Sie wissen schon, dass Berlin die Hauptstadt Deutschlands ist, aber wissen Sie, dass Berlin auch schon während (*during*) mehrerer vergangener (*past*) Regierungen Hauptstadt war? Lesen Sie die folgenden Texte, um etwas über diese vergangenen Regierungen zu lernen.

Was wissen Sie über die Geschichte, Wirtschaft, Politik und Bevölkerung von Berlin und Deutschland ...

- im 18. Jahrhundert?
- im 19. Jahrhundert?
- im 20. Jahrhundert?
- und heute?

A. Vor dem Lesen

Unterstreichen Sie in den Texten auf den nächsten Seiten einige Verben im Imperfekt. Erstellen Sie eine Liste mit diesen Verben.

Reguläre Verben	Irreguläre Verben	Englische Bedeutung
- - - - - - - - - -	Beispiel: *war*	*to be*

Bevor Sie die nächste Aufgabe beginnen, bearbeiten Sie bitte folgende Grammatikteile in *Grimm Grammar*:

Das Imperfekt (regelmäßige Verben)
Das Imperfekt:

Beispiel:

machen
ich machte
du machtest
er/sie/es machte

wir machten
ihr machtet
sie machten
Sie machten

Wiederholung:
Das Imperfekt (haben)

haben
ich hatte
du hattest
er/sie/es hatte

wir hatten
ihr hattet
sie hatten
Sie hatten

Wiederholung:
Das Imperfekt (sein)

sein
ich war
du warst
er/sie/es war

wir waren
ihr wart
sie waren
Sie waren

B. Das Königreich Preußen (1701-1870)

Zwischen 1740 und 1786 wurde Berlin unter der <u>Herrschaft</u> von Friedrich dem Großen (König Friedrich II) zu einer europäischen Metropole. Berlin war Teil des Königreichs Preußen, das <u>unabhängig</u> vom <u>Heiligen Römischen Reich</u> war. Das Königreich Preußen <u>steigerte</u> seine <u>Macht</u> und seinen <u>Grundbesitz</u> durch eine Reihe von Kriegen. Es war aber nicht nur für seine Kriege bekannt, sondern auch für seine <u>Fortschrittlichkeit</u> und <u>Aufgeklärtheit</u>. Zum Beispiel <u>führte</u> Friedrich der Große unter seiner Herrschaft (1740-1786) viele Reformen und größere religiöse Toleranz <u>ein</u>. Er war <u>Förderer</u> der Künste und mit dem Franzosen Voltaire eng befreundet.

Es folgte eine turbulente Zeit während der Napoleonischen Kriege. 1805 endete das Heilige Römische Reich und 1806 <u>zog</u> Napoleon <u>als Sieger</u> in Berlin <u>ein</u>. Aber nach der <u>Schlacht</u> bei Waterloo (1815) wurde das Königreich Preußen immer mächtiger. Unter König Wilhelm I und <u>Ministerpräsident</u> Otto von Bismarck erreichte Preußen den <u>Höhepunkt</u> seiner Macht.

Vokabelhilfe

das Heilige Römische Reich – Holy Roman Empire	die Fortschrittlichkeit – progressiveness
unabhängig – independent	die Aufgeklärtheit – enlightenment
der Grundbesitz – land holdings	die Herrschaft – rule
die Macht – power	der Förderer – patron
steigern – to rise, grow	die Schlacht – battle
einführen – to introduce	der Ministerpräsident – prime minister
als Sieger einziehen – to emerge victorious	der Höhepunkt – peak/climax

---

Sind die Aussagen *richtig* oder *falsch*?

        richtig   **falsch**

1. Das Königreich Preußen war Teil des Heiligen Römischen Reichs.

2. König Friedrich II war gegen religiöse Toleranz.

3. Preußen war unter König Wilhelm I am mächtigsten.

Was wissen Sie über die Geschichte von Ihrem eigenen Land zu dieser Zeit? Wer war an der Macht? Wie war die Regierung in Ihrem Land (z.B. War es schon eine Demokratie? Ein Königreich?)

Was ist im 18. und im ersten Teil des 19. Jahrhunderts in Europa passiert? Welche Länder/Reiche waren an der Macht?

Das ist das ursprüngliche Wappen des Königreichs Preußen und der späteren Provinz Ostpreußen.

Work found at http://commons.wikimedia.org/?title=File:Wappen_Preu%C3%9Fen_2.png / CC BY-SA 3.0 (http://creativecommons. org/licenses/by-sa/3.0/)

C. Das Deutsche Reich (1871-1945)

Das zweite Reich/Das Deutsche Kaiserreich (1871-1918)

Am Ende des <u>Deutsch-Französischen Kriegs</u> gründete der Preußische König Wilhelm I das Deutsche Reich (1871-1945), bekannt als zweites Reich, weil das Heilige Römische Reich das erste war. Das zweite Reich <u>vereinte</u> zum ersten Mal die vielen deutschen <u>Staaten</u>, die seit dem Ende des Heiligen Römischen Reiches ihre Unabhängigkeit bekommen hatten. Im zweiten Reich wurde Wilhelm der erste Kaiser, Ministerpräsident Bismarck der erste <u>Kanzler</u>. 1971 wurde Berlin auch Hauptstadt des Deutschen Reichs.

Das zweite Reich <u>verfolgte</u> eine Politik des Expansionismus, genauso wie das ehemalige Königreich Preußen (jetzt der größte und mächtigste Staat unter den neuen Staaten des Reichs). Kaiser Wilhelm II <u>erweiterte</u> das Herrschaftsgebiet des Reichs, indem er einige Territorien in Afrika und Inseln im Pazifik kolonialisierte. Die imperialistischen Bestrebungen des Reichs sowie die imperialistischen <u>Bestrebungen</u> anderer europäischer Mächte führten schließlich zum 1. Weltkrieg. <u>Vereinfacht</u> gesagt, kämpften das Deutsche Reich und Österreich-Ungarn gegen die Alliierten (Frankreich, Großbritannien, Russland und später die USA). Die Alliierten siegten.

Vokabelhilfe

der Deutsch-Französische Krieg – Franco-Prussian War	verfolgen – to pursue
vereinen – to unite	erweitern – to extend
der Staat – state	die Bestrebung – effort
der Kanzler – chancellor	vereinfachen – to simplify

Sind die Aussagen *richtig* oder *falsch*?

	richtig	falsch
1. Das zweite Reich konnte die deutschen Staaten nicht vereinen.		
2. Wilhelm I wurde 1871 zum Kaiser des Reichs.		
3. Der Imperialismus des Reichs hatte mit dem 1. Weltkrieg nichts zu tun.		

Was wissen Sie über die Geschichte Ihres Landes zu dieser Zeit? Wer war an der Macht? Wie war die Regierung in Ihrem Land (z.B. War es schon eine Demokratie? Ein Königreich?)

Was ist am Ende des 19. und am Anfang des 20. Jahrhunderts in Europa passiert? Welche Länder/ Reiche waren an der Macht?

Otto von Bismarck (kurz für Otto Eduard Leopold von Bismarck-Schönhausen) beeinflusste die Gründung des Deutschen Reiches und war erster Reichskanzlervon 1871 bis 1890.

Quelle: Bundesarchiv

D. Die Weimarer Republik (1919-1933)

Die Novemberrevolution im Deutschen Reich und in Österreich-Ungarn <u>stürzte</u> die Monarchie, es kam zur Gründung der Weimarer Republik. (Weimar war die östliche Stadt, in der die neue <u>Verfassung</u> des Reichs geschrieben wurde. Rechts sehen Sie Philipp Scheidemann bei der Ausrufung der Republik am 9. November 1918).

Noch <u>schwer</u> vom Krieg <u>gezeichnet</u>, war die Weimarer Zeit voll von Instabilität. <u>Angriffe</u> von rechts (der Kapp-<u>Putsch</u> (1920) und der Hitler-Putsch (1923) sind vor allem bekannt, aber auch von links <u>gefährdeten</u> die schwache Demokratie. Die <u>Wirtschaftslage</u> im Deutschen Reich wurde katastrophal. Es gab zum Beispiel eine große Inflation, die so schlimm wurde, dass es billiger war, Papiergeld zu verbrennen, als <u>Brennholz</u> zu kaufen. Die Leute waren arm und hoffnungslos.

Quelle: Bundesarchiv

Vokabelhilfe

stürzen – to overthrow	der Angriff – attack
die Verfassung – constitution	der Putsch – coup
schwer gezeichnet – profoundly shaped	gefährden – to endanger
das Brennholz – firewood	die Wirtschaftslage – economic situation

---

Sind die Aussagen *richtig* oder *falsch*?

	richtig	falsch
1. Die Weimarer Republik war eine Monarchie.		
2. Linksextreme allein waren für die vielen Angriffe verantwortlich.		
3. Eine katastrophale Wirtschaftslage bedeutet, dass die Menschen sehr arm sind.		

Was wissen Sie über die Geschichte von Ihrem eigenen Land zu dieser Zeit? Wer war an der Macht? Wie war die Regierung in Ihrem Land (z.B. War es schon eine Demokratie? Ein Königreich?)

Wie war die Wirtschaftslage in Ihrem Land zu dieser Zeit? Wie war die politische, soziale Lage? Gab es eine Verbindung (*a connection*) zwischen der Wirtschaftslage und der politischen/sozialen Lage in Ihrem Land? Wenn ja, welche?

Karte des Deutschen Reichs

„Weimarer Republik"/„Drittes Reich" 1919-1937

Work found at http://commons.wikimedia.org/wiki/ File:Karte_des_Deutschen_Reiches,_Weimarer_Republik-Drittes_Reich_1919%E2%80%931937.svg / CC BY-SA 3.0 (http://creativecommons.org/licenses/by-sa/3.0/)

E. Das Dritte Reich (1933-1945)

Aufgrund der Instabilität im Lande konnte der Nationalsozialismus im Deutschen Reich Fuß fassen. Die Nazis blendeten die Bevölkerung mit Versprechen und änderten geschickt das Regierungssystem, so dass Adolf Hitler zu großer Macht kommen konnte. 1933 führten sie eine totalitäre Diktatur ein. Hitler wurde Führer dieses sogenannten Tausendjährigen Reichs (das aber in der Tat nur zwölf Jahre dauern würde).

Hitler und die Nazis machten verschiedene Gruppen für die Probleme im Land verantwortlich – Homosexuelle, Kommunisten, aber vor allem die Juden. Nach den Nürnberger Gesetzen (1935) begannen die Nazis der grausamen Ermordung von rund 6 Millionen Juden. Widerstandsbewegungen hatten wenig Erfolg, da die Nazis sie brutal unterdrückten.

Der Einmarsch Hitlers in Polen löste dann den 2. Weltkrieg aus. Italien, Japan und Deutschland führten Krieg gegen die Sowjetunion, England, Frankreich und die USA. Letztere siegten glücklicherweise. Im 2. Weltkrieg kam es zu großen, beinahe unvorstellbaren Verwüstungen. Allein in der Sowjetunion starben über 20 Millionen Menschen. Etwa 4,5 Millionen Menschen ließen in Polen ihr Leben, 7,5 Millionen Menschen fielen dem Krieg in Deutschland zum Opfer. Auch die anderen Länder hatten unglaublich hohe Todesraten.

Was bedeuten die folgenden Vokabeln in diesem Kontext? Suchen und unterstrechen Sie die Vokabeln aus dem Kasten zuerst im Text und kreisen Sie dann jeweils die richtige Definition ein. Überlegen Sie auch einmal, was die übrigen Begriffe auf Deutsch sein könnten.

Vokabeln	Definitionen		
1. *Fuß fassen*	to trample underfoot	to gain footing	to grab one's foot
2. *blenden*	to annoy	to blend in with	to bedazzle
3. *Versprechen*	promises	money	worries
4. *geschickt*	stupidly	fashionably	cleverly
5. *in der Tat*	in actuality	surprisingly	possibly
6. *verantwortlich machen für*	to owe	to sympathize with	to blame
7. *Widerstandsbewegung*	religious movement	resistance movement	peace movement
8. *unvorstellbar*	imaginable	usual	unimaginable
9. *Verwüstungen*	ravages	problems	odds
10. *zum Opfer fallen*	to fall over	to fall victim to	to survive

Was wissen Sie über die Geschichte von Ihrem eigenen Land zu dieser Zeit? Hat es an dem 2. Weltkrieg teilgenommen? Wenn ja, welche Rolle spielte Ihr Land in diesem Konflikt?

Quelle: Bundesarchiv

Wie viele deutsche Städte, war auch Berlin fast komplett zerstört worden.

Links sehen Sie wie das Wohnen am Küstriner Platz in Berlin aussah.

F. Die Bundesrepublik Deutschland BRD und die Deutsche Demokratische Republik (DDR) (1949-1990)

Mit dem Ende des 2. Weltkriegs endete das Deutsche Reich (gegründet 1871). Die vier Siegermächte teilten das Reich in vier Besatzungszonen auf: Großbritannien besetzte die nordwestliche Zone, Frankreich die südwestliche, die USA die südöstliche und die Sowjetunion die nordöstliche. Auch Berlin teilten die Siegermächte in vier Besatzungszonen auf, weil die Stadt Hauptstadt Nazideutschlands war.

Es gab aber viele Uneinigkeiten zwischen der Sowjetunion und den anderen Siegermächten. 1948 verhängte die Sowjetunion eine Blockade über ganz Berlin und Großbritannien und die USA mussten West-Berlin beinahe ein Jahr lang aus der Luft versorgen (die Berliner Luftbrücke, 1948-1949). Im Mai 1949 gründeten Großbritannien, Frankreich und die USA aus ihren Besatzungszonen die BRD und West-Berlin. Später, im Oktober 1949, gründete die Sowjetunion aus ihren Besatzungszonen die DDR und Ost-Berlin. Bonn wurde Hauptstadt der BRD, Ost-Berlin (inoffizielle) Hauptstadt der DDR.

Während das Regierungssystem der BRD sich an dem amerikanischen Regierungssystem orientierte, orientierte sich das Regierungssystem der DDR an dem sowjetischen Regierungssystem. 1961 erbaute die DDR-Regierung die Berliner Mauer, um die vielen unzufriedenen Menschen, die die DDR verlassen wollten, aufzuhalten. (Einer der Kontrollpunkte am Grenzübergang – „Checkpoint Charlie" – wurde besonders berühmt.) Spannungen zwischen der BRD und der DDR spiegelten und hatten zugleich selbst Anteil an diesem Konflikt zwischen den USA und der Sowjetunion: der Kalte Krieg.

Wie zuvor in Aktivität E, finden Sie die passenden Definitonen zu den Vokabeln. Diesmal sind die Begriffe bereits im Text unterstrichen.

Vokabeln	Definitionen		
1. Siegermächte	victors	losers	neutrals
2. Besatzungszonen	neutral zones	countries	occupation zones
3. Uneinigkeiten	similarities	agreements	disagreements
4. versorgen	to supply	to worry	to attack
5. Grenzübergang	bridge	elevator	border crossing
6. Spannungen	civilities	tensions	conversations

Was wissen Sie über die Geschichte von Ihrem eigenen Land zu dieser Zeit? Wer war an der Macht? Wie war die Wirtschaftslage, und die soziologische/politische Lage in Ihrem Land?

Wenn Ihr Land am 2. Weltkrieg teilgenommen hat, wie hat es sich von dessen Auswirkungen (*effects*) erholt (*recovered*)? Hat jemand Ihrem Land geholfen? Wenn ja, wer und wie?

YOU ARE LEAVING
THE AMERICAN SECTOR
ВЫ ВЫЕЗЖАЕТЕ ИЗ
АМЕРИКАНСКОГО СЕКТОРА
VOUS SORTEZ
DU SECTEUR AMÉRICAIN
SIE VERLASSEN DEN AMERIKANISCHEN SEKTOR
US ARMY

Schild am *Checkpoint Charlie* in Berlin

Eine Nachbildung (*reconstruction*) des Postens kann man heute an der selben Stelle in Berlin besichtigen.

G. Das vereinte Deutschland (1990 bis zum heutigen Tag)

Im Laufe der DDR versuchten viele, über die Berliner Mauer drüber zu kommen. Rund 5000 Menschen hatten damit Erfolg, aber nicht alle waren so glücklich. Mindestens 136 Menschen ließen sogar ihr Leben dabei und diese Tode hatten eine starke abschreckende Wirkung. Das heißt, zum größten Teil wurde es mit der Mauer erreicht, Ostdeutsche in Ost-Berlin (und damit auch Ostdeutschland) festzuhalten.

Die sich verschlechternde politische und wirtschaftliche Lage der DDR führte 1989 zu weit verbreiteten Protesten und am 9. November 1989 öffnete die Regierung die Grenze zwischen Ost- und West-Berlin. Die ganze Nacht lang feierten die Ost-Berliner und West-Berliner an der Mauer. Für die DDR war dies der Beginn des Endes einer fast dreißigjährigen Ära. In den nächsten Monaten ließ die Regierung die Mauer abbauen. Nach dem Fall dieser Regierung kam schließlich die lang ersehnte Vereinigung Deutschlands. Am 3. Oktober 1990 wurden Ost und West offiziell eins: Ost- und West-Berlin und Ost- und Westdeutschland. Heute feiern die Deutschen den 3. Oktober als „Tag der Deutschen Einheit".

Finden Sie auch hier wieder die passenden Definitonen.

Vokabeln	Definitionen		
1. *über etw. drüber kommen*	to cross	to jump over	to visit
2. *abschreckende Wirkung*	positive effect	deterrent effect	little effect
3. *verschlechternd*	deteriorating	improving	encouraging
4. *die Grenze*	dialogue	animosity	border
5. *abbauen*	to build up	to maintain	to dismantle
6. *ersehnt*	detested	longed-for	mocked

Gibt es in Ihrem Land eine ähnliche Situation wie zwischen dem ehemaligen Ost- und Westdeutschland oder bestehende Konflikte wie zwischen *Ossis* und *Wessis*? Wie lange dauert es Ihrer Meinung nach, bevor zwei Bevölkerungsgruppen friedlich und ohne Konflikte zusammen leben können? Ist es überhaupt möglich?

Schauen Sie sich einige deutsche Informationsmedien (Zeitungen, Magazine, die Tagesschau zum Beispiel) an und finden Sie heraus, ob in den Artikeln immer noch von „Ost" und „West" von „Ossis" und „Wessis" die Rede ist. Ist das immer noch ein aktuelles Thema?

Links:
Bild der Mauer 1986 mit Graffiti auf der Westseite und ohne Graffiti auf der Ostseite.

Rechts:
Menschen verlassen den Osten nach dem Fall der Mauer 1989.

Work found at http://commons.wikimedia. org/wiki/File:Berlinermauer.jpg / CC BY-SA 3.0 (http://creativecommons.org/licenses/ by-sa/3.0/)

Work found at http://commons.wikimedia. org/wiki/File:Fall_of_the_Berlin_ Wall_1989,_people_walking.jpg / CC BY-SA 3.0 (http://creativecommons.org/ licenses/by-sa/3.0/)

Mehr Informationen zur deutschen Geschichte finden Sie zum Beispiel unter:
* http://www.tivi.de/fernsehen/logo/index/00087/index.html
* http://www.berlin.de/berlin-im-ueberblick/geschichte/index.de.html

Oder schauen Sie sich einen der folgenden Filme an:
* Der Hauptmann von Köpenick (1931)
* Triumph des Willens (1934)
* Goodbye Lenin (2003)
* Rosenstraße (2003)
* Sophie Scholl (2005)
* Das Leben der Anderen (2006)

Grimm Grammar

Bitte gehen Sie zu *Grimm Grammar* und bearbeiten Sie folgende Grammatikteile:

Das Imperfekt (unregelmäßige Verben)

Beispiel:

gehen
ich ging
du gingst
er/sie/es ging

wir gingen
ihr gingt
sie gingen
Sie gingen

Das Imperfekt (gemischte Verben)

Beispiel:

bringen
ich brachte
du brachtest
er/sie/es brachte

wir brachten
ihr brachtet
sie brachten
Sie brachten

Aktivität 6. Der Stil der Erzählung: das Imperfekt

In den vorangegangenen Texten konnten Sie einiges über die deutsche Geschichte lesen. Wählen Sie aus jedem Abschnitt zwei Sätze, die die Geschichte Berlins gut zusammenfassen (*summarize*). Merken Sie sich die Zeitform der meisten Verben: das Imperfekt (*simple past*). Schreiben Sie jeweils den Satz auf, dann das Verb im Imperfekt und im Infinitiv.

Das Königreich Preußen (1701-1870)	das Imperfekt	der Infinitiv
1. *Berlin war Teil des Königreichs Preußen …*	*war*	*sein*
2.		

Das zweite Reich/Das Deutsche Kaiserreich (1871-1918)		
3.		
4.		

Die Weimarer Republik (1919-1933)		
5.		
6.		

Das Dritte Reich (1933-1945)		
7.		
8.		

Die Bundesrepublik Deutschland (BRD) und die Deutsche Demokratische Republik (DDR) (1949-1990)		
9.		
10.		

Das vereinte Deutschland (1990 bis zum heutigen Tag)		
11.		
12.		

Aktivität 7. Die Geschichte Ihres Landes

Während Sie die Texte über die Geschichte Deutschlands lasen, haben Sie sich über Ihr eigenes Land Notizen gemacht. Benutzen Sie jetzt möglichst viele der zwölf Verben, die Sie auf der vorigen Seite aufgeschrieben haben, um eine kurze Geschichte Ihres Heimatlandes zu schreiben.

Aktivität 8. Die Geschichte Deutschlands

Wählen Sie ein Thema der deutschen Geschichte (berühmte Personen, Ereignisse, Orte, Kriege, Kunst, Filme, Erfindungen usw.) aus und bereiten Sie ein Referat vor. Sie sollten dafür natürlich weitere Informationen sammeln (aus dem Internet, in der Bibliothek, in Büchern usw.) und Ihr Referat auf Deutsch halten. Benutzen Sie Musik und Bilder, wo möglich, und nennen Sie natürlich Ihre Forschungsquellen (*sources of information*). Wenn die anderen Studenten ihre Referate halten, hören Sie bitte gut zu und machen Sie sich Notizen.

Thema des Referates

Notizen (z.B. wichtige Figuren, Datum, Ort, warum war diese Figur/dieses Ereignis wichtig in der dt. Geschichte, was hat mich besonders überrascht [*surprised*] – was wusste ich nicht)?

_____   _____

_____

_____

_____

_____

Aktivität 9. Lieblingsepoche in der deutschen Geschichte

A. Berna, Erin und Jan: Welche sind ihre Lieblingsepochen?
Hören Sie sich die Interviews von Berna, Erin und Jan an ("Lieblingsepoche")
und markieren Sie die richtigen Aussagen. (Tipp: Es kann sein, dass mehrere
Aussagen richtig sind, nicht nur eine.)

Bernas Lieblingsepoche ist

❑ der 2. Weltkrieg.
❑ das 20. Jahrhundert.
❑ das Ende des 20. Jahrhunderts und der Beginn des 21. Jahrhunderts.

Sie interessiert sich für

❑ Immigranten.
❑ die Politik.
❑ den Holocaust.
❑ kulturelle Identitäten.
❑ die Minoritäten in Deutschland.

(QR 10.2 p.483)

Erin gefällt

❑ die Deutsche Demokratische Republik
❑ die Weimarer Republik
❑ die Vereinigung Deutschlands

wegen (*because of*)

❑ der Filme.
❑ der Kunst.
❑ der Ideen.
❑ der Musik.
❑ der Hoffnung.

(QR 10.3 p.483)

Am liebsten mag **Jan**

❑ das 20. Jahrhundert.
❑ das Königreich Preußen.
❑ das 18. Jahrhundert.

Er findet diese Epoche

❑ am wichtigsten.
❑ am interessantesten.
❑ sehr ereignisreich.

(QR 10.4 p.483)

B. Jans Interview

Hören Sie sich Jans Interview noch einmal an und beantworten Sie folgende Fragen:

Das „schlimmste, barbarischste" Extrem dieser Epoche wäre vielleicht _____

_____, weil _____.

Das „schönste" Extrem dieser Epoche wäre vielleicht _____

_____, weil _____.

C. Jetzt sind Sie dran!

Sie wissen jetzt mehr über die neuere Geschichte Deutschlands. Haben Sie eine Lieblingsepoche? Wenn ja, warum? Wenn nein, warum nicht? Welche Epoche interessiert Sie am meisten? Warum? Beantworten Sie diese Fragen in einem kurzen Absatz.

D. Umfrage

Fragen Sie zwei Kommilitonnen, was ihre Lieblingsepochen in der neueren deutschen Geschichte sind und warum diese Epochen ihnen gefallen.

Name:		
Was ist deine Lieblingsepoche in der neueren deutschen Geschichte?		
Warum gefällt dir diese Epoche?		

Aktivität 10. In Berlin, um Berlin und um Berlin herum – die Berliner Mauer

Die Berliner Mauer ist wohl eines der bekanntesten und verhasstesten Symbole des Kalten Krieges. In der Nacht, in der sich plötzlich die Mauer öffnete, empfing die Bevölkerung West-Berlins begeistert die DDR-Bürger. Viele Kneipen in der Nähe der Mauer schenkten spontan Freibier aus und der Kurfürstendamm war überlaufen von Menschenmassen und hupenden Autos. In der Euphorie dieser Nacht bestiegen Menschen von beiden Seiten das Wahrzeichen des Kalten Krieges. Eindrücke finden Sie in vielen Videos auf youtube, wenn Sie die Begriffe „Mauerfall", „Fall der Mauer", „Berlin", „1989" usw. eingeben.

A. Vor dem Schauen

Der Mauerfall steht Synonym auch für „Freiheit"? Was fällt Ihnen zu dem Wort ein? Wa bedeutet „Freiheit" für Sie?

B. Bei dem Schauen – ohne Ton

Finden Sie nun den Song „Freiheit" von Marius Müller-Westernhagen auf youtube und schauen Sie es ohne Ton an.

• Welche Personen sind in dem Video?
• Wie sehen die Personen aus? Welche Gefühle drücken diese PErsonen aus?
• ...

C. Bei dem Schauen – mit Ton

Schauen und hören Sie sich das Video nun mit Ton an:

• Welche Gefühle weckt das Lied in Ihnen?
• Wie wirkt das Lied auf Sie?

D. Nach dem Schauen

Sprechen Sie mit einem Partner/einer Partnerin:

• Welche Personen hat Ihr Partner/Ihre Partnerin in dem Video gesehen?
• Welche Gefühle hat Ihr Partner/Ihre Partnerin in dem Video festgestellt?
• Welche Gefühle hat das Lied in Ihrem Partner/Ihrer Partnerin geweckt?

Freiheit

Die Verträge sind gemacht
und es wurde viel gelacht
und was Süßes zum Dessert
Freiheit Freiheit

Die Kappelle rum-ta-ta
und der Papst war auch schon da
und mein Nachbar vorneweg
Freiheit Freiheit
ist die einzige die fehlt
Freiheit Freiheit
ist die einzige die fehlt

Der Mensch ist leider nicht naiv
der Mensch ist leider primitiv
Freiheit Freiheit
wurde wieder abbestellt

Alle die von Freiheit träumen
sollten's Feiern nicht versäumen
sollen tanzen auch auf Gräbern
Freiheit Freiheit
ist das einzige was zählt
Freiheit Freiheit
ist das einzige was zählt.

Aktivität 11. Die Mauer

A. Wie sah die Berliner Mauer aus?

Wie stellen Sie sich vor, dass die Mauer aussah? Zeichnen oder skizzieren Sie die Berliner Mauer auf einem Extrablatt.

Und hier sehen Sie noch einmal, wie Ost und West aufgeteilt waren.

Berliner Mauer

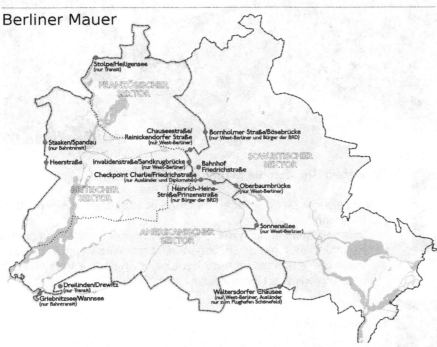

Die Karte zeigt die Sektoren und die Lage der Berliner Mauer, die West- von Ostberlin trennte.
Work found at http://commons.wikimedia.org/wiki/File:Karte_berliner_mauer_de.png /
CC BY-SA 3.0 (http://creativecommons.org/licenses/by-sa/3.0/)

Und diese Karte zeigt die Lage von Westberlin in der DDR.
Work found at http://commons.wikimedia.org/wiki/File:Map_FRG_GDRsvg.svg /
CC BY-SA 3.0 (http://creativecommons.org/licenses/by-sa/3.0/)

B. Haben Sie sich die Mauer so vorgestellt?

- Vergleichen Sie Ihre Mauerzeichnung oder Skizze mit einem Partner/einer Partnerin.
- Finden Sie jemandenim Kurs, der eine ähnliche Vorstellung hatte wie Sie. Was ist ähnlich an Ihren Zeichnungen/Skizzen? Was ist unterschiedlich?
- Finden Sie jemanden im Kurs, der eine völlig andere Vorstellung hatte. Was ist unterschiedlich an Ihren Zeichnungen/Skizzen?

C. Mauern in der Welt

Kennen Sie andere, vergleichbare (*comparable*) Mauern in der Welt oder wissen Sie von anderen, vergleichbaren Mauern in der Weltgeschichte? Diskutieren Sie darüber mit einem Partner und machen Sie sich Notizen.

Land/Ort	Unterschiede	Ähnlichkeiten

Aktivität 12. Die Phantasie benutzen

Am 9.November ist der Jahrestag des Mauerfalls. Stellen Sie sich vor, Sie wären ein ehemaliger DDR-Staatsbürger und müssten für eine Zeitung einen Bericht über Ihre Erlebnisse zu der Zeit des Mauerfalls schreiben.

- Wie haben Sie von der Maueröffnung gehört? Wo waren Sie?
- Wie haben Sie den Tag/die Nacht verbracht? Was haben Sie gemacht?
- …?

Aktivität 13. Symbole der Stadt: das Reichstagsgebäude

Wenn Berlin ein Symbol Deutschlands ist, ist das Reichstagsgebäude ein Symbol Berlins. („Der Reichstag" war der ehemalige Name des deutschen Parlaments. Heute heißt das Parlament „der Bundestag", aber das Gebäude selbst heißt immer noch „das Reichstagsgebäude".)

Seit dem Bau des Gebäudes im 19. Jahrhundert ist hier sehr viel passiert. Welches Bild gehört zu welchem Teil der Geschichte? Ordnen Sie den Bildern die entsprechenden Texte zu und füllen Sie die Lücken mit den angegebenen Verben im Imperfekt.

1.

a. Am 27. Februar 1933 _____ das Reichstagsgebäude in Flammen _____ (aufgehen). Nach diesem Feuer _____ (können) Hitler und die Nazis die Macht ergreifen. Es ist noch heute unklar, wer an dem Feuer schuld _____ (sein). Im Dritten Reich _____ (sein) der Reichstag kein echtes Parlament, da Hitler mit solchen demokratischen Institutionen nichts zu tun haben _____ (wollen). Im 2. Weltkrieg _____ (beschädigen) Bomben das Gebäude noch weiter. Die Rote Armee _____ (erobern – *to capture*) am 30. April 1945 das Reichstagsgebäude und kaum eine Woche später kapitulierte Deutschland.

2.

b. Nach fast 40-jähriger Teilung _____ am 3. Oktober 1990 die Vereinigung Deutschlands am Reichstagsgebäude _____ (stattfinden). Erst acht Monate später _____ (nennen) der Bundestag die neue Hauptstadt: Berlin. Aber ein Umbau des Gebäudes _____ (sein) nötig und zwar unter der Aufsicht des britischen Architekten Sir Norman Foster. Das Reichstagsgebäude _____ (eröffnen) wieder am 19. April 1999. Foster _____ (errichten) eine neue Kuppel (*cupola*) aus Stahl und Glas, die sofort eine beliebte Berliner Sehenswürdigkeit _____ (werden).

3.

c. „Dem deutschen Volke" lautet (*reads*) die Inschrift, die 1916 über dem Haupteingang des Reichstagsgebäudes eingraviert wurde. Die Inschrift _____ (gefallen) dem imperialistschen Kaiser Wilhelm II überhaupt nicht. Am Ende des 1. Weltkriegs, als Wilhelm II abdanken (*to abdicate*) _____ (müssen), _____ Philipp Scheidemann die neue Republik aus einem Fenster des Reichstagsgebäudes _____ (ausrufen).

4.

d. Architekt Paul Wallot _____ (gewinnen) 1882 den Wettbewerb, ein Gebäude für den Reichstag zu bauen. Seine Pläne _____ (fordern) ein sechsgeschossiges Gebäude im Stil der italienischen Hochrenaissance mit einer großen Kuppel (*cupola*) aus Stahl und Glas. Am 9. Juni 1884 _____ (legen) Kaiser Wilhelm I den Grundstein des Gebäudes. Zehn Jahre später sein Nachfolger, Kaiser Wilhelm II, den Schlussstein.

III. Berlin heute: Berlin besichtigen

Mit solch einer spannenden Geschichte ist es kein Wunder, dass es in Berlin viel zu sehen gibt! Aber wo sollen Sie anfangen? Nach diesem Teil des Kapitels werden Sie einige Ideen haben ...

Aktivität 14. Berlin Mitte mit dem Bus *100*

Berlin Mitte ist der Bezirk, in dem sich viele der berühmtesten und wichtigsten Sehenswürdigkeiten der Stadt befinden. Wenn man diesen Bezirk besichtigen, aber dabei nicht viel Geld ausgeben möchte, sollte man unbedingt den Bus *100* nehmen. Die Route dieses Doppeldeckerbusses überbrückt (*to bridge*) die ehemalige Kluft (*divide*) zwischen West- und Ost-Berlin, indem er vom Zoologischen Garten (im ehemaligen West-Berlin) zum Alexanderplatz (im ehemaligen Ost-Berlin) und wieder zurück fährt. Man darf natürlich aussteigen und wieder einsteigen, wo man will, um die Sehenswürdigkeiten besser ansehen oder auch besuchen zu können.

A. Der Stadtplan

Die folgende Karte (auf Seite 460) zeigt verschiedene Sehenswürdigkeiten, die man vom Bus *100* aus sehen kann. (Unter http://www.welt-atlas.de/datenbank/karten/karte-1-166.gif finden Sie eine größere Kopie der Karte.)

a. Schauen Sie sich die Karte auf der folgenden Seite an, kreisen Sie die unten aufgelisteten Orte ein und schreiben Sie die dazugehörige (*matching*) Nummer auf.

b. Versuchen Sie dann, die Busroute einzuzeichnen (*to trace*).

---

1. Breitscheidplatz • 2. Europa-Center • 3. Zoologischer Garten • 4. Tiergarten
5. Siegessäule • 6. Schloss Bellevue • 7. Kongresshalle • 8. Reichstag • 9. Brandenburger Tor
10. Unter den Linden • 11. Humboldt-Universität • 12. Neue Wache
13. Museumsinsel • 14. Berliner Dom • 15. Fernsehturm

BUS 100 S+U Zoologischer Garten ◄► S+U Alexanderplatz

BVG

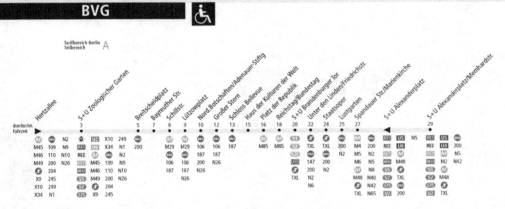

Diesen und andere Streckenpläne finden Sie direkt auf der Website der BVG (Berliner Verkehrsbetriebe) auf http://www.bvg.de unter „Linien, Netze und Karten"

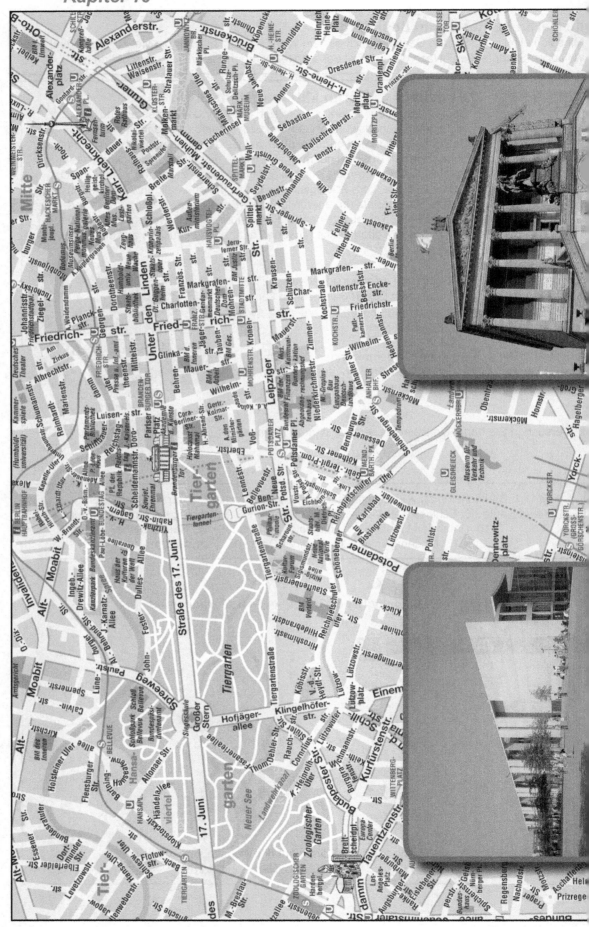

Aktivität 15. Ausgewählte Sehenswürdigkeiten mit der Linie *100*

Sie wissen jetzt Bescheid, wo die aufgelisteten Sehenswürdigkeiten auf dem Stadtplan zu finden sind. Aber was sind das für Sehenswürdigkeiten? Warum sind sie so berühmt und wichtig? Informationen zu diesen Sehenswürdigkeiten können Sie auf der folgden Website finden:
http://www.bus100.de/diestationen/

A. **Bushaltestelle 1: Zoologischer Garten Berlin**

Wenn Sie sich für Tiere interessieren, müssen Sie den Zoologischen Garten Berlin unbedingt sehen. Deutschlands ältester Zoo – gegründet 1844 – bietet Besuchern den größten Artenreichtum (*diversity of species*) aller Zoos weltweit mit fast 1.400 verschiedenen Tierarten.

Knut – die berühmteste Persönlichkeit des Zoologischen Gartens

Work found at http://commons.wikimedia.org/wiki/File:Knut012.jpg / CC BY-SA 3.0 (http://creativecommons.org/licenses/by-sa/3.0/)

Knuts Geschichte – eine Debatte

Der beliebte Knut hatte eine ziemlich ungewöhnliche Kindheit. Er und sein Bruder wurden am 5. Dezember 2006 im Zoologischen Garten Berlin geboren. Da es seit mehr als 30 Jahren keine Eisbärengeburt in einem Berliner Zoo gegeben hatte, wurde diese Geburt besonders groß gefeiert. Leider wollte Knuts Mutter Tosca ihre Kinder nicht annehmen und ein paar Tage später starb der eine Bär. Zu dieser Zeit entschied sich der Zoologische Garten Berlin Knut von seiner Mutter zu trennen und beauftragte (*to task*) den Tierpfleger (*zookeeper*) Thomas Dörflein mit dem Aufziehen des Tieres. Dörflein zog Knut von Hand auf. Er wohnte sogar eine Zeitlang im Zoo, damit er besser auf Knut aufpassen konnte.

Die einzigartige (*unique*) Geschichte Knuts verbreitete sich weltweit und allein im Jahr 2007 besuchten ungefähr 500.000 mehr Menschen als in den vorherigen Jahren den Zoologischen Garten. Knut wurde ein Weltstar. Aber – wie es bei vielen Weltstars der Fall ist – kam sein Erfolg vielleicht zu schnell. Knut gewöhnte sich an die Menschenmassen (*crowds of people*) und fing an, immer mehr Aufmerksamkeit (*attention*) zu verlangen (*to demand*). Er benahm sich nicht, wie ein „normaler" Eisbär sich benehmen sollte!

Schon bevor Knut am 23. März 2007 zum ersten Mal der Öffentlichkeit (*public*) vorgeführt (*to present*) wurde, meinten einige Tierrechts-Aktivisten (*animal rights activists*), ein Tier von einem Menschen aufziehen zu lassen, sei unnatürlich und Knut solle deshalb getötet werden.

Nach vier Jahren als Quasi-Celebrity in Berlin ertrank Knut im März 2011 in seinem Gehege. Sein Tod kam sehr unerwartet und ganz Berlin trauerte um ihn. Es war eine Tragödie nicht nur für Berliner und Touristen, sondern auch für viele Betriebe und Firmen. Einer Studie zufolge brachte Knut fast 100 Millionen Euro für Firmen wie Haribo, Steiff und Ravensberger ein. Im Frühjahr wurde heftig diskutiert, ob man Knuts Pelz ausstopfen lassen und dadurch noch mehr vom Bärchen profitieren soll. Was meinen Sie? Wie weit darf ein Zoo ein Tier ausnutzen, um Besucherzahlen zu erhöhen und den Zoo profitabler zu machen?

Lesen Sie zum Beispiel den folgenden Artikel bei *Spiegel-Online*: http://www.spiegel.de/wissenschaft/natur/0,1518,472520,00.html.

Was denken Sie darüber? Sind Sie für oder gegen die Handaufzucht eines Tiers wie Knut? Was wären die Pro- und Kontra-Argumente für so eine Entscheidung? Debattieren Sie diesen Punkt in Gruppen von drei oder vier und listen Sie mindestens vier Pro- und Kontra-Argumente auf. Nach 15 Minuten sollten Sie als Gruppe EINE Meinung haben (das heißt, Sie müssen debattieren, bis alle Mitglieder der Gruppe derselben Meinung sind).

Pro	Kontra

B. **BUS** **Bushaltestelle 2: der Breitscheidplatz**

Auf dem Breitscheidplatz befindet sich eine der faszinierendsten Kirchen der Stadt: die Kaiser-Wilhelm-Gedächtniskirche. Besuchen Sie folgende Website und machen Sie sich Notizen über die Geschichte dieser Kriche: http://www.berlin.de/orte/sehenswuerdigkeiten/kaiser-wilhelm-gedaechtniskirche/. Besprechen Sie mit zwei anderen Studenten, was Sie herausgefunden haben.

C. BUS Bushaltestelle 7: der Tiergarten und die Siegessäule

In der Mitte der Stadt liegt der Tiergarten – Berlins Version von New Yorks Central Park – und in der Mitte des Tiergartens steht die beeindruckende Siegessäule (*victory column*). Lesen Sie zuerst die Beschreibungen dieser Sehenswürdigkeiten unter
http://www.berlin.de/orte/sehenswuerdigkeiten/tiergarten/
und
http://www.berlin.de/orte/sehenswuerdigkeiten/siegessaeule/
und beantworten Sie dann folgende Fragen.

Die Siegessäule

1. Wer ließ den Tiergarten anlegen (*to design*)?

2. Was passierte dem Tiergarten im 2. Weltkrieg und nach dem Krieg?

3. Wann und wo wurde die Siegessäule ursprünglich aufgestellt (*to erect*)? Wer verlegte (*to relocate*) die Siegessäule auf den Großen Stern?

4. Die Siegessäule erinnert an welche drei Feldzüge (*military campaigns*)?

D. BUS Bushaltestelle 12: das Brandenburger Tor

Das Brandenburger Tor ist vielleicht die bekannteste Sehenswürdigkeit in Berlin. Erweitern Sie Ihr Wissen über dieses wichtige Monument der deutschen Geschichte und entscheiden Sie, ob folgende Aussagen richtig oder falsch sind.

Das Brandenburger Tor

Aussagen	richtig	falsch
1. Das Brandenburger Tor befindet sich am Ende der Straße *Unter den Linden*.		
2. Napoleon brachte 1806 die Quadriga (*quadriga sculpture*) mit sich nach Paris.		
3. Während des Kalten Kriegs blieb das Brandenburger Tor offen.		
4. Die Quadriga musste nach den Vereinigungsfeiern restauriert werden.		

E. Ein Reiseführer-Eintrag

Es gibt auch viele andere Sehenswürdigkeiten auf der Bus-100-Route. Wählen Sie eine dieser Sehenswürdigkeiten aus der unten stehenden Liste. Suchen Sie weitere Informationen zu diesem Ort (und natürlich auch Fotos!) und bereiten Sie dann einen kleinen Reiseführer-Eintrag (*travel guide entry*) vor. Konzentrieren Sie sich in Ihrem Eintrag auf die folgenden Punkte:

- die Geschichte des Orts
- was man dort sehen oder tun kann
- warum dieser Ort berühmt/wichtig ist

BUS Bushaltestelle 12: Unter den Linden   **BUS** Bushaltestelle 15: der Berliner Dom

BUS Bushaltestelle 13: Neue Wache   **BUS** Bushaltestelle 16: die Museumsinsel

BUS Bushaltestelle 14: der Bebelplatz   **BUS** Bushaltestelle 17: der Fernsehturm

Mein Reiseführer-Eintrag:

_____

_____

_____

_____

_____

_____

_____

_____

F. Liniennetz der U- und S-Bahnen

Der folgende Plan zeigt das Liniennetz (*network of routes*) für die U- und S-Bahnen, die durch den Bezirk Berlin Mitte fahren. Stellen Sie sich vor, Sie hätten den Bus 100 vom Zoologischen Garten zum Alexanderplatz genommen und Sie müssten jetzt am Alexanderplatz aussteigen. Schauen Sie den Plan an und beantworten Sie die folgenden Fragen.

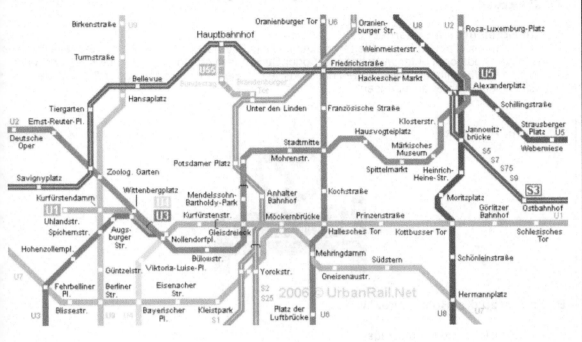

1. Welche Route würden Sie nehmen, um am besten (d.h. mit den wenigsten Haltestellen) wieder zum Zoologischen Garten zurückzufahren?

2. Sie sind jetzt wieder am Zoologischen Garten und wollen unbedingt noch heute beim Kaufhaus Karstadt einkaufen. Sie wissen, dass das älteste Karstadt sich am Hermannplatz befindet. Wie fahren Sie am besten dorthin?

3. Bei Karstadt treffen Sie zufällig einige Freunde aus Ihrem Würzburger Seminar. Ihre Freunde haben das Brandenburger Tor noch nicht gesehen und fragen Sie, ob Sie es ihnen zeigen könnten (da Sie jetzt ein Experte sind). Wie fahren Sie am besten dorthin?

4. Ihre Freunde erzählen Ihnen von einem guten Restaurant, das in der Nähe vom Moritzplatz ist. Sie haben Hunger und würden das Essen dort gerne mal probieren. Wie fahren Sie am besten dorthin?

Aktivität 16. Unterkunft
Schön und gut, dass wir jetzt einige Sehenswürdigkeiten kennen und uns über die öffentlichen Verkehrsmittel informiert haben, aber wir brauchen noch einen Platz zum Schlafen – auf der Parkbank ist das schließlich nicht erlaubt. Wir müssen eine Unterkunft finden.

A. Auf Hotelsuche im Internet
Surfen Sie im Internet und finden Sie tagesaktuelle Hotelübernachtungsangebote. Webseiten wie das Berliner Stadtportal unter www.berlin.de, oder Suchmaschinenen wie www.hotel.de oder www.hrs.de sind hierfür hilfreich. Beim Surfen notieren Sie hier Begriffe, die benutzt werden, um die Hotels bzw. die Zimmer anzupreisen.

Hotelinformationen   *Zimmerinformationen*

B. Fragen zu drei Hotels Ihrer Wahl

1. Gibt es kostenlosen Internetzugang?

2. Ist Frühstück im Preis enthalten?

3. Sind die Hotels typisches? Warum (nicht)?

4. Welche Sehenswürdigkeiten liegen in der Nähe der Hotels:

_____   _____   _____

5. Welches Hotel hat Ihrer Meinung nach das beste Preis/Leistungsverhältnis (*cost/vaue comparison*)? Warum?

C. Meine Hotelwahl

Suchen Sie sich ein Hotel aus, das Ihnen am besten gefällt. Welches Hotel wählen Sie? Was bietet das Hotel? Wie viel kostet das Hotel? Ist Frühstück inklusive? Warum haben Sie dieses Hotel gewählt?

D. Ankunft im Hotel

Sie kommen müde im Hotel an und wollen nur noch schlafen. Zuerst müssen Sie aber noch Ihren Koffer auspacken und Ihre Sachen ordentlich aufräumen.

Überlegen Sie zuerst was diese Verben bedeuten und sagen Sie dann wo Sie ihre Sachen hin tun.

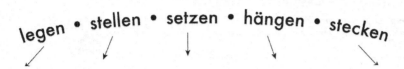

legen • stellen • setzen • hängen • stecken

In der nächsten Aufgabe werden die Wechselpräpositionen (2-Way Prepositions) benötigt. Bitte gehen Sie zu *Grimm Grammar* und lesen Sie folgende Grammatikteile:

Wechselpräpositionen

Review:
Akkusativ
und
Dativ

an – at, by (vertical)
auf – on top of
hinter – behind
in – in, within
neben – next to
über – above
unter – under
vor – in front of
zwischen – between

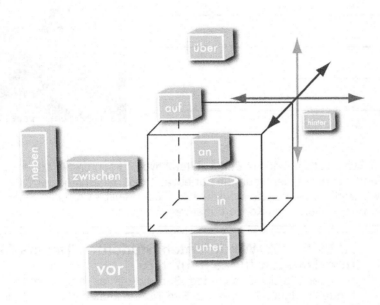

Wohin tun Sie die Sachen?
~~die Jacke~~
die Schuhe
das Buch
die Digitalkamera
der Reisepass
der Laptop
das Geld
der Teddybär

Beipiel:

Ich hänge meine Jacke über den Stuhl.

_____

_____

_____

_____

_____

E. Stress am Morgen

Das Aufräumen war umsonst. Sie haben sich mit Ihren Freunden am Tierpark verabreitet, aber Sie haben verschlafen. Wo sind alle Ihre Sachen? Benutzen Sie die Sätze aus Aufgabe 16B und schreiben Sie auf, wo Ihre Sachen sind.

Was bedeuten diese Wörter?

liegen • stehen • sitzen • hängen • stecken

Beipiel:

Die Jacke hängt über dem Stuhl.

_____

_____

_____

_____

_____

Abends in Berlin. Was gibt's abends in Berlin zu tun? Wohin könnten Sie gehen, wenn Sie etwas Kulturelles machen möchten? Oder wenn Sie nur etwas Spaß haben möchten? Es gibt natürlich in einer Großstadt wie Berlin unbegrenzte Möglichkeiten. Zum Beispiel könnten Sie in die Oper oder ins Theater gehen oder vielleicht ins Konzert oder ins Restaurant ...

Aktivität 17. Wie könnten Studenten Tickets für Shows und Theaterstücke kaufen?

Schauen Sie sich Evas Video „Showtickets" an und finden Sie heraus, wie Studenten laut (*according to*) Eva Tickets kaufen können. Schreiben Sie Ihre Antworten unten auf.

_____

_____

_____

_____

(QR 10.5 p.483)

Aktivität 18. Was will ich machen?

Gehen Sie auf die Internetseiten der Attraktionen, Sehenswürdigkeiten und Orte über die Sie in diesem Kapitel bereits gelesen haben und die im Folgenden aufgelistet sind. Was wollen Sie machen? Stellen Sie ein Abendprogramm zusammen. In welches Restaurant werden Sie gehen? Wo ist das Restaurant? Was gibt es dort zu essen und zu trinken? Was trinken und essen Sie? Welche Shows werden Sie sich ansehen? Was kosten die Karten? Welche Bars werden Sie besuchen? Was gibt es in den Bars? Wo gehen Sie tanzen? Welche Musik wird dort gespielt? Begründen Sie Ihre Auswahl!

Restaurants

Zur letzten Instanz
http://www.zurletzteninstanz.de/index2.htm

Die Gaststätte ist das älteste Restaurant unserer Hauptstadt. Sein Ursprung geht in das Jahr 1621 zurück, als ein ehemaliger Reitknecht des Kürfürsten hier eine Branntweinstube eröffnete.

Haus Berlin
http://www.haus-berlin.net/

An einem geschichtsträchtigen Boulevard im Herzen der Stadt erwartet Sie ein Ort der Gastlichkeit. Gehobene deutsche und internationale Küche mit gutem Preis/Leistungsverhältnis wird ergänzt durch typische DDR-Gerichte.

Fernsehturm Restaurant
http://www.tv-turm.de/de/restaurant.php

An einem Tisch in unserem Restaurant ist die Stadtrundfahrt inklusive: In einer halben oder manchmal in einer Stunde dreht sich das Telecafé einmal um seine eigene Achse. Nirgendwo sonst bekommen Sie so schnell einen Überblick über Berlin!

Bars

Spagos
http://www.spagos.de/

Die aufregende Loungeadresse für Menschen mit hohem Anspruch und außergewöhnlichem Sinn für aktive Ästhetik und Lifestyle.

Carambar
http://www.carambar.de/

Wolltest du schon immer wissen, wie sich Berlins Herzschlag anhört? Dann lausche dem Sound des neuen Partylabels Berlins: „Heart Beat", denn so klingt Berlins wahrer Herzschlag.

Um welches Getränk handelt es sich, wenn man in Berlin ein „Berliner Kindl mit Schuss" bestellt?

Zwischen welchen Farb- beziehungsweise Geschmacksrichtungen kann man wählen?

Wie alt muss man in Deutschland sein, um das Getränk probieren und trinken zu dürfen?

Theater/Kinos/Galerien

Lufttanz
http://www.lufttanz.com/

Das Lufttanz Theater lässt aus Akrobatik und Tanz betörende Welten entstehen. Mit Seiltanz, Luftartistik, Stelzenakrobatik und Schwebevehikeln spielen wir Solos und Duos und kreieren daraus Shows, Walkacts und Arealbespielungen. In einem Kosmos aus faszinierender Körperkunst, Multimedia, Lichtdesign und Pyrotechnik entstehen atemberaubende Inszenierungen.

Berliner Kriminal Theater
http://www.kriminaltheater.de/

Die Kriminal-Bühne von Berlin garantiert mit ihren Aufführungen knisternde Spannung und bietet den krimisüchtigen Zuschauern aufregende Unterhaltung. Ob Gift oder Schlinge, Pistole oder Messer, ein herabfallender Blumentopf oder ein Würgeengel die Ursache sind – ein Mord muss sein! Und selbstverständlich ein Kommissar. Wer ist der Täter? Diese Frage ist nach wie vor die meistgestellte im Kriminal Theater! Denn: Nicht immer ist der Mörder der Gärtner!

Theater im Kino
http://www.theater-im-kino.de/

Neben klassischen, modernen, absurden und selbst geschriebenen Stücken gibt es bei uns Lesungen, Konzerte und neuerdings auch das Intermezzo zu erleben. Diese Form des offenen Abends soll jedem, der Lust und Laune, vor allem aber Ideen hat, die Möglichkeit geben, den Einstieg in unser Theater zu erleichtern, sich ein Bild von unserem Verein zu machen und sich kreativ auszuleben. Hier ist fast alles erlaubt.

Kino International
http://www.yorck.de/

Das architektonisch herausragende Premierenkino im Herzen Berlins ist in vielerlei Hinsicht eine Ausnahmeerscheinung in der Stadt. Hier können Sie Kino in seiner schönsten Form erleben.

East Side Gallery
http://www.eastsidegallery.com

Ein internationales Denkmal für die Freiheit. Die East Side Gallery ist ein 1,3 km langer Abschnitt der Berliner Mauer nicht weit von Berlins Mitte. Mehr als 100 Bilder von Künstlern aus der ganzen Welt formen dieses Denkmal der Freiheit und machen es zur größten 'Open Air'-Galerie der Welt.

A. Mein Nachtprogramm:

_____

_____

_____

_____

_____

_____

_____

_____

B. Was machen die anderen?
Bilden Sie eine Gruppe von vier Personen. Erzählen Sie Ihrer Gruppe von Ihrem Abend-/Nachtprogramm. Was machen die anderen Studenten in Ihrer Gruppe? Vergleichen Sie Ihre Pläne.

Nachtprogramm von:

Name:	Name:	Name:

C. Das beste Programm
Diskutieren Sie in Ihrer Gruppe, wer den besten Plan für den Abend hat. Warum? Sie können auch Elemente von allen Ideen in der Gruppe verwenden und das ultimative Programm erstellen. Denken Sie daran Ihre Antwort zu begründen.

Unser Nachtprogramm:

_____

_____

_____

_____

_____

_____

_____

_____

_____

_____

_____

_____

D. Präsentation

Stellen Sie Ihr Abendprogramm der Klasse vor. Machen Sie sich Notizen, wenn die anderen Gruppe vortragen. Die Klasse muss am Ende wählen, welche Gruppe das beste Programm hat.

Notizen zu

Gruppe:	Gruppe:	Gruppe:	Gruppe:

Das beste Programm hat Gruppe _____, weil. ..

Aktivität 19. In die Oper gehen

Neben den vielen möglichen Veranstaltungen, die man auf der Website www.eventim.de aussuchen und buchen kann, gehören natürlich auch Opern. Was sagt Erin über Opern? Was sagen Sie?

A. Erin

Hören Sie sich Erins Videoclip an und entscheiden Sie, ob folgende Aussagen richtig oder falsch sind.

(QR 10.6 p.483)

Aussage	richtig	falsch
1. Erin war schon mehrmals in der Oper.		
2. Erin mag Opern nicht.		
3. Erin findet es teuer, in die Oper zu gehen.		

B. Jetzt sind Sie dran!

Besprechen Sie jetzt folgende Fragen mit einem Partner/einer Partnerin.

1. Warst du schon einmal in der Oper?

2. Warum warst du in der Oper? Warum warst du noch nie in der Oper?

3. Was hast du gesehen?

4. Wie hat es dir gefallen?

Aktivität 20. Ins Theater gehen

Wenn Sie noch niemals in der Oper waren, iwaren Sie vielleicht schon mal im Theater. Was sagen Jan und Erin über das Theater? Was sagen Sie?

Grimm Gramma

A. Jan und Erin

Q: Gehst du gern ins Theater oder in die Oper?

> Lieber _____,
> und _____ schau' ich
> mir gerne _____ Stücke an, von
> _____ zum Beispiel, oder von ...
> Ich schau' auch gerne_____, also _____
> Sachen guck' ich mir gerne an.

(QR 10.7 p.483)

Q: Was war das letzte Theaterstück, das du gesehen hast?

> Das letzte
> Theaterstück, das ich gesehen
> habe, war in _____. Das war
> _____. Es war ein bisschen ... Sie
> haben ganz viel _____ und die Zuhörer oder
> die Zuschauer haben das nicht erwartet und ... also ich habe das
> nicht erwartet. Also es war ganz _____,
> aber es
> könnte nicht so sein.

(QR 10.8 p.483)

B. Jetzt sind Sie dran

Arbeiten Sie mit einem Partner und stellen Sie sich gegenseitig die folgenden Fragen über das letzte Theaterstück, das Sie gesehen haben.

1. Gehst du gern ins Theater? (Wenn ja, warum? Wenn nein, warum nicht?)

2. Was war das letzte Theaterstück, das du gesehen hast?

   Wo hast du es gesehen?

3. War es gut, schlecht, so lala? Was hat dir daran besonders gut gefallen, und was hat dir (gar) nicht gefallen?

Sidebar (Grimm Grammar):

In den nächsten Übungen sind Adverbien der Narration sehr wichtig. Bitte gehen Sie zu *Grimm Grammar* und bearbeiten und wiederholen Sie Grammatikteile:

Adverbien der Narration

Adverbien: Wann?

Adverbien: Wie?

Bearbeiten Sie folgend Grammatikteile in *Grimm Grammar:*

Wiederholung: Modalve ben im Präsens

Wiederholung: Modalve ben im Imperfekt

Grimm Grammar

Grimm Grammar

In dieser Aufgabe wird der Imperativ wiederholt. Bitte gehen Sie zu Grimm Grammar und lesen Sie folgende Grammatikteile noch einmal:

Imperativ

Aktivität 21. Ich möchte ins Theater gehen

Sie möchten ins Theater! Aber Ihre Freunde wollen nicht. Schreiben Sie eine Geschichte und erzählen Sie Ihren Freunden vom Theater: Wann finden dort Aufführungen statt? Was können Sie dort sehen? Wie ist das Theaterstück? Warum wollen Sie das Theaterstück sehen? Warum sollten Ihre Freunde das Theaterstück sehen? Schreiben Sie 6-8 Sätze und benutzen Sie dabei viele Adverbien, um Ihre Geschichte stilistisch besser zu machen.

Adverbien

Zum Beginnen: (zu)erst · am Anfang · neulich · früher ...
Im Text: dann · danach · inzwischen · jetzt · plötzlich · später ...
Am Ende: schließlich · am Ende · zum Schluss · seitdem · zuletzt ...
Adverbien der Zeit: bisher · heute · morgen · später · sofort ...
Adverbien der Häufigkeit: manchmal · oft · immer · nie · selten · fast nie ...
Adverbien der Intensität: sehr · total · fast · wirklich · wahnsinnig ...
Adverbien der Art und Weise: gern · lieber · fleißig · langsam · wütend · hoffentlich · freiwillig ...

Modalverben

müssen   dürfen   können   sollen   mögen

_____

_____

_____

_____

_____

Aktivität 22. Wie komm´ ich dahin?

Sie wissen jetzt zwar, was es in Berlin so zu tun und zu sehen gibt, aber es ist oft sehr schwer, sich in einer fremden Stadt zu orientieren, und man muss deshalb nach dem Weg fragen. Für die Wegbeschreibungen brauchen Sie die Vokabeln aus diesem Kapitel und den Imperativ, den Sie schon gelernt haben – achten Sie auf den formalen und nicht-formalen Gebrauch!

Mögliche Ziele:

Neue Wache

Alte Nationalgalerie

DDR-Museum

Palast der Republik

S-Bahnstation Friedrichstraße

Berliner Dom

Jungfernbrücke

Pergamonmuseum

Komische Oper

U-Bahnstation Friedrichstraße

A. Wie komme ich ...?

Arbeiten Sie mit einem Partner zusammen und wählen Sie drei Sehenswürdigkeiten aus, die Sie besichtigen möchten. Beschreiben Sie, wie Sie von einer Sehenswürdigkeit zur anderen kommen. Am Ende wollen Sie zum Zooeingang gehen, wie kommen Sie dorthin? Danach suchen Sie nach Restaurants oder Imbisse in der Gegend, wo Sie Frühstück, Mittagessen und Abendessen bekommen können. Zur Krönung des Tages brauchen Sie auch ein Abendprogramm. Wo geht es hin?

Startpunkt: InterCityHotel, Berlin Ostbahnhof

Notizen:

	Welche Bus-/U-Bahn-/S-Bahnlinie nehmen Sie?	An welcher Haltestelle müssen Sie umsteigen?	Wo müssen Sie aussteigen?
Sehenswürdigkeit 1			
Sehenswürdigkeit 2			
Sehenswürdigkeit 3			
Zooeingang			
Restaurants:			
Frühstück			
Mittagessen			
Abendessen			
Abendprogramm:			

IV. Schluss

Wie Sie in diesem Kapitel gesehen haben, hat Berlin seinen Besuchern sehr viel zu bieten. Berlin ist ein Symbol der deutschen Geschichte und der deutschen Kultur und ist deshalb ein passendesr Abschluss für Ihrem Besuch in Würzburg. Sie haben viel über die deutsche Sprache und auch über Deutschland selbst gelernt. In den folgenden drei Aufgaben werden Sie Ihre neuen Kenntnisse darüber zum letzten Mal ausprobieren.

Aktivität 23. Was man wissen muss ...

Welche drei Dinge sollte jeder amerikanische Student über Deutschland wissen? Hören Sie sich folgende Interviews an und tragen Sie ein, was jeder amerikanische Student laut Eva, Erin, Jan und Berna über Deutschland wissen sollte. Dann geben Sie an, ob diese Dinge Sie überrascht haben oder nicht.

Drei Dinge: **Überraschend?**

1.

2.

3.

(QR 10.9 p.483)

Drei Dinge: **Überraschend?**

1.

2.

3.

(QR 10.10 p.483)

Drei Dinge: **Überraschend?**

1.

2.

3.

(QR 10.11 p.483)

Drei Dinge: **Überraschend?**

1.

2.

3.

(QR 10.12 p.483)

Aktivität 24. Abschlussspiel: Hätten Sie's gewusst?

In den vergangenen Kapiteln (6-10) haben Sie viel über Deutschland gelernt! Nun ist es an der Zeit, dieses Wissen auf die Probe zu stellen. Jeder Student schreibt zu Hause sieben Fragen in sechs verschiedenen Schwierigkeitsstufen (*difficulty level*) auf. Zu jeder Frage gibt er auch vier mögliche Multiple-Choice-Antworten an. Falls Ihnen keine Fragen einfallen, suchen Sie einfach in den letzten Kapiteln nach Informationen!

Die einfachste Frage, Level 1, ist 500 Punkte wert, es folgt die 1.000-Punkte-Frage (Level 2), dann die 2.000-Punkte-Frage (Level 3), dann die 4.000-Punkte-Frage (Level 4), dann die 6.000-Punkte-Frage (Level 5), dann die 8.000-Punkte-Frage (Level 6) und schließlich die schwierigsten Fragen, die 10.000 Punkte wert (Level 7) sind.

Der Lehrer, der Moderator der Quiz-Show, sammelt die Karten mit den Fragen in sieben Stapeln (alle Level-1-Fragen, Level-2-Fragen usw.) und mischt sie innerhalb der Stapel. Jeweils drei bis vier Studenten bilden ein Team und versuchen, sieben Fragen aus verschiedenen Schwierigkeitsstufen ihrer Wahl zu beantworten. Gemeinsam versucht jedes Team, mehr Punkte als alle anderen Teams zu sammeln. Jedes Team hat einen Joker und darf die Klasse um Hilfe bitten (die ausgewählte Antwort der Studenten wird durch Melden signalisiert – eine Art "Ask-the-Audience-Lve-Line").

(Kapitel 10, Aufg. 4f) 4.000 Punkte

Wann fiel die Berliner Mauer?

A: 1961   B: 1990

C: 1989   D: 1980

(Kapitel 6, Aufg. 9) 500 Punkte

Wenn sie singt, versinken Schiffe.

A: Lola   B: Lolita

C: Loreley   D: Lena

(Kapitel 6, Aufg. 9) 2.000 Punkte

Die Hauptstadt der Insel Sylt heißt:

A: Traumland   B: Westerland

C: Osterland   D: Norderland

Mögliche Ausdrücke für den Moderator:

- Welche Antwort wählt ihr/wählen Sie?
- Wir haben nicht ewig Zeit, was soll es denn nun sein?
- Wirklich?
- Sicher?
- Letzte Chance, eure/Ihre Antwort zu ändern!
- Seid ihr euch/ sind Sie sich auch ganz sicher?
- Möchtet ihr/möchten Sie den Joker einsetzen?
- Seid/Seien Sie vorsichtig!
- Also das klingt ja nicht sehr überzeugend.
- Ich würde den Joker einsetzen.
- Diese Frage ist wirklich kinderleicht.
- Das ist eine sehr schwierige Frage …
- Ich frage mich, ob ich auf das Publikum hören würde …
- Ruhe im Publikum! Hier wird nicht geschummelt!
- Richtig! Das sind 1.000 Punkte mehr auf eurem/Ihrem Konto.
- Euer/Ihr Punktestand beträgt _____ Punkte. Mal sehen, ob das noch ein Team schlagen kann.

Mögliche Ausdrücke für den Teilnehmer:

- Ich wähle Antwort B.
- C ist totaler Schwachsinn.
- Ich bin mir total unsicher.
- Das ist einfach, das weiß ich!
- Ich glaube/Wir glauben, es ist C, aber ich bin mir/wir sind uns nicht sicher …
- Ich möchte den Joker einsetzen.
- Warum bekommen wir immer diese schwierigen Fragen?
- Als nächste Frage möchte ich/möchten wir eine Frage mit dem Schwierigkeitslevel 3.
- Ich weiß die Antwort! Diese Karte habe ich nämlich selber erstellt.
- Wie ist unser Punktestand im Augenblick?
- Wie viele Punkte hat das führende Team?

Aussprache

Please go to the Deutsch
im Blick website, Kapitel 10

Aussprache
German Dialects Spoken in the US

In the previous three chapters we took a brief look at the dialect varieties in Germany, Switzerland and Austria. However, German dialects are not only spoken in these European countries. As a result of German immigration before 1800 and in the mid 19th century, the US also has several German speaking areas. Their heritage, history, linguistic status and features are incredibly rich, and we cannot do them justice in a mere mini-segment. Therefore, please read the following information only as an introduction, and do search for more information on the Internet about these dialects, especially if your heritage is German and you live in the US!

For the sake of space, time and clarity, in this chapter we will take a look at:
1. Texas German
2. Pennsylvania Dutch, and
3. Wisconsin German.

A. Texas German

Quelle: Google 2013

Texas German is a dialect spoken by German immigrants in the Texas Hill country. These German settlers emigrated from various regions of Germany to the Hill country (in Central Texas, around Austin) during the mid-19th century. Town names like Boerne, Fredericksburg, New Braunfels or Schulenburg all point to the German heritage of their founding fathers.

However, while Texas German is commonly thought of as a single dialect, this is in fact erroneous -- it is really more a collection of dialects. For example, the Texas German you hear from one Texas German speaker may be vastly different than the Texas German you hear from another speaker! Why is this? Primarily, this is due to the fact that, as mentioned above, the settlers came to Texas from such disparate areas of Germany.

Although German was spoken almost exclusively in the Hill Country settlements before World War I and World War II, anti-German sentiments during these wars led to the decline of German. Texas German speakers stopped teaching their language to their children and used more and more English in their communication with each other. Today the dialect is almost extinct, spoken only by a few aging members of this speech community.

Speakers of German usually do not have too much of a problem understanding Texas German varieties. However, there are some words that were either invented or "Germanized" from English over the last century and a half because they did not exist in the vocabulary of the early immigrants but were needed by following generations. Here are some examples:

Note: For more information please visit the Texas German Dialect Program located at the University of Texas at Austin. (http://www.tgdp.org/)

You can also find an articles about Texas German on Dr Boas website. He provides pdfs for the German articles featured in the magazines *Stern* and *Der Spiegel*. (http://sites.la.utexas.edu/hcb/press/)

Here are some examples:

Texas German	Literal translation	Standard German	English
Stinkkatze	Stinkkatze	Stinktier	Skunk
Luftschiff	Airship	Flugzeug	airplane
Blanket	Blanket	Decke	blanket

B. Pennsylvania Dutch/Deitsch/German/Deutsch

Speakers of Pennsylvania Dutch are descendents of German immigrants who, for religious reasons, came to Pennsylvania as early as the 17th century and settled primarily in the southeastern part of Pennsylvania. Scholarly consensus holds that the term Dutch does not refer to the people of the Netherlands but rather reflects the adjective 'Deutsch' meaning German. The immigrants who settled in southeast Pennsylvania came not only from Germany (Rheinland-Westphalen) but also from Switzerland and the Alsace. However, Pennsylvania Dutch is a "daughter-language" of Palatine German (a West-Franconian dialect), spoken in Southwestern Germany.

Pennsylvania Dutch is spoken even today (often because the communities that speak it live in relative isolation from the dominant English-speaking linguistic environment). Communities can be found in Pennsylvania - obviously - as well as in a wider range around Pennsylvania: Maryland, West Virginia, North Carolina, Ohio, and Indiana. You can hear some Pennsylvania Dutch in the movie The Witness with Kelly McGillis and Harrison Ford.

Similarly to Texas German, Pennsylvania Dutch has incorporated a number of English loan words. In addition, Pennsylvania Dutch speakers also use words which do not exist in standard High German but are adaptations from German dialects or words they have coined (neologisms).

Pennsylvania Dutch	Literal translation	Standard German	English
juscht			just
tschumbe		springen	jump
Maschiin	Maschine	Auto	car
Welschkorn	foreign corn	Mais	foreign corn
gleiche	to be similar	gleichen	to like

Note: For more information on Pennsylvania Dutch please visit the following websites: http://csumc.wisc.edu/AmericanLanguages/

C. Wisconsin German

By the 1860s Germans made up the largest number of foreigners in Wisconsin. Most of these German immigrants came from Prussia. From 1881 to 1884 a second wave of German immigrants arrived in Wisconsin. Swiss immigrated to a much lesser extent to Wisconsin and founded cities like New Glarus. Some of the dialects spoken are Wisconsin High German, Kölsch, Pommerisch, Glarner Swiss German, Lëtzenbuergesch and Oberbrüchisch.

The following link at the University of Wisconsin-Madison gives you a good overview of the German dialects spoken in Wisconsin with available audio material. Check it out.
http://csumc.wisc.edu/AmericanLanguages/german/states/wisconsin/german_wi.htm

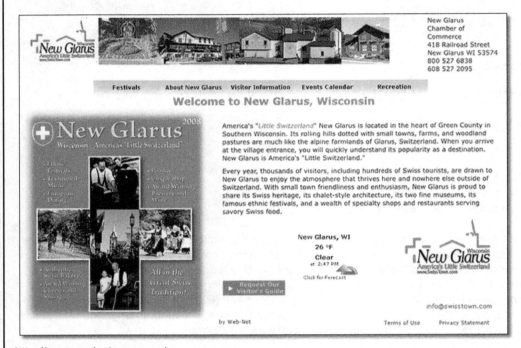

http://www.swisstown.com/

Meinungsumfragen
Klicken Sie auf „Meinungsumfragen" auf der *Deutsch im Blick*-Website. Die Themen in diesem Kapitel sind

Geschichte, Politik und eine Frage zu sozialen Themen.

WebQuests
Zu diesem Kapitel gehören vier mögliche WebQuests, die sie wie gewohnt auf der *Deutsch im Blick*-Website finden und bearbeiten können:

1. *Die Geschichte von Berlin*
2. *Der Euro*
3. *Soziale und politische Systeme in Deutschland*

(QR 10.1 p.483)

(Deutsche) Geschichte	(German) History
auswandern (wanderte aus - ausgewandert)*	to emigrate
die Berliner Mauer	the Berlin Wall
die Bundesrepublik Deutschland (BRD)	the Federal Republic of Germany (BRD)
die Deutsche Demokratische Republik (DDR)	the German Democratic Republic (DDR)
die ehemalige Sowjetunion/UdSSR	former Soviet Union/UdSSR
die ehemalige DDR	former East Germany
die Epoche (Epochen)	era/the epoch
das Ereignis (Ereignisse)	event/the incident
die Gegenwart	present
gründen (gründete - gegründet)	to establish
das Heilige Römische Reich	the Holy Roman Empire
hoffen	to hope
die Hoffnung (Hoffnungen)	hope
die Inflation	inflation
der Imperialismus	imperialism
das Interesse (Interessen)	interest
das Jahrhundert (Jahrhunderte)	century
das Jahrtausend (Jahrtausende)	millennium
die Jahrhundertwende (-wenden)	turn of the century
der Kaiser (Kaiser)	emperor
die Kaiserin (Kaiserinnen)	empress
der Kanzler (Kanzler)	chancellor
die Kanzlerin (Kanzlerinnen)	female chancellor
die Kirche (Kirchen)	church
der König (Könige)	king
die Königin (Königinnen)	queen
kritisieren (kritisierte - kritisiert)	to criticize
die Krone (Kronen)	crown
die Krönung (Krönungen)	coronation/the crowning
krönen	to crown
die Kultur (Kulturen)	culture
der Mauerfall	the fall of the Berlin Wall
die Neuzeit	modern times
das Reich	empire
das Dritte Reich	the Third Reich
der Staat (Staaten)	state/country/federal state
die Sünde (Sünden)	sin
die Vergangenheit	past
die Weimarer Republik	the Weimar Republic
der Wiederaufbau	reconstruction
die Wiedervereinigung	the (German) reunification
die Wirtschaft	economy
das Wirtschaftswunder	economic miracle
die Wirtschaftskrise (Wirtschaftskrisen)	economic crisis/the depression
die Zukunft	future

---

* *Imperfekt* and the past participle forms of regular verbs follow the same pattern: stem-t-ending for the impefect, and ge-stem-t for past participles. Thus, only irregular forms are given here.

Make it a habit to study all three forms together. Go back through *Kapitel 1 - 9* and add the forms to all verbs. You will feel accomplished and you will now be able to use many German verbs in multiple contexts. *Wunderbar!*

Krieg und Frieden	War and Peace
der/die Allierte	the allied power/ally (m/f)
die Alliierten	the allied powers/the Allies
angreifen (griff an - angegriffen)	to attack
der Angriff (Angriffe)	attack
die Armee (Armeen)	army
der Augenzeuge (-zeugen)	eye witness
die Besatzung (Besatzungen)	occupation (also: the crew)
die Besatzungszone (-zonen)	zone of occupation
der Erfolg (Erfolge)	success/achievement
jemanden erschießen (erschoss - erschossen)	to shoot somebody
die Europäische Union (die EU)	the European Union
furchtbar	terrible/awful
die Gewalt	violence
grässlich	dreadful/ghastly
die Grausamkeit (Grausamkeiten)	cruelty
der Frieden	peace
die Hilfe/Hilfeleistung (Hilfen/Hilfeleistungen)	help
jemanden hinrichten	to execute somebody
der Kampf (Kämpfe)	fight
kämpfen	to fight, battle
die Kapitulation (Kapitulationen)	capitulation/the surrender
kapitulieren (kapitulierte - kapituliert)	to surrender
das Konzentrationslager (-lager)	concentration camp
der Krieg (Kriege)	war
der erste Weltkrieg	World War I
der zweite Weltkrieg	World War II
die Macht (Mächte)	power
mächtig sein	to be powerful
marschieren (marschierte - marschiert)	march
das Opfer (Opfer)	victim/casualty
regieren (regierte - regiert)	to reign
der Sieg (Siege)	the victory/the win
siegen	to win
der Sieger (Sieger)	winner
die Siegerin (Siegerinnen)	female winner
die Sinnlosigkeit (Sinnlosigkeiten)	pointlessness
sterben (starb - gestorben)	to die
der Tod (Tode)	death
töten	to kill
die Todesstrafe (-strafen)	death penalty
sich umbringen (brachte um - umgebracht)	suicide
jemanden umbringen	to kill somebody
jemanden verhaften	to arrest somebody
verlieren (verlor - verloren)	to lose
der Verlierer (Verlierer)	loser
die Verliererin (Verliererinnen)	female loser
die Verzweiflung (Verzweiflungen)	desperation
die Waffe (Waffen)	weapon

Über berühmte Personen sprechen	Talking about Famous People
bekannt sein	to be known/to be famous
beliebt sein	to be popular
berühmt sein	to be famous
der Dichter (Dichter)	poet
der Dichterin (Dichterinnen)	female poet
dichten	to compose/to write poetry
das Gedicht (Gedichte)	poem
der Komponist (Komponisten)	composer
das Konzert (Konzerte)	concert
das Klavierkonzert	piano concert
die Literatur	literature
der Maler (Maler)	painter
die Melodie (Melodien)	melody
der Philosoph (Philosophen)	philosopher
der Roman (Romane)	novel
der Schriftsteller (Schriftsteller)	author/writer
die Sinfonie (Sinfonien)	symphony
das Unglück (Unglücke)	disaster/accident/catastrophe
unglücklich sein	to be unhappy
vergessen (vergaß - vergessen)	to forget

Rund um Deutschland und die Deutschen	On Germany and the Germans
arrogant sein	to be arrogant
bauen	to build/to construct
bewundern (bewunderte - bewundert)	to admire
der Bürger (Bürger)	citizen (male)
die Bürgerin (Bürgerinnen)	citizen (female)
der/die Deutsche (Deutschen)	German (m/f)
die Disziplin (Disziplinen, but typically no plural)	discipline
der Einwohner (Einwohner)	resident (male)
die Einwohnerin (Einwohnerinnen)	resident (female)
das Fremdbild (-bilder)	outsider's perception on somebody
die Gesellschaft (Gesellschaften)	society
das Gewichtsproblem (-probleme)	weight problem
keinen Humor haben	to have no sense of humor
jammern	to whine/to moan/to complain
pünktlich sein	to be on time
überpünktlich sein	to be overly punctual/to be exceedingly on time
die Sitte (Sitten)	custom/convention
das Stereotyp (Stereotypen)	stereotype
tauschen	to swap/to trade
die Tradition (Traditionen)	tradition
die Umfrage (Umfragen)	survey/the poll
das Vorurteil (Vorurteile)	prejudice

Opern und andere Sehenswürdigkeiten — **Operas and other Objects of Interest**

die Aufführung (Aufführungen)	performance/act/showing
die Uraufführung	world premiere/the first release
die Gestalt (Gestalten)	a person/a shape/a figure
das Kunstfest (-feste)	art festival
die Oper (Opern)	opera
die Ruhe (Ruhen)	silence/the calm
die Ruhe vor dem Sturm	quiet/calm before the storm (fig.)
die Suche (Suchen)	search
suchen	to search
unsichtbar sein	to be invisible
die Vorstellung (Vorstellungen)	screening/the show/the performance
beeindruckend	impressive
sich befinden (befand - befunden)	to be located
gegründet	founded/started
der Reiseführer (-führer)	travel guide

Nach dem Weg fragen — **Asking for directions**

Entschuldigen Sie/Entschuldigung!	Excuse me, pardon me.
Ich kenne mich hier nicht aus.	I don't know my way around.
Können Sie mir vielleicht helfen?	Could you help me?
Wie komme ich zum Zoo?	How do I get tot he zoo?
Wo ist der Zoo?	Where is the zoo?
Vielen Dank.	Thank you.

Wegbeschreibungen — **Giving directions**

auf der rechten/linken Seite.	On the right/left side.
Biegen Sie rechts/links ab.	Turn right/left.
Der Zoo ist in der Nähe von …	The zoo is near the …
Zum Zoo sind es ungefähr zehn Minuten	It's about 10 minutes to the Zoo
zu Fuß/mit dem Bus.	by foot/by bus.
Fahren Sie mit dem Bus/mit der U-Bahn.	Take the bus/the subway.
Gehen Sie geradeaus (bis zum/zur …, dann …)	Go straight ahead (until the …, then …)
Gleich da drüben.	Right over there
Gehen Sie an der nächsten Kreuzung rechts/links./	Take a right/left on the next intersection.
Biegen Sie an der nächsten Kreuzung rechts/links ab.	